Praise for *Web Application Design Patterns*

This is the type of book you'll want to read with your entire team and a flip chart because every page will produce a list of actionable changes for the applications you're developing. Pawan Vora has produced an amazing catalogue of the essential patterns for designing today's web-based applications.

— Jared Spool, Founding Principal, User Interface Engineering

A generation has watched the Internet work its way into every part of society as talented designers and developers have explored new user interfaces and as the most robust design patterns have emerged through the refining fire of hundreds of millions of users. Pawan Vora has done a wonderful service in capturing these best practices in *Web Application Design Patterns*. This book will be valuable to people ranging from those putting together their first website to those shaping corporate web experiences, and from practitioners to researchers benchmarking existing patterns as new interface paradigms are created.

— Arnie Lund, User Experience Director, Microsoft

Web Application Design Patterns is a must-read if you are in the business of designing web applications, or you simply want to understand the elements of a well-designed web application. Pawan Vora has condensed best practices, along with research and his solid experience, to create a useful reference about designing web applications. Even if you skim the book and look at the designs, it will spark creative design ideas.

— David Dick, Senior Member of STC, User and UX Special Interest Group

Excellent! A very complete and exhaustive overview of patterns for web applications with many previously undocumented patterns. This book is written in a very accessible way and will tell you (nearly) everything you need to know when designing web applications. A must-have for any designer!

— Martijn van Welie, Pattern Author, Philips Design

Web Application Design Patterns

Pawan Vora

AMSTERDAM • BOSTON • HEIDELBERG • LONDON
NEW YORK • OXFORD • PARIS • SAN DIEGO
SAN FRANCISCO • SINGAPORE • SYDNEY • TOKYO

Morgan Kaufmann Publishers is an imprint of Elsevier

Morgan Kaufmann Publishers is an imprint of Elsevier.
30 Corporate Drive, Suite 400, Burlington, MA 01803

This book is printed on acid-free paper.

Library of Congress Cataloging-in-Publication Data
Application submitted.

ISBN: 978-0-12-374265-0

For information on all Morgan Kaufmann publications,
visit our Web site at *www.mkp.com* or *www.books.elsevier.com*.

Printed in Canada
09 10 11 12 13   10 9 8 7 6 5 4 3 2 1

Dedication

To my little princess, Sumi

Contents

Acknowledgments

My sincere and heartfelt thanks to:

- The technical reviewers—Wendy Castleman, David Dick, Kaaren Hanson, Arnie Lund, and Dave Rogers—for taking the time and offering advice and constructive feedback. Their insightful suggestions have improved this book several-fold. Any errors or shortcomings, however, are my own and likely caused by not heeding their advice.

- Len Beasley, for assisting with research and helping with endless rounds of editing drafts of the book's chapters.

- The team at Elsevier: Mary James, my editor, for being patient as I experienced the first-time author struggles and for helping me stay focused and on (revised) schedule; Denise Penrose and Diane Cerra, for giving me the opportunity to write a book on a topic I am so passionate about; and the production team, including copyeditor Jodie Allen and proofreader Deborah Prato, for their talents in clarifying content and designing and laying out the book.

- Clients, colleagues, and friends, who continue to teach, guide, listen, and encourage.

- Sona, my dear wife, for her support and putting up with me during my extended work during the writing and review schedule and for not letting me give up when the going got tough.

- And, Sumi, my little princess, for understanding that daddy needed time by himself to finish the book and for offering to write it so that he had time to play with her.

Pawan Vora

About the Author

Pawan Vora is the founder and president of Alpha Cube, Inc., a user experience design consultancy focused on designing, reviewing, and evaluating user interfaces for software and web-based applications.

He has been a user experience professional for more than 14 years and has designed user interfaces for a range of applications for business-to-consumer, business-to-business, consumer-to-consumer, and business-to-employee environments. He has published and conducted a number of tutorials and in-house training workshops on web site design, web application design, and design patterns in the United States and internationally.

Pawan has a Ph.D. and M.S. in industrial engineering from the State University of New York at Buffalo in addition to his bachelor's degrees in production engineering and mechanical engineering from Victoria Jubilee Technical Institute in Mumbai, India.

CHAPTER 1

Introduction

INTRODUCTION

Increasingly, software applications are built using web technologies and made accessible via web browsers (e.g., Internet Explorer, Firefox, Safari, and Opera). They are commonly referred to as *web applications*, or hosted applications—applications based on a software as a service (SaaS) model[1] or cloud computing.[2] These web applications are different from more traditional web sites in that their emphasis is on allowing users to accomplish tasks such as send email, make travel reservations, find homes, pay bills, transfer money, buy products, send invitations, and so forth (Figures 1.1 through 1.4). Web sites, on the other hand, are content oriented and are designed to facilitate browsing and consumption of rather static information (Figure 1.5).

BENEFITS OF WEB APPLICATIONS

The trend in favor of web applications is understandable in view of the benefits these applications offer, as described in the following sections (Baxley, 2003; Turnbull, 2006).

Ease of access

Typically, the only software users need to access and use web applications is a browser such as Internet Explorer, Firefox, Safari, and Opera. Users do not need to download and install separate software to use different web applications, although there are instances when they have to download helper applications

---

[1]SaaS is a software application delivery model where a software vendor develops a Web-native software application and hosts and operates it (either independently or through a third party) for use by customers over the Internet. Customers do not pay for owning the software; they subscribe to it and pay a regular subscription fee for using it.
[2]Web applications are considered to be a form of "cloud computing" because applications and files are hosted in the Internet "cloud," which consists of thousands of computers and servers, all linked together and made accessible via the Internet.

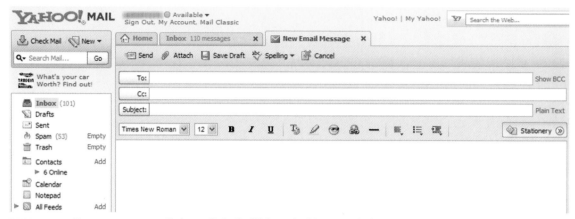

FIGURE 1.1 Users can manage their email via the Web, as in this example from Yahoo! Mail, which is similar to its desktop counterparts such as Microsoft Outlook, Mozilla Thunderbird, and Eudora.

FIGURE 1.2 Users can search for travel options and make reservations using web applications like Expedia.

or plug-in modules, such as Adobe Flash, Java, Microsoft Silverlight, and so forth, to access all or part of a web application.

Moreover, because both the application and information are stored on servers of the application's providers and not on users' computers, users can access web applications from almost anywhere, as long as the computer they use has a web browser and Internet connectivity. This remote data storage also facilitates sharing and collaboration among users; for example, users can share bookmarks with applications such as Delicious (*www.delicious.com*) and Furl

FIGURE 1.3 Users can find homes for sale, assess the value of a home, and see recent sales of homes in a neighborhood on sites such as Zillow.com.

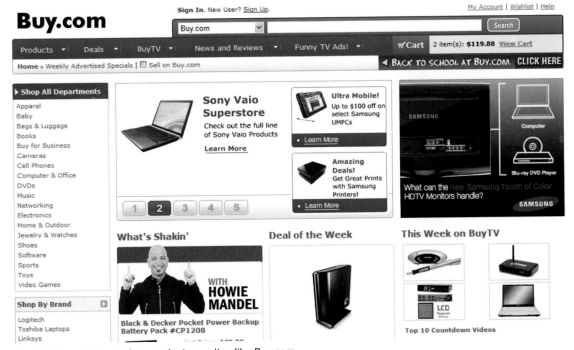

FIGURE 1.4 Users can buy products on sites like Buy.com.

FIGURE 1.5 Ultragrain allows users to access static information about the company and its products on its web site (*www.ultragram.com*).

(*www.furl.net*), and remotely collaborate on the same documents using productivity applications such as Google Docs and Spreadsheets (*docs.google.com*) and Zoho (*www.zoho.com*).

Ease of deployment

Web applications are also popular with businesses and software developers because they can be developed, updated, and maintained remotely without requiring users to install (or reinstall) them. A related advantage of web applications is that they *can* perform as specified regardless of the operating system on users' computers. They can be built once and deployed to almost any user, rather than creating separate versions of applications for Microsoft Windows, Macintosh OS X, GNU/Linux, and other operating systems.

"Trained" user base

The Web's growth and widespread adoption (from 16 million users in December 1995 to almost 1.5 billion users in June 2008, according to Internet World Stats; *www.internetworldstats.com*) has made the Web style of interaction familiar to a large number of users. Most Internet users can now be expected to be familiar with web browser terminology such as home, back, forward, bookmarks, hypertext links, submit buttons, and so forth. With this knowledge, and the fact that using web applications does not require elaborate installations, barriers to their use (or at least to try them out) are much lower. Further, it helps that many popular web applications are now available for free or have a free trial period.

Maturity and reliability of network connectivity and web technologies

An important roadblock for earlier web applications was unreliable network connectivity and significantly inconsistent web standards support—that is, HTML, CSS, and JavaScript—in web browsers. This is no longer the case. Adherence to web standards is improving, and browser inconsistencies that used to cause frustration for web developers are decreasing. In addition, network connectivity and broadband access is becoming more reliable, more ubiquitous, and cheaper to use. According to Website Optimization the use of broadband Internet access grew to 57 percent in US homes in March 2008 and was 90 percent among active Internet users (*www.websiteoptimization.com/bw/0807/*). This stable platform has also spawned the availability of visual development tools and frameworks to facilitate web application development.

CHALLENGES TO DESIGNING INTERFACES FOR WEB APPLICATIONS

Despite these benefits and increasing use, designing interfaces for web applications remains difficult. Challenges in creating usable interactions are mainly related to the underlying "loosely coupled" web architecture, a limited set of interactive controls natively supported in web browsers, and the lack of design guidance as to how user interactions should be implemented.

"Loosely coupled" web architecture

An important challenge faced by web application designers is caused by the "loosely coupled" or "stateless" nature of the Web. The Web's interaction paradigm is very simple: Users request web pages with web browsers, and servers respond by sending the requested pages to the browsers or informing users if there are problems retrieving those pages. However, once a user's request is satisfied by the web server, by sending the web page to the browser, the connection between the web server and the web browser is severed. When a user makes a subsequent request, the connection is established again with the server until the new web page is "reloaded" in the user's browser.

Each page reload, or page refresh, is marked by perceptible delays caused by the need to establish the connection, the server to respond to the request, the network to receive the page, and the browser to reload the page. This creates a jumpy and discontinuous experience for web application users. For example, a user browsing a hierarchical tree structure of items may have to wait after every click to expand, or collapse, a data node for the page to reload and see the expanded, or collapsed, view. Although this problem is addressed to a great extent by the use of scripting technologies such as JavaScript and Rich Internet Applications (see Chapter 8), it's an important user experience issue faced by most web applications.

Limited set of controls, or widgets, to support application design

In the current version of HTML (version 4.01), native support for controls is limited to text boxes, radio buttons, checkboxes, dropdown lists, and command or action buttons. It does not offer support for sophisticated interactions common in desktop applications such as spin controls, calendars, wizards, tabs, toolbars, drag-and-drop, floating palettes, dialog boxes, context-sensitive menus, and so forth, which are available in even basic desktop applications. Although such controls can be developed using JavaScript and Cascading Style Sheets (CSS), a lack of inherent support for them has led to a variety of implementations with inconsistent presentations and interactions.

Inconsistent interaction approaches

Both the underlying technological architecture of the Web and the limited set of controls available make it difficult to create interactions for web applications comparable to desktop applications. Additionally, because most web applications are designed to be browser-agnostic, interactions and appearance cannot be simulated to match all operating systems; for example, tabs in the Macintosh OS X Aqua interface are visually quite different than the tabs in the Windows Vista interface (Figure 1.6).

Although the Web's relatively unrestricted development environment offers considerable creativity and flexibility to designers, the resulting diversity and inconsistency in user interfaces and interaction approaches in web applications is often challenging for users. This is due to the fact that users are faced with a variety of styles of interfaces and interactions, each with its own vocabulary of objects, actions, and visuals mixed together in the same application (see Tidwell, 2006). Figure 1.7 shows an example of changing the tab name in Zoho Notes (a note-taking web application like Microsoft OneNote) and Zoho Sheet (a worksheet web application like Microsoft Excel). To change the tab name in Zoho Notes, users must double-click the tab name and a Rename dialog pops up. In order to change the tab name in Zoho Sheet, users must right-click the

NOTE

The next version of HTML (version 5) will support additional form elements that are currently part of the World Wide Web Consortium's (W3C) Web Forms 2.0 (*www.w3.org/TR/web-forms-2/*). This new version offers additional form controls (e.g., the **<datalist>** element to create combo-boxes and the **<output>** element to show values derived from other form controls) as well as an extension to existing form controls (e.g., **<input type="date" />**, **<input type="email" />**, etc.), which makes web application development a little easier. Opera (version 9 and above) currently supports Web Forms 2.0 enhancements and offers a good platform to develop interactive prototypes.

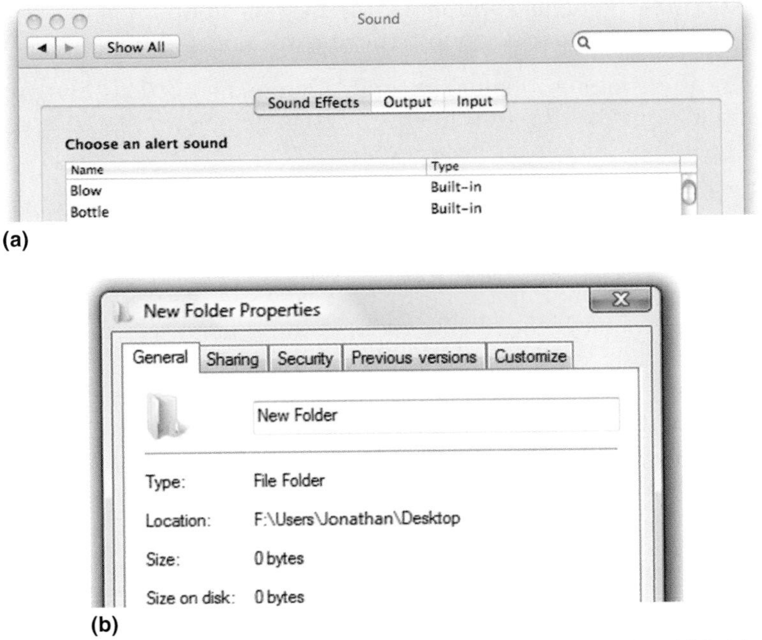

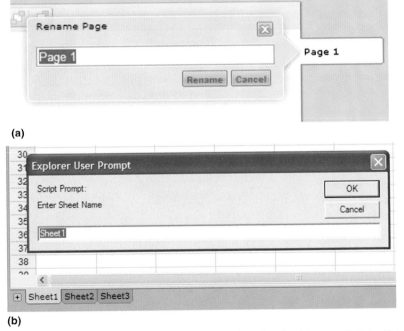

FIGURE 1.6 Tab controls in the Macintosh OS X Aqua interface (a) and Windows Vista interface (b).

FIGURE 1.7 Two different interaction approaches for changing the tab name in Zoho Notes (a) and Zoho Sheet (b).

tab and select the "Rename" option, which displays a pop-up window to allow users to change the tab name; double-clicking just selects the text.

To address these design challenges and accompanying usability problems, many corporations develop user interface design guidelines and style guides to manage the web application's "look and feel."

Applying design guidelines to develop usable web applications is not easy, however. Design guidelines are limited in their effectiveness, as they often advocate high-level principles (e.g., make system status visible; recognition is better than recall; prevent errors) or offer very specific guidance (e.g., align table headings to match the alignment of column data). On the other hand, design style guides focus on branding and visual design aspects and are usually specific to a platform (e.g., Macintosh OS X Aqua and Windows Vista) or to applications developed by a specific corporation (e.g., "Oracle Browser Look and Feel [BLAF] Guidelines," 2004), and do not necessarily provide detailed guidance for developing usable interactions.

Design guidelines and style guides are also quite lengthy and difficult to follow, because implementing one interaction requires user interface designers to be familiar with several sections within the document. For example, Apple's "Human Interface Guidelines" document is about 400 pages long, and to create a dialog with form controls, a designer would have to be familiar with several sections within "Part III: The Aqua Interface" (Figure 1.8), which has about 250 pages allocated to it.

Finally, design guidelines and style guides can also become too esoteric to be useful to those not familiar with human–computer interaction. This can limit their effectiveness as a means of communication among web application development team members, including customers, subject matter experts, clients, requirement analysts, software developers, product managers, and marketers, who are unlikely to be well-versed in human–computer interaction and usability.

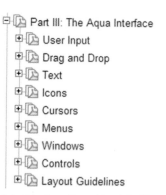

FIGURE 1.8 "Part III: The Aqua Interface" section of Apple's "Human Interface Guidelines" comprises about 250 out of the document's 400 pages.

Using design patterns addresses many of these concerns and can complement design guidelines and style guides to create better, and consistent, interface designs and improve usability of web applications.

DESIGN PATTERNS

The notion of patterns was introduced in the field of architecture by Christopher Alexander and his colleagues in *A Pattern Language* (Alexander et al., 1977) and *The Timeless Way of Building* (Alexander, 1979). They explained the nature of patterns as follows:

> Each pattern describes a problem that occurs over and over again in our environment, and then describes the core of the solution to that problem, in such a way that you can use this solution a million times over, without ever doing it the same way twice. (Alexander et al., 1977, p. x)

Thus, patterns explicitly focus on the problem within the context of use and guide designers on when, how, and why the solution can be applied. Patterns are practical and describe instances of "good" design while embodying high-level principles and strategies.

Patterns have recently become attractive to user interface and software designers[3] as well for their following benefits:

Proven design solutions and guidance for their use. Patterns identify real solutions and not abstract principles or guidelines. In addition, by making the context and problem explicit and summarizing the rationale for their effectiveness, patterns explain both how a problem can be solved and why the solution is appropriate for a particular context. However, because it's a generic "core" solution, its use can vary from one implementation to another without making it look "cookie-cutter" or discouraging creativity.

Improved design process. Identifying design patterns and cataloging them can help user interface designers increase productivity by reducing time spent "reinventing the wheel." Furthermore, if user interface components are built for patterns in the form of a design pattern library (see Chapter 13), designs can be developed, tested, and iterated rapidly, and can help shorten release cycles.

Reusability and consistent interfaces. Developing a library of reusable user interface components can also facilitate development of consistent interfaces both within and across applications. This is particularly useful in

---

[3]Inspired by Alexander's work in the field of architecture, the concept of patterns was applied and became popular in the field of software after the publication of *Design Patterns: Elements of Reusable Object-Oriented Software* (1994) by Erich Gamma, Richard Helm, Ralph Johnson, and John Vlissides (commonly referred to as the Gang of Four or simply GoF). Subsequently, patterns also became popular in the field of human–computer interaction from the works of Tidwell (*www.designinginterfaces.com*), Welie (*www.welie.com*), Borchers (2001), Graham (2003), and Van Duyne et al. (2002, 2006).

large corporations with multiple and distributed design teams, where different solutions may be applied for the same problems by different design groups, leading to inconsistent interfaces among designs produced within the same company. By cataloging and communicating design patterns, teams can increase consistency, predictability, and usability of their designs (Leacock et al., 2005) and can serve as a corporate memory of design expertise (Borchers, 2001).

A common, shared language. Patterns help support and improve communication among team members from diverse disciplines by developing a common language or vocabulary when explaining and discussing the design solutions (Borchers, 2001; Erickson, 2000). This is very important because user interface designers often work in an interdisciplinary team with developers, application domain experts, and users or user representatives, and these groups typically lack a common terminology to exchange design ideas and opinions.

Effective teaching aid and reference tool. Patterns also can be an effective way for experienced designers to offer design guidance to those without a formal background in design (Chen, 2003). Because of the approach used in documenting patterns, by providing visual and textual description, it is easier for novice interface designers to see examples of their successful usage.

Usable web applications. Finally, because patterns are based on a history of successful usage, their use can make the web application usable because interactions afforded by patterns would be familiar to users.

DOCUMENTING PATTERNS

It's important that patterns are documented to convey what they are, why they work, and how they should be applied to solve a design problem to reap the aforementioned benefits. Interestingly, however, there is no "pattern" for documenting patterns (see Chapter 13). Pattern authors have used a range of approaches, from those following a more descriptive Alexandrian notation (Borchers, 2001; Graham, 2003; van Duyne et al., 2002, 2006) to those following a more structured, albeit casual and minimalist, approach (Laasko, 2003; Tidwell, 2006; *www.welie.com*).[4]

In this book, patterns are presented using a rather minimalist approach. Specifically, each pattern includes:

- *Pattern name.* A short title describing the design solution. Following the convention used in other pattern collections, pattern names are written in CAPITAL LETTERS to make them stand out from the rest of the text.

[4]To bring order to the varied and inconsistent forms pattern authors have used and to find a way to combine patterns and pattern languages from different authors into specific, thematic pattern collections, participants at the CHI 2003 (April 6–7) Workshop Perspectives on HCI Patterns: Concepts and Tools proposed an XML-based markup language called Pattern Language Markup Language (PLML; pronounced "Pell-Mell"). For more information, see Fincher (2003).

- *Problem.* A brief description of the design problem(s) the pattern solves and accompanying design challenges and trade-offs (referred to as "forces" by Alexander et al., 1977) faced by user interface designers.
- *Solution.* The core design solution to the problem. This is a brief statement about the solution (i.e., the pattern) accompanied by an example (i.e., a sensitizing image) illustrating its use in a web application.
- *Why.* Rationale for the design solution's effectiveness.
- *How.* A list of best practices describing the application of the solution and possible variations. One or more illustrative examples are included for each variation to demonstrate how the pattern can be applied effectively in a variety of situations.
- *Related design patterns.* Because it's so often the case that several patterns are used together to create a usable design solution, this section identifies related patterns that designers may want to consider either because they are used together or are relevant for the use of the given pattern.

ORGANIZATION OF THE PATTERNS IN THIS BOOK

The patterns in this book are organized by chapter, as follows.

Chapter 2: Forms. Forms are a distinguishing characteristic of web applications. It is through form elements such as text boxes, dropdown menus, radio buttons, checkboxes, and others that users provide information and interact with web applications. This chapter discusses patterns related to designing forms for web applications, to ensure that filling out forms is not cumbersome and that they help users accomplish their goals, including CLEAR BENEFITS, SHORT FORMS, LOGICAL GROUPING, LABEL ALIGNMENT, REQUIRED FIELD INDICATORS, SMART DEFAULTS, FORGIVING FORMAT, KEYBOARD NAVIGATION, INPUT HINTS/PROMPTS, ACTION BUTTONS, and ERROR MESSAGES.

Chapter 3: User Authentication. Web applications enable one-to-one interaction with users and store user-specific information. This requires that users create an account and access it using a unique set of credentials. This chapter describes design patterns related to accessing and exiting web applications, including REGISTRATION, CAPTCHA, LOG IN, LOG OUT, AUTOMATIC LOGOUT, and FORGOT USERNAME/PASSWORD.

Chapter 4: Application Main Page. Once users have logged in to the application, an important question for designers is what users should see or which page they should be taken to. This chapter discusses design patterns designers should consider as they take users to that "main" application page, including INBOX, CONTROL PANEL, DASHBOARD, PORTAL, PERSONALIZATION, CUSTOMIZATION, and BLANK SLATE.

Chapter 5: Navigation. Navigation is how users experience web applications. When designed effectively, navigation becomes transparent and users are able to accomplish goals quickly and without unnecessary backtracking.

This chapter focuses on design patterns for navigation systems, including PRIMARY NAVIGATION, SECONDARY NAVIGATION, UTILITY NAVIGATION, FACETED NAVIGATION, SUPPLEMENTARY NAVIGATION, TAG CLOUDS, BREADCRUMBS, and WIZARD.

Chapter 6: Searching and Filtering. For most web applications, accessing information using only navigation systems can become cumbersome and compromise usability. Therefore, information within web applications is made searchable to get users to their desired items quickly and efficiently. Unless search terms are very specific, users are likely to be faced with a large number of results. Designers must offer users options to narrow down such a result list to a manageable set of choices by providing filtering mechanisms. This chapter discusses design patterns related to searching and filtering in web applications, including SIMPLE SEARCH, PARAMETRIC SEARCH, ADVANCED SEARCH, SEARCH TIPS, SEARCH RESULTS, SORTING, PAGINATION, CONTINUOUS SCROLLING, FILTERING, FACETED SEARCH, and SAVED SEARCHES.

Chapter 7: Lists. Lists are used to present a collection of items to users. Depending on the nature of items in the collection, the presentation approach varies. This chapter discusses design patterns for different types of lists, including SIMPLE LIST, TABULAR LIST, HIERARCHICAL LIST, EVENT LIST, TIMELINES, IMAGE LIST/GRID, MAPS, LIST ACTIONS, and LIST UTILITY FUNCTIONS.

Chapter 8: Rich Internet Applications. Rich Internet Applications (RIAs) can deliver responsiveness and interactivity comparable to desktop applications because users need not wait for pages to refresh for basic data and layouts to update; therefore, their actions' results can be seen immediately. This chapter discusses commonly used RIA design patterns, including RICH-TEXT EDITOR, RICH FORM, AUTOSUGGEST/AUTOCOMPLETION, EDIT-IN-PLACE, OVERVIEW-PLUS-DETAIL, DYNAMIC QUERYING, LIVE PREVIEW, DRAG-AND-DROP, SLIDER, ANIMATIONS/TRANSITIONS, DELAY/PROGRESS INDICATOR, SPOTLIGHT/YELLOW-FADE, and CAROUSEL.

Chapter 9: Social Applications. A recent trend in web applications is the development of social applications, which not only encourage users to contribute and share content (e.g., photos, videos, bookmarks, and so forth), but also promote interaction and help build communities. This chapter describes design patterns that have emerged from such social applications, including ADD/UPLOAD CONTENT, TAGGING, RATING, REVIEWS, VOTE TO PROMOTE, USER PROFILE, REPUTATION, DISCOVER NETWORK MEMBERS, FRIEND LIST, GROUPS/SPECIAL INTEREST COMMUNITY, MESSAGING, PRESENCE INDICATOR, SHARING, and COLLABORATION.

Chapter 10: Internationalization. Internationalizing web applications is an important step toward localization—that is, adapting them to a specific region or language. It helps reduce the effort required for localization later and eliminates the need to develop region- and language-specific versions of applications. This chapter discusses design patterns that help incorporate necessary flexibility and adaptability in web applications during initial design stages, including EXTENSIBLE DESIGN, DATE FORMAT, TIME FORMAT, NUMBER FORMAT, CURRENCY AND CURRENCY FORMAT, GLOBAL GATEWAY, and LANGUAGE SELECTOR.

Chapter 11: Accessibility. Design patterns that are discussed in this chapter help make web applications accessible and support recommendations and regulations for web accessibility, such as W3C's Web Content Accessibility Guidelines and Section 508 of the Rehabilitation Act; they include PROGRESSIVE ENHANCEMENT, SEMANTIC STRUCTURE, UNOBTRUSIVE STYLE SHEETS, UNOBTRUSIVE JAVASCRIPT, ACCESSIBLE FORMS, ACCESSIBLE IMAGES, ACCESSIBLE TABLES, ACCESSIBLE NAVIGATION, and ACCESSIBLE ALTERNATIVE.

Chapter 12: Visual Design. The visual design of web applications plays an important role in how usable an application is perceived and how credible it is considered by its users. In this chapter the emphasis is on design patterns that influence the overall look and feel of web applications, including LIQUID-WIDTH LAYOUT, FIXED-WIDTH LAYOUT, PROGRESSIVE LAYOUT, GRID STRUCTURE, VISUAL HIERARCHY, HIGHLIGHT, and ICONS.

Chapter 13: Pattern Libraries. Despite the popularity of patterns and pattern libraries, currently there is no consensus of how patterns should be documented, maintained, and shared with others. Therefore, this chapter presents a pattern library as a pattern and identifies its core elements, as well as offers best practices for its development.

Web Appendix: Help. Despite adherence to basic design principles, processes, and patterns that create an interface that users can learn easily and use efficiently, it is necessary to provide help and make it available at all levels of user interaction. The appendix, posted at *www.elsevierdirect.com/9780123742650*, lists design patterns related to providing help in web applications, including CONTEXTUAL HELP, FREQUENTLY ASKED QUESTIONS, APPLICATION HELP, GUIDED TOURS, HELP WIZARDS, HELP COMMUNITY, and CLICK-TO-CHAT.

NOTE

This book includes many web application screenshots taken over a period of nine months. Although a majority of them were valid as of November 2008, a few may have changed after this book went to press. This is expected, since companies building web applications change features, introduce new services, and discontinue older interfaces.

USING PATTERNS IN THIS BOOK

This book provides practical user interface design guidance for developing web applications by offering a usable "working" starting point that designers can adapt and refine to develop creative solutions.

Consider patterns in this book as blueprints and not precise design solutions, and use them as they apply to your specific problem. Do not force a pattern to a problem just for the sake of using it! As pointed out by Graham (2003): "Patterns are abstract, core solutions to problems that recur in different contexts.... The actual implementation of the solution varies with each application. Patterns are not, therefore, ready-made 'pluggable' solutions" (p. 1). So, focus on the essence of a pattern and then consider how a problem might be solved with the pattern, as patterns do not dictate a single solution, but rather a strategy for solving the problem.

COMPANION WEB SITE

All the patterns in this book are also available on the book's companion web site (*www.elsevierdirect.com/9780123742650*). I will also use that site to list errata and additional information (and, perhaps more patterns) and use it as a way to answer your questions and respond to your comments.

CHAPTER 2

Forms

INTRODUCTION

Forms are a distinguishing characteristic of web applications. By using form elements (e.g., text boxes, dropdown lists, scrolling lists, radio buttons, checkboxes, and action buttons), web applications allow users to accomplish goals such as buying products and services, making flight reservations, finding directions, uploading and sharing photos, and so forth. To ensure that users can accomplish their goals successfully, it is important that forms are not cumbersome and are designed such that:

- Their purpose is clear (CLEAR BENEFITS).
- They ask for only relevant and a minimal amount of information (SHORT FORMS).
- Their organization clearly conveys the relationship among form elements (LOGICAL GROUPING).
- Labels and corresponding form elements are aligned to improve scanning and completion (LABEL ALIGNMENT).
- They clearly indicate what is expected from users (REQUIRED FIELD INDICATORS, INPUT HINTS/PROMPTS).
- They minimize user input and do not require users to enter the same information twice (SMART DEFAULTS).
- They make completing a form efficient (SMART DEFAULTS, FORGIVING FORMAT, KEYBOARD NAVIGATION).
- They clearly indicate how to complete a task (ACTION BUTTONS).
- They clearly guide users when errors occur (ERROR MESSAGES).

Although selection of appropriate form elements (i.e., when to use a checkboxes or radio buttons) is extremely important for usable form design, it's not discussed here because excellent resources to address this topic already exist; for example, see Mayhew (1991), Galitz (2002), Apple OS X's "Human Interface Design Guidelines" (2007), and Windows Vista's "User Experience Guidelines" (2007).

It's important, however, to remember that web applications are developed using HTML and do not offer all the form controls available on popular platforms such as Windows and Macintosh. Specifically, the interaction in web applications is limited to the following form elements: text fields (single line and multiline), radio buttons, checkboxes, dropdown lists, scrolling lists, buttons (including image buttons), and a special control to browse files. Some of the missing controls are spin control, combo-box, tree control, and tabs. Although these controls have been implemented using some clever combinations of HTML, CSS, and JavaScript, they are workarounds and not true controls because they are not available as part of the basic markup language.

CLEAR BENEFITS

Problem

When presented with a form, users may not understand how filling it out and submitting it helps them accomplish their goals and tasks.

Solution

When designing, clearly indicate benefits of filling out and submitting forms. This is particularly important when users are creating a new account (i.e., registration forms), which is the first step before many web applications allow them access to their functionality (Figure 2.1).

Why

Users may not want to fill out forms and provide personal information unless they understand the benefits they will get in return and how it helps them

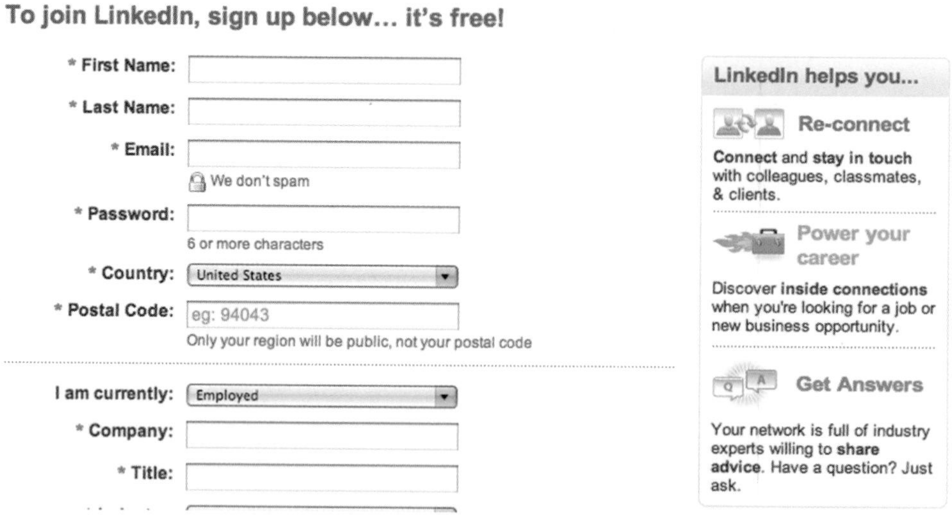

FIGURE 2.1 LinkedIn clearly lists the benefits of registering in the section "LinkedIn helps you...."

achieve their goals. In addition, they may be concerned about the security of their personal information, since they may not know how it will be used. Clearly indicating benefits and addressing users' concerns about security and privacy are the first steps in ensuring that users will not abandon the forms.

How

Users should be made aware of the benefits of filling out forms, even if it's just a one-field form like signing up for email newsletters (Figure 2.2).

EXPLAIN THE BENEFITS OF REGISTERING ON LOGIN FORMS

When users view the login form, and if they are not registered application users, it's a perfect opportunity to describe registration benefits to them. This makes it easy for users to decide whether they want to register or not (Figure 2.3).

EXPLAIN THE BENEFITS BEFORE LEADING USERS TO THE FORM

In many cases, users have to be led to a form. If they don't know the benefits, they may not bother to click the link or button that leads them to the form. Therefore, it's important that the form's benefits are described before users

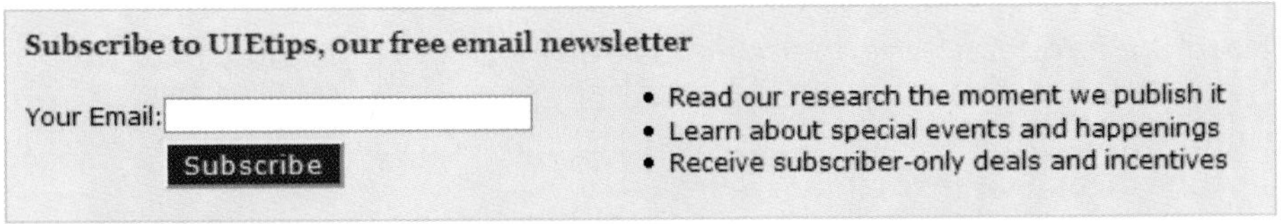

FIGURE 2.2 User Interface Engineering (UIE) lists benefits of signing up for their email newsletter, "UIEtips."

FIGURE 2.3 Blockbuster lists the benefits of signing up with Blockbuster.com and offers a "free" trial period as an added incentive for registering.

Not a member yet?

Sign up and get the only online address book and
calendar that syncs with Microsoft, Google, Yahoo!,
Apple, AOL — and your mobile phone.

Sign up *It's free!*

Learn more ▶   Video demo ▶

FIGURE 2.4 Plaxo describes the benefits of becoming a member alongside the sign-up button, and for new and unfamiliar concepts, they offer users the opportunity to learn more through a demo or a tour.

FIGURE 2.5 Prosper (a marketplace for money borrowers and lenders) provides information about how borrowing and lending works using "How to Borrow" and "How to Lend" links.

get to the form. One way to accomplish this is with clear link labels, such as "Transfer Money" or "Pay Bills," instead of generic link labels, such as "Learn More" or "Continue." When benefits may not be clear to users, it helps to describe them near the action (Figure 2.4).

Increasingly, web applications offer functionality and benefits that may be difficult to explain with just a few statements. Or, even when the benefits are clear, users may want to learn more about how the benefits are realized when using the application. To explain such functionality in detail, offer users options to learn more about how the web application works and reduce their anxiety about filling out any required forms (Figures 2.5 and 2.6).

Related design patterns

For many complex web applications and those that require users to pay upfront, consider offering a "CLICK-TO-CHAT" option (see Web Appendix: Help), which allows users to ask questions directly to a qualified company representative.

SHORT FORMS

Problem

The more information users provide, the easier it is to understand their profiles and tailor the application to better suit their needs and provide more relevant

FIGURE 2.6 In addition to showing the benefits of blogging (publish thoughts, get feedback, etc.), Blogger provides information about blogging through the "Take a Quick Tour" option.

Choose a plan that fits your needs

Plans can be changed at any time, so feel free to start using Crazy Egg with a free plan.

	Basic $9 / month	**Grab an account now**	
Visits you can track per month	10,000	Email	
Pages you can track at once	10		
Advanced Features	✓	Password	Re-type password
Live Reporting	✓	☐ I have read and agree to the Terms of Use and the Privacy Policy.	
	SIGN UP	CANCEL	SUBMIT ▸

FIGURE 2.7 Signing up with Crazy Egg requires users to enter only three pieces of information and agree to the terms of use and privacy policy. Furthermore, by integrating the form with corresponding benefits, users clearly know what they are going to receive in return.

and personalized information. However, long forms increase the chance of users not filling out the form or providing false information.

Solution

Make forms as short as possible (Figure 2.7). Do not ask users for any information that "may be useful" in the future. If additional information fields may help and cannot be removed, offer them as optional and indicate them as such (see the REQUIRED FIELD INDICATORS pattern later in this chapter for more information).

Why

A study reported by Relevant Ads showed that shorter forms had higher conversion rates (Figure 2.8). Making forms shorter also reduces the potential for errors, since users have to respond to fewer form elements. This further increases the chance of successful form completion, resulting in a higher conversion rate.

How

Analyze each form element for its importance and the downside of not including it in the form. In addition, consider how easy it would be for users to provide the information. If users have to think about how to respond to an item in the form, consider it as an obstacle to completing the form, and then consider removing it. The most quoted "simple" form page is probably Google's, which on its search page simply presents a text entry field and search button (Figure 2.9).

Jottit is another example of the shortest and perhaps most effective form (Figure 2.10). To create a Web page, users simply type in what they want on their page and click "Create a Page."

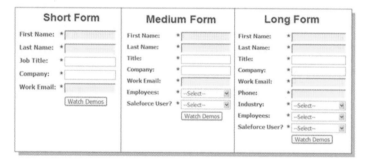

	Short Form	Medium Form	Long Form
Conversion Rate	13.4%	12.0%	10.0%
Cost Per Conversion	$31.24	$34.94	$41.90

FIGURE 2.8 In a study reported by Relevant Ads, the conversion rate decreased with an increase in the number of form fields. (*Source:* "Form Conversion Analysis: Less Is More," *www.relevantads.com/results/Form-Conversion-Analysis.aspx*.)

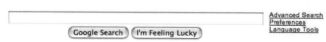

FIGURE 2.9 Google's search form is the simplest and shortest. Although it includes the "I'm Feeling Lucky" button, many people usually enter their search terms and click "Google Search" or press "Enter" on their keyboard.

(a)

> **That was easy!** <u>Remove this message</u>
> Here's your new site. Be sure to bookmark it so you can find it again. To change it, just press the edit button at the bottom of the page. Enjoy!

This is my test page... to see how this really works.

changed 10 seconds ago <u>history</u> <u>edit</u>

(b)

FIGURE 2.10 On Jottit, to create a Web page, users simply enter text and click the "Create a Page" button (a). Users then get their Web page and an option to edit it (b).

DIVIDE LONG FORMS INTO MULTIPLE PAGES WITH SHORTER FORMS

Group information in a long form so that each group is focused on a subtask, and present form elements related to each group on a separate page (Figure 2.11). In addition, order groups so that the most important and required information is presented first and optional information later. Splitting forms makes filling out each page faster, and users are more likely to perceive them to be shorter as compared to the entire form presented on one page.

Related design patterns

Once forms are made as short as possible, make them appear even more manageable by indicating to users the required information (REQUIRED FIELD INDICATORS), grouping and ordering form elements logically (LOGICAL GROUPING), and ensuring that users are aware of the benefits of filling out the form (CLEAR BENEFITS). In addition, consider using the WIZARDS pattern for forms that are split into multiple pages (see Chapter 5).

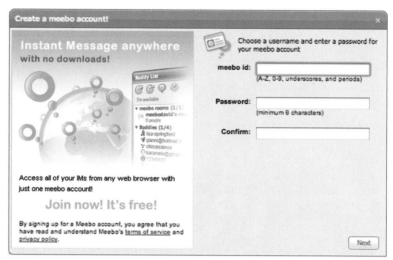

FIGURE 2.11 Meebo divides the registration form into several pages. It shows the most important, the sign-up portion of the form, upfront and uses subsequent pages to help users set up their accounts and preferences.

LOGICAL GROUPING

Problem

To complete a task, users have to fill out a rather long form. However, designers want to give users an impression that the form is easy to fill out so that they are not reluctant to complete it.

Solution

Group form elements such that it is clear to users the type of information required by each group (e.g., shipping information, payment information, and so forth; see Figure 2.12).

Why

Grouping information such that users can clearly see what is expected from each group and how form elements relate to their corresponding group can make forms appear easy to fill out and manageable. Users are more likely to think of the form in terms of the smaller collection of groups instead of a larger collection of individual form elements.

How

Group form elements according to their functions such as shipping address, billing address, contact information, and so forth. For each group, ensure that the order of elements matches users' mental model of how information should be entered. For example, for users in the United States, organize address-related form elements so that users are asked first for street address, then city, and then

1. Tell us about yourself...

My Name [First Name] [Last Name]

Gender [– Select One – ▼]

Birthday [– Select Month – ▼] [Day] [Year]

I live in [United States ▼]

Postal Code [ ]

2. Select an ID and password

Yahoo! ID and Email [ ] @ [yahoo.com ▼] (Check)

Password [ ] Password Strength ☐☐☐☐

Re-type Password [ ]

3. In case you forget your ID or password...

Alternate Email [ ]

Security Question [– Select One – ▼]

Your Answer [ ]

FIGURE 2.12 Yahoo! groups registration form elements and divides them into logical groups, which makes the form appear manageable and easier to complete.

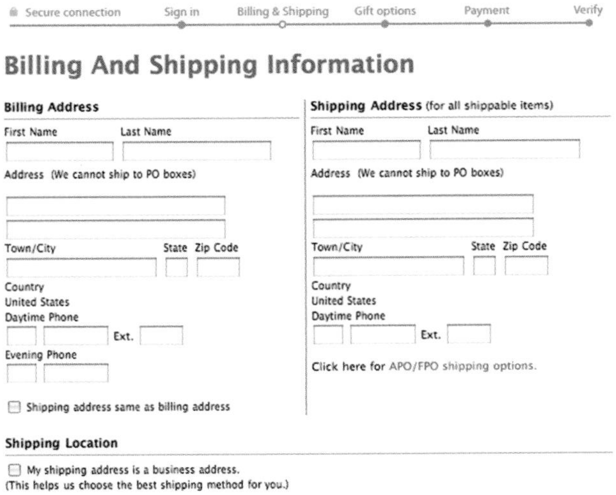

⊞ Secure connection   Sign in   Billing & Shipping   Gift options   Payment   Verify

Billing And Shipping Information

Billing Address

First Name   Last Name
[ ]   [ ]

Address (We cannot ship to PO boxes)
[ ]
[ ]

Town/City   State Zip Code
[ ]   [ ] [ ]

Country
United States
Daytime Phone
[ ] [ ]   Ext. [ ]

Evening Phone
[ ] [ ]

☐ Shipping address same as billing address

Shipping Address (for all shippable items)

First Name   Last Name
[ ]   [ ]

Address (We cannot ship to PO boxes)
[ ]
[ ]

Town/City   State Zip Code
[ ]   [ ] [ ]

Country
United States
Daytime Phone
[ ] [ ]   Ext. [ ]

Click here for APO/FPO shipping options.

Shipping Location

☐ My shipping address is a business address.
(This helps us choose the best shipping method for you.)

FIGURE 2.13
Apple makes checkout forms appear more manageable first by dividing them into several pages and then by logically grouping elements on each page.

state and zip code, or for setting up account information, ask for username (or email address) first and then password (Figure 2.13).

Once groupings and form elements in each group are identified, order them according to user tasks and system requirements. For example, in an e-commerce checkout flow, it is better to ask for shipping information first because it can be used to calculate tax and shipping charges, so that on the billing page users can be shown the total price and an option to indicate that their billing address is the same as their shipping address (Figure 2.14).

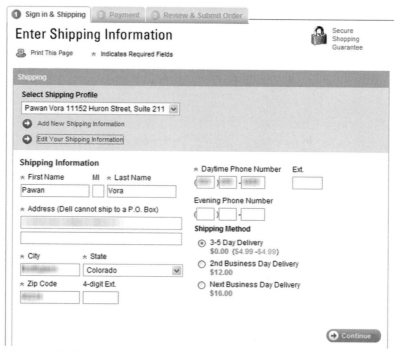

FIGURE 2.14 Dell, like many e-commerce applications, presents shipping and payment information in separate steps to make forms appear shorter and allows users to focus on one chunk of information at a time.

Related design patterns

Grouping form elements may suggest that the form be split up into multiple pages to make it appear shorter (SHORT FORMS) or that it be structured so that data entered by users in earlier groups prepopulate fields in later groups (SMART DEFAULTS) so that users don't have to go back and refer to previously entered information.

LABEL ALIGNMENT
Problem

Labels and corresponding form elements need to be clearly associated with one another to make form filling easier and to minimize user input errors.

Solution

There are three acceptable placements for labels in relation to form elements: above the element, with their left edges aligned with the elements; to the left, with their left edges aligned with other labels; and to the left, with their right edges aligned to other labels (Figure 2.15).

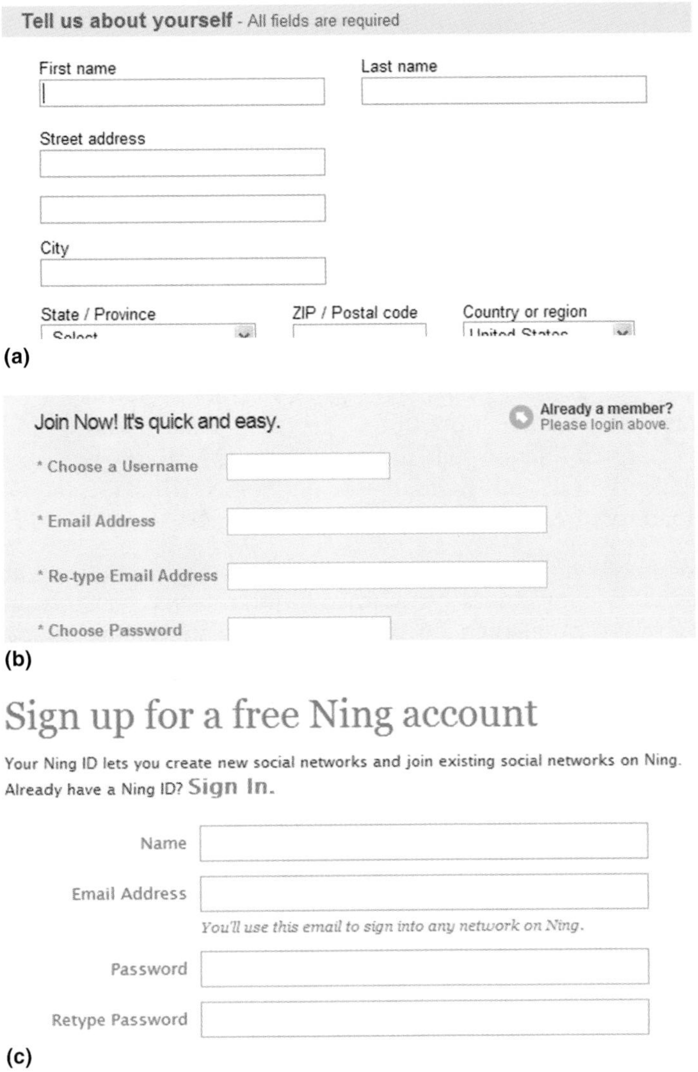

FIGURE 2.15 The common placement for labels are above the form elements (a), left aligned (b), and right aligned (c).

Why

The faster users are able to associate labels to corresponding form elements, the faster they will be able to fill out forms. In an eye-tracking study, Penzo (2006) found that users are able to easily associate labels with form elements with any of the three common label placements shown in Figure 2.15. However, the eye-tracking data showed that when field labels are left aligned, excessive distances between some labels and their input fields (which happen because not all labels are the same length—for example, "Company Name" compared to

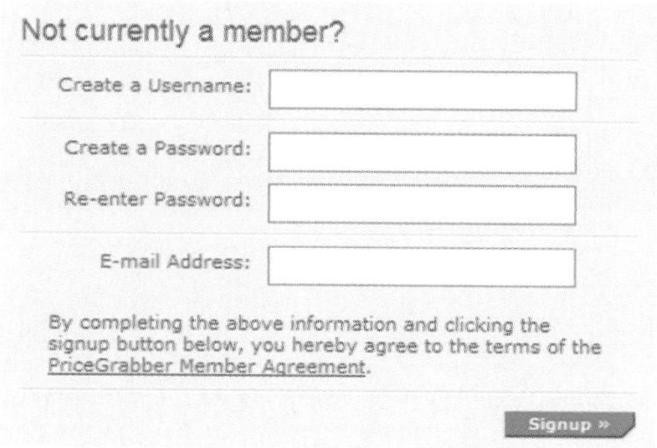

FIGURE 2.16
PriceGrabber places
labels to the left of
form elements but
right aligns them.

"City") cause users to take more time to interact visually with the form. When compared with left-aligned field labels, the overall number of fixations was reduced by nearly half with right-aligned field labels, thus greatly reducing the cognitive load required for users to complete the task.

The same study also demonstrated benefits of placing field labels above form elements; this style had the shortest form-filling times. One downside of placing labels above form elements is the additional vertical space that it requires. However, if the form is to be translated into different languages, it maintains the layout's visual integrity because different languages require different lengths for the same labels. Placing labels above form elements thus allows for necessary text expansion of labels when localizing the application (see the EXTENSIBLE DESIGN pattern in Chapter 10).

How

To associate labels correctly with corresponding form elements (for languages that read left-to-right), place labels either to the left or above the form control (Penzo, 2006; Wroblewski, 2008). When placing field labels to the left of form elements, right align the labels so that they are closer to each other (Figure 2.16).

When placing labels above form elements, it's important to provide enough visual separation between the label for the next form element from the previous form element (Penzo, 2006); Wroblewski (2008) recommends a separation of about 50–75 percent of the height of a single input field. In addition, Penzo (2006) recommends using plain-text labels over bold-text labels because the latter are a little difficult to read (Figure 2.17).

USE EMBEDDED LABELS SPARINGLY

Embedded labels are acceptable for forms that have just a few input fields (typically one) and when most users are expected to be familiar with the nature of the input such as search terms (Figure 2.18). Because embedded labels are in the fields themselves and have to be removed when users focus on them, they are not visible once users have entered data in them. Therefore, they are not

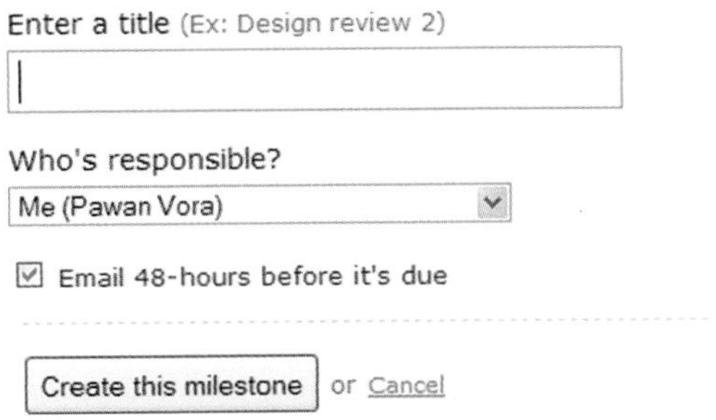

FIGURE 2.17 Basecamp uses plain-text labels above the input fields.

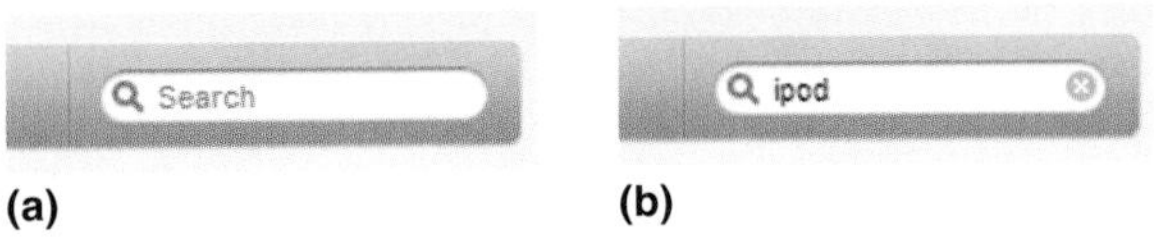

(a)　　　　　　　**(b)**

FIGURE 2.18 Apple uses an embedded label for the search field (a). The label disappears when users click in the search field or start entering search terms (b).

useful for long forms or forms where users are less likely to be familiar with data they are expected to enter.

Related design patterns

Labels in forms are generally accompanied by indicators for required information (REQUIRED FIELD INDICATORS).

REQUIRED FIELD INDICATORS

Problem

Users must provide certain information to complete a task successfully. For example, when setting up an account, users often must provide email addresses and passwords. However, to improve user interaction, forms may ask for additional optional information, which users may not want to provide or may not know at the time. Leaving out required information would lead to error messages and increase the time it would take users to accomplish tasks.

Solution

Clearly indicate required information on forms so that users can complete a task successfully and reduce the chance of encountering "missing required information" messages (Figure 2.19).

Why

Not only does visually distinguishing required fields save users time from deciding what information to provide, but it also saves them time dealing with

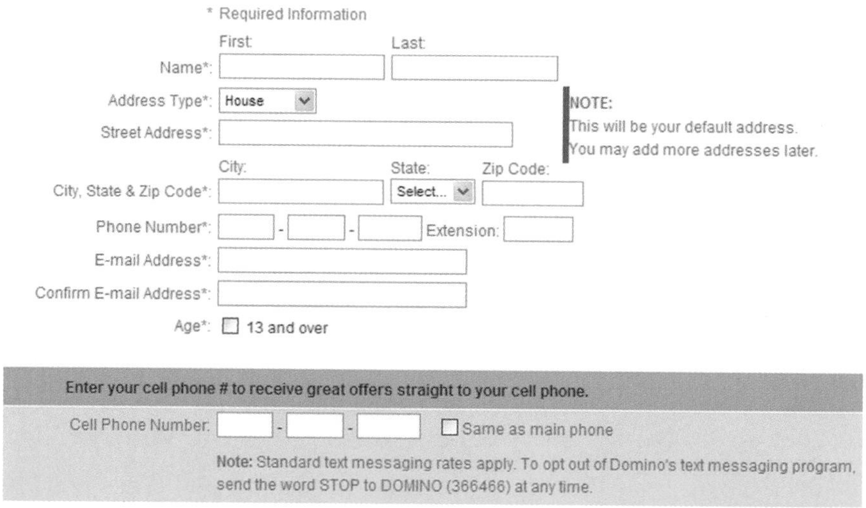

FIGURE 2.19 Dominos identifies required information using red asterisks, thus making it clear to users that a cell phone number is optional. It also indicates how providing a cell phone number would benefit users.

error messages, identifying missed information, and resubmitting forms to complete the task.

How

Using asterisks (typically red) next to field labels to identify required information is common in web applications. Red asterisks are effective because they do not rely on color alone to communicate information to users; because the asterisks have both shape and color coding, they are accessible to people with color-vision deficiencies as well. Other forms of indicating required information (e.g., making the field label red and bold) is not preferred because often such visual styles are used to indicate errors within the page. In addition, changing colors may not be accessible to screen readers, and people with color deficiencies may have trouble distinguishing between required and optional information.

Although there may be other ways to indicate required fields with both shape and color encodings, using a red asterisk is recommended because most users' experience on other web applications have likely habituated them to associate red asterisks with required information; the asterisk's color may be different depending on the page's background color.

TIP
On login pages, users know that both usernames and passwords are required. Therefore, indicating them as required is not necessary.

Write a hotel review

Thank you for writing a hotel review. By taking a few minutes to share your opinions, you are helping other travelers make informed decisions. Your review is subject to our review guidelines.

* **Name of Hotel:**

* **Hotel's Location:**   Ex. "Rome, Italy", "Miami South Beach"

* **Review Headline:**

> Show examples

* **Your Rating:**   Click numbers to rate the hotel

| 1 | 2 | 3 | 4 | 5 | 6 | 7 | 8 | 9 | 10 | ?

> Show detailed scoring

FIGURE 2.20 TravelPost shows required field indicators to the left of labels, which are positioned above the form elements. However, note that they make labels bold, which is not recommended, since bold labels increase the time it takes to complete a form (Penso, 2006).

SHOW THE REQUIRED FIELD INDICATOR LEGEND

Although most Web users will recognize red asterisks next to field labels as an indication of required fields, some web applications use this symbol to indicate optional information. Therefore, it helps to be clear and indicate at the top of the form that items marked with an asterisk (*) are required.

PLACE REQUIRED FIELD INDICATORS CONSISTENTLY ON ALL FORMS

There is no clear evidence about the efficacy of required field indicators' location in relation to field labels; they are found in any of the following areas: after field labels, before field labels, before input form elements, and after input form elements.

However, considering that when filling out forms, users' eyes are near form elements, showing required fields closer to form elements makes the most intuitive sense. In addition, placing them in a consistent location helps users quickly scan forms and identify required information. This may be accomplished by placing required field indicators to the left of form elements when labels are placed to their left and aligned right (see Figure 2.19). For top-aligned labels, place required field indicators to the left of labels (Figure 2.20), as they would then be closer to both field labels and form elements where users enter or select data; placing them to the left of form elements may become confusing when showing checkboxes or radio buttons, as users may feel that selecting that option is required.

DO NOT INDICATE OPTIONAL FIELDS

In situations where a form has fewer optional fields, there is a tendency to mark optional fields, as opposed to required fields, to reduce clutter. This is a poor practice. Because of users' familiarity with other applications, most of which use required field indicators, they are more likely to consider them as required or at least be confused about what is expected of them.

PROVIDE INSTRUCTIVE TEXT FOR REQUIRED SENSITIVE INFORMATION

If information asked of users is personal in nature, such as their birth date, gender, or race, clearly indicate why the information is required. In addition, provide a link to the "Privacy Policy" informing users how their information will be used.

Related design patterns

Even when a form clearly shows required fields, designers should still strive to minimize the total number of fields on a form—both optional and required fields (SHORT FORMS). In addition, when users fail to provide required information, show them a message on the same page as the form with the required information (ERROR MESSAGES).

SMART DEFAULTS

Problem

With every additional form element, both the total time it takes users to fill out the form and chances of potential errors increase. In addition, for multipart forms, if users have to reenter the same information, not only would it increase the time required to complete the form, but also require the application to check that the information was entered identically each time.

Solution

Use appropriate default values based on what users are most likely to choose or enter; this may be based on their previous input or selections (Figure 2.21). However, do not prepopulate form elements required for confirmation (e.g., reentering password, or users agreeing to have read terms and conditions of use) or related to security (e.g., resetting password).

Why

Providing good default values minimizes the need for users to enter or select data. This decreases the total time to complete the task and reduces data input errors. In some instances, using defaults may completely eliminate the need to fill out the form and reduce users' task to simply verifying information. For example, on e-commerce applications, users who have previously provided shipping and billing information (and consented to saving the information) need not go through the entire checkout process. Instead, they can be presented with a review/confirmation page with a "Place Order" button. Because most users are not likely to change shipping and billing information

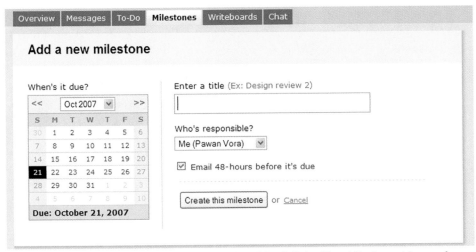

FIGURE 2.21 Basecamp defaults today's date for "When's it due?" and the logged-in user for "Who's responsible?," and it checks the "Email 48-hours before it's due" to make it easy to add a new milestone.

frequently, the checkout time is substantially reduced; however, users should be offered the option to change their shipping and billing information.

Providing default values serves another purpose: It provides users with an example of the type and format of data to enter and minimizes the potential for data entry errors (van Duyne et al., 2006).

How

Analyze every form element—text fields, radio buttons, dropdown lists, and so on—and if any reasonable data can be assumed about them, either based on users' previous choices or task context, prepopulate them with those values. Smart defaults can be applied to task flows as well; for example, if users completed task X, which is likely to be followed by task Y, take users directly to the page for task Y (Figure 2.22).

DO NOT USE DEFAULT VALUES FOR SENSITIVE INFORMATION

For sensitive information such as gender, salutation, age, race, and so forth, do not use default values, as they could offend some users or be perceived as biased. For example, for gender, showing male or female as the default may make users feel that the application is biased in favor of that gender; the same is true if the salutation is defaulted to Mr. or Ms.

Additionally, when it's unclear as to why certain types of personal information would be relevant for an application, it's better to make that information optional or offer users a choice to not disclose such information. For instance, on

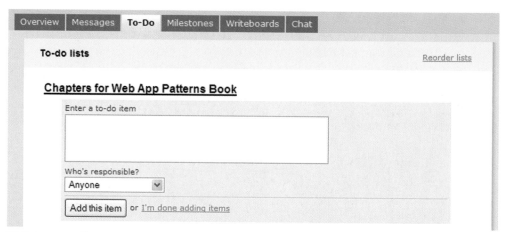

FIGURE 2.22 Basecamp uses smart defaults to improve task flows. After users create a "To-do" list, the page shows users the form "Enter a to-do item" without requiring them to click "Add a To-Do" item.

match-making applications, it would be clear to users why their gender information would be appropriate. However, for an email application, it may be difficult for users to understand how their gender information would be relevant.

DO NOT DEFAULT OPT-IN OPTIONS

When presenting opt-in options, such as those for newsletters or other communications from the company or third parties, make sure the default selections are not in favor of the company. If users don't read forms carefully, they may sign up for services or communications they would not have chosen otherwise. Later, they would consider any follow-up communication received from the company as spam or would distrust the company for such practices.

Related design patterns

Using smart defaults is another way to make forms appear shorter and faster to fill out (SHORT FORMS). In addition, they minimize the chances of error and reduce the need for error messages (ERROR MESSAGES).

FORGIVING FORMAT
Problem

Forms often require users to provide information such as phone numbers, credit card numbers, dates, and so forth, which may be entered in a variety of formats and syntax. For example, when entering a phone number, various options are available to users: without spaces (e.g., 3035555555), separated by spaces or dashes (e.g., 303 555 5555 or 303-555-5555), and entered with appropriate

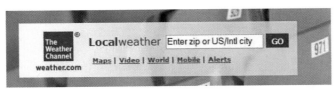

FIGURE 2.23 The Weather Channel allows users to enter either zip codes or city names to get weather information. It also uses only one text field instead of separating the input into two separate text fields.

separators (e.g., (303) 555-5555). Even when an example is provided to users, it is possible that they may not follow the format exactly as specified. Showing an error message may slow down the form-filling task and frustrate users if there are several form elements with stringent formatting requirements.

Solution

Allow users to enter data in a variety of formats and design web applications so that it can accept them without having to show an error message (Figure 2.23).

Why

For several types of information (e.g., dates, phone numbers, zip/postal code, etc.) there are several "correct" ways of entering data. When filling out forms, rather than putting the burden of formatting on users, it is easier for the application to accept multiple, yet unambiguous, data formats and parse them as necessary to meet application requirements.

How

Consider alternative ways a user might enter data and then design the application to accept them as long as they are unambiguous and can be parsed correctly. For ambiguous inputs, offer users alternatives to choose from so that they do not feel they have made an error and that they are making progress (Figure 2.24). This may also be accomplished by suggesting valid choices to users (Figure 2.25; see also the AUTOSUGGEST/AUTOCOMPLETION pattern in Chapter 8).

PROVIDE INPUT HINTS/PROMPTS

Even when applications are designed to accept multiple formats, show an example of at least one acceptable format (see the INPUT HINTS/PROMPTS pattern later in this chapter). Such formatting instructions eliminate doubts in users' minds about the appropriate way to enter data.

Related design patterns

Allowing users to enter data in a variety of formats is just one of the ways to minimize user input errors and make form filling easier. Input errors can also be minimized by providing necessary formatting instructions and

FIGURE 2.24
Expedia asks users
to choose from likely
options for the airport
when the input (San
Francisco, in this
example) has multiple
possibilities.

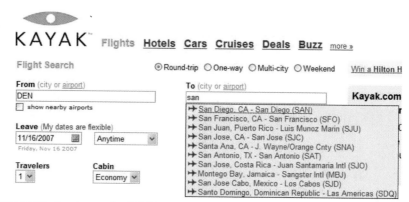

Please help us with a little more information

> 1 We found more than one airport that matched 'San Francisco'. Please select an airport from the list below.

Going to:

○ San Francisco, CA (QSF-All Airports)
○ Oakland, CA (OAK-Oakland Intl.)
○ San Francisco, CA (SFO-San Francisco Intl.)
○ San Jose, CA (SJC-San Jose Intl.)
Or
○ Enter a new location or use Airport lookup

FIGURE 2.25 Kayak uses the AUTOSUGGEST/AUTOCOMPLETION pattern to offer valid choices to users and minimize errors.

prompts (INPUT HINTS/PROMPTS) and by suggesting valid choices as users are entering data (see the AUTOSUGGEST/AUTOCOMPLETION pattern in Chapter 8).

KEYBOARD NAVIGATION

Problem

When filling out forms, users often move between fields using the Tab key or use the keyboard keys to select an option from a dropdown. Requiring users to switch between the mouse and keyboard to fill out certain parts of forms can not only become frustrating but may also make the form inaccessible to users with assistive technologies.

Solution

Allow users to use the Tab key to move from one form element to another. In addition, ensure that users can press the Enter key to submit the form; and, if it improves interaction efficiency, allow them to navigate using keyboard short-cuts (Figure 2.26). Also make sure that the dropdown lists are accessible using the keyboard keys, especially those implemented using JavaScript.

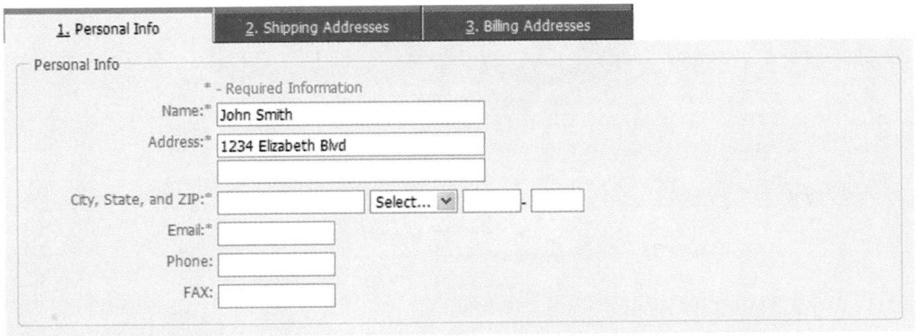

FIGURE 2.26 In this example, users can both navigate the form using the "Tab" key and navigate to different tabs using keyboard shortcuts. For example, users can navigate to the "Billing Address" by pressing "Alt + 3" (on Windows) or "Ctrl + 3" (on a Mac).

Why

Allowing users to interact with forms with a keyboard is a good practice, not just for improving accessibility of forms, but also for making form filling faster, since users do not need to switch between the keyboard and mouse to fill out a form.

How

Enable keyboard navigation for all forms; that is, users should be able to use forms using either the keyboard or mouse. Pay particular attention to navigating between fields. By default, web browsers provide a default tab sequence to navigate among page elements (tabs, form elements, and links) based on their order of appearance in the HTML code. In most well-structured pages, designers do not have to specify the tab sequence. But in cases where the HTML code doesn't match the users' task flow (that is, how users are going to fill out the form), override the default tab sequence using the **tabindex** attribute, as in this example:

```
<input type="text" name="fieldname" id="fieldname" tabindex="110" />
```

This is often necessary when forms are presented using multicolumn layouts, where it is important that the "Tab" key moves the cursor to the next logical form element, not simply from left to right or top to bottom in the order of occurrence of form elements in the HTML code.

> **NOTE**
>
> The **tabindex** attribute can take a value between 1 and 32,767. When coding forms and using the **tabindex** attribute, increment the **tabindex** value by 10. If the need arises to change the form and insert one or more form elements between existing elements, it's possible to use numbers between existing **tabindex** values without affecting the rest of the form.

Table 2.1	Browser Keyboard Shortcuts
F	Invokes File menu in IE and Firefox
E	Invokes Edit menu in IE and Firefox
V	Invokes View menu in IE and Firefox
A	Invokes Favorites menu in IE
T	Invokes Tools menu in IE and Firefox
H	Invokes Help menu in IE and Firefox
B	Invokes Bookmarks menu in Firefox
S	Invokes History menu in Firefox

BE CAREFUL WHEN PLACING CURSOR IN FIRST FORM FIELD

When the primary task for users is to fill out a form (e.g., search, register, login, etc.), it's usually acceptable to place the cursor in the first field when the page loads so that they can start filling out the form right away.

However, for pages with navigational elements that allow users to access other areas of the application, or with content users may need to read (e.g., instructions for filling out the form or error messages), avoid placing the cursor in a form field. Automatic placement of the cursor in such instances would render the page unusable to screen reader users because they are likely to miss the information above the form field.

CONSIDER OFFERING KEYBOARD SHORTCUTS

Offer keyboard shortcuts for applications that are going to be used regularly and the primary focus is on interaction efficiency (e.g., applications for customer support centers). Keyboard shortcuts can be implemented in HTML using the **accesskey** attribute, as in this example:

```
<input type="button" value="buttonName" accesskey="k" />
```

By specifying the **accesskey** attribute, users can navigate directly to that form element by pressing the "Alt" key (or the "Ctrl" key on a Mac) plus the letter or number specified in the **accesskey** attribute.

When assigning keyboard shortcuts, it's important to not implement and redefine commonly used browser shortcuts. See Table 2.1 for a list of these shortcuts.

Related design patterns

Allowing keyboard navigation not only helps in filling out forms quickly but is also essential for making web pages accessible (see the ACCESSIBLE FORMS pattern in Chapter 11).

INPUT HINTS/PROMPTS

Problem

For certain input fields, users may be unsure of what is expected of them or if they must adhere to specific syntax or formatting requirements. Users may then provide information that is either incorrect or is in an incorrect format.

Solution

Provide necessary hints, prompts, or formatting instructions to educate users on how they should enter d ata (Figure 2.27). In situations where it is possible to enter data in multiple ways, use a FORGIVING FORMAT (discussed earlier).

Why

A prompt that describes what is expected from users eliminates guesswork and reduces the chances of errors, which makes form filling faster.

How

There are several ways to provide hints and instructions to users (Figure 2.28):

- *Provide examples* of how to enter data. For instance, if an email text field accepts multiple emails, show an example of multiple emails separated by a comma or another delimiter.

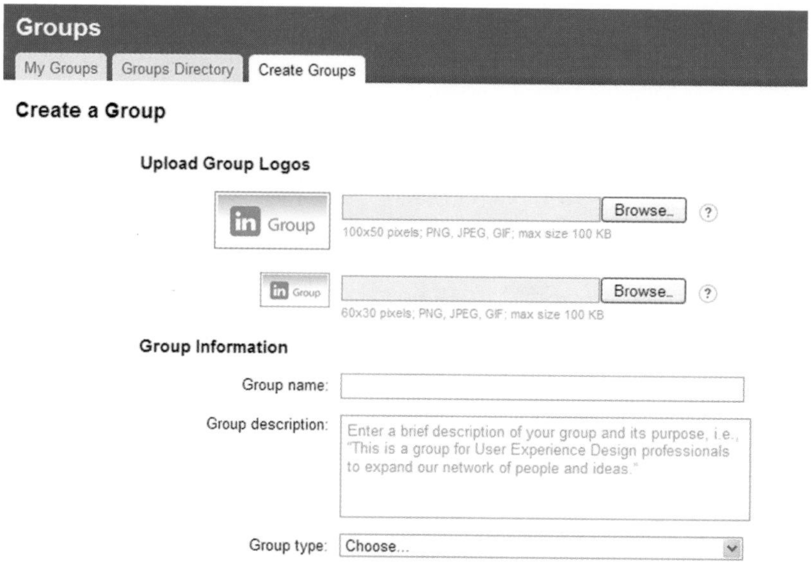

FIGURE 2.27 When creating groups on LinkedIn, users are offered necessary hints and requirements for Group Logos, such as dimensions, file formats, and file sizes, and are shown an example of a group description embedded within the text field.

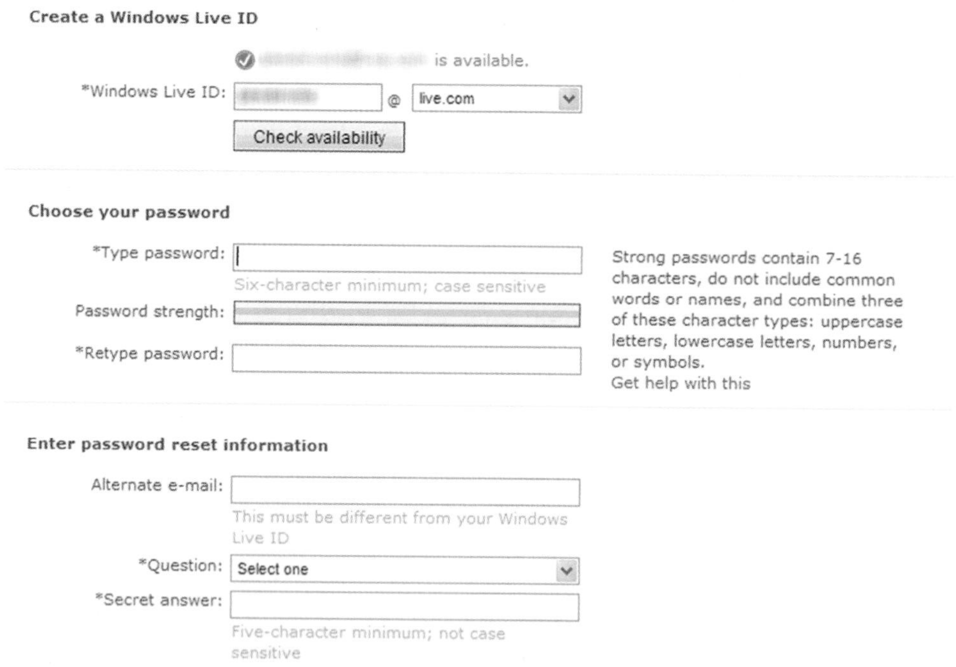

FIGURE 2.28 The Windows Live sign-up form shows users prompts for passwords, alternate email, and the secret answer. In addition, when users focus on a field, they are offered additional information and the option to get more help with a "Get help with this" link.

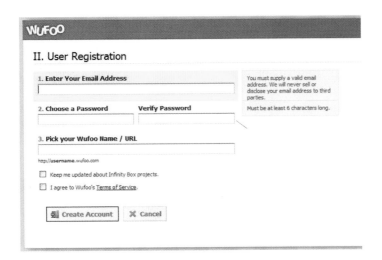

FIGURE 2.29
Wufoo shows
prompts on both
hover and focus.

- *Show accepted formats* for information such as dates, phone numbers, credit card numbers, and so forth. For dates, show acceptable formats as **mm/dd/yy**, **dd/mm/yy**, or **mm/dd/yyyy**; for phone numbers in the USA, use **xxx-xxx-xxxx**; and so forth).
- *Show constraints* for fields such as a minimum or maximum number of characters. For example, for a password field, users may be asked to enter at least six characters with at least one special character other than a space.

Make hints or prompts brief—no longer than a few words or a sentence—to avoid having users ignore them. In addition, put input hints or examples closer to the corresponding form elements. To clearly distinguish input hints from labels, make them less salient by using a lighter color and/or a smaller font.

CONSIDER DYNAMIC CONTEXTUAL INSTRUCTIONS

When hints or prompts need to include elaborate or detailed instructions, consider showing prompts dynamically for the form element (or group of elements) that has focus or the element users have hovered the cursor over (Figure 2.29). One downside of this approach is that it requires users to focus on a specific element (or group of elements) to see instructional text.

MATCH TEXT FIELD SIZES TO THE EXPECTED DATA

Do not make text field sizes appear longer (or shorter) than the expected length of data to be entered; in cases where the data length cannot be accurately predicted, make its size large enough to show a majority of the data entry. Field sizes can work as subtle hints for users and suggest the length of the data input expected from them. For example, if users are going to enter their zip code and the text field size is five characters long, most users will not consider entering the add-on code. In addition, if only five characters of the zip code are stored in the database, not only make the text field show only five characters but also restrict users' input to five characters. This can be accomplished in HTML as follows:

```
<input type="text" size="5" maxlength="5" />
```

In the preceding example, size="5" controls the text field length as it appears to users, and maxlength="5" restricts the number of characters users can enter to five.

In addition, having different lengths for text fields serves as a cue for the nature of the data in the text fields and makes it easier to find information on a page, especially when users are editing information (Mayhew, 1991).

Related design patterns

Reducing errors is an important aspect of designing effective forms. In addition to INPUT HINTS/PROMPTS, use the REQUIRED FIELD INDICATORS, FORGIVING FORMAT, and SMART DEFAULTS patterns to minimize user errors and reduce the time it takes to fill out forms.

ACTION BUTTONS

Problem

Users must "submit" the form after filling it out to continue with the next step in the workflow or to complete the task. It's important that users choose the appropriate action so that they can move forward with the task and avoid any data loss.

Solution

Allow users to submit forms using action buttons; they are also referred to as *command* buttons (Galitz, 2002). Use meaningful labels that clearly describe the action, such as "Save Changes," "Register," "Log In," and so forth. In addition, make the primary action button on the page salient so users don't miss it (Figure 2.30).

Why

Buttons are typically identified with taking actions such as submitting form data, in contrast to links, which afford navigation between pages. Because of their "pushbutton-like" shape (i.e., a raised appearance), buttons invite "clicking" or "pressing." In addition, because of users' familiarity with them in desktop applications, they make a suitable choice for performing actions.

How

Use action buttons (or images that resemble buttons) for submitting form data. In addition, ensure that they have a higher visual saliency than secondary

FIGURE 2.30 LinkedIn clearly indicates the primary action "Send" on this "Compose your message" form.

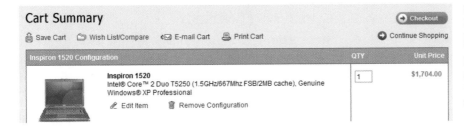

FIGURE 2.31
Dell shows the primary action "Checkout" as a button, but the secondary action "Continue Shopping" as a link.

actions such as "Cancel," "Preview," and so forth. Reducing the visual prominence of buttons with secondary actions minimizes their inadvertent selection and potential errors (Wroblewski, 2008).

A recent trend is to show secondary actions as links to reduce their visual emphasis (Figure 2.31). But eye-tracking studies by Wroblewski (2008) did not find any added benefit for such a practice when compared with showing them as action buttons (even with the same emphasis as primary actions); however, they did not cause additional errors either.

Too many action buttons may clutter the interface and can make it difficult for users to decide which action is appropriate to perform a task. In such instances, consider changing a few action buttons into links (or links with icons),

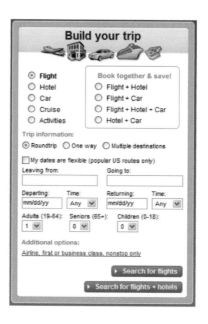

especially if they are of secondary importance. Additionally, try grouping related buttons to make three or fewer visually distinct groups.

LABEL BUTTONS CLEARLY AND CONCISELY

Use labels to clearly convey actions to minimize any confusion as to the outcome. Because buttons are used to perform a task or accomplish a goal, use a verb in the button's label to represent that task or goal. Avoid using labels such as "Submit," which only signify the act of *submitting* the form data; rather, use labels such as "Save Changes," "Search for Flights," or "Find Users" (Figure 2.32).

Following are two additional guidelines for labeling action buttons:

Using "Remove" and "Delete." Use "Delete" when data elements will be permanently deleted and will not be available without having to create a new data element. Whereas, use "Remove" when data elements are removed only from that context but are still available in other contexts. For example, in email applications, to remove a document from a list of attachments, use "Remove attachment" or "Remove." But to delete a message from a list of messages, use "Delete message" or "Delete."

Using "Add" and "New." Use "New" when creating a completely new record (or data element). Use "Add" when selecting or relating existing data elements to another data element. For example, to create a new user account, use "New user" or "New," but to add another user's calendar, use "Add calendar" or "Add."

✔ Please log in first and then we'll send you right along.

Username: |

Password: [   ] (I forgot my password/username)

☐ Remember me on this computer

[Sign in]

FIGURE 2.33
Basecamp's login
screen aligns the
primary action
"Sign in" with
form elements.

ALIGN PRIMARY ACTION BUTTONS WITH FORM INPUT ELEMENTS

Align primary action buttons with form input elements (Figure 2.33). In an eye-tracking study conducted by Wroblewski and Etre (2007), aligning action command buttons with form input elements lead to faster form completion times, as it provided a clear path to completion for users.

ENABLE PRIMARY ACTION WHEN USERS PRESS "ENTER"

The primary action for a form should be the default action when users press the "Return" or "Enter" key. This is particularly important for forms with only one input field, such as "Search." This can be accomplished in HTML by setting the primary action button type to "Submit," as shown in the following examples:

```
<input type="submit" value="Save Changes" /> or
<button type="submit">Save Changes</button>
```

BE CAREFUL WHEN DISABLING THE PRIMARY ACTION

On short forms, it may be acceptable to disable the primary action button until users have filled in the required fields (Figure 2.34). Such a practice can avoid errors caused by inadvertent submission of forms without all the required information. However, such a practice may be inappropriate for longer and complex forms because users may not know why the primary action is unavailable. They may then incorrectly conclude that the form is not working properly and abandon the form.

DISABLE THE ACTION BUTTON AFTER THE FIRST CLICK

Performing the same action multiple times (by repeatedly clicking the action button) could have undesirable consequences. For example, repeatedly clicking the action button may place an order multiple times or place buy/sell orders on stocks multiple times. In such instances, disable the action button or remove the action button and replace it with text such as "Processing ..." or "Please Wait...." This will acknowledge users' actions and indicate that the web application is waiting for a response (Figure 2.35).

Create your Campfire account

When you sign up for Campfire you start off on the **free** plan. You can stay on the free plan as long as you'd like or upgrade to a paying plan later on. It's up to you.

Full name

Email address

Time zone (GMT-06:00) Central Time (US & Canada)

Every Campfire site has its own unique web address. This is where you'll login. For example, if you wanted your Campfire site to be at acme.campfirenow.com you'd enter acme in the field below.

Campfire URL http:// .campfirenow.com

Letters and numbers only, no spaces please.

Password

Password again

☐ Yes, I agree to the terms of service and the privacy policy

Sign me up and let me in!

FIGURE 2.34 Campfire disables the "Sign me up …" button until all fields are filled in.

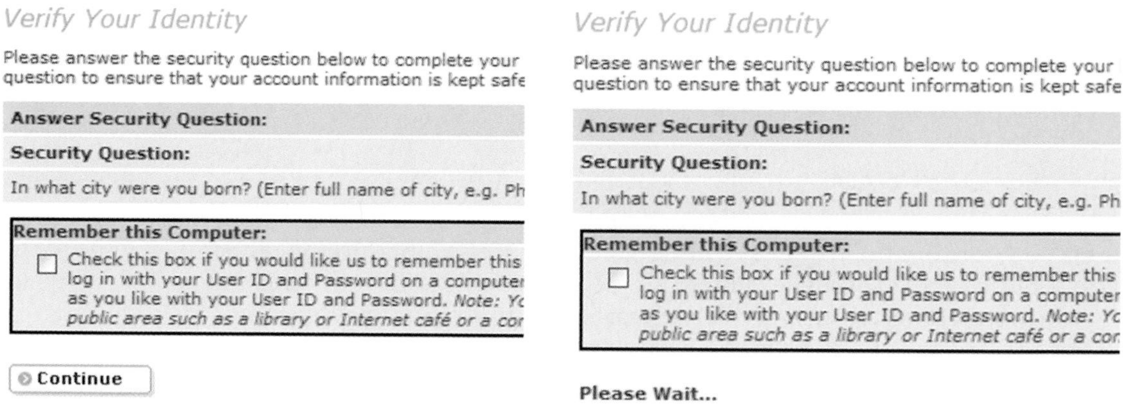

Verify Your Identity

Please answer the security question below to complete your question to ensure that your account information is kept safe

Answer Security Question:

Security Question:

In what city were you born? (Enter full name of city, e.g. Ph

Remember this Computer:

☐ Check this box if you would like us to remember this log in with your User ID and Password on a computer as you like with your User ID and Password. *Note: Yc public area such as a library or Internet café or a cor*

○ Continue

Verify Your Identity

Please answer the security question below to complete your question to ensure that your account information is kept safe

Answer Security Question:

Security Question:

In what city were you born? (Enter full name of city, e.g. Ph

Remember this Computer:

☐ Check this box if you would like us to remember this log in with your User ID and Password on a computer as you like with your User ID and Password. *Note: Yc public area such as a library or Internet café or a cor*

Please Wait…

FIGURE 2.35 Advanta replaces the "Continue" button with "Please Wait …" text to let users know that their action was submitted and the application is now waiting for a response.

ELIMINATE RESET BUTTONS

A "Reset" button reverts a form to its original state. If users start with a blank form, clicking "Reset" after filling out all or part of the form will cause them to lose all their entered data, and if they start with a filled-in form to make changes, clicking "Reset" will undo all their changes. This loss of changes cannot be undone. Therefore, do not use the "Reset" button (Nielsen, 2000).

Related design patterns

When submitted, form data usually require some form of validation. If the form fails validation, users must be informed of the reasons for its failure. This is usually accomplished using ERROR MESSAGES.

ERROR MESSAGES

Problem

Errors are inevitable, even with the most usable form design. Despite appropriate labels and instructions, not all users will submit the form with accurate and complete information every time. The following types of errors are particularly common:

- *Missing information.* This is when users fail to provide one or more pieces of required information.
- *Formatting errors.* This is when users' input does not match the desired format—for example, mismatched data types (numerical versus alphabetical), length errors (either shorter or longer input than desired), date format errors, decimal errors, and so forth.
- *Invalid information.* This is when information provided is incorrect—for example, incorrect user ID and password, "to" date before the "from" date in a date range, and so forth.

Solution

Show users an error message and clearly indicate the reasons for the error(s) and appropriate instructions for fixing them. Additionally, show error messages on the same page as the form and retain the user-entered data (Figure 2.36). This approach has two important benefits:

1. Users can refer to the error message while correcting the error(s).
2. Users don't have to reenter correct data.

Why

When errors are managed gracefully, users can quickly fix problems and are not distracted from their main task (or goal).

How

Most important, ensure that users know that an error occurred right away. Grab users' attention to the error by showing messages in a salient color (either the background color or the text color). In addition to color, consider using an alert

FIGURE 2.36
Adobe Buzzword shows an error message above the "Sign In" area.

icon (or any other appropriate icon) to draw attention to the error message and/or the form elements that caused the error(s) (Figure 2.37).

PROVIDE INSTRUCTIONS TO FIX THE ERROR

This could be as simple as asking users to do something simple and specific (e.g., "Reenter your username and password. Then click Log In") to offer suggestions to fix the error (e.g., "Username is case-sensitive. Check the Caps Lock key on your keyboard").

SHOW ERROR MESSAGES ON THE SAME PAGE AS THE FORM

Web applications that show error messages on a different page force users to memorize the error(s) and the instructions to fix them before returning to the form page containing errors. If there are several errors on a page, this can become cumbersome, because users may have to go back and forth several times to fix all the errors. Showing error messages on the same page as the form eliminates the need to return to the page with the error message and makes it easier for users to fix errors.

RETAIN USER-ENTERED INFORMATION

When showing error messages, it's important that user-entered information is not lost. Asking users to enter the same information again is annoying and may lead them to abandon the form (Figure 2.38).

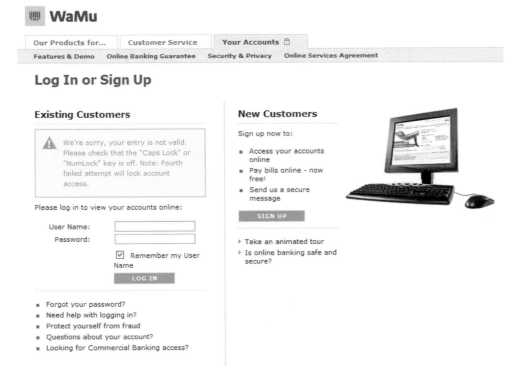

FIGURE 2.37 Washington Mutual's login form clearly indicates that an error occurred and uses an alert icon to grab users' attention to the error.

FIGURE 2.38 SugarSync retains user information when presenting errors. Because passwords are not echoed back to users, it is acceptable to remove passwords if they are the cause of the error.

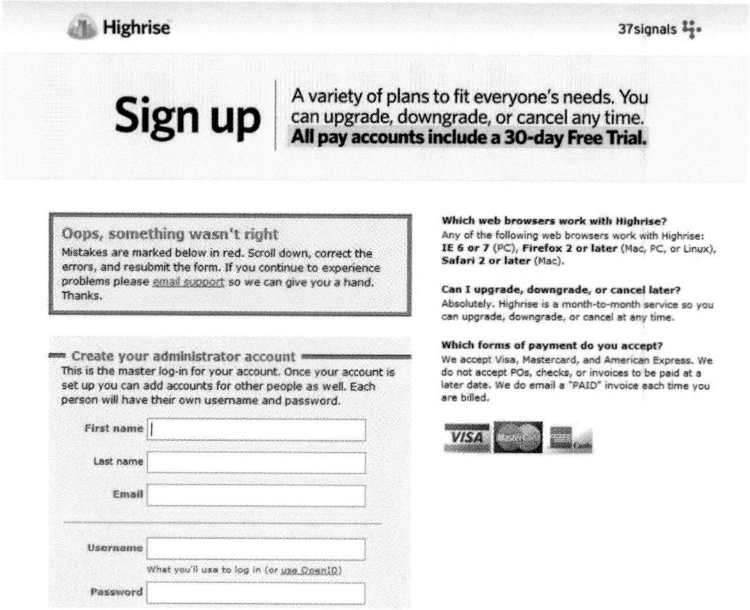

FIGURE 2.39 Highrise shows the error message on the same page and clearly indicates what needs to be done to fix the error.

IDENTIFY "PROBLEM" AREAS

In addition to showing the error message, clearly identify the specific form elements that caused the errors. This is particularly helpful for longer forms in which users may have to search for the form element(s) that caused the error (Figure 2.39).

Related design patterns

Although error messages are an important part of form design, every step should be taken to prevent errors. This can be accomplished by clearly indicating required fields (REQUIRED FIELD INDICATORS), providing appropriate instructions for formatting and the type of data expected from users (INPUT HINTS/PROMPTS), minimizing user data input using appropriate defaults (SMART DEFAULTS), and allowing users to accept data in common formats (FORGIVING FORMAT).

CHAPTER 3

User Authentication

INTRODUCTION

When web applications enable one-to-one interaction and store user-specific information, they require users to create an account (REGISTRATION) and choose unique credentials to access the web applications. Registering may require users to enter a set of alphanumeric characters from a distorted image to prevent spam and ensure that registering users are human and not automated computer programs (*CAPTCHA*, Completely Automated Public Turing test to tell Computers and Humans Apart).

Once unique credentials are established, users can identify themselves (LOG IN) and store and access their personal information. After logging in and accomplishing desired tasks, users often need a way to exit the application to ensure that unauthorized users cannot access and modify their account information (LOG OUT). Many applications also have provisions for automatically logging out users after a certain period of inactivity (AUTOMATIC LOGOUT).

Because many web applications are used occasionally, users often forget their login information and need a way to retrieve it. Depending on the security level of the applications, users may be asked to provide one or more pieces of unique information about their account. It can be as simple as providing the email address associated with the account or answering one or more security questions that were established during registration (FORGOT USERNAME/PASSWORD).

REGISTRATION

Problem

Web applications often need to uniquely identify users. The reasons include preventing unauthorized access to personal and sensitive information (e.g., financial or health records), increasing convenience (e.g., storing billing and shipping addresses), and enabling sharing (e.g., photos). Despite such benefits, users often hesitate when providing personal information and often shy away from applications that require them to set up an account.

Choose a plan that fits your needs
Plans can be changed at any time, so feel free to start using Crazy Egg with a free plan.

FIGURE 3.1
Crazy Egg has one of the shortest and simplest registration forms. To register, users only need to provide their email address and password and agree to the terms of use and privacy policy.

Solution

Delay registration for as long as possible and allow users to explore the application so that they fully understand the benefits of setting up an account. In addition, if users are willing to forego some convenience, make it possible for them to transact without registering. Topix.net found a significant increase in the number of posts and a substantial improvement in their quality when they removed the registration requirement from their discussion forums (Blake, 2006). When registration unavoidable, clearly indicate the benefits of registration and ask users only for the information necessary to set up an account (Figure 3.1).

Why

For most applications, setting up an account or registering is not one of the users' goals. Their goals typically include purchasing an item, sharing information, paying bills, and so forth. Asking users to register is usually an interruption in their interaction experience, since it distracts them from their primary goals. Therefore, registration should be delayed as long as possible. This is common in e-commerce applications (e.g., Amazon, Buy.com), content portals (e.g., Yahoo!, MSN, Morningstar), and content-sharing applications (e.g., Flickr, YouTube, SlideShare), which allow users to explore content without a user account. Only when users want to make a purchase, add content, make comments, or customize an application's look and feel do these web applications require users to register. Thus, delaying registration also allows users to experience the application's benefits and better understand the need and value of setting up an account.

How

First and foremost, keep registration forms as short as possible and ask only for essential information (Figure 3.2). For most applications, this includes a unique username (or user ID or email address) and associated password.

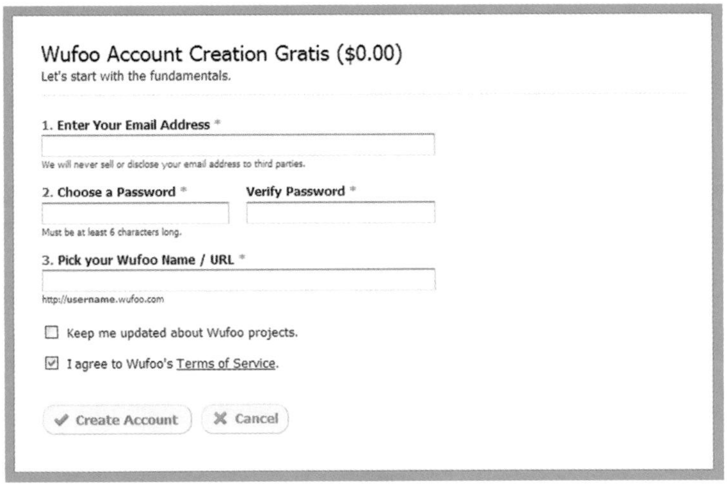

FIGURE 3.2
Wufoo, an online form-builder application, uses a simple registration form that asks only for the essential information for creating an account.

Because users cannot see the password they entered, ask them to confirm the password by reentering it. In addition, if required for legal reasons, ask them to agree to the usage terms and conditions.

When users need to set up an account, it's important that forms are as short as possible and ask only for relevant information so that users are distracted only for a very short period of time and can continue to accomplish their goals. Asking for nonessential information increases the time it takes to register and increases the chances of user errors. This may cause a user to abandon registration or provide incorrect or nonsensical data.

When asking users for any personally sensitive information, such as birth date, gender, race, and so forth, clearly indicate why the information is needed and how it will be used (Figure 3.3).

CONSIDER USING AN EMAIL ADDRESS FOR A USERNAME

When registering, users are often required to choose a unique identifier for their account such as a username or email address. Email addresses are often a better choice because they are always unique and are easier to remember even when users have multiple email accounts. In addition, when users have to be reminded of their login credentials, it's easier to send the reminder information to their registered email address (see FORGOT USERNAME/PASSWORD pattern later in this chapter).

USE CAPTCHA TO ENSURE REGISTRATION BY HUMANS

An increasing number of automated web crawlers have made it difficult to distinguish them from legitimate human users. Use CAPTCHA as part of the registration form to minimize registration by such automated agents (Figure 3.4).

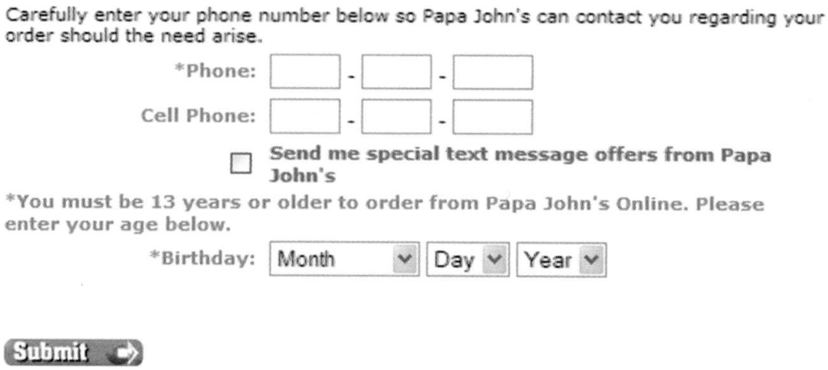

Carefully enter your phone number below so Papa John's can contact you regarding your
order should the need arise.

*Phone: [ ] - [ ] - [ ]

Cell Phone: [ ] - [ ] - [ ]

☐ **Send me special text message offers from Papa John's**

*You must be 13 years or older to order from Papa John's Online. Please enter your age below.

*Birthday: [Month ▾] [Day ▾] [Year ▾]

Submit ⟶

FIGURE 3.3 Papa John's registration form justifies asking users to enter their birth dates by indicating that they must be 13 or older to place an online order.

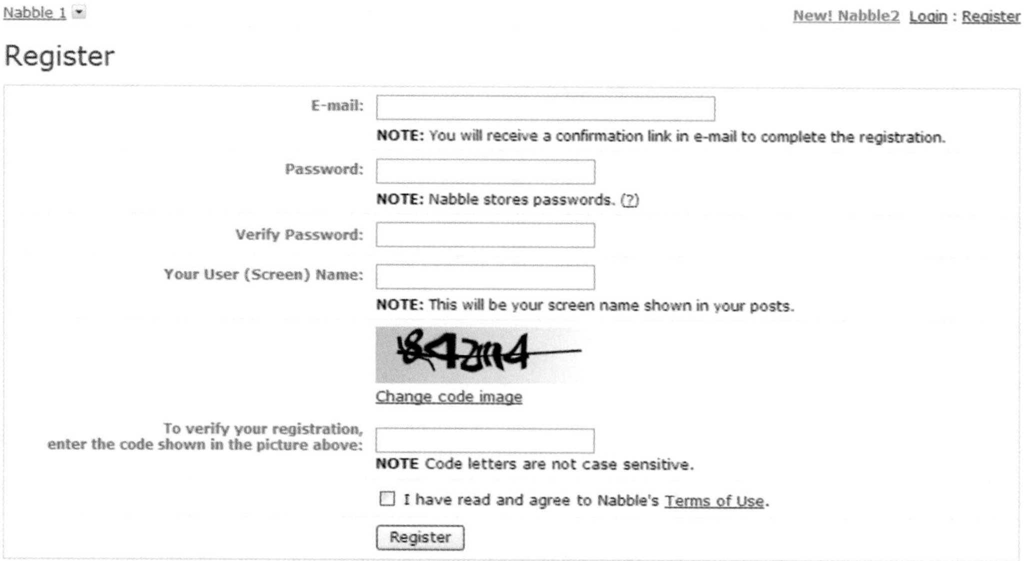

Nabble 1 ▾ New! Nabble2 Login : Register

Register

E-mail: [ ]
NOTE: You will receive a confirmation link in e-mail to complete the registration.

Password: [ ]
NOTE: Nabble stores passwords. (?)

Verify Password: [ ]

Your User (Screen) Name: [ ]
NOTE: This will be your screen name shown in your posts.

Change code image

To verify your registration, enter the code shown in the picture above: [ ]
NOTE Code letters are not case sensitive.

☐ I have read and agree to Nabble's Terms of Use.

[Register]

FIGURE 3.4 Nabble asks users to respond to a CAPTCHA image when registering.

CAPTCHA requires users to type characters from a distorted image containing letters and/or numbers before they can register. The ability to correctly identify characters from the distorted image is used as sufficient evidence that the user is human and not an automated agent (see the CAPTCHA pattern next).

Although the use of CAPTCHA is becoming common, it is yet one more piece of information users have to provide and should be avoided, if possible.

Calbucci (2008) found that removing CAPTCHA from the registration form improved the conversion rate by 9.2 percent on Sampa (*www.sampa.com*).

CONSIDER THE "LAZY" REGISTRATION APPROACH

As mentioned, registration is often an interruption in users' interaction experience. Therefore, delay registration as much as possible and allow users to explore the application before asking them to register. For instance, Morningstar asks users to register or log in only when they land on a page that requires them to provide sensitive information (e.g., creating an investment portfolio) or when they are accessing content reserved for paying customers.

To make the registration process as efficient as possible, even when it is delayed, an option is to use a *"lazy" registration* approach, which is collecting information about users using browser cookies as they interact with the application. As Mahemoff (2006) states:

> As the user interacts with the application, the account accumulates data. In many cases, the data is explicitly contributed by the user, and it's advisable to expose this kind of information so that the user can actually populate it. In this way, the initial profile may be seen as a structure with lots of holes. Some holes are eventually filled out automatically and others by the user himself. (p. 475)

By collecting information in the background, when users are presented with the registration form, some of the registration fields can be prepopulated, requiring users to verify collected information rather than enter it. For example, if a user signs up for an email newsletter, the application has the user's email address, which it can prepopulate on the registration form.

CONSIDER ELIMINATING REGISTRATION

Offer users the option to have access without registering in applications where they may just want to complete transactions quickly. This is common in e-commerce applications, especially those that support gift registries, where users may just want to purchase a gift and leave the application (Figure 3.5). Users may be prompted to register at the end of the transaction (or checkout process) with clearly listed benefits for doing so (e.g., track the order).

CLEARLY INDICATE REGISTRATION BENEFITS

For web applications where it's not possible to delay registration, clearly indicate registration benefits to users (Figure 3.6).

For many applications, listing benefits may not be sufficient, especially when registering is not free. In such instances, offer users the option to take a guided tour that explains the benefits of using the application and/or allow them to set up a free-trial account for a limited time period or with restricted functionality (Figure 3.7).

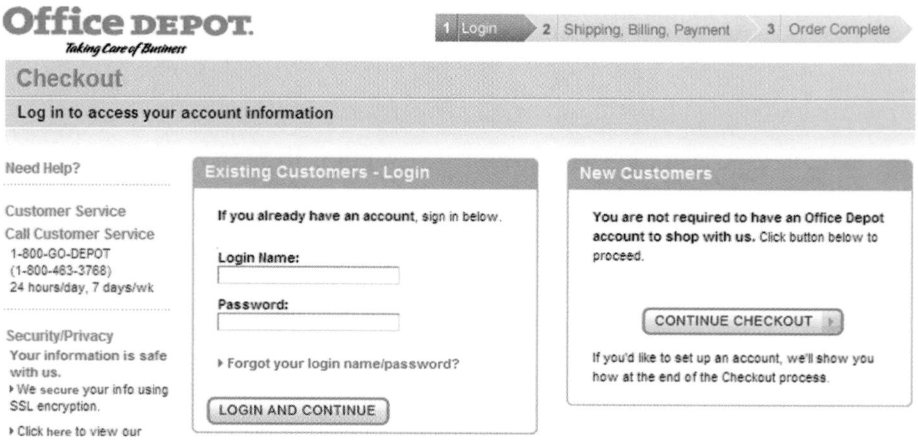

FIGURE 3.5 Office Depot offers users the option to purchase without registering. It also allows users to defer the registration decision until later, indicating that they can set up an account at the end of the checkout process.

FIGURE 3.6
Netflix not only lists registration benefits but also indicates on the same page how Netflix works. It offers links to users who want to learn more about the free trial offer or about movie selection and goes a step further by offering a phone number for users to call in case they have any questions.

CONSIDER USING "UNIFIED REGISTRATION" SERVICES

Remembering login information for more than a few applications can be difficult for users and lead to practices that could compromise the security of their personal information (e.g., writing down login information or using very simple passwords). Even when security is not a concern, forgetting login information could result in unnecessary delays in accomplishing tasks. Therefore, if feasible, allow users to register using "unified registration" services such as OpenID or Windows CardSpace.

An OpenID is an open standard that allows users to create and use one set of username and password to log in to any OpenID-enabled web application; for more information, visit *www.openid.net*. Thus, enabling support for OpenID can

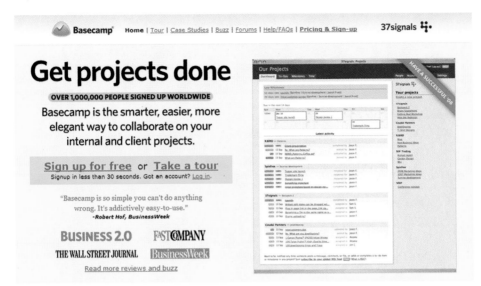

FIGURE 3.7 Basecamp (from 37Signals) offers users an application tour so they can explore its functionality and benefits. It also allows users to sign up for a free-trial account so they can experience the application firsthand. Although the free-trial account has restricted functionality it makes it possible for users to easily understand the benefits of having an account.

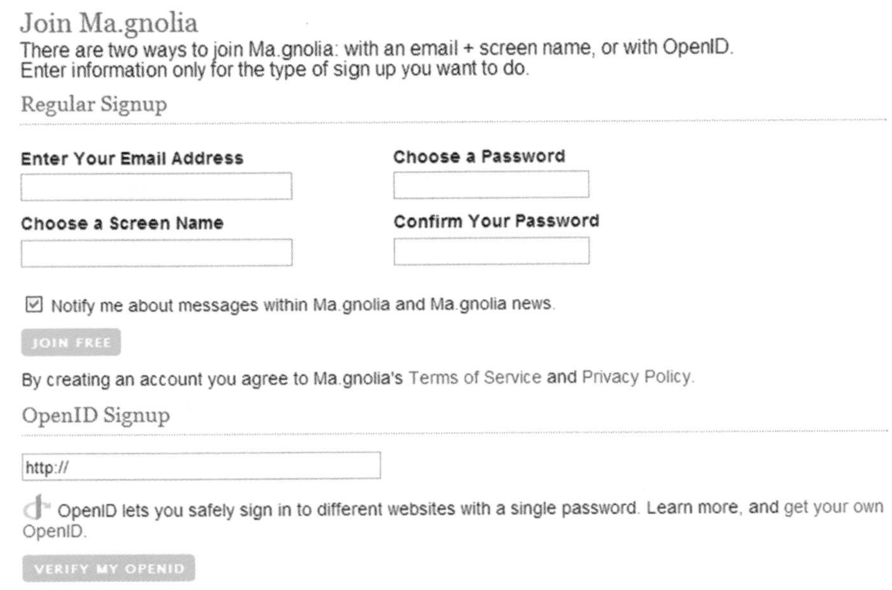

Join Ma.gnolia

There are two ways to join Ma.gnolia: with an email + screen name, or with OpenID. Enter information only for the type of sign up you want to do.

Regular Signup

Enter Your Email Address

Choose a Password

Choose a Screen Name

Confirm Your Password

☑ Notify me about messages within Ma.gnolia and Ma.gnolia news.

`JOIN FREE`

By creating an account you agree to Ma.gnolia's Terms of Service and Privacy Policy.

OpenID Signup

`http://`

OpenID lets you safely sign in to different websites with a single password. Learn more, and get your own OpenID.

`VERIFY MY OPENID`

FIGURE 3.8
Ma.gnolia offers users a regular registration process where they choose their login credentials, as well as supports registration using OpenID.

either eliminate the need for registration or at least minimize the information required from users to set up an account (Figure 3.8). Because not all users can be expected to have OpenID accounts, supporting a normal registration process is still important.

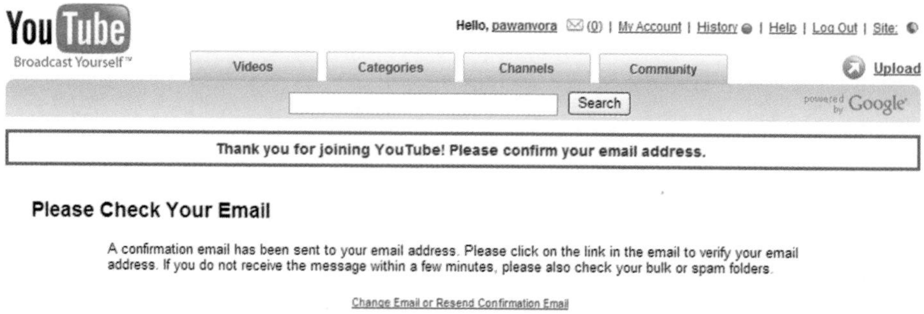

FIGURE 3.9 YouTube asks users to click the confirmation link in the email to complete their registration and then to check their spam folders if they don't see the message appear in their inbox within a few minutes.

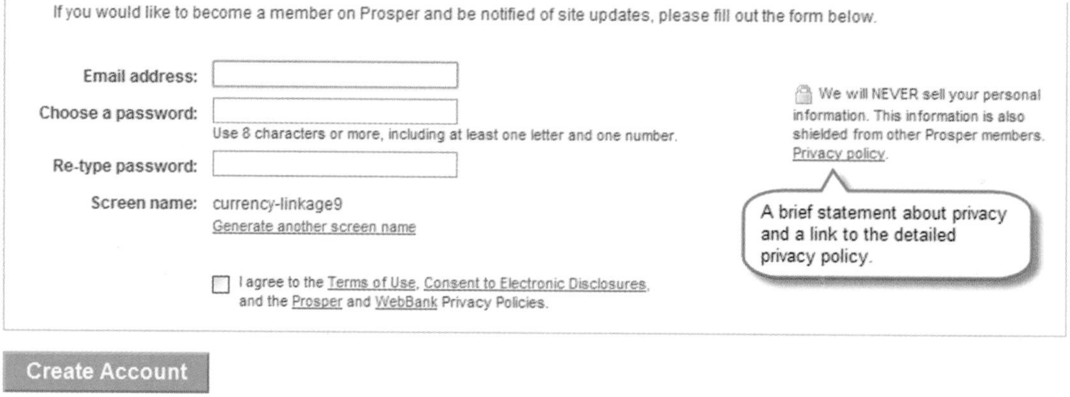

If you would like to become a member on Prosper and be notified of site updates, please fill out the form below.

Email address: [_____]

Choose a password: [_____]
Use 8 characters or more, including at least one letter and one number.

Re-type password: [_____]

Screen name: currency-linkage9
Generate another screen name

🔒 We will NEVER sell your personal information. This information is also shielded from other Prosper members. Privacy policy.

A brief statement about privacy and a link to the detailed privacy policy.

☐ I agree to the Terms of Use, Consent to Electronic Disclosures, and the Prosper and WebBank Privacy Policies.

Create Account

FIGURE 3.10 Prosper provides a brief summary of their privacy policy on the registration form, as well as offers a link to a detailed privacy policy.

VERIFY REGISTRATION

If necessary, require users to verify their registration to prevent fraud and ensure legitimate user accounts. This is commonly accomplished by sending a message with a confirmation link to the email address provided by users during registration. Only after users have returned to the application by clicking the confirmation link (or by pasting the registration URL in their browser address field) do they consider their registration complete. To ensure email reaches users' email inboxes, ask them to check their spam folders (Figure 3.9).

ALLAY USERS' PRIVACY CONCERNS

Users may be hesitant to register because they may not know how their personal information will be used. Include a brief privacy statement (e.g., "Your information will not be sold or shared") followed by a link to a detailed privacy policy statement to address such concerns (Figure 3.10).

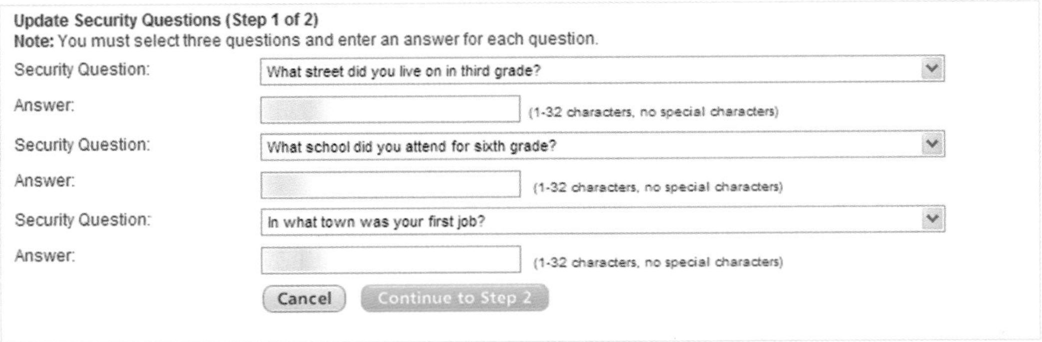

FIGURE 3.11 When setting up an account, CapitalOne requires users to set up security questions.

SET UP SECURITY QUESTIONS WHEN STORING SENSITIVE INFORMATION

Use security questions for web applications that require a higher level of security, such as for financial applications (Figure 3.11). Security questions can then be used to establish users' identities when they log in and/or when they need help retrieving their forgotten login information (see the FORGOT USERNAME/PASSWORD pattern later in this chapter).

OPT-IN

Ask users to opt in instead of opt out if the company supporting the web application plans to communicate with them in the future or send promotional information (Figure 3.12). This is the first step to making sure email sent to users is CAN-SPAM[1] compliant (Dixon, 2004; see also the Federal Trade Commission's SPAM home page at *www.ftc.gov/spam/*). The better practice is to use double opt-in, where upon opting in, users are sent an email confirmation with a link that they must click to finish the opt-in process.

In addition, set users' expectations by explaining how frequently they will receive communication and what kind of messages will be sent. With the possibility of email communication being stopped by spam filters, ask users to adjust their spam filter settings appropriately or add the "from email address" to their contact lists.

RETURN USERS TO THE NEXT LOGICAL STEP IN THE INTERACTION SEQUENCE

Upon the completion of registration, return users to the "page of departure"—that is, the page from where they chose to register or were required to register.

---

[1]CAN-SPAM is a commonly used acronym for Controlling the Assault of Non-Solicited Pornography and Marketing Act of 2003. It became a law on January 1, 2004, and applies to most businesses in the United States that send commercial email. It provides email recipients with the right to opt out (unsubscribe).

FIGURE 3.12
Evite offers users a
clear opt-in option
for sending party
tips and planning
ideas.

For example, in an e-commerce application, if users are asked to register at checkout, return them to the page they are likely to see if they were already registered or logged in, such as the shipping information page.

Related design patterns

For many web applications, registration may be the first form users encounter. To create a successful user experience, it's important to follow the patterns identified in Chapter 2—CLEAR BENEFITS, SHORT FORMS, REQUIRED FIELD INDICATORS, and ERROR MESSAGES. When presenting the registration form to users, it is important that they be given an option to LOG IN since they may have registered previously. In addition, because CAPTCHA often accompanies registration, follow the best practices identified in the following pattern.

CAPTCHA

Problem

The application needs to make sure that the action (e.g., register, provide feedback, send comment, and so forth) is initiated by a human rather than an automated agent to prevent creation of fraudulent accounts and fake responses.

Solution

Ask users to type characters from a distorted image that contains letters and/or numbers before they can register or provide comments or feedback (Figure 3.13).

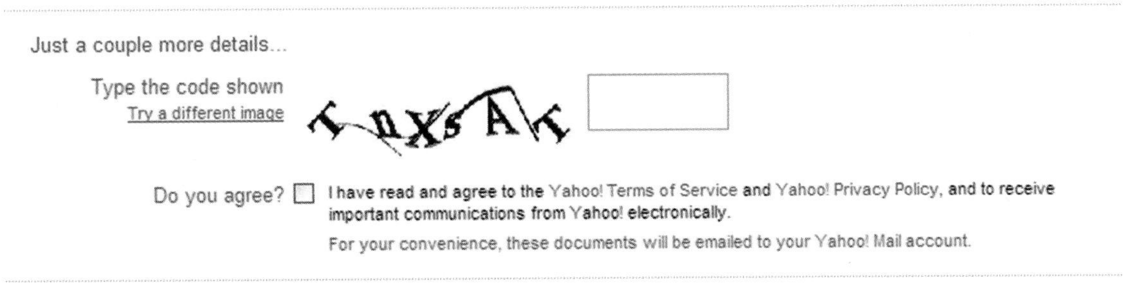

Just a couple more details...

Type the code shown
Try a different image

Do you agree? ☐ I have read and agree to the Yahoo! Terms of Service and Yahoo! Privacy Policy, and to receive important communications from Yahoo! electronically.

For your convenience, these documents will be emailed to your Yahoo! Mail account.

FIGURE 3.13 CAPTCHA on Yahoo!'s registration page.

Decoding distorted images is used as a validation that a user is human and not an automated agent, since automatically decoding a distorted image is computationally intensive. This method is referred to as CAPTCHA, which stands for Completely Automated Public Turing test to tell Computers and Humans Apart (Ahn, Blum, and Langford, 2004).[2]

Why

An increasing number of automated crawlers on the Web have made it difficult to distinguish them from legitimate human users. By asking users to do something that is relatively easy for humans to do but difficult for automated crawlers, the use of CAPTCHA makes it difficult, if not impossible, for bots and crawlers to interact with the application and submit forms.

How

CAPTCHA images typically have about four to five distorted alphanumeric characters; the alphabetical characters in the image may include both uppercase and lowercase ones. In addition, they may have lines through them, more than one distorted word, noisy backgrounds, and so forth (Figure 3.14). Users are asked to decode the image and enter the alphanumeric characters in the correct order (they may or may not be case sensitive) before submitting the form. Upon form submission, the response is verified, and users are either taken to the next step or presented with an error.

Recently, some sites have included simple math problems in CAPTCHA images such as 2 + 4 or 4 × 2 that users must answer (Figure 3.15).

ALLOW USERS TO CHANGE THE CAPTCHA IMAGE

Users may find some CAPTCHA images too distorted to distinguish between some characters (e.g., the number 1 versus a lowercase *l*, or the number 9 versus

---

[2]Many CAPTCHA images on the Web use the free CAPTCHA service offered by Carnegie Mellon University as part of their reCAPTCHA project, which helps digitize books by sending users digitized words as CAPTCHA that cannot be read by their OCR (optical character recognition) programs. For more information, visit *www.recaptcha.net*.

FIGURE 3.14 Examples of CAPTCHA images.

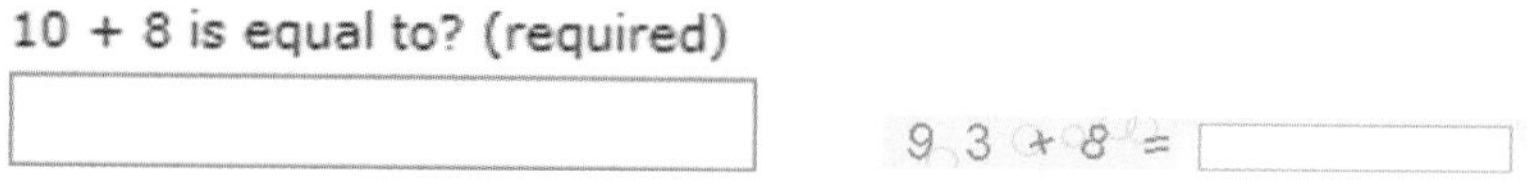

10 + 8 is equal to? (required)

9 3 + 8 =

FIGURE 3.15 Two examples of math CAPTCHA.

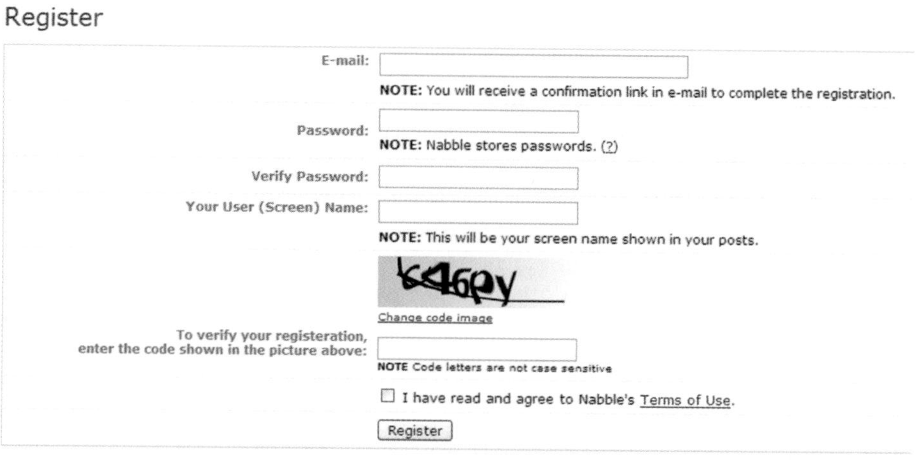

Register

E-mail:	
	NOTE: You will receive a confirmation link in e-mail to complete the registration.
Password:	
	NOTE: Nabble stores passwords. (?)
Verify Password:	
Your User (Screen) Name:	
	NOTE: This will be your screen name shown in your posts.

Change code image

To verify your registeration,
enter the code shown in the picture above:

NOTE Code letters are not case sensitive

☐ I have read and agree to Nabble's Terms of Use.

Register

FIGURE 3.16 Nabble offers users the option to change the CAPTCHA image.

a lowercase *g*). Therefore, users should be offered the option to change the CAPTCHA image by clicking on a "refresh" or "change" link (Figure 3.16).

OFFER AUDITORY CAPTCHA TO MAKE APPLICATIONS ACCESSIBLE

Because CAPTCHA is based on decoding the image, it presents an obvious obstacle for blind users or those with visual disabilities. They should be offered

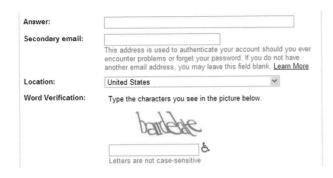

FIGURE 3.17 Gmail offers both visual and auditory CAPTCHA.

a voice CAPTCHA—an audio version of CAPTCHA—that allows them to interact with the application (Figure 3.17).

Related design patterns

Use of CAPTCHA is common during registration, as most applications try to avoid fraudulent registrations by automated web crawlers (REGISTRATION). They are also common in discussion forums or blogs, where users can make comments or participate in communities (see the GROUPS/SPECIAL INTEREST COMMUNITY pattern in Chapter 9).

LOG IN

Problem

Users need to identify themselves so that they can access their account information and/or see customized or personalized versions of the web application. For example, users may want to check their emails (e.g., Hotmail, Yahoo! Mail), access their account to see the order status on an e-commerce application (e.g., Amazon, Dell), or see the customized version of their content portals (e.g., My Yahoo!, iGoogle).

Solution

Ask users to identify themselves by providing a combination of a unique identifier (e.g., username or email address) and password that they either chose when registering with the application or that was provided to them by the system administrator. Universal identity services that uniquely identify users, such as OpenID or Windows CardSpace, can be used as well to allow users to access a web application (Figure 3.18). In addition, to make it easy to access the application, consider offering users an option to let the application remember their login information.

Why

When a web application allows users to access their personal and/or sensitive information, it is important that users identify themselves by logging in with

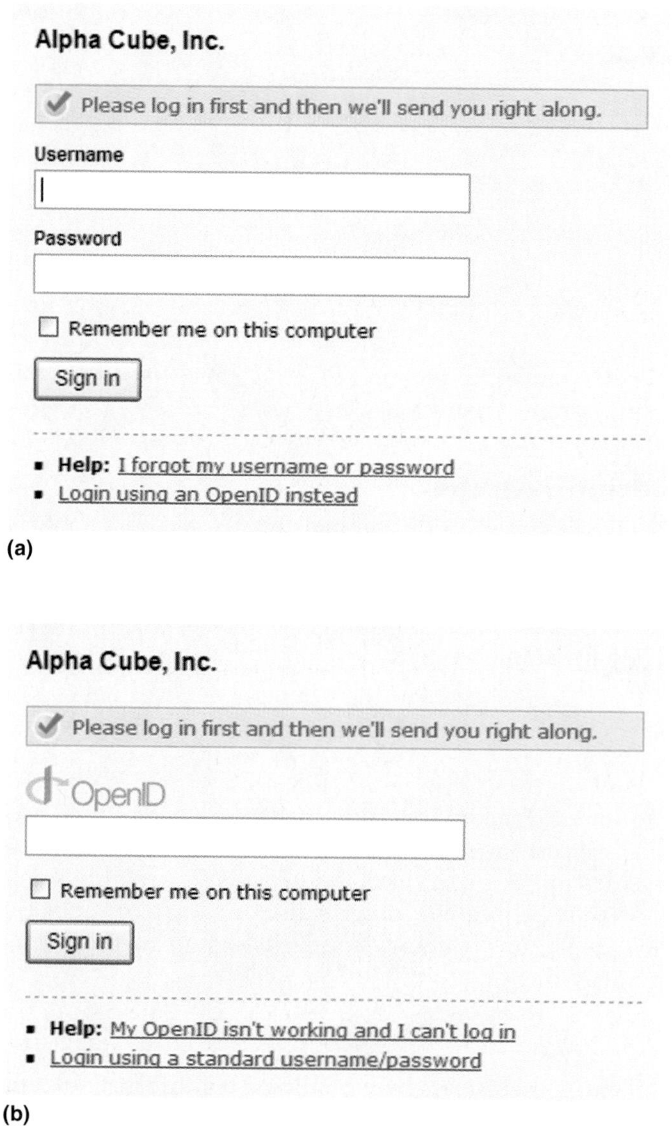

(a)

(b)

FIGURE 3.18 Basecamp allows users to log in using the username and password they chose during registration (a) or with their OpenID (b). Users may also choose to let the application remember their login information.

a unique set of credentials that they established while registering with the application. While logging in is an important task to secure account information and avoid unauthorized access, users may consider it an obstacle to accomplishing their goals. In addition, for applications not visited frequently, users may forget their login credentials and may be locked out for some time period. Therefore, where feasible, users should be offered the option to let the

Sign In

What is your e-mail address?

My e-mail address is [   ]

Do you have an Amazon.com password?

○ **No, I am a new customer.**

⦿ **Yes, I have a password:** [••••••]

[Sign in using our secure server ▶]
Forgot your password? Click here
Has your e-mail address changed since your last order?

FIGURE 3.19 Amazon lets users know they are logging in using their secure server.

application remember their login information. Offering users a "remember me" option eliminates the need to log in and makes it easier for them to accomplish their goals without unnecessary interruptions.

How

Require users to log in using their username or email and the password they provided during registration. However, like registration, logging in is an interruption to a user's interaction experience. Therefore, delay it as much as possible. When logging in cannot be delayed for business reasons—for example, users must log in to select their delivery or pick-up store for ordering from food chains such as Domino's or Pizza Hut for franchise obligations—consider alternative means for getting users closer to their goal—for example, ask them to provide their street address and/or zip code.

ECHO USERS' PASSWORDS WITH NONCHARACTERS

Use the HTML tag **<input type="password" />** for the password field. It instructs the web browser to echo users' input as asterisks or bullets in the password field. However, because users don't receive any feedback on what they are entering, when a login error occurs, remove users' input from the password fields. In addition, ask them to check the "Caps Lock" key if passwords are case-sensitive.

WHEN NECESSARY, OFFER SECURE LOGIN

When allowing users to access personal information that is sensitive in nature, make the login process "secure" by transmitting the information over a Secure Sockets Layer (SSL) connection. Also, let users know they are logging in using a secure protocol (Figure 3.19). This can help increase users' trust in the web application.

OFFER USERS AN OPTION TO REGISTER

Designers usually strive to make their web applications more convenient to repeat users and typically ask users to log in only when they need to identify

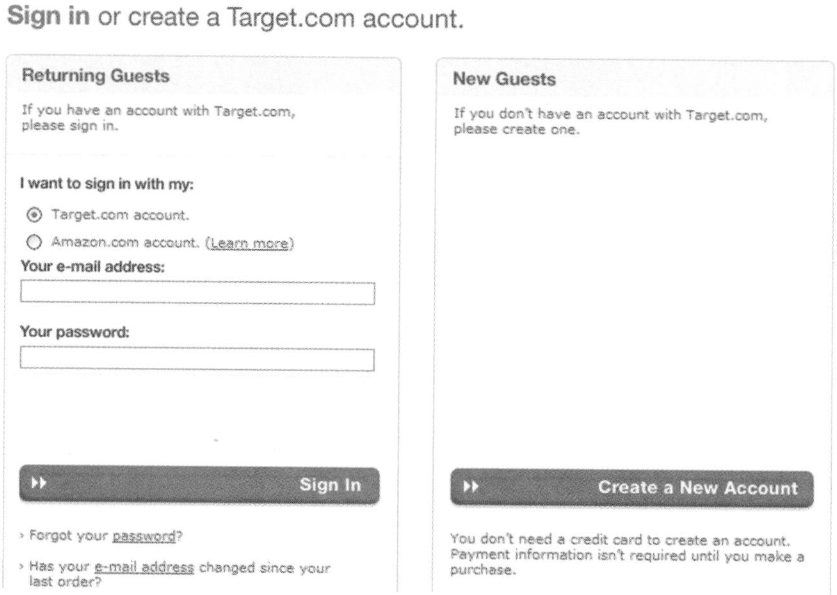

Sign in or create a Target.com account.

FIGURE 3.20
Target offers users the option to register on the sign in (i.e., log in) page.

themselves. Considering that users may not have registered with the web application, it's important that they be offered an option to register (Figure 3.20).

ENABLE USERS TO RETRIEVE FORGOTTEN LOGIN INFORMATION

Users often forget their login information, especially when they do not access a web application frequently. Help users to retrieve forgotten login information by offering options such as "Forgot password?" and/or "Forgot username or password?" (Figure 3.21); see the FORGOT USEERNAME/PASSWORD pattern later in this chapter.

CONSIDER A TWO-STEP LOGIN FOR HIGHER SECURITY

For security reasons, many financial applications require a two-step login to verify a user's identity. The first step is very similar to the login process described so far—that is, asking users to provide their username or user ID and password. The second step requires users to answer a security question. The answer must match the one provided during registration for them to successfully log in and access their account (Figure 3.22). Although many financial institutions require users to respond to a randomly selected security question, it may become annoying for users to answer security questions every time they log in. To minimize frustration, offer users the option to skip the additional step by registering the computer they typically use to log in.

FIGURE 3.21 Yahoo! offers a "Forgot your ID or password?" link below the "Sign In" button and offers new users an option to register using a "Sign Up" link.

SINGLE SIGN-ON (SINGLE LOGIN)

Many web applications, especially business-to-business (that is, extranet) and business-to-employee (that is, intranet) applications, allow users to access one or more related applications based on their access rights. Such additional applications should be enabled for single sign-on (commonly referred to as SSO) so that once users have logged in, the same credentials are used to verify their identity with other applications. Users' transition from one application to another should be seamless, and they should feel they are using the same application. For instance, once users have logged in to their Google Mail account, they do not have to log in again for accessing related applications such as Google Calendar and Google Documents.

CONSIDER ALLOWING THE USE OF "UNIVERSAL LOGIN" SERVICES

As mentioned earlier, allow users to log in using "universal login" services such as OpenID and Windows CardSpace (Figure 3.23). Such services allow users to create a unique digital identifier and use it to log in to any application supporting its use. This is similar to the SSO approach, except that users' credentials are maintained by a third-party identity provider rather than the web application provider.

Cardmember Log In

Enter your User ID and password to access your account.

Primary Cardmember Information

The information below is requested for your security and protection, and we keep it confidential. For more information, please

| User ID: | | Required |
| Password: | | Required |

[⊚ **Log In**] 🔒

Forgot Your User ID or Password?
Not Yet Registered?
Need Help?

(a)

Verify Your Identity

Please answer the security question below to complete your log in. Because we do not recognize this computer, we ask this question to ensure that your account information is kept safe and secure.

Answer Security Question:

Security Question: **Answer:**

In what city were you married? (Enter full name of city, e.g. Philadelphia) [   ]

Remember this Computer:

☐ Check this box if you would like us to remember this computer. You will not have to answer a security question if you log in with your User ID and Password on a computer we remember. You can have us remember as many computers as you like with your User ID and Password. *Note: You should NOT check this box if you are using a computer in a public area such as a library or Internet café or a computer you don't expect to use in the future.*

[⊚ **Continue**]

SECURED BY
RSA

(b)

FIGURE 3.22 Advanta (a credit card company) asks users to verify their identity after they have logged in (a) by asking them to respond to one of the security questions they set up during registration (b). They also offer users an option to skip the additional verification step in the future by allowing them to let the application remember the computer they used to log in.

REMEMBER LOGIN INFORMATION

Like registering, logging in often distracts users from their goals and tasks. To minimize distractions, offer users the option to allow the application to remember their login information on their computers. Depending on the level of security and privacy concerns, such "remember me" options can be implemented in one of two ways:

1. *Remember both username and password* (Figure 3.24). This eliminates the login step completely for users as long as they use the same computer. Because browser cookies that are used to remember log in preference are stored on computers used to log in, users don't have to log in as long as they access the application using the same computer or until the cookies expire or users delete them. For security reasons, the "remember me" function may be set to expire after a certain time period, such as two weeks or 30 days.

2. *Remember only the username* (Figure 3.25). This partial remembering option still requires users to enter their password to log in, but eliminates the need to enter their username. E-commerce applications

Login
Get in there and join the party.

Login	OpenID
Email	
Password	

Login

New to IconBuffet?
Sign up for a free account.

Forgot your password?
Send an email to yourself with with your password and login information.

(a)

Login
Get in there and join the party.

| Login | **OpenID** |

OpenID lets you safely sign in to different websites with a single password. Get an OpenID.

OpenID URL

Login

New to IconBuffet?
Sign up for a free account.

Forgot your password?
Send an email to yourself with with your password and login information.

(b)

FIGURE 3.23 IconBuffet offers users the option to login with either a regular account (a) or with an OpenID (b).

Sign in to Gmail with your
Google **Account**

Username:
Password:
☑ Remember me on this computer.
Sign in

I cannot access my account

Sign up for Gmail

About Gmail   New features!

FIGURE 3.24
Gmail offers users the option to remember their login information.

(e.g., Amazon) typically use this approach and require users to enter their password before making any purchases.

When the security of user information is critical, as in financial applications (e.g., Fidelity, CitiCards), it's acceptable to trade-off user convenience for the prevention of misuse and identity theft and not offer the "remember me" option.

FIGURE 3.25 Dominos offers users the option to save their username on their computer.

FIGURE 3.26 Gmail shows a user's email address along with a "Sign out" link in the top-right corner of the page to indicate that the user has successfully logged in.

CONFIRM LOGIN

Clearly indicate to users when they have successfully logged in. This may be accomplished by a "Welcome, username" message or by simply showing a username (typically placed at top right of the page; Figure 3.26). This is especially important when users have opted to be remembered on a computer.

LOCKING USERS' ACCOUNTS

When security is of utmost importance (e.g., finance applications), it is a reasonable precautionary measure to lock users out of their account after a certain number of unsuccessful login attempts. Users should be forewarned about this scenario after their first unsuccessful attempt (Figure 3.27). When locked out, users should be offered the phone number to call or the steps that they need to follow to unlock or reactivate their account.

Related design patterns

When asked to log in, users often realize they have forgotten their login information (FORGOT USERNAME/PASSWORD). In addition, if users have not created an account, they should be offered the option to set up one (REGISTRATION).

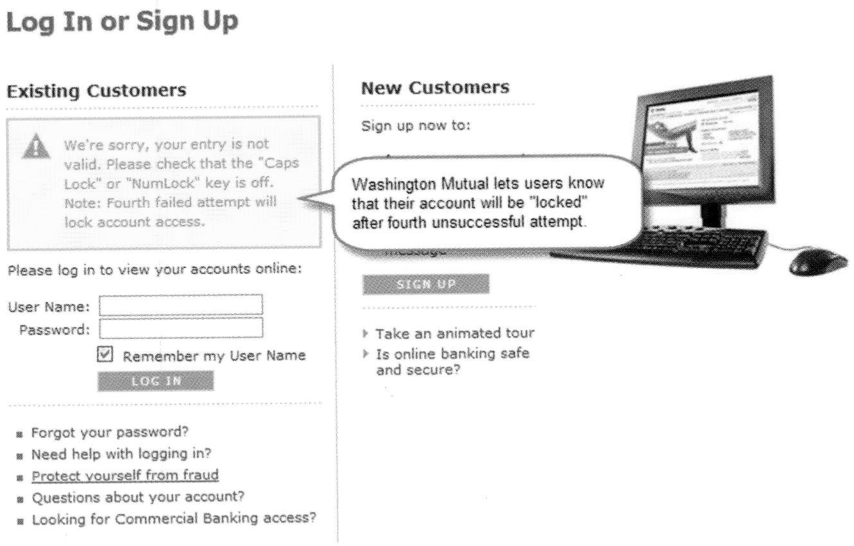

Log In or Sign Up

Existing Customers

⚠ We're sorry, your entry is not valid. Please check that the "Caps Lock" or "NumLock" key is off. Note: Fourth failed attempt will lock account access.

Please log in to view your accounts online:

User Name: [ ]
Password: [ ]

☑ Remember my User Name

[LOG IN]

- Forgot your password?
- Need help with logging in?
- Protect yourself from fraud
- Questions about your account?
- Looking for Commercial Banking access?

New Customers

Sign up now to:

Washington Mutual lets users know that their account will be "locked" after fourth unsuccessful attempt.

[SIGN UP]

▸ Take an animated tour
▸ Is online banking safe and secure?

FIGURE 3.27 Washington Mutual indicates to users that their account access will be blocked after the fourth failed attempt.

The LOG IN pattern is almost always accompanied by the LOG OUT pattern so that users can explicitly end their session with the application.

LOG OUT

Problem

After logging in and accomplishing desired tasks, users may want to end their session with the web application. They may want to do so for a variety of reasons:

- To prevent unauthorized users from accessing their personal information.
- To log out of one account and log in to another.
- To indicate that they have completed their task and no longer need access to the application.

Solution

Allow users to end their session by logging out (Figure 3.28).

Why

When users' account information can be misused, it's important that they be offered the option to log out. The ability to log out is particularly important for web applications because they are not installed on a specific computer and

FIGURE 3.28 CitiCards offers a "Log Out" link to allow users to end their session.

FIGURE 3.29 Buy.com uses a "Not pawan.vora? Click here" link to allow users to log out and log in as a different user.

are accessible from anywhere as long as users have access to the Internet and a web browser. On one hand, this offers users the flexibility to access their information from anywhere (e.g., libraries, shared computers at work, Internet cafes, and so forth), but on the other hand, this ease of access opens opportunities for misuse and fraud. Therefore, users must be offered an explicit way to end their session.

How

Offer users a log out option. Typically, the "log out" option is placed in the top-right portion of the page or closer to the username. Consumer web applications where login information is saved for future visits, especially e-commerce applications, do not offer an explicit logout but provide users with an option to log in as another user or offer options such as "Not username?" They greet users with the message "Welcome, username" to indicate that the user is recognized (Figure 3.29). When an explicit logout option is not offered to users, ensure that users have to log in for any financial transactions (e.g., checkout) or account updates (e.g., change password).

USE LABELS CONSISTENTLY

Although this has minor usability implications, a relevant design issue is labeling the action that ends user sessions with the application. The common options are logout, log out, sign out, logoff, log off, and sign off. As the link represents an action, appropriate usage is log out, sign out, log off, or sign off. In the absence of any research evidence, a common practice is to complement the action users used when accessing the web application: For most consumer applications, Sign Out (to complement Sign In) is used, and for many business and technical applications, Log Out (to complement Log In) is used.

ACKNOWLEDGE LOGOUT

Clearly indicate to users that they are logged out. The acknowledgment may be in the form of:

- A dedicated "You're Logged Out" page with appropriate choices for users to navigate to.
- The login page with the appropriate message indicating that the user is logged out.
- A non-logged-in visitor version of the page (this is common on content portals such as Yahoo!, MSN, iGoogle, and so forth).
- A combination of these choices—for example, a dedicated page with an automatic redirect after a certain time delay (Figure 3.30).

The choice often depends on the "initial" conditions for login. If a user is required to log in to access the application, return users to the login page when they log out with a message acknowledging logout because that typically doesn't require confirmation unless users are going to lose data. This also allows users to log in again if they logged out by mistake. Alternatively, if users started with a version of the page for non-logged-in visitors before logging in, then return them to a similar page when they log out.

Related design patterns

The LOG OUT pattern accompanies the LOG IN pattern because when users have to log in to access the application, they are usually offered the option to log out.

AUTOMATIC LOGOUT

Problem

After logging in, users have stopped interacting with the application for a duration longer than expected, suggesting that they are either distracted or have abandoned the application but have forgotten to log out. By leaving their account in a logged-in state, users are exposed to misuse and abuse of their personal or sensitive data.

Solution

After a predetermined period of inactivity (e.g., 15–45 minutes), end users' sessions by logging them out (Figure 3.31).

Why

Not only do automatic logouts help reduce the chances of unauthorized account accesses, but they also reduce the burden on the web server that maintains users'

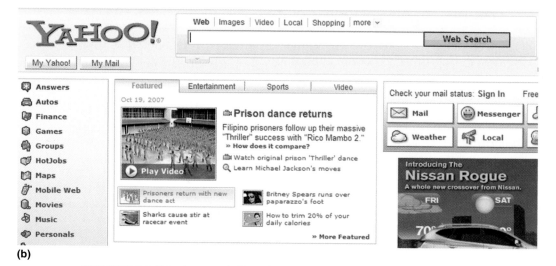

FIGURE 3.30 Yahoo! uses a dedicated page indicating that users have signed out (a). After a brief delay, users are taken to the non-logged-in visitor version of the page (b).

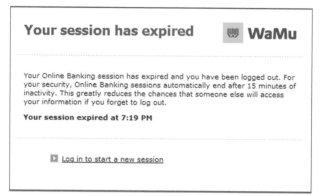

FIGURE 3.31 Washington Mutual logs users out after an inactivity period of 15 minutes. They also make it easier for users to start a new session by offering a link to log in again.

session information. Automatic logouts are particularly important with new browsers, which allow tab-based browsing. Many users open multiple tabs and access several web applications and often forget to log out of their sessions.

How

For applications with security and/or privacy concerns, automatically log out users after a certain period of inactivity (i.e., session timeout). Typical session timeouts are 15- to 45-minute durations depending on the sensitivity of the data that may be exposed. As the session timeout is approaching, offer users a warning and give them an opportunity to stay logged in. Confirmation is especially useful in instances where user tasks are likely to take some time (e.g., in cases of multistep tasks like checkout) and likely data loss could be frustrating to users (Figure 3.32).

When session timeout occurs, the following are quite common:

- Users are taken to the Login page with a message that the session timed out (or suspended) and that they must log in to start a new session. This approach is useful when the data available on the screen are sensitive.
- Users are kept on the same page with a pop-up that indicates that the session was suspended and whether or not their data were saved (say, for example, in a "draft" status). This approach is not recommended when data available on the screen (behind the pop-up) are personal and/or sensitive.

For some applications, sessions can end if the browser window used to access the application is closed.

SAVE USERS' INFORMATION

When automatically logging out users, consider saving their information. It could be annoying for users to have their session time out and discard all their data when they intended to finish what they started but were distracted for

FIGURE 3.32 As session timeout approaches, Bellco prompts users and offers them an option to continue their current session. It also shows how users can change the session's timeout duration.

FIGURE 3.33 Rally Community Edition allows users to set their session timeout duration for up to four hours. The default timeout is set to one hour.

some reason. For example, Gmail saves users' incomplete emails in the "draft" state and marks them to indicate that they have a pending response.

ALLOW USERS TO SET DURATION OF SESSION TIMEOUTS

Users may want some web applications to have longer or shorter session time-out duration than the one defaulted by the application. This is common for applications that users may to use all day, such as email, office productivity applications (e.g., word processing, spreadsheets), and status-monitoring applications (e.g., investment tracking). If timeouts are set for such applications, offer users an option to change the duration (Figure 3.33).

Related design patterns

AUTOMATIC LOGOUT is a fallback measure where users may forget to log out and therefore expose personal or sensitive information. It's quite possible that users may not know how to log out of an application because the available option is hidden or not located where users expect it to be (LOG OUT).

FORGOT USERNAME/PASSWORD

Problem

Users often forget login information (username and/or password) and without it are unable to access the application.

Solution

Offer users options to remember or retrieve forgotten login information (Figure 3.34).

Why

Users often forget usernames and/or passwords, especially when they are accessing an application that they rarely use. Therefore, it's important that users

FIGURE 3.34 Gmail offers an "I cannot access my account" link.

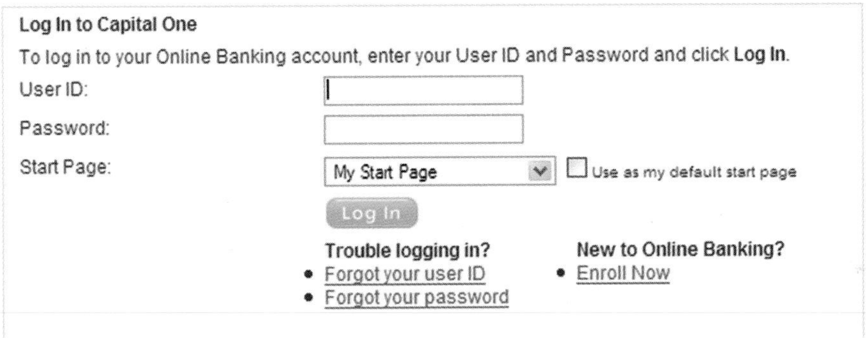

FIGURE 3.35 Capital One offers links for "Forgot your user ID" and "Forgot your password" below the Log In button.

have a way to remember that information or retrieve it. Because users typically realize that they have forgotten their credentials when asked to log in, the options to retrieve them should be provided near the login area. In situations where user accounts are not tied to private or sensitive information, sending a link to reset passwords via email is acceptable. However, when dealing with sensitive information, it's important to take additional steps to verify identity before allowing users to reset or access their log in credentials.

How

Provide a "Forgot User ID (or Password)" link near the login area (Figure 3.35); if users' email addresses are used for logging in, the "Forgot Password" link is sufficient.

SEND PASSWORDS TO REGISTERED EMAIL ADDRESS

If the web application being accessed doesn't store personal information about users that can be misused (e.g., health-related or financial information), ask users to provide their username or the email address they used to register. Once verified, passwords can be emailed to them. For improved security,

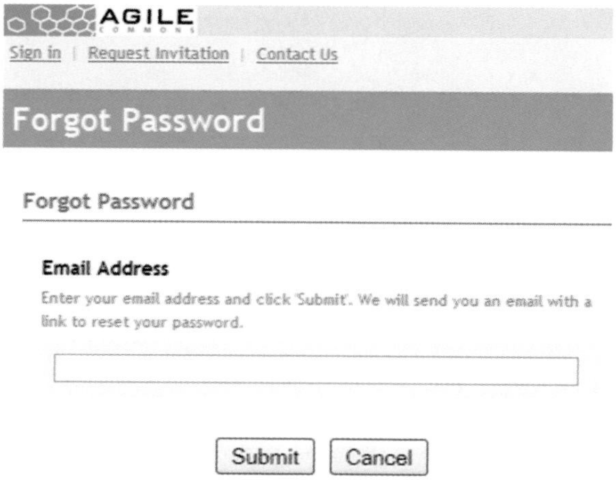

FIGURE 3.36 Agile Commons (hosted by HiveLive) emails the link to reset the password after verifying the email address (a). Clicking the link displays the reset password page (b).

instead of emailing the current password, assign users a temporary password that they can change as soon as they log in. Alternatively, users may be emailed a link to reset their password (Figure 3.36).

CONFIRM USER IDENTITY WITH SECURITY QUESTIONS

If the web application stores sensitive information, additional layers of security may be necessary to verify the identity of the user claiming to have lost log in information. Additional identification questions may include information that only the account owner knows, such as the last four digits of his or her Social Security number, account number, and so forth (Figure 3.37). The identification

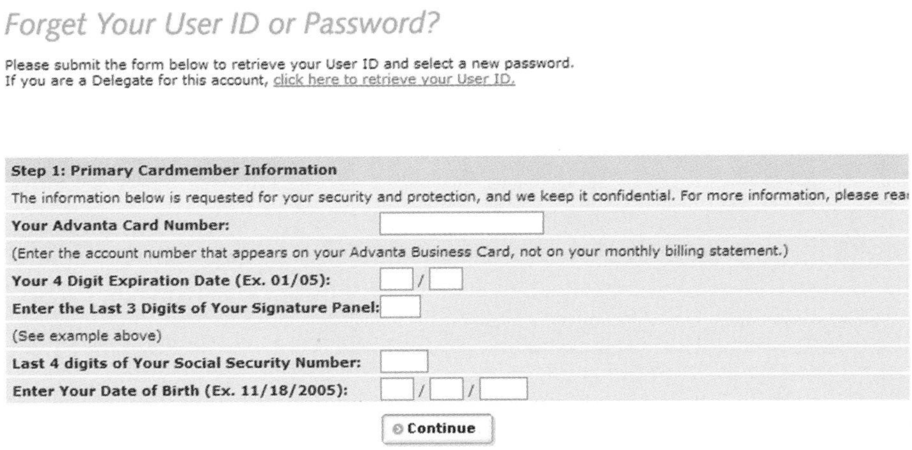

Forget Your User ID or Password?

Please submit the form below to retrieve your User ID and select a new password.
If you are a Delegate for this account, click here to retrieve your User ID.

Step 1: Primary Cardmember Information
The information below is requested for your security and protection, and we keep it confidential. For more information, please rea
Your Advanta Card Number:
(Enter the account number that appears on your Advanta Business Card, not on your monthly billing statement.)
Your 4 Digit Expiration Date (Ex. 01/05):
Enter the Last 3 Digits of Your Signature Panel:
(See example above)
Last 4 digits of Your Social Security Number:
Enter Your Date of Birth (Ex. 11/18/2005):

⊙ Continue

FIGURE 3.37 Advanta, a credit card company, asks for several identification-related questions before resetting user ID and password.

may also require users to answer one or more security questions set up during registration.

Related design patterns

Users may realize that they have forgotten their username and/or password when they are prompted to log in. Therefore, options to retrieve them should be presented along with fields that are required to log in (LOG IN).

CHAPTER 4
Application Main Page

INTRODUCTION

An important decision for designers is what users should see or which page they should be taken to after they log in to the application.

For web applications that allow access without logging in (e.g., consumer e-commerce applications), users either remain on the same page or are taken to the next page in the sequence. For example, if users decide to log in on a product details page, they remain on the same page. However, if they log in during the checkout process, they are taken to the next page in the sequence—the shipping information page.

On the other hand, applications that require users to log in before accessing their functionality may show one of the following, depending on the nature of the application:

- An INBOX, where users can see a list of items to view or act on.
- A CONTROL PANEL, which serves as a launch page to access application functionality.
- A DASHBOARD, with an at-a-glance view of the most important performance indicators.
- A PORTAL, which aggregates information from several sources and serves as a launching place for information and applications users may access. PORTAL pages often incorporate some aspects of CONTROL PANEL and DASHBOARD in order to enable users to quickly access functionality and content supported by one or more applications.

Application main pages are typically personalized based on user profiles, interests, and information needs with the intention of presenting the most relevant content and filtering out the not-so-relevant information. However, PERSONALIZATION driven by business rules or some form of social filtering may not be able to accurately predict the information users may need. Thus, applications often offer users CUSTOMIZATION options to allow them to tailor the application to their preferences and compensate for personalization shortcomings. Customization is not limited to information and task-related needs; it often extends to a choice of colors, logos, themes, fonts, and page layouts.

An often-overlooked design aspect of many web applications is what first-time users will see (BLANK SLATE). This is particularly important for applications that rely on users to fill in the application with appropriate data.

INBOX

Problem

It is essential that users know the items they need to work on or the activities that have happened since they last logged in.

Solution

Show users a list of items they can act on or need to review. For example, for email applications, show users a list of emails; for defect-tracking applications, show users a list of defects; and so forth (Figure 4.1).

Why

Applications focused on managing items of one type (e.g., emails, defects, files, accounts, support calls, timesheets, etc.) benefit from showing users items that they can interact with as soon as they login. This does not mean that the application does not allow users to manage other types of items or allow quick

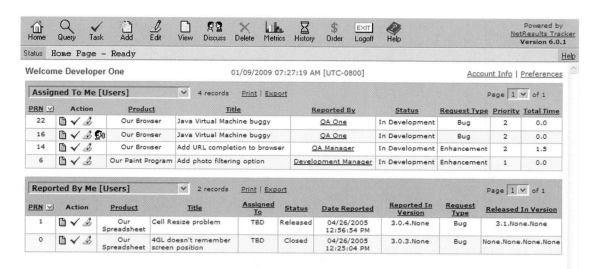

FIGURE 4.1 NetResults tracker shows developers a list of bugs and enhancements assigned to them when they log in.

access to other functionalities within the application—it's just that they are secondary in nature. For example, email applications allow users to manage contact lists even though managing contacts is not its primary purpose. Therefore, when users log in, they are first shown a list of emails, both past and new. The term *inbox* is appropriate, since these are typically items that users need to attend to when they log in to the application.

How

Show users a list of items for which the application was primarily designed—emails, defects, files, accounts, to-dos, and so on—highlighting the items that users need to immediately attend to or be reminded of, such as new emails, new files, new defects, and so forth (Figure 4.2).

ALLOW USERS TO SET UP REMINDERS

If the application is not going to be accessed frequently and if users prefer to be reminded of changes in the state of one or more items (e.g., payment due or a new to-do item), allow them to set up reminders (Figure 4.3).

Related design patterns

The INBOX pattern typically uses lists, either TABULAR LISTS or IMAGE GRIDS. In addition, like lists, they often need SORTING and FILTERING to make it easy for users to find relevant information (see Chapter 7 for further discussion on lists).

CONTROL PANEL

Problem

After users have logged in, they may want to access different application functions to perform a variety of tasks. However, which function they may want to access cannot be reliably predicted.

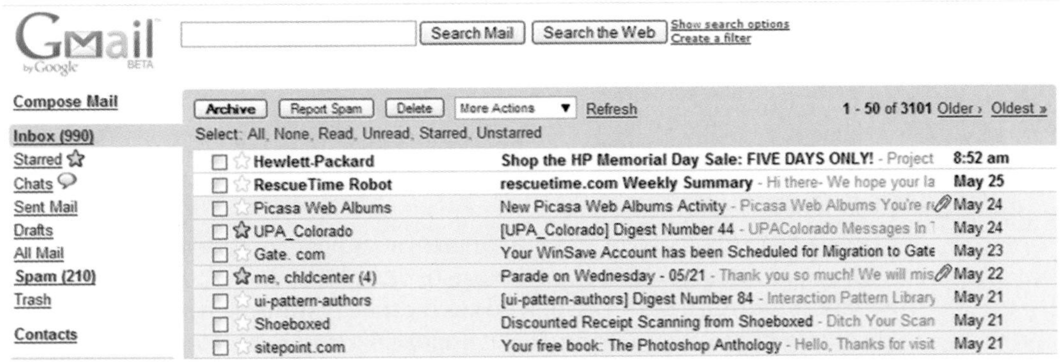

FIGURE 4.2 Users see their email inbox after they have logged in to Gmail. New items in the inbox are in bold.

FIGURE 4.3 Remember The Milk offers users the option of setting reminders daily as well as a preset number of minutes before the task is due. It also allows users to be reminded via email, instant messengers, and mobile text messages.

Solution

Show users a page with all available application functions, any one of which they can quickly access (Figure 4.4).

Why

For many web applications, users need a place that serves as a launch pad for accessing its functions (i.e., mini-applications) that are rather independent of each other. Although users need access to all functions, they do not need to navigate from one function to another. However, they need a place to return to when they feel lost or disoriented (similar to a "home page" on web sites).

How

Provide a "launch" page from which users can access all application functions or mini-applications. Control panels are designed using a hub-and-spoke user-interface approach (Baxley, 2003; Tidwell, 2006), where users can reach the self-contained mini-applications (i.e., "spokes") from one central "hub" page such that users can access a mini-application, accomplish desired tasks, and return to the hub page to perform another task using another mini-application.

FIGURE 4.4 1&1, a web site hosting company, gives users the ability to access all functions related to their account on their control panel page. Because there are a number of options, it groups them into two separate areas, "Administration" and "Account."

Control panels have quite a few similarities with home pages on content-oriented web sites:

- They set an expectation of the application's scope and provide quick access to its most important features and functionality.
- They establish an overall information design approach for pages within the application in terms of its layout, placement of navigation, search functionality, and so forth.
- They inform users of new features and functions.

Control panels are also useful for account overview pages where users can access all of their account-related functions in one place. For example, e-commerce applications use account overview pages to allow users access to their orders, shipping addresses, payment information, and so forth (Figure 4.5).

HIGHLIGHT ITEMS THAT NEED ATTENTION

Like with the INBOX, a CONTROL PANEL is a place to inform users of, or direct their attention to, changes in application functionality and content. As soon as users have landed on the control panel page, it is important to direct them to items that need their attention. Because users may not be expecting them, it's necessary that items serving as notifications or announcements

FIGURE 4.5 Dell's "My Account" page provides a summary of account information and serves as a launch page allowing access to user-specific information such as saved items, coupons, shopping cart, order status, and so forth.

are made salient. A good notification example is a message about a planned application outage, although this should also be done on the login page. For items that serve only an informational purpose (i.e., announcements) and do not require any user action, offer users an option to dismiss them.

Related design patterns

Use the BLANK SLATE design pattern, especially on "spoke pages," to avoid showing users empty pages and to ensure that they are not confused as to what to do after logging in for the first time. This also helps them get comfortable using the application, especially for applications that rely on users to provide data.

DASHBOARD

Problem

Information that helps users make decisions and monitor information about the "state of their world" is available, but requires users to visit several different application areas. In addition, available information is not presented in a format that helps users make decisions and/or determine their next steps.

Solution

Offer users a single-page "dashboard" view of information and metrics that they need to track. In addition, allow users to "drill" down to detailed content from the dashboard view (Figure 4.6).

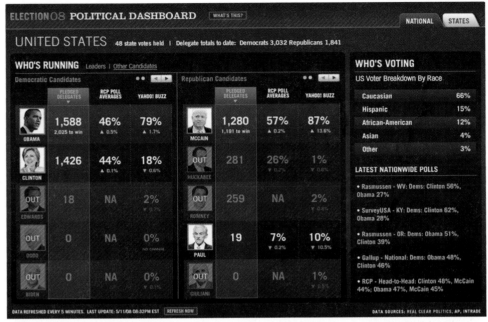

(a)

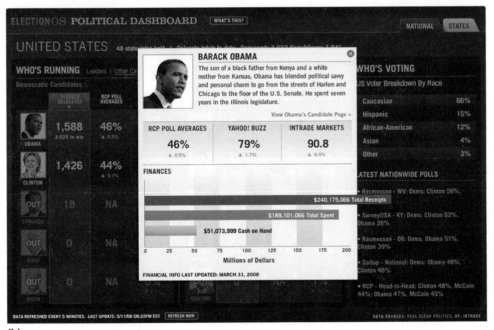

(b)

FIGURE 4.6 Yahoo!'s Election 08 Political Dashboard shows at-a-glance information about the current status of each candidate at the national level (a). Additionally, it allows users to click on candidates and get detailed information about the candidate including recent poll averages, money raised, and so forth (b).

Why

Requiring users to navigate several application pages or run reports to monitor items' status and determine actions to take is not only inefficient but also may cause users to overlook important information. In addition, integrating information sources from several places for every visit can become quite cumbersome for users.

Dashboards, when properly designed, are "presented in a way that allows them [users] to monitor what's going on in an instant" (Few, 2006). By using appropriate visualizations for important measures (often referred to as key performance indicators or KPIs) along with exception conditions and alerts, dashboards provide at-a-glance information about current status and facilitate identification of necessary corrective and preventive actions.

How

Dashboards typically serve three important functions for users:

1. They monitor and track important metrics.
2. They provide analysis to determine trends and exception conditions.
3. They report information to facilitate diagnosis and identify corrective actions as necessary.

FIGURE 4.7 Data display methods.

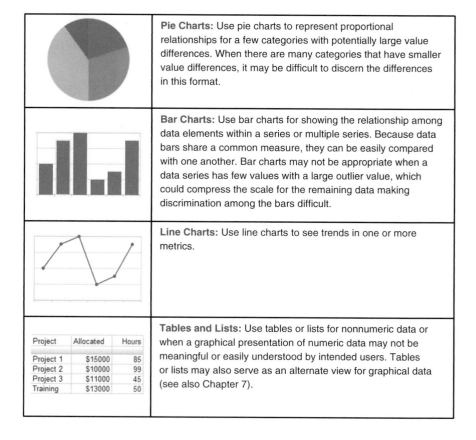

Pie Charts: Use pie charts to represent proportional relationships for a few categories with potentially large value differences. When there are many categories that have smaller value differences, it may be difficult to discern the differences in this format.

Bar Charts: Use bar charts for showing the relationship among data elements within a series or multiple series. Because data bars share a common measure, they can be easily compared with one another. Bar charts may not be appropriate when a data series has few values with a large outlier value, which could compress the scale for the remaining data making discrimination among the bars difficult.

Line Charts: Use line charts to see trends in one or more metrics.

Tables and Lists: Use tables or lists for nonnumeric data or when a graphical presentation of numeric data may not be meaningful or easily understood by intended users. Tables or lists may also serve as an alternate view for graphical data (see also Chapter 7).

To help users understand data, relationships, trends, and diagnose problems, report summarized and abstracted data on dashboards using approaches such as pie charts, bar charts, line charts, tables or lists, and so forth. To ensure that data are understood correctly, employ data visualization or charting methods that are suitable for the type of data and their intended use (Figures 4.7 and 4.8).

MATCH EXCEPTION CONDITIONS TO USERS' TASKS

Match dashboard icons and indicators to users' monitoring tasks (Figure 4.9). For example, use indicators, such as alert or traffic light icons, if users need to know only the current state of a metric. However, if users need to also know trends, use trend icons, such as up and down arrows, with appropriate colors may be more appropriate; they may be supplemented with spark lines to show a quick snapshot of the historical trend.

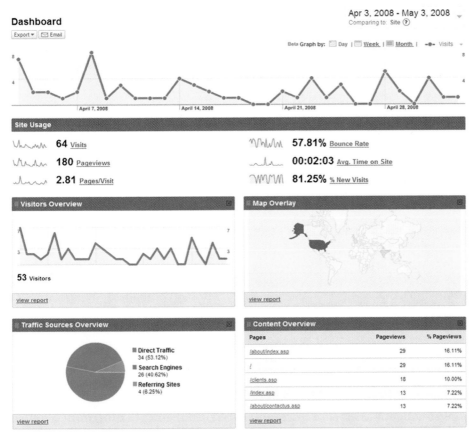

FIGURE 4.8 Google Analytics' dashboard uses a variety of charting methods to convey web site performance metrics. It uses a trend chart to show "Visitors Overview," numbers and spark lines to show "Site Usage," and tabular data to show "Content Overview."

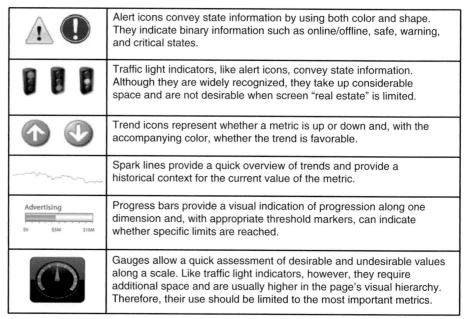

	Alert icons convey state information by using both color and shape. They indicate binary information such as online/offline, safe, warning, and critical states.
	Traffic light indicators, like alert icons, convey state information. Although they are widely recognized, they take up considerable space and are not desirable when screen "real estate" is limited.
	Trend icons represent whether a metric is up or down and, with the accompanying color, whether the trend is favorable.
	Spark lines provide a quick overview of trends and provide a historical context for the current value of the metric.
	Progress bars provide a visual indication of progression along one dimension and, with appropriate threshold markers, can indicate whether specific limits are reached.
	Gauges allow a quick assessment of desirable and undesirable values along a scale. Like traffic light indicators, however, they require additional space and are usually higher in the page's visual hierarchy. Therefore, their use should be limited to the most important metrics.

FIGURE 4.9 Dashboard visualizations.

SHOW INFORMATION IN CONTEXT

Because dashboards show monitored data (i.e., metrics) as abstractions or summaries, include their historical context to help users identify whether:

- A metric is up or down.
- The trend is increasing or decreasing (and favorable or unfavorable).
- The metric is too close to the acceptable variance levels.
- The metric has reached the desired benchmark; and so forth.

Showing data in context offers users at-a-glance insights that simple measures by themselves can't provide. Knowing the nature of contextual information that needs to be provided can also help identify appropriate charting methods and exception indicators. For example, trend information can be presented using line charts, area charts, or spark lines accompanied by trend icons (Figure 4.10).

DISPLAY ALL REQUIRED INFORMATION ON ONE SCREEN

Whenever possible, avoid scrolling on dashboards (Few, 2006). This is especially true for dashboards that present real-time data and are used primarily for monitoring. The main purpose of dashboards is to provide an overview of the current state for selected metrics and emphasize metrics that need users' attention. In addition, ensure that every dashboard widget is allocated space and positioned relative to its importance to users.

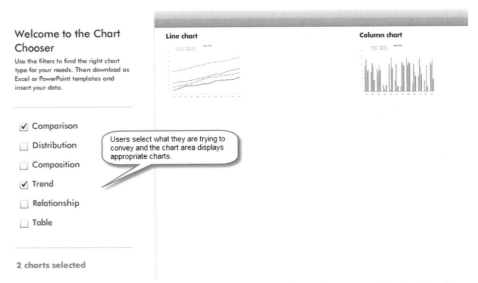

FIGURE 4.10 Chart Chooser from Juice Analytics helps determine appropriate chart type(s) based on what users want to convey using the chart, such as a comparison, distribution, composition, trend, relationship, or table. In addition, it allows users to download corresponding Excel and PowerPoint templates. (Source: *www.juiceanalytics.com/chartchooser/*.)

ALLOW USERS TO CUSTOMIZE DASHBOARDS

Although dashboards are often personalized to meet the needs of specific user roles, it's possible that the same layout and design may not satisfy all users in a given role. For example, while some users may like the default chart format, others may prefer a tabular view. In addition, some users may want to reorganize the information presented to better match their needs. Accommodate such individual differences by allowing users to customize their dashboard layouts (see the CUSTOMIZATION pattern later in this chapter).

ALLOW USERS TO "DRILL" DOWN TO VIEW DETAILED INFORMATION

When viewing dashboards, users may need additional information either to better understand the summary views or before making decisions on corrective actions. Therefore, from the dashboard, allow users to "drill" down to the detailed information that formed the basis of the summary view (Figure 4.11).

ALLOW USERS TO TRANSFER OR SHARE DATA

Users may want to download dashboard data locally to do further analysis and/or share them with others. This can be accomplished by enabling actions such as downloading a detailed report in formats such as PDF, Excel, or XML, or sending emails to other users from the dashboard (Figure 4.12; see also the LIST UTILITY FUNCTIONS pattern in Chapter 7).

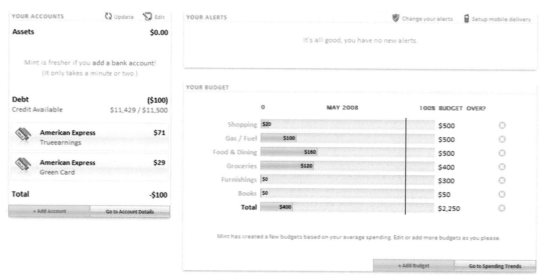

FIGURE 4.11 Mint's dashboard shows users their assets, debt, alerts, and budget. Users can click on individual areas to get further details—for example, users can click on "American Express Green Card" and get a list of transactions amounting to a balance of $29.

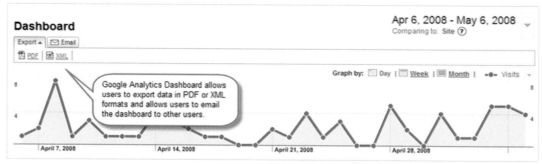

FIGURE 4.12 Google Analytics' dashboard allows users to export data in PDF or XML formats and allows users to email the dashboard to other users.

Related design patterns

The goal in laying out an effective dashboard is to have the most important business information as the first thing to grab users' attention (see the VISUAL HIERARCHY pattern in Chapter 12).

PORTAL

Problem

The information and functionality that users would like to access are dispersed over several web sites and web applications. For example, within a corporation,

FIGURE 4.13 iGoogle, a web portal, allows users to access content and functions from several different sources.

employees may need to access a wide variety of information to accomplish tasks such as enrolling for benefits, managing personal information, reporting time and expenses, completing performance reviews, and so forth, each of which require them to access a separate application.

Solution

Provide a central application that aggregates content and functionality from several different sources and not only presents users a unified look and feel, but also serves as a single launch pad or access point for those applications (Figure 4.13). In addition, enable users to select content and customize its presentation, and if required for security and privacy reasons, restrict access to certain content and functions based on their roles and access rights.

Why

Portals aggregate a disparate set of applications and offer a unified interface to users to access relevant content and applications that otherwise would have to be discovered and accessed independently. Portals also improve user experience by providing a consistent appearance and navigation (and single sign-on, SSO) when accessing a range of applications (see the LOG IN pattern in Chapter 3). For many companies, a single launch point can help improve information sharing and collaboration among its users, which may include employees, customers, and partners. In addition, portals designed for self-service benefit both companies and users (employees or customers), as they help reduce costs for the former and increase convenience for the latter.

How

Portals organize individual pieces of content and/or functions into their own windowlike areas, commonly referred to as *portlets*. Portlets behave as smaller windows within a web page; they often support functionalities such as minimize, maximize, close, and so forth (Figure 4.14).

When supporting several functional areas, portals usually organize them by grouping related content and application and then present them as separate pages, allowing users to navigate among them (see Figure 4.15).

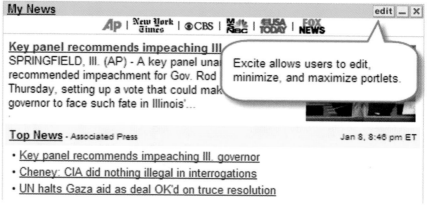

FIGURE 4.14 Excite allows users to edit, minimize, and maximize portlets.

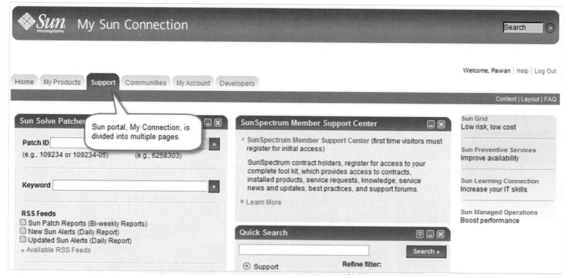

FIGURE 4.15 Sun's portal, My Sun Connection, is divided into multiple pages: "Home," "My Products," "Support," "Communities," "My Account," and "Developers."

FIGURE 4.16 My Yahoo! allows users to add their own portal pages by clicking the "Add Page" button. In this example, the user has created a "Finance" page.

ALLOW TAILORING OF CONTENT BASED ON USERS' ROLES AND NEEDS

Portals typically allow access to a large amount of content, only a small portion of which the typical user would be interested in. For example, a system administrator in the information technology (IT) group would be interested in completely different types of content and applications on an intranet portal than a recruiting specialist in human resources (HR). Similarly, for many extranet portals, end users (customers) would need access to completely different content than partners and resellers. Therefore, portals should allow personalization and customization of content based on users' roles and needs (see the PERSONALIZATION and CUSTOMIZATION patterns later in this chapter). For public portals (e.g., iGoogle, My Yahoo!, and My MSN), users are typically offered a default portal page to which they may add pages as necessary (Figure 4.16).

MAINTAIN A CONSISTENT APPEARANCE

Although portals allow users to access a variety of applications, they should strive to provide a consistent user experience. This can be achieved to a certain extent by maintaining a consistent "look and feel" throughout the portal.

AUTOMATICALLY SIGN-IN USERS TO APPLICATIONS

A portal should not only look unified based on its appearance. It should behave in a unified manner, too. Once logged in to the portal, unless additional security is required, allow users to access different applications seamlessly without requiring them to log in separately; that is, the portal should support single sign-on (SSO) (Figure 4.17; see also the LOG IN pattern in Chapter 3).

Although SSO is feasible for enterprise portals, many web portals allow the incorporation of other applications using web services to which users may have to log in separately. For example, iGoogle allows users to view their Jott (*www.jott.com*) reminders in its own portlet, which requires them to log in separately. In such instances, offer a "remember me" option so that users do not have to log in every time they access the portal.

ALLOW USERS TO CUSTOMIZE PORTAL'S APPEARANCE

Unlike many web applications, portals are designed for regular and frequent use. To ensure that users are as productive as possible with the portal, and to

FIGURE 4.17 On iGoogle, users can view Google Finance Portfolios, Google Calendar, and Gmail information, as they all use the same login information.

feel that it's their personal workspace, allow them to customize its appearance and change the placement of content (see the CUSTOMIZATION pattern later in this chapter).

Related design patterns

Although portals offer a common "look and feel," typically users can "reskin" a portal by changing its appearance. Users are also allowed to customize content and layout (see CUSTOMIZATION). Because portals are designed to aggregate content from disparate sources, some content may also appear in a DASHBOARD style, thereby giving users a view of the current status (or health) of certain key metrics.

PERSONALIZATION

Problem

For web applications with an extensive amount of content (e.g., a large number of products in e-commerce applications), finding content or items that are relevant or of interest may become difficult for users. In addition, because new items are being added at a rate users are likely to find difficult to keep up with (and not all of them are going to be of interest to them), showing every new item is neither desirable nor feasible.

Solution

Tailor users' experience by showing them personalized information based on their profiles, interaction patterns, and/or stated (or inferred) preferences and interests (Anand and Mobasher, 2005; Koch and Rossi, 2002) (Figure 4.18).

FIGURE 4.18
Netflix, an online movie rental web application, recommends movies based on users' rental history and their ratings of movies they have watched. Netflix also personalizes recommendations based on users' age and gender.

Why

Personalization is becoming increasingly common in helping users manage access to almost an unlimited amount of information. Rather than presenting "all" information, users are only offered information that meets their unique needs and interests (Anand and Mobasher, 2005; Koch and Rossi, 2002; Rossi et al., 2001). Thus, personalization helps in two ways: It reduces "clutter" by eliminating items that users are not likely to be interested in and it exposes users to new items they might not have discovered or sought out on their own. Furthermore, because the personalized (or recommended) list of items is based on users' interests and behaviors, users would have less anxiety in considering them for purchase or engaging in other transactions.

How

Personalized experiences can be offered at two levels:

1. Based on known facts about users such as their demographic information or stated interests (*explicit personalization*).
2. Based on inferred interests from users' past interaction and transaction history (*implicit personalization*).

EXPLICIT PERSONALIZATION

At its most basic level, an application can offer personalization simply by welcoming users with their name (Figure 4.19).

FIGURE 4.19 Morningstar greets users with a "Welcome [first name]" message log in.

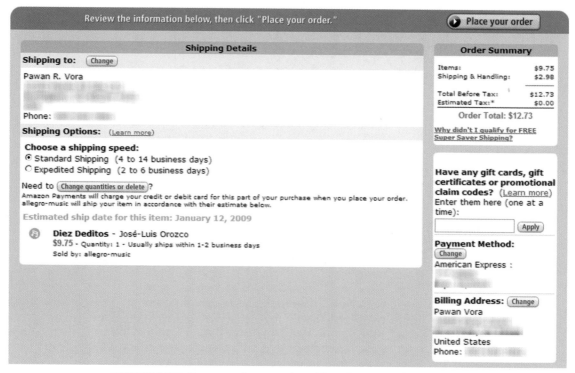

FIGURE 4.20 Once users have purchased from Amazon, subsequent checkout experiences are personalized based on their past shipping and billing information.

Another common form of explicit personalization is saving users' profiles and account information, such as shipping and billing information, and prepopulating them as needed to improve returning users' experience—for example, when checking out in e-commerce applications (Figure 4.20).

Yet another form of personalization is showing different views of the application to guest users (those who have not logged in or do not have an account) and logged-in users (Figure 4.21).

A comparable personalization approach for logged-in users is based on user roles, where they are presented different application content areas and thus a different navigation structure, based on their access rights and permissions within the application. For example, only users with administrative rights may have access to user management functionality (Figure 4.22).

IMPLICIT PERSONALIZATION

Personalization inferred from users' preferences and needs (implicit personalization) is typically in the form of recommendations, which consider users' past transactions and interaction behaviors. Such personalization is common in e-commerce applications where users are recommended products based on

(a)

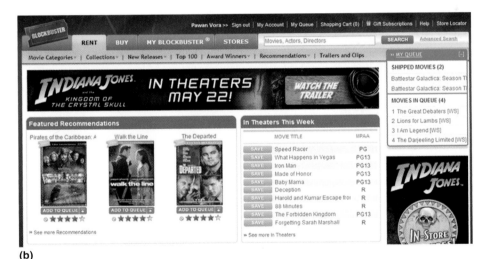

(b)

FIGURE 4.21 Blockbuster offers different versions of their home page: one for new users (a) and another for repeat logged-in users (b).

their past purchases or previously viewed items. Such personalization often adopts a social filtering approach, in which recommendations are based on similarities in behavior and interests among the application users (Goldberg et al., 1992) (Figure 4.23). It can also be seen in social applications where users are recommended people to "friend" with based on the commonality among other friends in their networks (see Chapter 9).

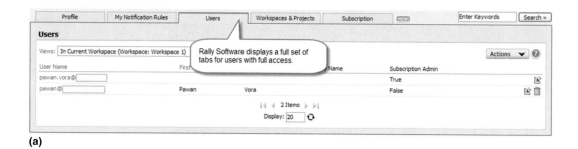

(a)

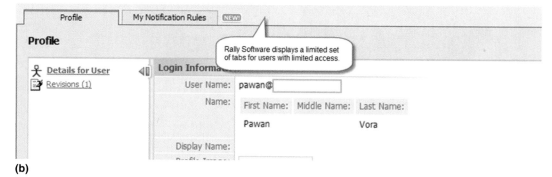

(b)

FIGURE 4.22 Rally Software shows different sets of tabs for users with subscription access rights (a) and for those without such rights (b).

ALLOW USERS TO ADJUST THEIR PERSONALIZATION PREFERENCES

Although implicit personalization has its value, it often falls short because not all users' interactions and transactions are for themselves. For example, some of users' purchases on e-commerce applications may be gifts or made on behalf of friends and family members. To improve the quality of recommendations, allow users to either state their preferences (Figure 4.24) or adjust their preferences by having them indicate if an item should be excluded when generating recommendations (Figure 4.25).

Related design patterns

Because users' needs can never be accurately predicted, personalization can never be perfect. Therefore, consider using CUSTOMIZATION approaches to let users tailor the content and interface to their needs. In addition, some personalization can be based on users' location—for example, users can be shown country-specific pages based on where they are accessing the application. Therefore, consider the GLOBAL GATEWAY pattern in Chapter 10 as well.

CUSTOMIZATION
Problem

From all the content offered by a web application, users may only be interested in a very small subset. However, considering varied needs and preferences of

Recommended for You

Missed Fortune: Dispel the Money... Paperback by Douglas R. Andrew
(Why is this recommended for you?)

Don't Make Me Think: A Common Sense... Paperback by Steve Krug
(Why is this recommended for you?)

Buffalo Technology LPV3-U2 Network...
(Why is this recommended for you?)

Missed Fortune 101: A Starter Kit to... Hardcover by Douglas R. Andrew
(Why is this recommended for you?)

> See more recommendations

(a)

What Do Customers Buy After Viewing This Item?

90% buy the item you viewed

6% buy this alternative

3% buy this alternative

2% buy this alternative

Designing for the Social Web Paperback by Joshua Porter

Designing the Moment: Web Interface... Paperback by Robert Hoekman Jr.

Landing Page Optimization: The... Paperback by Tim Ash

Subject To Change: Creating Great... Hardcover by Peter Merholz, Todd...

> View or edit your browsing history

(b)

Customers Who Bought This Item Also Bought

Page 2 of 10 (Start over)

The Myths of Innovation by Scott Berkun
★★★★★ (29) $16.49

Designing Interactions by Bill Moggridge
★★★★☆ (13) $26.37

Communicating Design: Developing Web Site... by Dan Brown
★★★★☆ (22) $29.69

Thoughts on Interaction Design by Jon Kolko
★★★★★ (7) $30.00

Designing the Moment: Web Interface Design... by Robert Hoekman Jr.
★★★★★ (1) $25.99

(c)

FIGURE 4.23 Amazon offers several forms of recommendations based on (a) users' past purchases, (b) users' recent browsing behavior, and (c) related items based on the purchase history of other people with similar interests.

users, it's difficult to effectively match and prioritize content. In addition, users may want to tailor the application to match their company's standards or individual preferences. Although personalization is an option, users know what they want and are able to clearly specify their needs.

Please share some information so that we can provide you with a personalized site.

Year of Birth   19

Gender ○ Male
        ○ Female

(a)

STEP 1 STEP 2 STEP 3

Rate these types of movies by **clicking the stars**

Help us understand your movie tastes (you will be able to modify your ratings later).

	Hate it	Love it
Action & Adventure		☆☆☆☆☆
Anime & Animation		☆☆☆☆☆
Children & Family		☆☆☆☆☆
Classics		☆☆☆☆☆
Comedy		☆☆☆☆☆
Documentary		☆☆☆☆☆
Drama		☆☆☆☆☆
Faith & Spirituality		☆☆☆☆☆
Foreign		☆☆☆☆☆
Horror		☆☆☆☆☆
Independent		☆☆☆☆☆
Music & Musicals		☆☆☆☆☆
Romance		☆☆☆☆☆
Sci-Fi & Fantasy		☆☆☆☆☆
Sports & Fitness		☆☆☆☆☆
Television		☆☆☆☆☆
Thrillers		☆☆☆☆☆

Continue

(b)

Cirque du Soleil: Dralion

Add
★★★★☆
⊘ Not Interested
No Opinion

Cirque du Soleil: Alegria

Add
★★★★☆
⊘ Not Interested
No Opinion

Baby Shakespeare: World of Poetry

Add
★★★★☆
⊘ Not Interested
No Opinion

Cirque du Soleil: Saltimbanco

Add
★★★★☆
⊘ Not Interested
No Opinion

The Secret

Add
★★★★☆
⊘ Not Interested
No Opinion

(c)

FIGURE 4.24 Netflix offers users an option to state their preferences explicitly by asking them to provide their birth year and gender during registration (a), rating movie genres (b) and specific movies in the "Movies You'll Love" section (c).

Solution

Offer users customization features such as adding or removing content, choosing page layouts, adjusting appearance (color schemes, fonts, and so forth), and, if necessary, adding or importing their own content (Figure 4.26).

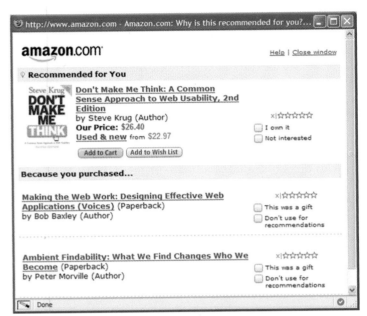

FIGURE 4.25 Amazon allows users to indicate whether their past purchases were gifts and/or shouldn't be used for generating recommendations. It also allows users to identify products they currently own so that they can be removed from "Recommended for You."

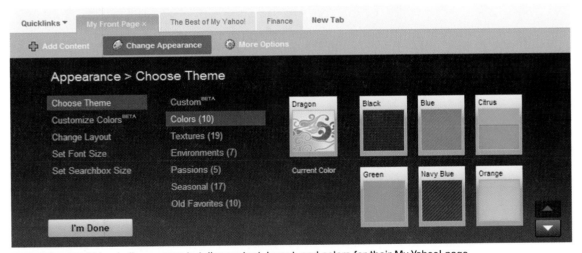

FIGURE 4.26 Yahoo! allows users to tailor content, layout, and colors for their My Yahoo! page.

Why

Allowing users to customize an application to match their content needs, color and layout preferences, and its components affords necessary flexibility to users. In addition, it reduces the burden on designers, as they can defer some of these decisions to users. For example, designers can focus on one application look-and-feel and not worry about coming up with a visual design that satisfies the needs of all users. Through customization options, users can then change the appearance of pages if they prefer a different set of colors, fonts, themes, and so forth. However, this should not be a reason to avoid difficult design decisions. Even when customization options are offered, many users do not choose to customize (Mackay, 1991). In addition, having too many customization options is likely to add complexity to the interface and may make it difficult for users to customize it.

How

Offer users customization options at the content, appearance, and application levels.

CONTENT-LEVEL CUSTOMIZATION

Content-level customization is useful when users are interested in only a very small subset of application content. Allow users to choose content appropriate for their needs and interests from a list of available content. In addition, when possible, categorize content to make it easy for users to narrow down choices and select content quickly (Figure 4.27).

Other ways to help users choose from available content is to provide detailed descriptions and user ratings (see the RATINGS pattern in Chapter 9). Incorporating personalization as part of customization is another way to help users discover useful content. For example, when users add a content module in

FIGURE 4.27 When users click "Add Stuff" on iGoogle, they are shown a categorized list of "Gadgets" that they can add on to the iGoogle pages. When users choose a gadget, iGoogle offers recommendations of things users may like based on the choice of gadget. By doing so, iGoogle makes it easier for users to discover relevant content.

FIGURE 4.28
iGoogle offers an
"I'm feeling lucky.
Automatically add
stuff based on the tab
name" option when
users are adding
a new tab to their
iGoogle portal.

iGoogle (referred to as a "gadget"), they are offered a "You also might like ..."
link to view related content. Another way iGoogle helps users is by offering
them an option to add content automatically based on the tab's name when
they add a tab to their portal (Figure 4.28).

APPEARANCE CUSTOMIZATION

Customization at the appearance level is related to changing the application's
"look and feel"—that is, its page layout, colors, skins, and themes (Figure 4.29).

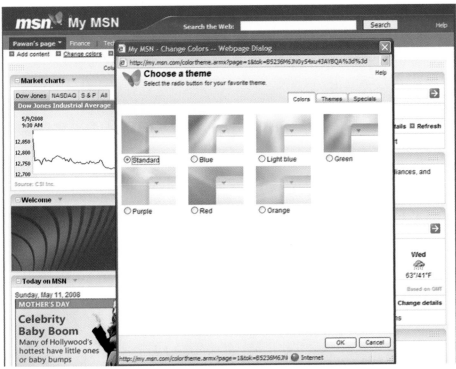

FIGURE 4.29 My MSN offers users several choices for changing appearance, based on colors,
themes, and special occasions such as Valentine's Day, Mother's Day, New Year's Day, and so on.

Most users are not designers, however. When offered a wide selection of colors, their choices may not be visually pleasing and may make pages difficult to use. Therefore, consider offering preset color schemes to choose from. However, this is not to suggest that customization options should be restricted to an existing set. Allow users to choose their own colors as well (Figure 4.30).

APPLICATION CUSTOMIZATION

For enterprise-level web applications, it may be impossible to anticipate and accommodate diverse user needs without compromising usability. For such applications, offer customization options at the application level such as allowing creation of custom reports or even custom fields. Users can then tune the application to conform to their current way of working (Figure 4.31). It's important to remember that such customization at the application level may not be used frequently, so offer users necessary assistance, such as step-by-step guidance using wizards (see the WIZARDS pattern in Chapter 5).

MINIMIZE CUSTOMIZATION CHOICES DURING REGISTRATION

Without interacting with the web application, users may not know whether they would like to customize it and, if so, to what extent. Therefore, limit the customization options to a minimum during the registration process.

FIGURE 4.30 Basecamp offers users preset color schemes to choose from; it also offers a "custom" option that can be chosen to specify colors different from those suggested in a preset scheme.

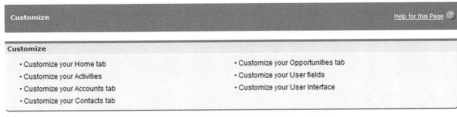

(a)

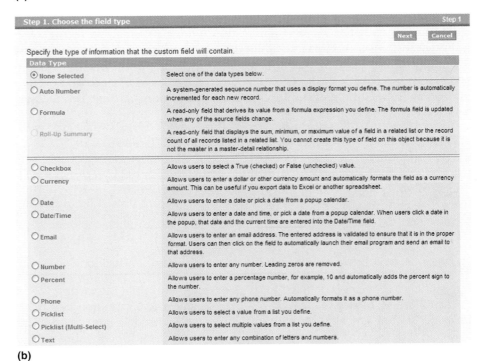

(b)

FIGURE 4.31 SalesForce offers users several customization options, including options to customize user interface elements (a). When customizing user interface elements, users can even specify the type of field such as currency, date/time, email, pick list (i.e., dropdown list), text, and so forth (b). SalesForce uses a wizard approach and offers users detailed assistance on every customization step.

ENSURE THAT CUSTOMIZATION IS OPTIONAL

As mentioned, users are not likely to customize the interface often, and many users won't customize at all (Mackay, 1991). Therefore, it's important that the web application be useful and usable without any customization.

Related design patterns

Because PORTALS usually have a need to support a large amount of content, they typically allow users to customize content and appearance. However, customization requires effort on the users' part. Therefore, if it's possible to infer their needs and content can be personalized—for example, based on information provided by them—consider complementing customization with PERSONALIZATION approaches.

BLANK SLATE

Problem

Many web applications start out empty because they rely on users to provide data (e.g., a defect-tracking application, online calendar, to-do list, etc.). Although the application pages will fill up eventually, the first time users access the application (or a new functionality within the application) they'll see an empty page—a "blank slate." They may be confused as to what to do next and may get an impression that the application is not working as desired when they see a page without content.

Solution

On the blank-slate page, answer questions that first-time users would have such as how to get started, what to do next, and what will the page look like when filled in with data (37signals, 2006). This can be accomplished by explaining to users the best ways to get started via tutorials and help texts and/or show a typical screenshot of the page filled with content (Figure 4.32).

Why

Any guidance that can be offered to users during their initial interaction with a web application makes them feel comfortable with the application and helps them get started quickly. In addition, when faced with an empty page, users may find it difficult to determine scope and the extent of functionality offered by the web application, thus limiting the degree to which they are able to interact with the application.

Having a blank-slate page serves several purposes for users: it sets appropriate expectations, encourages taking action, familiarizes them with what the page will eventually look like, and creates a positive first impression of the application (Hoekman, 2008; 37signals, 2006).

How

An important design feature of an effective blank-slate page is one or more prominently displayed action(s) that would remove the blank slate and get users familiar with the application (Figure 4.33).

The actions may be accompanied by messages informing users why they are not seeing any content. For example, Basecamp uses messages such as "Create the first writeboard for this project" with "first" implying that users have not created a writeboard (Figure 4.34).

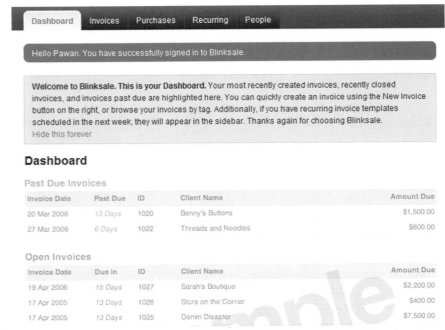

FIGURE 4.32 Blinksale, an invoice management application, provides a brief explanation of the dashboard and shows an example dashboard page demonstrating to users what the dashboard will look like when filled in.

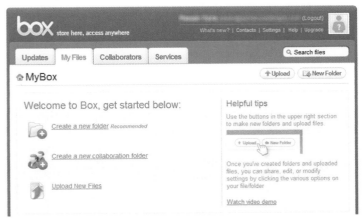

FIGURE 4.33 On its blank-slate page, Box.net offers users several options (e.g., create a new folder, create a new collaboration folder) to get started. It also offers an option to "Watch video demo."

OFFER USERS RELEVANT TUTORIALS OR DEMOS

Make users understand the steps involved in using a web application or a piece of functionality by offering them tutorials or demos (see Figure 4.34). Make them targeted and short in duration so that users can start using the application quickly.

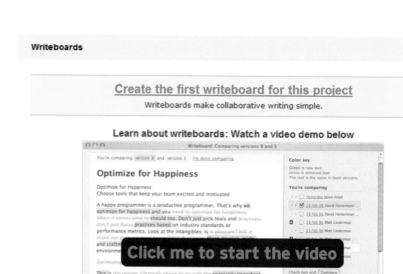

FIGURE 4.34 Basecamp shows the message "Create the first writeboard for this project" to indicate that users haven't created any writeboards. It also shows what a writeboard looks like and offers users a video demo (approximately 2 minutes) to learn more about writeboards.

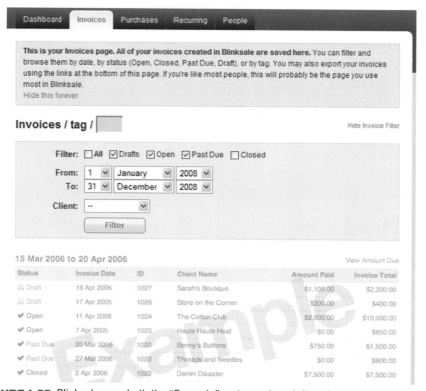

FIGURE 4.35 Blinksale uses both the "Example" watermark and dims the screenshot on the blank-slate page.

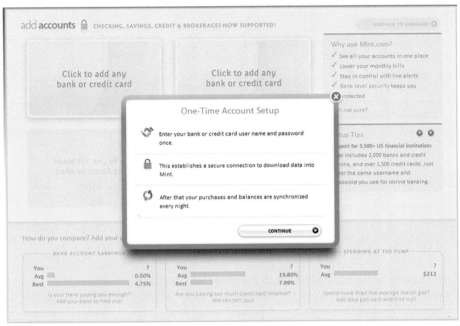

FIGURE 4.36 Mint offers users help with initial account setup. They show the page without content dimmed with some sample data to give users a general idea of what the "Account" page will eventually look like.

SHOW USERS AN EXAMPLE SCREENSHOT

Set clear expectations of what the page will look like when filled by showing a screenshot with sample content. Make it clear to users that they are not seeing real data by inserting watermarks, such as "Sample data" or "Example," or dim the screenshot to make it recede into the background (Figure 4.35).

ASSIST USERS IN THE INITIAL SETUP

If there are certain tasks users must do before they can use the web application, offer options to guide them through the initial setup process. For example, for a financial application, users can be offered to set up accounts (Figure 4.36).

Related design patterns

BLANK SLATE offers necessary guidance to new users of the application so that they can become productive with the application quickly. The need for assisting users does not completely go away after they have interacted with the application and filled it with data. It's important to continue assisting users throughout their interaction with the application using CONTEXTUAL HELP, FREQUENTLY ASKED QUESTIONS, and APPLICATION HELP (see the Web Help Appendix at *www.elsevierdirect.com/9780123742650* and the INPUT HINTS/PROMPTS pattern in Chapter 2).

CHAPTER 5

Navigation

INTRODUCTION

Designing navigation is about establishing relationships between various application parts (i.e., content and functionality) and conveying their importance and hierarchy to efficiently and effectively facilitate completion of user tasks. This includes organization, labeling, and presentation of content and functionality. This chapter focuses on patterns related to the types of navigation systems and their presentation; to learn about the organization and labeling of navigation systems, see Morville and Rosenfeld (2006), Kalbach (2007), and Fleming (1998).

Most web applications are organized hierarchically and thus allow users access to its content and functionality using levels of navigation. At the highest level, PRIMARY NAVIGATION, or *global navigation*, shows top-level categories or groupings that users can access from anywhere within the application. By making it available throughout the application, it also helps orient users within the application. SECONDARY NAVIGATION, or *local navigation*, shows users second and subsequent levels of navigation options for the selected primary navigation option. In addition to primary and secondary navigations, users also need a quick way to access a few key functions (e.g., login, logout, language selector, etc.) and content (e.g., help, cart, account, etc.). Like primary navigation, these key functions and content areas need to be made available throughout the application (UTILITY NAVIGATION).

Although primary and secondary navigation are useful in supporting an application's hierarchical structure, content in many applications is multidimensional and does not afford a unique hierarchical navigation scheme. FACETED NAVIGATION has emerged as an effective approach to allow maximum flexibility and support a variety of tasks by offering the ability to navigate using multiple attributes and not restricting users to only one (e.g., a facet) with which to start navigation.

In addition to the hierarchical navigation approaches, users also benefit from nonhierarchical ways to access information using indexes, related items lists, recommendations, and so forth (SUPPLEMENTAL NAVIGATION). Supplemental navigation systems are intended not only as alternative ways of accessing content but also to encourage exploration. More recent applications, especially those that rely on user-generated and user-contributed content, allow users to discover new content by offering a navigation approach based on *folksonomies*—a structure derived from user-provided labels describing application content (TAG CLOUDS).

Another important function of navigation is that of orienting users and letting them know where they are within the application. Support for orientation is usually provided by location trails, commonly referred to as BREADCRUMBS.

While most application navigation is intended to get users to their desired content or function, there are instances where navigation is used to help users accomplish tasks by guiding them one step at a time (WIZARDS). This is particularly the case for infrequent, yet important, multistep tasks that have dependencies that users may be unfamiliar with.

PRIMARY NAVIGATION

Problem

The most common functionality and high-level categories (or objects) within web applications need to be readily available and understood by users. Additionally, users should be able to navigate quickly among major sections from anywhere within the web application.

Solution

Offer users a consistent way to navigate to main application functions and place them in a consistent and salient manner on all application pages (Figure 5.1).

Why

For web applications, primary navigation plays a crucial role in facilitating navigation and orientation. It serves as both a table of contents by exposing high-level application functions and an orientation mechanism that lets users know where they are within the application's structure (see also the BREADCRUMBS pattern later in this chapter).

FIGURE 5.1 LinkedIn uses a tab-based approach that allows users access to important application features and functionalities.

How

Place primary navigation either horizontally at the top of the page or vertically running down the page, either on the left or right side. Web applications have typically favored placing primary navigation horizontally (Figure 5.2); Adkisson (2002) found that 87 percent (65 of 73 sites) of e-commerce applications placed the primary navigation horizontally at the top of the page. This is understandable, since placing primary navigation vertically reduces available horizontal space. For web applications presenting tabular data with many columns, vertical placement of primary navigation could result in horizontal scrolling or make tabular data appear cluttered.

Placing primary navigation horizontally, however, limits the number of navigation options it can offer users before requiring them to scroll horizontally. To avoid horizontal scrolling, web applications often resort to having a "more" option (usually depicted as an arrow icon) to allow users to see additional navigation choices (Figure 5.3); this is similar to toolbars in desktop applications

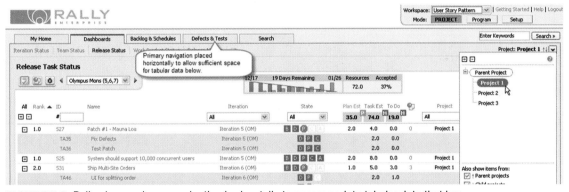

FIGURE 5.2 Rally places primary navigation horizontally to accommodate tabular data that has several columns.

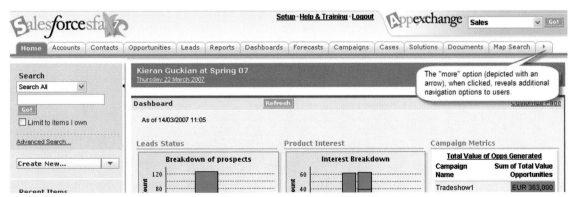

FIGURE 5.3 SalesForce uses an arrow tab that allows users access to additional primary navigation options that could not be accommodated horizontally.

Table 5.1	Benefits and Limitations of Horizontal and Vertical Placement of Primary Navigation	
	Horizontal Placement	**Vertical Placement**
Benefits	Allows more horizontal space for content. Beneficial if the web application requires showing tabular data with several columns.	Is easier to scale. Can easily accommodate 10–15 menu options without requiring users to scroll on monitors with 1024 × 768 resolution. Allows multiple levels of navigation options as a hierarchical structure.
Limitations	Difficult to scale. Cannot typically accommodate more than 8–10 navigation options on monitors with 1024 × 768 resolution. If multiple navigation levels are desired and shown as cascading levels, horizontal navigation breaks down beyond two to three levels. Also, with multiple cascading levels, content gets pushed down.	Requires horizontal space limiting the space available for application content.

such as Microsoft Word, Firefox, and others. Table 5.1 summarizes the benefits and limitations of horizontal and vertical placement of primary navigation.

Regardless of the placement of primary navigation, it is important that it be positioned consistently and made available throughout the application.

MAKE PRIMARY NAVIGATION VISUALLY SALIENT

Because users rely on primary navigation to access the main functionality of the web application, make it salient and clearly differentiated from the page content (Figure 5.4).

HIGHLIGHT THE SELECTED NAVIGATION OPTION

Highlight the selected navigation option to let users know where they are within the application. This can be accomplished by visually distinguishing the selected navigation option from others by varying its font, background, color, and/or border (Figure 5.5).

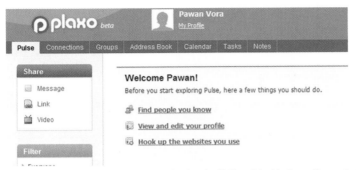

FIGURE 5.4 Plaxo uses global navigation that is clearly distinguishable from the rest of the page.

FIGURE 5.5 Backpack makes the selected option appear like a tab to visually distinguish it from other navigation options.

REMOVE PRIMARY NAVIGATION FOR TASKS WITH SELF-CONTAINED NAVIGATION

Typically, primary navigation should be placed in and made available consistently throughout the application. However, for multistep tasks with their self-contained navigation (e.g., wizard-based), to minimize distractions or to prevent data loss (e.g., checkout, initial setup, or registration) primary navigation may be removed (Figure 5.6). Because wizardlike tasks are often supported by their own navigation, removing primary navigation also avoids potential confusion among multiple navigation mechanisms (see the WIZARDS pattern later in this chapter).

ESTABLISH A CORRECT INFORMATION "SCENT" THROUGH EFFECTIVE LABELING

Primary navigation labels are very important for establishing a correct information "scent" for the application. The notion of an information "scent" is based on the *information foraging theory*, which explains mechanisms used by people when searching for information (Chi et al., 2000; Pirolli and Card, 1999). This

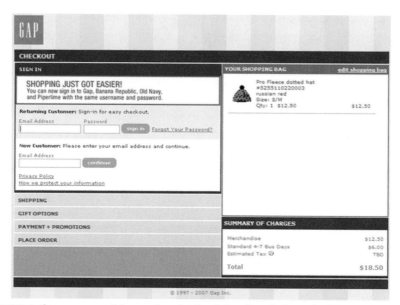

FIGURE 5.6 Gap removes all forms of navigation (other than that required for purchasing items) as soon as users begin the checkout process. This site uses the accordion[1] approach to navigate for sign in, shipping, payment, and so forth.

theory suggests that, when faced with a variety of options, users choose the one offering them the strongest indication or "scent" that will take them closer to the desired information. When applied to primary navigation, if labels representing navigation options fail to provide a strong "scent," not only will users take longer to decide which option to choose, but they may also navigate down the wrong paths, leading to inefficient interaction and a frustrating experience. Simply stated, from navigation labels, users should be able to form correct expectations of information they will be able to access and tasks they will be able to accomplish by choosing a navigation option without actually selecting it.

> **TIP**
> The need to establish a correct information
> "scent" applies to all types of navigation systems,
> not just primary navigation.

[1]The *accordion* approach shows users content for only one navigation option at a time. Clicking another navigation option expands the content within it and collapses other choices. The accordion interface is similar to a tab-based navigation in that both the approaches show content within only one navigation option at a time. The main difference is in the accordion menu's visual representation and the accompanying "sliding" animation effect for revealing content within each navigation option.

Related design patterns

Most web applications support hierarchical navigation, requiring both primary navigation and SECONDARY NAVIGATION. For deeper navigation hierarchies, consider using BREADCRUMBS to orient users and show them where they are in the application.

SECONDARY NAVIGATION

Problem

Users need a way to access navigation options in the application's hierarchy at levels below the primary navigation.

Solution

Show users secondary navigation that corresponds to the selected primary navigation option. In addition, clearly show the hierarchical relationship between the primary and each secondary level of navigation (Figure 5.7).

Why

Navigation in most web applications is designed to support its hierarchical structure,[2] which is typically two to three levels deep. Secondary navigation complements primary navigation and makes it easy for users to navigate the application's structure at levels below the primary navigation. Although secondary navigation options change based on the selected primary navigation, their placement within the application should be consistent to encourage exploration.

How

Clearly indicate the primary navigation option to which the secondary (and deeper) levels of navigation belong. When primary navigation is placed horizontally, secondary navigation options are either placed horizontally nested below the primary navigation (see Figure 5.6) or vertically as either left or right navigation bars (Figure 5.8).

FIGURE 5.7 Rally shows secondary navigation nested below the selected primary navigation option. Although not common, Rally allows users to add their own secondary navigation option.

---

[2]This doesn't exclude other navigation approaches such as quick links to related items, alphabetical indexes, breadcrumbs, and so forth (see the SUPPLEMENTAL NAVIGATION pattern later in this chapter). However, hierarchies are simpler to understand and offer a familiar way to organize information. Therefore, they are the preferred approach for structuring information (Morville and Rosenfeld, 2006).

FIGURE 5.8 Gap uses an inverted-L navigation layout by placing primary navigation horizontally at the top of the page and secondary navigation vertically on the left.

Placing secondary navigation vertically on the left or right is usually preferred when the total number of secondary navigation options cannot be accommodated horizontally or when the navigation choices are available at even deeper levels. Vertical placement of secondary navigation allows for necessary scalability as users navigate down the hierarchy. Although an inverted-L navigation layout—that is, placing secondary navigation on the left and primary navigation at the top of page—is quite common, Kalbach and Bosenick (2003) did not find any evidence of its benefits when compared to its placement on the right. When showing deep hierarchies, it's common to show navigation in an indented list in a treelike structure (Figure 5.9)

The use of menus similar to desktop applications for showing secondary navigation options is becoming popular for web applications (Figure 5.10); they are also referred to as dynamic menus, fly-out menus, pop-up menus, and dropdown menus.

Menus have the benefit of not taking up additional space and allowing users to explore navigation hierarchy without requiring them to select a primary navigation option. However, menus have several downsides as well. Most important, users prefer to have all choices visible instead of hidden in dropdown menus. Bernard and Hamblin (2003) found a strong dislike as well as longer search times for horizontal placement of menus when compared with vertical placement. In addition, they may be difficult for users who use assistive technologies (e.g., screen readers) if they are activated by mouse hovers. For improving accessibility, they should be activated by a click of the mouse, and navigation options should be accessible via keyboard. They also may be disorienting to users, since the context of the selected option would be missing; this concern

FIGURE 5.9
Wal-Mart uses a treelike navigation scheme for second and third levels of secondary navigation.

(a)

(b)

FIGURE 5.10 PriceGrabber (a) and Sony (b) use menus to show secondary navigation options. Because Sony has a deeper navigation structure, it also uses cascading menus.

can be alleviated to a certain extent by the use of location breadcrumbs (see the BREADCRUMBS pattern later in this chapter).

HIGHLIGHT SELECTED PRIMARY AND SECONDARY NAVIGATION OPTIONS

To orient users with the application, highlight the currently selected navigation option, both primary and secondary, in some way, such as by a combination of font size and weight, foreground and background colors, and border size and colors (see Figure 5.10).

Related design patterns

Because an application's hierarchical structure is made accessible through its navigation system, SECONDARY NAVIGATION cannot be considered without the PRIMARY NAVIGATION. Use of BREADCRUMBS is also recommended, as they not only make an item's placement in the hierarchy visible, but they also allow an efficient way to backtrack to a higher level in the hierarchy.

UTILITY NAVIGATION

Problem

Users need access to certain functions and tools, such as their shopping cart, help, log in, log out, account information, preferences, language selections, country selections, text-size selections, and so forth, on all application pages. Although they are key functions and need to be accessed from anywhere in the application, they are typically not used frequently.

Solution

Group such functions and tools (i.e., utilities) and allow users access to them from all pages within the application. Because they need to be accessible from anywhere in the application, place them in the header region (Figure 5.11).

Why

Utility navigation allows users quick access to important and key application functions. By placing them in a consistent, expected location throughout the application, users can find them easily. However, they are not the primary mechanism for navigating the application and should be given less visual prominence when compared with the primary navigation.

FIGURE 5.11 Snapfish separates utility navigation functions—"log out," "help," "your cart," and "your account"—in the top-right area of the page.

FIGURE 5.12 Buy.com uses an icon for the cart and uses orange to visually distinguish "View Cart" from other navigation options.

FIGURE 5.13 Rally Agile Pro allows users to switch workspaces by selecting a different workspace from a dropdown list in the utility navigation area.

How

Place utility navigation in the header region (preferably in the top-right corner of the page) of all web application pages. In addition, give it less visual prominence over the primary navigation.

EMPHASIZE COMMONLY ACCESSED FUNCTIONS

For utility functions accessed more frequently than others (e.g., shopping carts for e-commerce applications), make them salient by supplementing their labels with icons and/or by using a visual treatment that clearly distinguishes them from other utility navigation options (Figure 5.12).

USE UTILITY NAVIGATION TO ALLOW SWITCHING AMONG WORKSPACES OR APPLICATIONS

Web applications that allow users to create and access multiple workspaces— for example, multiple projects—often use a utility navigation to allow them to switch between workspaces (Figure 5.13).

Similarly, application suites, such as those offered by Google and Zoho, allow users to switch among applications using utility navigation (Figure 5.14).

INCLUDE A LANGUAGE SELECTOR IN UTILITY NAVIGATION

Web applications supporting multiple languages usually include options to change the language (or the country) as a utility navigation option (Figure 5.15; see also the LANGUAGE SELECTOR pattern in Chapter 10).

Related design patterns

Utility navigation options discussed here are "global" in nature (e.g., they apply to the entire page) and are placed in the header region. However, there

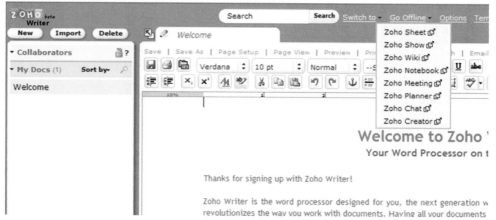

FIGURE 5.14 Zoho allows users to change applications using the "Switch to" dropdown list in the utility navigation.

FIGURE 5.15 Dominos' online ordering application allows users to switch between English and Spanish (labeled "Español") as a utility navigation option.

are utility functions that are "local" in nature and apply to the content within the page, such as export to Excel or XML, printer friendly, email to a friend, and so forth, and are placed closer to the content to which they apply (see the LIST UTILITY FUNCTIONS pattern in Chapter 7). In addition, options to change the page language or country are offered in the utility navigation region (see the LANGUAGE SELECTOR and GLOBAL GATEWAY patterns in Chapter 10).

FACETED NAVIGATION

Problem

Items such as wines, diamonds, recipes, cameras, computers, and many others can be classified along several attributes. For example, wines can be classified based on its type (e.g., red, white), region (e.g., California, France, Spain, Australia), price (e.g., less than $20, $20–$30, etc.), and several others. Thus, there is no one widely accepted hierarchical structure that can be used for navigation. In fact, a navigation scheme can be devised for each attribute it carries. Designing a navigation approach based on just one attribute would make navigation inefficient and unsatisfactory to a large number of users.

Solution

Offer users a faceted navigation approach where users can choose any facet (i.e., attribute) of the item to navigate. With each selection of a facet, show users additional navigation choices based on facets that are valid for the remaining items (Figure 5.16).

(a)

(b)

FIGURE 5.16
Wine.com uses a faceted navigation approach to help users navigate. With each selection, there are fewer available facets based on valid attributes for the remaining items. Therefore, navigation choices available for (a) Red Wine > Cabernet Sauvignon are different from those for (b) Red Wine > Cabernet Sauvignon > $20–$40 (price range).

Why

In contrast to hierarchical navigation based on only one attribute, faceted navigation offers users the ability to navigate to desired items based on several attributes. In addition, users can select any available attribute to start their navigation. Another important benefit is that an empty result set is not possible with faceted navigation. Because faceted navigation is generated from "facets" (or attributes) of the remaining items themselves, users see at least one choice at the end of the navigation. In fact, this is one important difference between faceted navigation (or faceted searching) from filtering (see the FILTERING and FACETED SEARCH patterns in Chapter 6).

How

Show users all available facets to start their navigation (Figure 5.17). After users have selected the initial facet, show them items belonging to the selected facet along with the updated navigation choices derived from the remaining items' facets. Additional facets may be placed vertically to the left or horizontally above the items list depending on the total number of facets available and the overall application design; horizontal placement may be limiting for items with several facets (Figure 5.18).

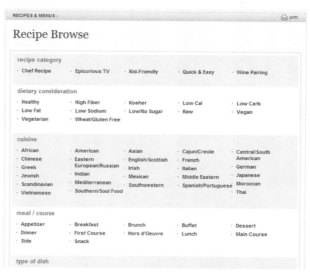

FIGURE 5.17 Epicurious offers users several facets to choose from to browse recipes.

KEEP USERS INFORMED OF THEIR SELECTIONS

Avoid disorientation by showing users their selections with mechanisms such as BREADCRUMBS above the item list (Figure 5.19). (See the BREADCRUMBS pattern later in this chapter.)

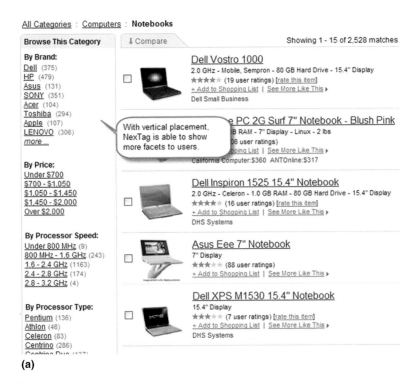

(a)

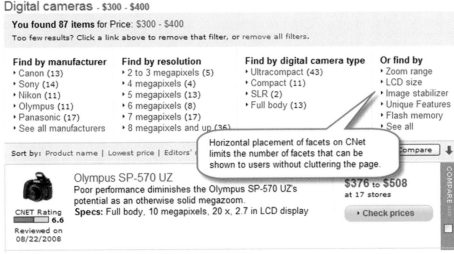

(b)

FIGURE 5.18 NexTag places facets on the left (a) and CNet places them at the top (b).

Related design patterns

As mentioned, BREADCRUMBS can be used to indicate users' choices when using faceted navigation. In addition, applications using faceted navigation usually support FACETED SEARCH as well (see Chapter 6).

FIGURE 5.19 Wine.com presents users' selections in a breadcrumbs format above the items list. Users can also see selections in the left navigation area where their choices are highlighted. In addition, instead of using "Home," the common first choice in a breadcrumb format, Wine. com uses "Start Over," which makes it easy for users to start at the beginning and avoid potential confusion with a link labeled "Home."

SUPPLEMENTARY NAVIGATION

Problem

Although PRIMARY and SECONDARY NAVIGATION provide an effective way to navigate the application's hierarchy, they do not provide adequate means for users to discover new content or encourage exploration. This may result in both poor utilization of a web application's functionality and fewer transactions (e.g., purchases, downloads, quotes, and so forth).

Solution

Offer users supplementary navigation mechanisms such as alphabetical or alphanumeric indexes, recommendations, related items, and so forth to facilitate discovery of new information and provide direct access to relevant information (Figure 5.20).

Why

Supplementary navigation can allow users direct access to content as well as encourage discovery of new content. However, it's important to remember they neither replace an application's navigation structure as instantiated by primary and secondary navigation nor minimize the impact of poorly designed information architecture (Morville and Rosenfeld, 2006).

How

Following are a few ways to incorporate supplemental navigation in web applications and provide direct access to application content or functionality.

FIGURE 5.20 The "Sun Downloads" page offers users several navigation options to get to a specific software download page.

FIGURE 5.21 PDRHealth (Physician's Desktop Reference) makes it easy to find specific drugs by offering alphabetical indexes of prescription drugs, over-the-counter (OTC) drugs, and herbals and supplements.

INDEXES

Indexes are alphabetical or alphanumeric lists of items in an application or its high-level categories. When users know a specific item that they are looking for, using an alphabetical index may be a more efficient way to get to it when compared with navigating the application hierarchy.[3]

For large applications, the alphabetical index may be divided over multiple pages with one or more pages representing a letter of the alphabet or a number (Figure 5.21). Because most people are familiar with alphabetical indexes in other information sources, their use typically does not require any instructions.

---

[3]Another way to quickly get to a known item is by searching (see Chapter 6 for patterns related to searching).

Customers Who Bought This Item Also Bought

Thinking Points:
Communicating Our
American Values and Vi... by
George Lakoff
★★★★☆ (10) $8.00

Metaphors We Live By by
George Lakoff
★★★★☆ (29) $10.88

The Political Brain: The Role
of Emotion in Deciding the...
by Drew Westen
★★★★☆ (35) $17.79

The Post-American World by
Fareed Zakaria
★★★★☆ (111) $15.57

Moral Politics : How Liberals
and Conservatives Think by
George Lakoff
★★★★☆ (67) $14.96

FIGURE 5.22 Amazon offers users "Customers Who Bought This Item Also Bought" recommendations to facilitate the discovery of new items.

RECOMMENDATIONS

Recommendations are another way of introducing users to new content. This may be based on users' past browsing or purchasing behaviors and/or matching behaviors of users with similar interests and profiles (i.e., collaborative filtering), as Figure 5.22 shows (see also the PERSONALIZATION pattern in Chapter 4).

RELATED ITEMS

Many e-commerce applications use some form of related items promoting the discovery of new products and encouraging upsell and cross-sell (Figure 5.23). The related items may be in the form of similar products, product accessories, services and warranties, and so forth.

Related design patterns

As the name suggests, supplementary navigation supplements, rather than replaces, PRIMARY NAVIGATION and SECONDARY NAVIGATION. In addition, because supplementary navigation approaches bypass the hierarchical navigation structure, incorporating BREADCRUMBS may help users understand where they are in the application structure. TAG CLOUDS are also another form of supplemental navigation and should be considered for applications that rely on user-contributed content.

TAG CLOUDS

Problem

Web applications that allow access to user-generated or user-contributed content, such as photos, videos, music, and so forth, typically allow users to label (i.e., *tag*) items they are viewing or adding (see the TAGGING pattern in Chapter 9). When an item is tagged by many users, tags created by them are likely to be dissimilar because of the differences in their interests, familiarity with the item, and usage context. Such diversity in tags can make it difficult for users to find those same items in the future. In addition, users may want to find items that are similar to the ones they are interested in. For example, after

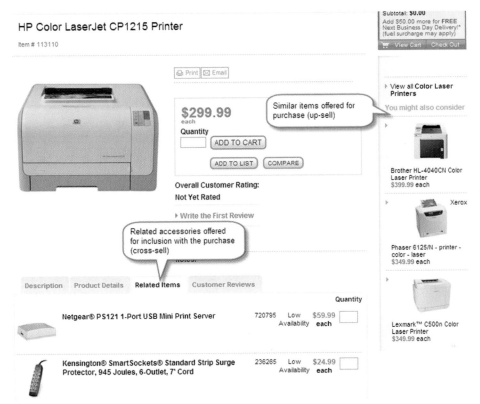

FIGURE 5.23 OfficeDepot shows users related items both for up-sell and cross-sell.

watching a video of an Olympics' swimming event, users may be interested in watching other videos with the same athlete in other Olympics.

Solution

Use *tag clouds* to show users the tags for individual items they are viewing along with their "strength" or importance in describing those items. In addition, allow users to navigate the information space using the tags in the tag clouds (Figure 5.24).

Why

Unlike navigation approaches discussed so far, which are designed to be persistent and support both navigation and orientation, tag clouds work as an associative navigation mechanism and facilitate the discovery of new content (Kalbach, 2007). This associative navigation supports three forms of information exploration (Smith, 2007):

- *Pivot browsing.* Users may choose a new reference point, a *pivot*, for exploring the information space.

FIGURE 5.24 Last.fm uses tag clouds for individual items (e.g., music group, artist, or album).

FIGURE 5.25
NexTag uses a
tag cloud to show
popular searches
on its comparison
shopping application.

- *Popularity-based navigation.* Tag clouds, by emphasizing frequently used or viewed tags, show the most popular ones (Figure 5.25). Users may then use them to judge the nature, quality, and importance of resources in the application.
- *Filtering.* Each label in the tag cloud can be used as a filter and allows users to "drill" down and view only the items tagged with that label.

In addition, because several community users can tag an item, tag clouds can provide an at-a-glance overview—a semantic map of sorts—of tagged items (Rivadeneira et al., 2007), and, in some instances, the application as a whole (Figure 5.26).

FIGURE 5.26 WebDesignerWall, a blog, uses a tag cloud as a persistent yet dynamic navigation mechanism. Because it updates with each new blog article, it can provide useful information about the nature of articles. In addition, it uses them as a filtering mechanism that lets users view all items labeled with a tag.

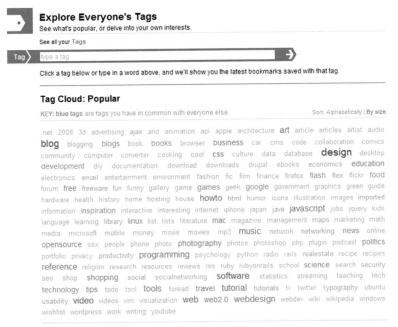

FIGURE 5.27 Delicious uses font size to indicate the tag's popularity and uses color to discriminate a user's tag set from the entire community's tag set.

How

The most popular method of showing tags is as a cluster of related concepts—tag clouds. The purpose of a tag cloud is to not only show related concepts to users but also clearly indicate a tag's importance (or frequency or popularity). This is accomplished more commonly by text size, weight (bold versus normal), and/or colors (Figure 5.27). Typically, higher contrast is used to indicate popularity

> **NOTE**
>
> When specifying the font sizes of tags in cascading style sheets (CSS), use relative text size units, such as "em," percentages, or "ex," (instead of "px" or "pt") to improve accessibility of tag clouds. This would allow users to change the browser page's text size without losing the importance and popularity of tags indicated by font size variability.

(or other similar measures) of a tag from others. Thus, less-popular tags have lower contrasts.

However, one has to be careful and not use too many colors or text sizes in a tag cloud. Using too many colors can make the tag cloud appear cluttered and difficult for users to distinguish among tags. In general, do not use more than three colors combined with text sizes to indicate tag popularity.

DETERMINE TAG ORDER BASED ON USERS' TASKS

Tags in tag clouds are generally ordered alphabetically. This makes finding a tag faster, especially as the tag set becomes larger (Halvey and Keane, 2007). However, a study by Rivadeneira et al. (2007) provides evidence in favor of a frequency-based layout over an alphabetical layout when the users' task is to form an impression about the "tagger," the person doing the tagging. In applications where users' tasks may vary, it may be useful to allow users to organize tags several different ways (Figure 5.28).

Related design patterns

Because of the associative nature of navigation, TAG CLOUDS should not be used as the only means of navigation within web applications. They should supplement PRIMARY NAVIGATION and SECONDARY NAVIGATION as well, if applicable.

   ▼ **tag options**
   » view as cloud | list
   » sort by alpha | freq
   » use minimum: 1, 2, 5
   » show | hide bundles
   » bundle tags
   » edit tags: rename | delete

FIGURE 5.28 Delicious allows users to view tags as clouds or lists, sort them alphabetically or by frequency, filter them by minimum number of occurrences, and so forth.

BREADCRUMBS

Problem

Users may lose track of where they are within applications that are several levels deep. Although users have an option to click a browser's "back" button to orient them or navigate to previous pages, frequent application users may find it cumbersome to click the "back" button several times or to start again from the home page just to return to a previous page. In addition, if users have "teleported" to a page using a search or other forms of deep linking, they may not know where the page resides in relation to other application pages (Spool, 2005).

Solution

Provide "breadcrumbs" starting from the application's main page leading up to the current page that indicate the current page's location within the application hierarchy. Link each page reference in the breadcrumbs trail, allowing users to return to any intermediate page (Figure 5.29).

Why

Although there are different implementations of breadcrumbs such as location breadcrumbs, path breadcrumbs, and attribute breadcrumbs (see sidebar, Types of Breadcrumbs), the most popular and advocated by usability experts is location breadcrumbs (Instone, 2002; Nielsen, 2007; Spool, 2005). By indicating the current page's relative position within the application structure, location breadcrumbs help orient users and help them understand the application's hierarchical structure. Furthermore, by linking parent pages, they serve an important, albeit secondary, navigation function by allowing users a quicker way to return to previous pages within the hierarchy.

How

On each application page, show location breadcrumbs by indicating the current page's position within the application hierarchy, starting from the "home"

FIGURE 5.29 Circuit City uses location breadcrumbs to indicate where users are within the application hierarchy. In addition, they link each page referenced in the breadcrumbs trail to make it easy for users to navigate directly to it.

TYPES OF BREADCRUMBS

Instone (2002) identified the following types of breadcrumbs.

Location breadcrumbs. Location breadcrumbs is perhaps the most commonly used type of breadcrumbs. They indicate a page's position within the application's hierarchy irrespective of the path—by browsing, searching, or deep linking from any page within the application—users take to reach it.

A variation of location breadcrumbs is the look-ahead breadcrumbs (LAB) developed by Teng (2003). For each page in a location breadcrumbs trail (except the current page), a dropdown list of links to the pages at that level in the hierarchy is included.

Path breadcrumbs. Unlike location breadcrumbs, path breadcrumbs are dynamic trails. They show the path taken by users within the application to reach the current page. Because users can take different routes (e.g., browsing, searching, etc.) to reach a page, several breadcrumbs exist for the same page.

Nielsen (2007) refers to path breadcrumbs as history trails and advocates against their use because they duplicate the functionality offered by the browser's "back" button, and they may be confusing if users have made unnecessary digressions along the way to the current page. Additionally, they do not help users visualize the current page's location within the application structure.

Attribute breadcrumbs. Many large sites, where the same page can be accessed through multiple paths (e.g., Amazon), employ breadcrumblike features describing meta-information about the current page within the site hierarchy (Figure 5.30).

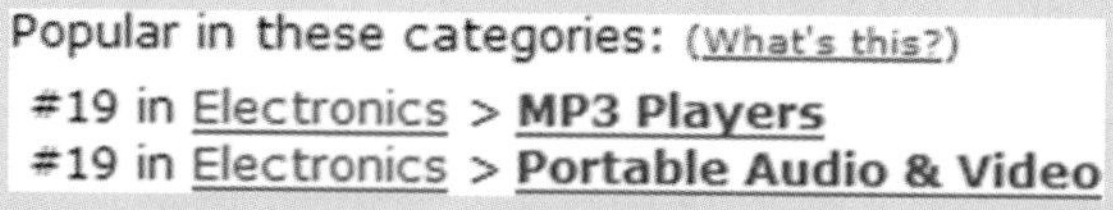

Popular in these categories: (What's this?)
#19 in Electronics > **MP3 Players**
#19 in Electronics > **Portable Audio & Video**

FIGURE 5.30 Amazon uses breadcrumblike features to indicate product meta-information. In essence, they indicate the current item's location from all places within the application structure.

page. In addition, allow users a quick way to jump to any page within the hierarchy by linking each page in the breadcrumb (except the one referring to the current page). Many location breadcrumbs do not show the current page in the breadcrumbs trail. However, several usability experts have recommended its inclusion (Instone, 2002; Krug, 2006; Nielsen, 2007).

SEPARATE EACH ITEM IN THE BREADCRUMBS TRAIL BY A SYMBOL

Separate each item in the breadcrumbs trail with a symbol to suggest a navigation path. The most commonly used separator symbol is the right arrowhead (>). Colter et al. (2002) found that among the applications using breadcrumbs, 47.10 percent used the > separator; Aery (2007) states that the use

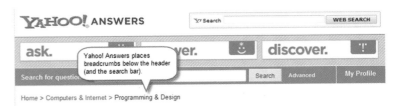

FIGURE 5.31 Yahoo! Answers places breadcrumbs just below the header and search area.

of > was even more prevalent among e-commerce sites (63.5 percent). Other commonly used separator symbols are /, :, |, », and →. Arrows and arrowheads are generally preferred because they clearly indicate movement from one level to another and users are familiar with their use in search directories (e.g., Yahoo!).

PLACE BREADCRUMBS BELOW THE PAGE HEADER

The most frequent placement of breadcrumbs is below the page header near the page title. If the primary navigation and/or search area is integrated with the page header, place the breadcrumbs trail below them (Figure 5.31). If a page has vertical navigation on the left, breadcrumbs may be placed to its right. Placement of breadcrumbs below the header is also found to have a higher usage than at the top of the page (Lida and Chaparro, 2003).

MATCH BREADCRUMBS TRAIL LINKS TO CORRESPONDING PAGE TITLES

Just like the recommended practice for link labels to match their destination page titles, parent pages in breadcrumbs should match their corresponding page titles. This also makes it easy for users to recognize them if they visited them on their way to the current page. If page titles are too long, shorten them with an ellipsis at the end, and provide the entire page title as a tool tip (or a hover tip).

MAKE LINKED BREADCRUMBS ELEMENTS LOOK LIKE LINKS

Because parent pages in breadcrumbs are links, they should appear as links. If they appear as buttons, they should look clickable. Without the necessary "click" affordance, breadcrumbs may fail to serve as an important navigation mechanism for users.

DESIGN BREADCRUMBS TO BE LOWER IN THE PAGE'S VISUAL HIERARCHY

Breadcrumbs are not the primary form of navigation for users. Therefore, they should be placed lower in the page's visual hierarchy (see the VISUAL HIERARCHY pattern in Chapter 12). This is typically achieved by using smaller, yet readable, fonts and using no more than a single line of text on a page. Because of their placement near primary and secondary navigations, breadcrumbs shouldn't visually compete for attention or distract users from the main navigation mechanisms.

Related design patterns

Breadcrumbs should be given lesser emphasis than other important elements on the page, such as the page title, PRIMARY NAVIGATION, and SECONDARY NAVIGATION (see VISUAL HIERARCHY pattern in Chapter 12).

WIZARDS

Problem

Users need to complete several steps in a specific order to complete a task (e.g., checking out an item on an e-commerce site, making reservations, filing taxes, and so forth). Because most users are going to perform the task occasionally, they may not acquire enough familiarity or expertise to remember the steps and their order for successfully accomplishing it.

Solution

Guide users through steps, one at a time, in a predetermined sequence (Figure 5.32). Such interfaces are commonly referred to as *wizards*.

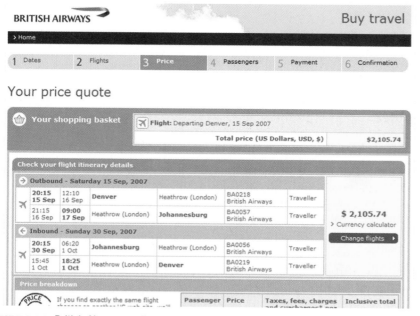

FIGURE 5.32 British Airways walks users through a wizard to help them make flight reservations.

Why

Wizards are useful when users must go through a specific sequence of steps and perform a set of individual tasks in succession (e.g., checkout for e-commerce applications or opening an account with a financial institution). They are also useful for complex tasks with branches or dependencies among elements, which require considerable domain knowledge to complete (Dryer, 1997).

By breaking such tasks into smaller steps and guiding users through each step, wizards hide the complexity of the underlying task. They require users to focus on only a few data elements at a time and let the application keep track of what they have done and still need to do. Additionally, by guiding users through each step, errors are minimized and the chances of users successfully accomplishing the task are improved. Finally, wizards are also useful when a task is critical for accomplishing users' goals (Wickham et al., 2002). For example, in e-commerce applications, checkout is a critical task for purchasing items.

How

As a first step, identify all information or groups of information and the order in which they need to be presented to users to complete the desired task. In addition, identify any dependencies or branches between them to ensure that the dependent tasks occur later in the sequence. For example, in an e-commerce checkout process, shipping information usually comes before payment information because the shipping address and shipping options (such as delivery timeframe, tax-exempt status, and so forth) are used to calculate tax and shipping charges, which contribute to the total price. Only after knowing the total price should users be asked for billing and payment information. Once information, grouping, and order are identified, break them up into individual steps so that logically related groups are together.

Once the steps, sequence, and branching decisions, if any, are made design pages in a wizard style—that is, present each step on a separate page and allow navigation between them with "next" or "continue" and "previous" or "back" actions (Figure 5.33).

Although typical wizard implementation has individual steps on separate pages, a recent trend is to consider an accordion interface design approach (Figure 5.34). This design shows all the steps on the same page but, like a wizard, makes only one step visible at a time. As users choose to go to the next step, the current step is collapsed and information corresponding to the next step is expanded and made available. Users may go to any previous step by clicking the corresponding step heading, which then expands that step and collapses the current step. This design approach is effective for wizards with just a few steps because the headings that represent steps and facilitate navigation can take up excessive space on the page, leaving little room for content in each step.

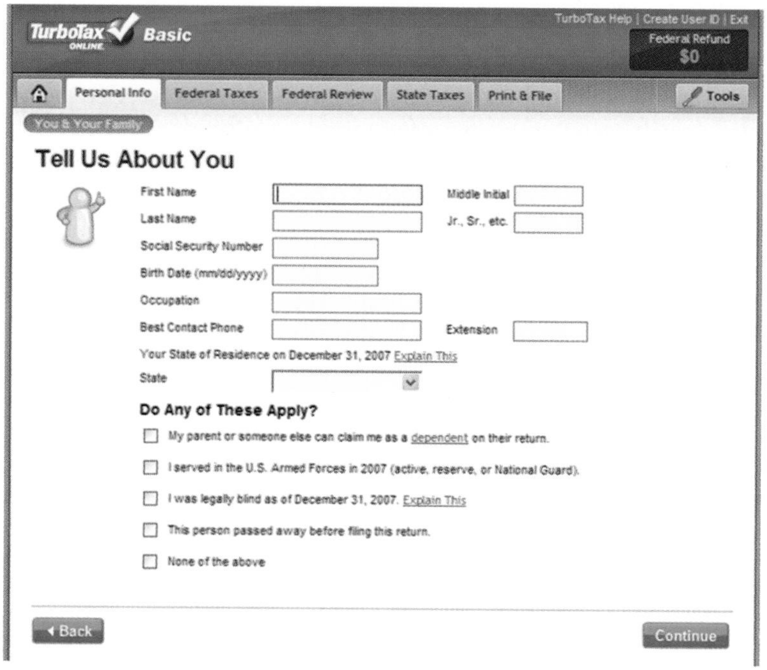

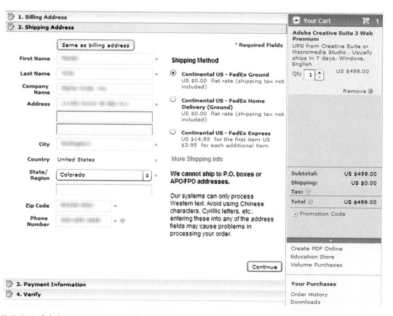

FIGURE 5.33 The TurboTax wizard uses "Back" and "Continue" actions to guide users to complete their taxes.

FIGURE 5.34 Adobe uses a wizard-style interaction, but as an accordian to show all the steps on the same page. After a step is completed and users click "Continue," the next step is revealed.

LIMIT THE NUMBER OF STEPS IN THE WIZARD

When developing wizards, the number of steps needed must be balanced with the amount of information asked from users on each step. Users should feel that they are making good progress through the wizard and that each page shows logically grouped information. At the same time, they shouldn't feel that most of their time is spent waiting for pages to refresh to go to the next step. Nor should they feel they have to backtrack often to change information provided in previous steps. Typically, wizards shouldn't require more than five to seven steps to accomplish a task (Wickham et al., 2002).

CLEARLY SHOW WIZARD STEPS

Show each step in the wizard as either a set of horizontal steps or tabs (Figure 5.35) or vertically as a list or table of contents. The latter is preferred when one or more steps may have substeps. Usability tests for desktop-application wizards have shown vertical placement of steps to be more effective than horizontal placement (Wickham et al., 2002). However, vertical placement does require additional space and may have to be traded off against content to be presented for each step.

BEGIN WITH AN OVERVIEW PAGE FOR VERY INFREQUENTLY USED WIZARDS

For wizards used very infrequently (perhaps, only once), such as initial configuration or application setup, use an overview page to explain and introduce the process and its steps (Figure 5.36).

FIGURE 5.35 Washington Mutual shows the steps for opening an account horizontally above the form.

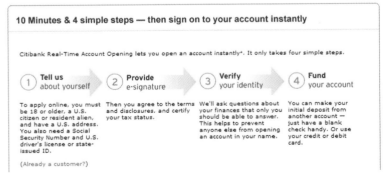

FIGURE 5.36 Citibank provides an overview page that outlines steps included in the wizard for opening an EZ Checking account.

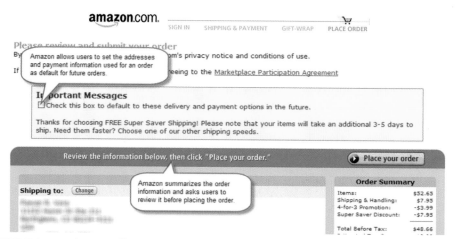

FIGURE 5.37 Amazon offers a summary page that asks users to review information before placing orders. In addition, it offers users the option to set defaults for current delivery and payment options, to minimize the number of steps they need to go through in future checkouts.

SUMMARIZE INFORMATION ON THE WIZARD'S LAST PAGE

On the last page of the wizard, summarize users' information and actions and explain what will happen when they press "Finish." Whenever possible, make the final action indicative of the task being completed—for example, "Place Order" or "Create Blog" (Figure 5.37).

INCLUDE AS MANY DEFAULTS AS POSSIBLE

Like any good web form, include as many defaults as possible (see the SMART DEFAULTS pattern in Chapter 2), especially in situations where users may have entered information in previous steps or during previous interactions. For example, in a checkout wizard, the billing address could be prepopulated with the shipping address from the previous step, or users can be offered an option to indicate that their billing address is the same as the shipping address.

CLEARLY INDICATE USERS' PROGRESS THROUGH THE WIZARD

Provide users a clear indication of where they are in the wizard, what steps they have completed, and how many remain. This way, users know what to expect and do not become impatient about the time it's taking them to complete the task (Figure 5.38).

REMOVE UNNECESSARY LINKS AND BUTTONS IN THE WIZARD

Users should not be distracted with extraneous links and buttons when completing a task using wizards. Therefore, remove all extraneous links, navigation,

FIGURE 5.38 Progressive's site shows where users are in the quoting process, the steps they have completed, and the remaining steps.

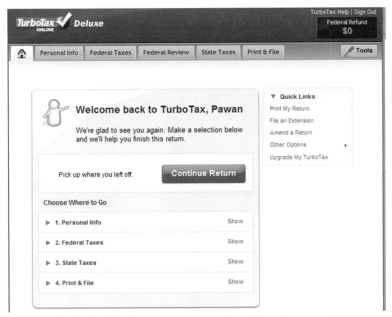

FIGURE 5.39 TurboTax Online allows users to save their information and offers them the option to return to the wizard from where they left off.

search bars, and buttons except those required for branding, privacy policy, and legal disclaimers.

ALLOW USERS TO SAVE INFORMATION AND RETURN TO WHERE THEY LEFT OFF

When an entire application uses a wizard-style interface or includes several "subwizards" within it, allow users to save their information so that in subsequent visits, they may start from where they left off and complete their tasks in multiple sessions. A good example is TurboTax Online, which allows users to do their taxes online using a wizard interface. Depending on the complexity and ready availability of information required to file the tax return, users may require interaction over a period of time to complete their taxes. To ensure usability of such applications, it's important that the information entered by users is saved and they are returned to the step where they left off when they return to the application at a later time (Figure 5.39).

Related design patterns

Because WIZARDS are just a way to present long and/or multistep forms, form-related patterns such as SMART DEFAULTS, REQUIRED FIELD INDICATORS, FORGIVING FORMAT, INPUT HINTS/PROMPTS, ERROR MESSAGES, and others are relevant (see Chapter 2).

CHAPTER 6

Searching and Filtering

INTRODUCTION

For web applications of a reasonable size, accessing information only by navigating the application hierarchy can become cumbersome and compromise usability. Therefore, it's important that information within web applications be made searchable to get users to desired items quickly and efficiently.

Searching can be done either in an unrestricted manner, where users enter their query as a set of keywords or key phrases in a search field (SIMPLE SEARCH), or in a directed and structured manner, where users specify desired values of the item attributes they are searching (PARAMETRIC SEARCH). Simple searches are usually sufficient for most users, but those who have more experience and prefer specifying their search precisely may benefit from using ADVANCED SEARCH, which allows the formulation of complex search queries. Regardless of the search mechanism offered, users can always benefit by getting some guidance on how they can improve their searches and formulate better queries (SEARCH TIPS).

After users have submitted their criteria, web applications show matched items ordered by relevance (SEARCH RESULTS). Although ordering by relevance is the most appropriate way to present search results, users may prefer to reorder them using other criteria (e.g., price when purchasing items) to get to desired items (SORTING).

For performance reasons and to not overwhelm users with too many items, search results are usually presented in subsets of 10 to 20 such that users can navigate through results using controls such as next, previous, first, last, and so forth (PAGINATION). An alternative emerging approach is CONTINUOUS SCROLLING, which also presents users a subset of search results at a time, but instead of pagination controls, it presents additional search results as users scroll to the bottom of the current set of results. Both approaches attempt to address a common problem with searching—too many search results.

Users are typically offered mechanisms such as FILTERING or FACETED SEARCH to narrow down the list of search results to a manageable number.

Both mechanisms remove items within the search results that do not match the selected filters or facets. The difference, however, is that in FILTERING, users are offered narrowing options that remain the same irrespective of the presented search results. FACETED SEARCH, however, is dynamic and the narrowing options offered to users are derived from search results themselves and continue to update as users narrow their result set.

After users have searched, filtered, and sorted results to their liking, consider allowing them to save their queries (SAVED SEARCHES) and set up alerts so that they can rerun saved queries and stay informed of new matches.

SIMPLE SEARCH

Problem

Navigating deep application hierarchies can be cumbersome and an inefficient way to get to known items in web applications. In addition, it may be unclear to users where the desired item is in the hierarchy given the available navigation options.

Solution

Allow users to search for items using keywords or key phrases and place the search feature in a consistent location throughout the application (Figure 6.1).

Why

When users know exactly what they are looking for, searching is easier and more efficient than navigating the application hierarchy; this is also referred to as a *known-item search*. Even when a search doesn't get users directly to the desired item, it may allow them to skip several levels of navigation to a point where they can navigate the rest of the hierarchy and get to the desired item quickly. Additionally, most users are not familiar with search concepts such as Boolean operators[1] (Nielsen, 1997) and feel more comfortable using simpler

FIGURE 6.1 A simple search box on Digg allows users to search information using keywords.

[1]Boolean queries are expressed in words or phrases, combined using the Boolean operators such as **AND**, **OR**, **NOT**, **XOR**, and so on.

keyword searches than advanced searches (Spink et al., 2001; see the ADVANCED SEARCH pattern later in this chapter).

A simple search may also benefit users in quickly determining if an item exists in an application. For example, users may want to know if an e-commerce application offers item X. Searching for item X to determine whether it is offered by the application can be far more efficient than navigating through the information hierarchy.

How

Allow users to search by entering one or more keywords into a search text field. In addition, let users search for key phrases by enclosing keywords within quotes; when searching for key phrases, users are shown results containing the exact phrase. In addition, avoid forcing users to click the "Search" button or tab to the "Search" button; rather, let users submit their search using the "Enter" or "Return" key.

PLACE SEARCH IN A CONSISTENT LOCATION

Place the search feature in a consistent location throughout the application to make it easier to find. Typically, it is placed in or near the page header (Figure 6.2) in one of the following locations:

- The top-right of the page.
- The center of the page in the header area or just below it (this is quite common in portals such as Yahoo!, MSN, and iGoogle).
- The top-left above browsing options (e.g., above product categories in e-commerce applications).

The top-right and top-left regions are preferred locations for placing search, since they closely match users' expectations of its placement on a page (Shaikh and Lenz, 2006).

With search available on all pages, users do not have to return to the home page or a dedicated search page to conduct their search. This allows users to begin new searches and reach specific content quickly from anywhere in the application.

SET THE SEARCH SCOPE

For applications with hundreds and thousands of items and several item categories, allow users to restrict search to a category by letting them specify the scope of their search. Depending on the number of scoping options available, use radio buttons, a dropdown list, images, or tabs (Figure 6.3). However, it's important that the page does not refresh when users choose a scoping option.

Do not scope search by default or require users to select a scoping category. Users may not know the category to which an item belongs, which may be the

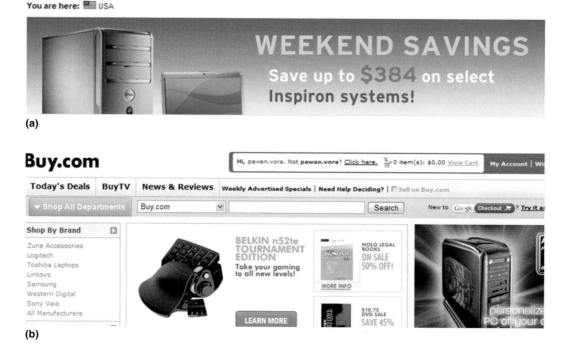

(a)

(b)

(c)

FIGURE 6.2 Common placement of search areas are (a) top-right corner, (b) in the center near the header area, and (c) top-left corner above the browse categories.

main reason they are searching. Therefore, default the search scope to "all" categories. As users navigate specific categories within the application (e.g., books, music, etc.), change the default search scope to that category but still allow users to change the scope.

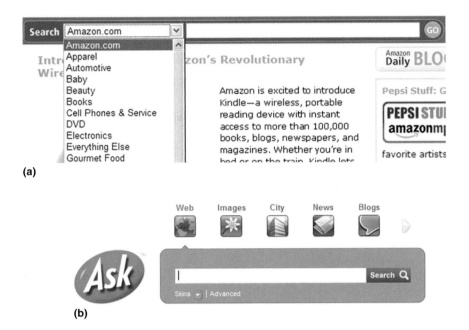

(a)

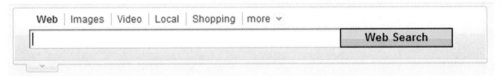

(b)

(c)

FIGURE 6.3 Amazon uses a dropdown menu to allow users to limit their search scope to a category (a). Ask and Yahoo! allow users to scope their search by showing categories as icons (b) or tablike links (c).

USE FAMILIAR LABELS FOR THE SEARCH BUTTON

Common options for action-button labels to execute a search are: "Search," "Find," "Go," and some form of an arrow graphic. When using "Go" or an arrow graphic, it's important that the search input box is prefaced with a "Search:" label. When using "Search" and "Find" as button labels, using separate field labels is unnecessary (Figure 6.4).

FIGURE 6.4 CNET uses a "Go" button to execute a search and uses the label "Search:" before the search input field.

FIGURE 6.5
Home Depot puts
the prompt within
the search field to
indicate to users
what they can enter.

FIGURE 6.6 Answers.com suggests matching search terms as users enter information in the search box. Users can click an item from the suggested list and go to the corresponding page.

Since users may not know what they can search on, offer a prompt and/ or examples of what they can enter in the search field. Because of the limited space available near most search areas, a common practice is to embed the search prompt within the search field (Figure 6.5). However, remove the prompt as soon as users focus on the search field so that they do not have to delete the prompt text before entering search terms.

SUGGEST EFFECTIVE KEYWORDS

Prompt users with appropriate keywords and search terms as they start typing in the search box to reduce typing errors and increase the relevance of search results (Figure 6.6; see also the AUTOSUGGEST/AUTOCOMPLETION pattern in Chapter 8).

SUPPORT COMPLEX SEARCHES WITHIN THE SIMPLE SEARCH FIELD

To allow expert users to enter more precise search queries in the simple search box, it's often useful to support a domain-specific search language that supports the ADVANCED SEARCH functionality (Figure 6.7).

`subject:"hello world"`	Messages with the phrase `hello world` in its `subject` only.
`subject:(hello world)`	Messages with `hello` and `world` in its `subject` only. Note the use of () to groups words together, rather than "" which denote a phrase.
`message:"hello world"`	Messages with the phrase `hello world` in its `message body` only.
`topic:(hello OR world)`	Messages in threads with either `hello` or `world` in its `topic` only.
`author:"Erik Hatcher"`	Messages of `Erik Hatcher` only.
`forum:Apache`	Messages in the `Apache` forum only.
`roam~`	Messages with `foam`, `roam`, and so forth. In essence, messages that match or sound like `roam`.

FIGURE 6.7 Nabble, a web application for forums, offers a specific search language to its members to allow them to enter precise queries. For example, to search in the "Apache" forum only, users can include "forum:Apache" in their query.

Related design patterns

If searching can be structured or directed, consider the use of PARAMETRIC SEARCH because it allows users to specify search criteria more precisely. For expert users, offer a separate ADVANCED SEARCH option and include SEARCH TIPS that explain ways in which users can improve search effectiveness.

PARAMETRIC SEARCH

Problem

Users may not know the best way to formulate their search queries as keywords or key phrases when looking for items with several attributes (e.g., prices of red-eye flights from Denver to San Francisco departing the following Wednesday and returning Friday). This may lead them to specify a search that is either too general, requiring them to wade through a large number of irrelevant results, or too specific, thereby eliminating many useful results.

Solution

Allow searching for items based on their characteristics (i.e., parameters). For example, when searching for flights, ask users to specify departure city, arrival city, departure and arrival dates, and so forth. In addition, where applicable, restrict users' search query by requiring them to choose from a predetermined set of options presented as dropdown lists, radio buttons, or checkboxes (Figure 6.8).

Why

Allowing users to specify their search in a structured manner makes it easy for them to formulate search queries and prevents them from making assumptions about which attributes are searchable. In some instances, searching by a set of parameters seems more natural than doing a free-form keyword search—for example, making flight, hotel, or car reservations; finding driving directions; finding homes to buy or sell; finding people with specific profiles and interests; and so forth.

FIGURE 6.8 Match.com, like many other dating service sites, allows users to formulate their search by asking for their gender, "seeking" gender, ages, and ZIP code. They also offer advanced options to allow users to indicate interests, income level, and so forth.

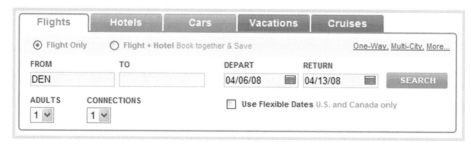

FIGURE 6.9 Yahoo! Travel shows users search parameters relevant only for the selected tab.

How

Ask users to enter search criteria in a form with clearly identified search parameters. Where appropriate, segment the form into multiple sections so that only appropriate search fields are shown to users (Figure 6.9).

HIDE NOT-SO-COMMON SEARCH PARAMETERS

Even when using a parametric search, it's important to keep the search simple and not overwhelm users by offering search parameters they are unlikely to use. Hide infrequently used options under "advanced options" or "more options" and make them available only when users request them (Figure 6.10).

Related design patterns

Although a PARAMETRIC SEARCH can help capture precise search criteria, it does not eliminate the possibility of large numbers of search results. Allow users to narrow down their search results by using either FILTERING or FACETED SEARCH.

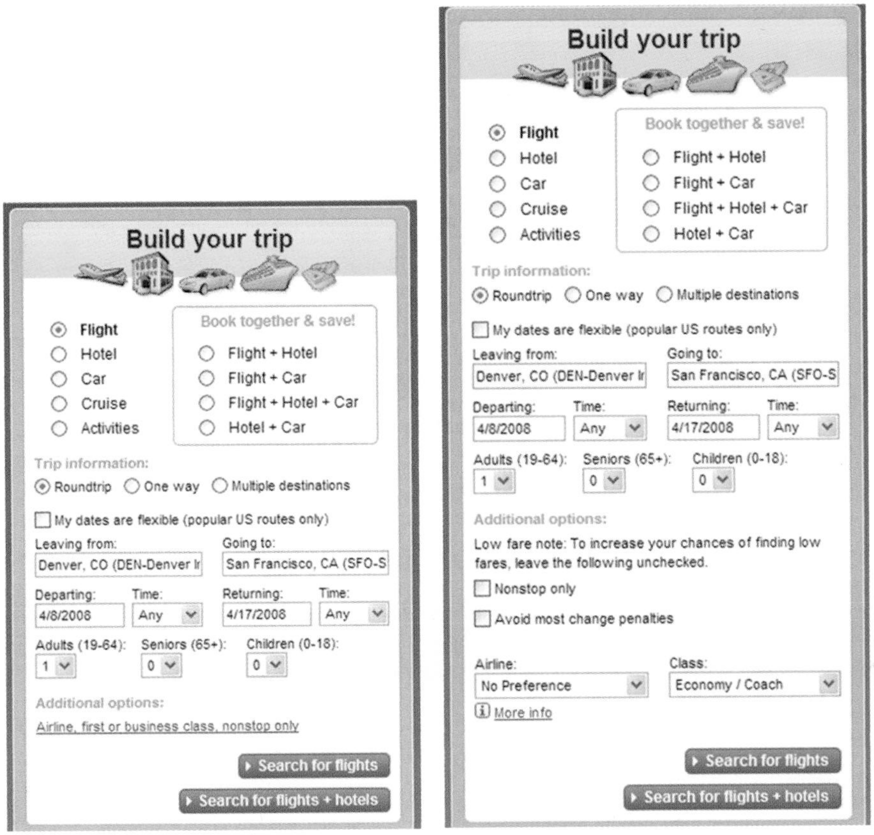

FIGURE 6.10 Expedia's "Build your trip" hides not-so-common options (a). It shows them only when users select the "Airline, first or business class, ..." link under "Additional options" (b).

ADVANCED SEARCH

Problem

An important problem faced by users when searching is a large number of search results, many of which are neither relevant nor useful to them. Narrowing and filtering options are useful, but they address the problem after users have been presented with search results (see the FILTERING pattern later in this chapter). In addition, because filtering options typically allow users to refine search results iteratively, it may take users several refinement steps before they can get to a manageable search result set.

Solution

Offer users an advanced search option so that they can precisely formulate their search query (Figure 6.11).

Advanced Search Options

SEARCH

Find Results

With all of the words:		in the body ▾
With the exact phrase:		in the body ▾
With any of the words:		in the body ▾
Without the words:		in the body ▾

Limit Search To

☑ Entire Site	☐ Individuals	☐ Internal Revenue Manual
☐ Forms and Instructions	☐ Businesses	☐ Tax Statistics
☐ Publications	☐ Charities & Non-Profits	☐ e-file
☐ Notices	☐ Government Entities	☐ Español
☐ IR Bulletins	☐ Tax Professionals (Includes Tax Regulations)	☐ FAQs

File Format

FIGURE 6.11 The IRS's "Advanced Search Options" page offers users various options, which allows users to specify their search query more precisely.

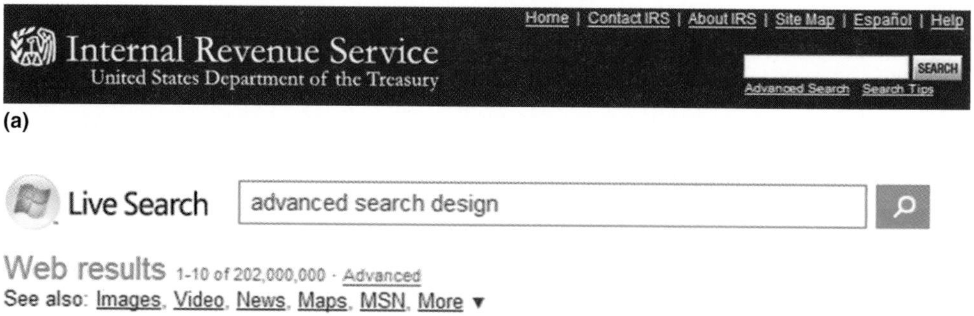

Home | Contact IRS | About IRS | Site Map | Español | Help

Internal Revenue Service
United States Department of the Treasury

SEARCH
Advanced Search   Search Tips

(a)

Live Search   advanced search design   🔍

Web results 1-10 of 202,000,000 · Advanced
See also: Images, Video, News, Maps, MSN, More ▾

(b)

FIGURE 6.12 The IRS offers an "Advanced Search" link near the simple search box (a), whereas MSN's Live Search offers the "Advanced" link on the search results page (b).

Why

No matter how well designed the search engine, users are likely to be faced with irrelevant results. Although FILTERING helps reduce the number of irrelevant search results, it helps only after the initial search query is run and results are presented. An advanced search allows users to be more precise when specifying search queries, thus reducing irrelevant results upfront.

How

Offer users an advanced search link near the search box (see the SIMPLE SEARCH pattern earlier in this chapter) or on the search results page (Figure 6.12). For most applications with complex or varied content, it makes sense to always have an advanced search link near the simple search box. However, if it's preferable to let users attempt a simple search before attempting an advanced

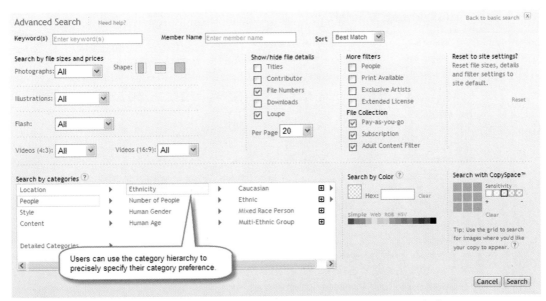

FIGURE 6.13 iStockphoto's "Advanced Search" offers users a variety of ways to precisely specify search criteria, including a search by type of media, color, type of information to show/hide on file details, and so forth. In addition, iStockphoto offers an interesting approach to hierarchically narrow down category options. This screenshot shows category and subcategory selections for "People" and "Ethnicity."

search, place the advanced search link on the search results page. This allows users to review search results before formulating a complex search query.

On the advanced search page, offer users options to precisely specify their query by allowing them to combine keywords with include (e.g., **AND, OR**) and exclude (e.g., **NOT**) options, and specify values for specific properties such as date ranges and content type. In addition, offer users control over output options such as information to include on the search results page, number of results per page, sorting of results, and so forth (Figure 6.13).

SIMPLIFY TERMINOLOGY

Although advanced search targets expert users, designers can only assume users' domain expertise and not necessarily their search expertise. Advanced search should still be easy to understand. For example, instead of asking users to specify their search criteria using Boolean operators such as **AND, OR, XOR**, etc., offer users options such as "all of these words," "any of these words," "none of these words," and so forth (Figure 6.14).

ALLOW USERS TO RETURN TO THE BASIC SEARCH PAGE

The wide variety of options offered on an advanced search page may be overwhelming to some users. Allow them to return to the simple search. If the advanced search overlays on the current page, like iStockphoto's in Figure 6.13,

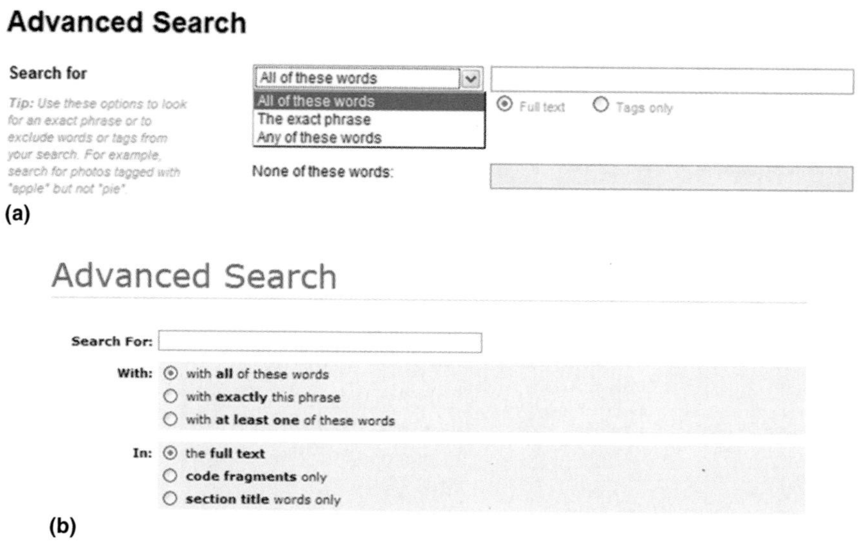

Advanced Search

Search for

Tip: Use these options to look for an exact phrase or to exclude words or tags from your search. For example, search for photos tagged with "apple" but not "pie".

| All of these words |
| All of these words |
| The exact phrase |
| Any of these words |

○ Full text   ○ Tags only

None of these words:

(a)

Advanced Search

Search For:

With: ○ with **all** of these words
○ with **exactly** this phrase
○ with **at least one** of these words

In: ○ the **full text**
○ **code fragments** only
○ **section title** words only

(b)

FIGURE 6.14 The "Advanced Search" pages from Flickr (a) and Safari Books (b) use simple terminology and avoid using Boolean operators.

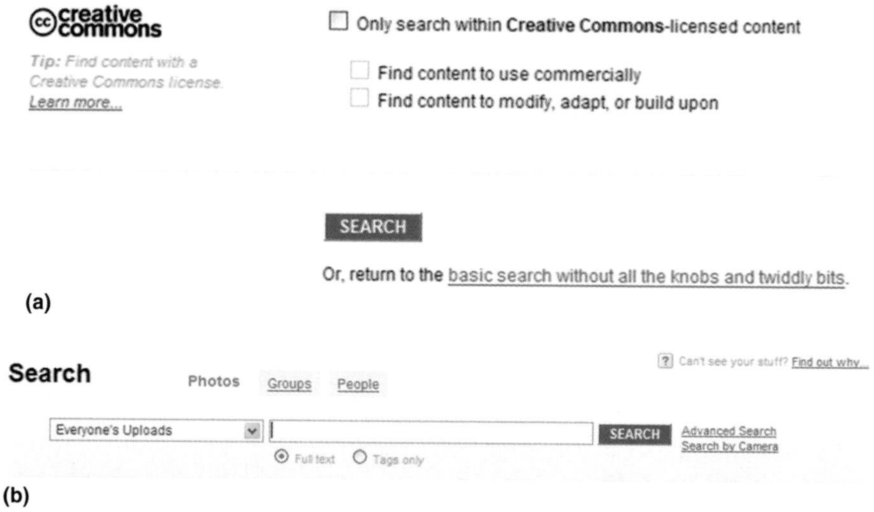

ⒸⒸ **creative commons**

Tip: Find content with a Creative Commons license.
Learn more...

☐ Only search within **Creative Commons**-licensed content

☐ Find content to use commercially
☐ Find content to modify, adapt, or build upon

SEARCH

Or, return to the basic search without all the knobs and twiddly bits.

(a)

Search   Photos   Groups   People

? Can't see your stuff? Find out why

| Everyone's Uploads |

SEARCH   Advanced Search
Search by Camera

○ Full text   ○ Tags only

(b)

FIGURE 6.15 Flickr offers a return to the basic search link below the "Search" button on the advanced search page (a) that takes users to the simple search page (b).

clicking "Back to Basic Search" can remove the overlay and return users to the original search. On the other hand, if the advanced search is a separate page, allow users to return to a dedicated basic search page (Figure 6.15). In order to avoid confusion, do not show both basic search and advanced search on the same page.

Related design patterns

Like PARAMETRIC SEARCH, use of ADVANCED SEARCH does not guarantee fewer search results and can benefit from FILTERING or FACETED SEARCH to help users narrow down SEARCH RESULTS.

SEARCH TIPS

Problem

The quality of search results often depends on how well users have been able to specify their search intent. There are typically a myriad of ways search engines allow users to make their intent clear. However, this information is usually unavailable to users, making it difficult for them to be precise when specifying their search criteria.

Solution

Offer users easily accessible search tips and explain different ways of specifying search criteria and formulating precise search queries (Figure 6.16).

Why

Search engines used by web applications vary in how they combine keywords and build precise search queries. Users cannot be expected to know the nuances of every search engine they encounter. Search tips can describe to users in a simple language ways to effectively use the search feature.

Search Tips

IRS.gov's search engine will help you find the information you are looking for, quickly and easily. Use these tips to help you maximize the effectiveness of your search.

Basic Searching and Choosing Search Terms
Advanced Searching
Search Results Page
In-Document Highlighting

- -

Basic Searching and Choosing Search Terms

Search Field: You can find the search field on the right side of the blue header on each page of the IRS.gov website. Type one or more terms in the search box, and select the "Search" button. The search engine will return a list of IRS.gov web pages and documents related to your search term(s).

Effective Search Terms: Specific words and multiple search terms will often help refine your search and provide more valuable results than general or single search terms.

Phrase Search: Search for complete phrases by enclosing them in quotation marks. ("employer identification number")

FIGURE 6.16 The IRS's "Search Tips" page offers guidance on how its search works and how users can improve their search queries. They offer search tips not only for simple and advanced searches, but also for the search results page. It also offers tips for conducting searches within PDF (Adobe Acrobat's Portable Document Format) documents (not shown here). This is important for IRS, as many of their available publications and forms are in the PDF format.

How

Make search tips easily accessible and visible by placing the corresponding link close to the search area (Figure 6.17).

Search tips may be presented to users in any of the following ways:

- They can be shown on a separate page if they are too elaborate to be included near the search feature. In most instances, this is appropriate considering that users can use the information provided in search tips and formulate their search queries in the persistent search box at the top of the page.
- They can be shown in a pop-up if users are likely to access tips from a search results page or the advanced search page and losing their current page (and search query) is of concern.
- They can be shown on the same page using an "expand-in-place" approach. For example, Nabble expands the search tips section and shows them between the search bar and the search results (Figure 6.18).

INCLUDE EXAMPLES OF APPROPRIATE SEARCH QUERIES

Because users are looking for assistance to improve search queries, include one or more examples with a brief description (see Figure 6.18). In addition, like any help system, avoid technical jargon and use plain language.

FIGURE 6.17 iStockphoto places the "Need help?" link in the search bar below the "Advanced Search" option.

FIGURE 6.18 Nabble uses the "Show Tips" link next to the "Go" button to make search tips easily accessible (a). Clicking "Show Tips" expands the tips below the search area and shows examples of how specific search queries relate to search results (b).

Related design patterns

SEARCH TIPS should be considered a part of help. Therefore, it's important they answer users' FREQUENTLY ASKED QUESTIONS (see the Web Appendix at *www.elsevierdirect.com/9780123742650*).

SEARCH RESULTS

Problem

Once users have specified and submitted their search criteria, search results should be presented in a meaningful manner so that users can quickly get to the most useful results without having to "pogo-stick"—that is, needing to return to the search results page to find a more suitable search result (Spool, 2008a).

Solution

Show users search results sorted by relevance with highly relevant items at the top. In addition, present search results in a manner suitable for quick scanning to facilitate identifying item(s) for further navigation and exploration (Figure 6.19).

Why

Users search because they are looking for either a specific item or want to explore a set of items related to their search terms. Therefore, items that closely match their search terms (i.e., with the highest relevance) should be shown at the top of the search results page. Any other way of presenting results would

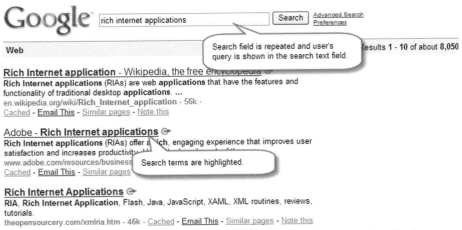

FIGURE 6.19 Google orders search results by relevance using its patented PageRank algorithm. It uses larger and bolder text for search results, highlights search terms, and repeats the search field prepopulated with users' search query to allow users to refine them. (*Note:* For each linked search result, Google uses the < h2 > tag, which improves the accessibility of the page by making it easy for screen reader users to jump from one search result to another. For more information about creating accessible web applications, see Chapter 11.)

confuse users or they would have to resort the results by relevance to get to the most appropriate matches. In addition, most users do not look beyond the second page of search results (Nielsen, 2001; Spool, 2008b). Therefore, unless users have specified that data be sorted differently (e.g., when using ADVANCED SEARCH), show search results sorted by relevance.

How

In addition to sorting search results by relevance, retain the keywords or key phrases users searched for in the search box to allow them to make changes to their query without having to retype the original search terms (Figure 6.20).

MAKE SEARCH TERMS CASE-INSENSITIVE

Users typically don't pay attention to the case of their search terms and may simply enter their search criteria in uppercase, lowercase, or mixed case. Unless indicated by users (e.g., when using ADVANCED SEARCH), ignore the search terms' case when presenting search results. For example, return the same results for the search keywords "WEB DESIGN," "Web Design," and "web design."

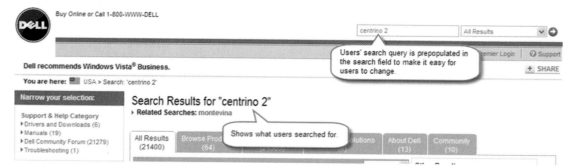

FIGURE 6.20 Dell's "Search Results" page shows what users searched for and shows users' query in the search box.

FIGURE 6.21 NexTag shows both the number of results on the current page and the total number of results. In addition, it shows how the results were sorted with a dropdown menu arrow to allow users to change the sorting method.

SHOW THE TOTAL NUMBER OF SEARCH RESULTS

On the search results page, clearly indicate the total number of search results and the number of results shown on the current page (Figure 6.21; see also the PAGINATION and CONTINUOUS SCROLLING patterns later in this chapter). Showing the total number of search results helps users decide if they want to change their query, make it more specific (or broad), or simply browse the search results.

SHOW DESCRIPTIVE INFORMATION WITH EACH SEARCH RESULT

It may not be clear to users whether a search result is relevant to their task based solely on its title. Users may need additional descriptive information about a search result to decide if navigating to it is worth the effort. For example, for books, users may want to know the author, the date published, a preview of the content, and a brief summary (Figure 6.22). For products, they may want to know the price, user ratings (if available), manufacturer, supplier, product image, and so forth. Therefore, consider users' most common tasks to determine the type of supplementary information to accompany each search result so as to improve its "information scent" (Pirolli and Card, 1999).

SHOW IMAGES OF ITEMS TO FACILITATE SCANNING

Include images in search results (Figure 6.23(a)) if they would help users recognize and differentiate items better than their textual descriptions (e.g., e-commerce and media applications). However, offer an alternate text-only version for the search results as well (Figure 6.23(b)); users may not be interested in images because of slower connection speeds (e.g., when accessing the application from remote areas or on mobile devices) or because they prefer to see a text-only view.

CONSIDER ALTERNATE VIEWS FOR PRESENTING SEARCH RESULTS

In addition to using text and image views for search results, there may be other appropriate views for showing results. For example, when users are searching

Title		Content Type	Chapter/Section Title	Publisher	Insert Date	Pub. Date
1.	**Easy Web Design** By Mary Millhollon; Jeff Castrina; Leslie Lothamer Slots: **1.0** Table of Contents	Book	1. Introducing Publisher as a Web Design Tool 2. Jeff Castrina, multimedia developer and Web designer 3. Mastering Web Design Basics **More...**	Microsoft Press	2006/10/04	2005/12/02
2.	**Designing Web Usability** By Jakob Nielsen Slots: **1.0** Table of Contents	Book	1. Conclusion: Simplicity in Web Design 2. Differentiating Intranet Design from Internet Design 3. Intranet Design **More...**	Peachpit Press	2006/01/21	1999/12/20

FIGURE 6.22 Safari (from O'Reilly) shows several descriptive book attributes on the search results page to make it easy for users to determine whether a book is appropriate for them.

for location-based information (e.g., restaurants in a city), consider showing search results in a map view (Figure 6.24; see the MAPS pattern in Chapter 7).

GROUP SEARCH RESULTS

If search results can be organized into independent categories, it helps to group search results by those categories. Each category could then serve as a narrowing option and reduce the number of search results to a manageable set (Figure 6.25).

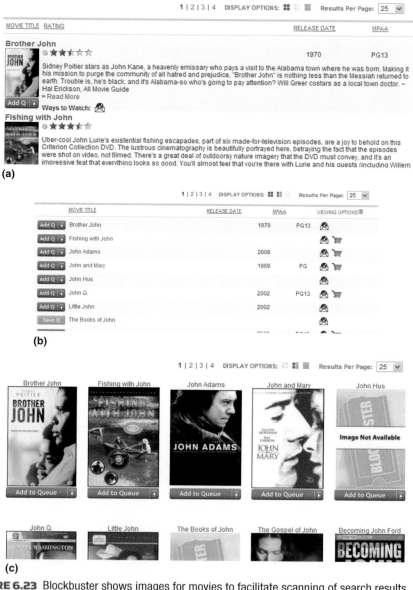

(a)

(b)

(c)

FIGURE 6.23 Blockbuster shows images for movies to facilitate scanning of search results (a). In addition, it offers users a text-only view (b), as well as an image-only view without any textual description (c).

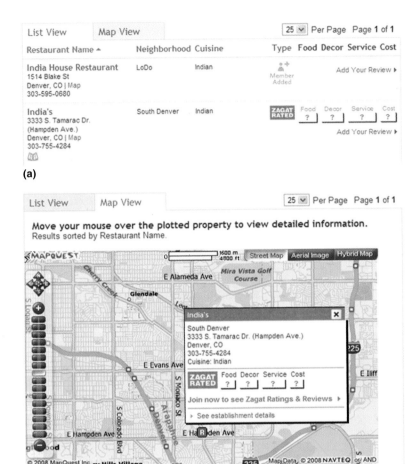

(a)

(b)

FIGURE 6.24 Zagat offers users to switch between a list view (a) and a map view (b) when showing restaurant information.

FIGURE 6.25 When searching for a keyword, Dell groups search results into "All Results," "Browse Products," "Support & Help," and so forth. This enables users to filter the results by those categories if needed. Dell also shows the number of search results in each category.

Search results categories may be based on either *grouping* or *clustering* mechanisms. Grouping is based on a predetermined set of categories, whereas clustering is dynamic in that categories are derived from the search results themselves and may change with each search that users perform. Being dynamic, users are never presented with a category of zero results with the clustering approach (Figure 6.26). However, clustering may be disconcerting for

(a)

(b)

(c)

FIGURE 6.26 Amazon uses a clustering mechanism to group search results. Categories shown for search on "harry potter" (a) are therefore quite different from those for "ipod" (b). Plaxo, on the other hand, uses the grouping mechanism and can have zero items in a category (c).

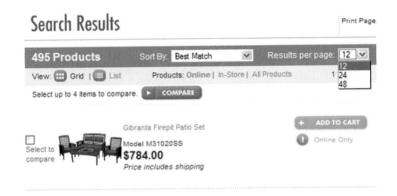

FIGURE 6.27
Home Depot shows
users 12 results per
page by default. For
users who would
rather see more, they
can choose 24 or 48
results per page.

searching datasets with just a few grouping possibilities, as users may be confused as to why categories do not appear consistently in search results.

ALLOW USERS TO CHANGE THE NUMBER OF SEARCH RESULTS PER PAGE

It is important to show results as quickly as possible and allow users to reframe their search query if they are not satisfied with their search results. One way to reduce delays in showing search results is to reduce the number of items on each search results page. An added benefit of showing fewer search results is that users scroll less to see all the items on a page. However, some users prefer to see more items on a screen because they have larger monitors, good connection speeds, or they find pagination cumbersome. To support such preferences, allow users to set the number of results on the page (Figure 6.27; see also the CONTINUOUS SCROLLING pattern later in this chapter).

SUGGEST ALTERNATIVES WHEN A SEARCH YIELDS NO RESULTS

There are two reasons why a user's search may not yield any results:

1. The content that the user is interested in is not available.
2. The search criteria formulated by the user is incorrect (e.g., misspellings or too specific search criteria).

Suggest alternatives as next steps when a search does not yield any results to account for the preceding possibilities. Suggestions may be in the form of alternate spellings, especially if users have likely misspelled the search term. If it is possible to make a reasonable guess as to what users may be looking for, show search results that match alternate keywords while indicating that matches were not found for the user-entered keywords (Figure 6.28). Other options are to show advanced search options (see the ADVANCED SEARCH pattern earlier in this chapter), suggest browsing the application using high-level categories within the application, and offer suggestions to improve search results.

Products <u>Mortgage</u> <u>Travel</u> <u>Degrees</u> <u>Real Estate</u> more ▾

kindella   **NexTag Search**

related: kinsella, sophie kinsella

<u>All Categories</u> : **kinsella**

Sorry, no exact matches found for kindella, showing matches for <u>kinsella</u>.

FIGURE 6.28 NexTag indicates that no results were found for the search query "kindella" and shows search results for the closest term, "kinsella." In addition, they show a few related items such as "kinsella" and "sophie kinsella."

Related design patterns

On the SEARCH RESULTS page, users may want to reorder results using criteria other than relevance (SORTING). In addition, when presented with a large number of results, they may want to narrow them down to a manageable set (FILTERING, FACETED SEARCH). PAGINATION or CONTINUOUS SCROLLING usually accompanies search results because in most applications they cannot be accommodated on one page.

SORTING

Problem

The order in which search results are presented to users may not match their preferences or expectations. For example, search results are typically ordered by relevance based on users' search criteria. However, users may want to order them based on other criteria such as popularity, dates, price, and so forth.

Solution

Allow users to sort search results on criteria other than relevance. For example, comparison-shopping sites may want to allow users to sort by popularity, product rating, and price (Figure 6.29).

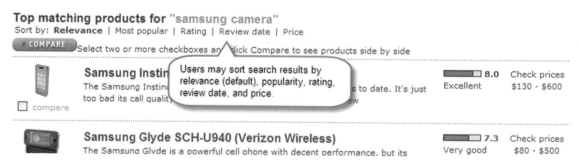

FIGURE 6.29 CNET allows users to sort results by "Relevance," "Most popular," "Rating," "Review date," and "Price".

Why

With keyword searches, the most common rule for ordering search results is by relevance. When viewing results, users may believe that changing the order in which items are presented will make it faster to get to the desired item(s) such as the least expensive item or the items with the highest user rating. Offering users the ability to reorder the search results by other criteria then makes it easy for them to view the search results in their preferred order.

How

Show users various sorting options near the search results either in the form of links, radio buttons, or dropdown lists (Figure 6.30). Links and radio buttons are usually better for showing options because they make it easy for users to see all available sorting options. On the other hand, dropdown lists are useful when there are several sorting options and showing them all would require considerable screen real estate. However, make sure sorting with dropdown lists is accessible by including a "Go" or the similar "action" button, and refrain from sorting the list as soon as an option is selected (see the UNOBTRUSIVE JAVASCRIPT pattern in Chapter 11).

For web applications offering ADVANCED SEARCH, ensure that sorting options match information presented on the SEARCH RESULTS page. This will make it possible for users to understand the results quickly, since they will be able to match them with the content presented in search results.

Related design patterns

If search results are presented as tabular lists, consider allowing users to sort by column headings (see the TABULAR LISTS pattern in Chapter 7).

PAGINATION

Problem

The number of search results presented to users is too large to be displayed on a page. Even when it's feasible to display all results on one page, response time could be several seconds or minutes, resulting in a suboptimal user experience.

Solution

Divide search results such that each page shows a fixed number of items (typically 10–20 items per page), and allow users to navigate among the pages of search results using controls such as "previous," "next," "first," and "last." Pagination controls may use numbered page links to allow users to navigate directly to individual pages within the search results (Figure 6.31).

Why

Dividing a large search result set into smaller and manageable groups allows users to navigate more effectively, since they can focus on one group (i.e., one

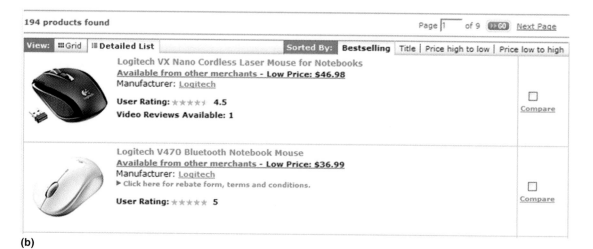

(a)

(b)

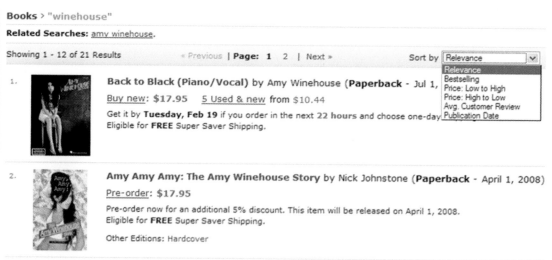

(c)

FIGURE 6.30 The three common approaches to show sorting options are (a) links (designed to appear as tabs), as on Buy.com's site; (b) radio buttons, as on Forrester Research's site; and (c) a dropdown menu, as on Amazon's site.

Books > "community"

Related Searches: neighborhood.

Showing 1 - 12 of 533,504 Results   « Previous | **Page: 1**   2   3   ... | Next »   Sort by [Relevance ▾]

1.   **Creating Community: Five Keys to Building a Small Group Culture** by Andy Stanley
and Bill Willits (**Hardcover** - Dec 31, 2004)

Buy new: ~~$19.99~~ $13.59   58 Used & new from $5.90

Get it by **Tuesday, Mar 4** if you order in the next 32 hours and choose one-day shipping.
Eligible for **FREE** Super Saver Shipping.

★★★★☆ (12)

FIGURE 6.31 When presenting a large set of search results, Amazon divides them into multiple
pages (with 12 results per page) and allows users to navigate them using pagination controls.

page) of results at a time. In addition, breaking down a large list into manageable
chunks makes page downloads faster and users can view results relatively quickly.

How

Divide search results into a sequence of pages and allow users to navigate
through them using, at a minimum, "next" and "previous" links.

MINIMIZE PAGING AS WELL AS SCROLLING

Deciding the number of items to show on a search results page is a trade-off
between scrolling and paging. Typically, for all text results with a minimal
description for each item, a search results page shows about 20 items at a time,
whereas for results that include images, users are typically shown no more
than 10 to 15 items. However, considering that users limit their exploration of
search results to just a few pages and they do not mind scrolling, a case can
be made for showing more search results on a page (Spool, 2008b). Showing
50 search results per page appears to be optimal as reported by Bernard et al.
(2002), who found the fastest search times and preference for 50 search results
at a time when compared with 10 or 100 search results.[2]

MAKE PAGINATION CONTROLS EASILY CLICKABLE

When numbered links are included in pagination controls to allow users to
jump directly to a specific search results page, they often present a very small
target for users to click. To ensure that pagination controls are easily clickable,
use a larger target size and provide sufficient space between them (Figure 6.32).
Doing so also helps distinguish one pagination link from another and minimizes inadvertent navigation to the wrong page.

---

[2]Interestingly, the study found slower search times and lower preference for 100 search results at
a time. This may be a case against showing an arbitrarily large number of search results.

| ‹ PREV | 1 | 2 | 3 | 4 | 5 | 6 | 7 | 8 | 9 | 10 | 11 | NEXT › |

FIGURE 6.32 A common design practice to increase the target size for pagination controls is to box pagination controls, as shown in this example from *UX Magazine* (*www.uxmag.com*).

SHOW THE PRESENCE OF MORE SEARCH RESULTS, IF APPLICABLE

In instances where the number of search results is excessive and cannot be enumerated as pagination controls, indicate the presence of additional results using either a "more" link or other indicators such as an ellipsis (Figure 6.33).

SHOW TOTAL NUMBER OF RESULTS AND RANGE USERS ARE VIEWING

Because pagination controls serve as both navigation and orientation mechanisms, they should clearly indicate to users the page they are viewing, the pages they have already viewed or skipped, and the pages they have yet to view. The page that users are on should be clearly distinguished from the rest of the pages, and it should not be clickable so that users can keep track of where they are (Figure 6.34).

ALLOW USERS TO NAVIGATE DIRECTLY TO THE FIRST PAGE OF SEARCH RESULTS

For really large datasets (more than 10–15 pages), allow users to jump to the first page, since it usually contains the most relevant results. Typically, users are also shown a link to the last page in the search results. However, recently, when showing a large number of search results, the link to the "last" page is disappearing. This is justified for two reasons. First, the last page contains the least-relevant results, and users are unlikely to jump to the results on the last page. Second, users typically do not go beyond a first few pages to find the items they need. According to Nielsen (2001), "Users almost never look beyond the second page of search results."

| « Previous | 1 | 2 | 3 | 4 | 5 | 6 | 7 | 8 | 9 | 10 | ... | 221 | 222 | Next » |

(a)

<<   previous | **1** 2 3 4 5 6 | next   >>

(b)

FIGURE 6.33 Digg uses ellipses between pagination controls to indicate the presence of additional search results (a). NexTag, on the other hand, indicates the presence of more pages with a + sign (b).

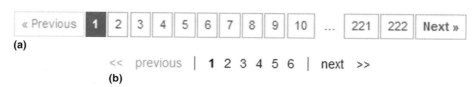

Showing 25-36 of 552 Results   Sort by: Relevance ▾

|◀ ◀ 1 2 3 4 5 6 ▶

FIGURE 6.34 When navigating search results from Dell, users know they are seeing "13–24 of 4525 Results" and that they are on the page 2 of the search results.

FIGURE 6.35 Digg disables "previous" and "next" controls on the first and last pages, respectively. In addition, they highlight the current page and don't link it to prevent unnecessary navigation.

However, there are situations where the last page link is both appropriate and necessary. If the resulting dataset can be sorted in multiple ways (e.g., alphabetically, chronologically, by price, and so forth), the last page link becomes relevant, as it allows users to quickly see the last page of items with a predictable set of search results—for example, items starting with Z, the most- or least-expensive item, and so forth.

REPEAT THE PAGINATION CONTROLS AT THE TOP OF THE PAGE

For short lists, pagination controls may be provided only at the bottom of the list. However, in pages where search results would require users to scroll extensively (e.g., when users are permitted to change the page size), repeat the pagination controls at the top of the page as well.

This technique can also be beneficial for search results accompanied by an alphabetical index. For example, users looking for an item beginning with the word "summit" might jump to the beginning of the "T" pages and then use pagination controls at the top of the page to go backward until they get to a page the first result of which is closest to the word "summit."

DO NOT LINK PAGINATION CONTROLS THAT ARE NOT RELEVANT

Like all navigation mechanisms, provide a clear indication to users as to where they are in the search results set and where they can go. Prevent unnecessary navigation actions by disabling pagination controls that do not navigate to other search results pages (Figure 6.35):

- On the first page, disable links to "first" and/or "previous" pages.
- On the last page, disable links to "next" and/or "last" pages.
- Instead of showing the current page as a link, make it plain text or highlight it in some fashion.

LABEL PAGINATION CONTROLS APPROPRIATELY

For most pagination controls, their labels and order are "first," "previous," "next," and "last." In applications where items are ordered chronologically, a more recent trend is to label them to reflect their chronological order—"newest," "newer," "older," and "oldest"—where "newest" is equivalent to "first" (Figure 6.36).

Messages **14180 - 14209** of 14209   Newest | < Newer | Older > | Oldest

Messages: Simplify | Expand   (Group by Topic)   Author   Sort by Date ▾

(a)

Messages **14180 - 14209** of 14209   Oldest | < Older | Newer > | Newest

(b)

FIGURE 6.36 Yahoo! Groups orders messages chronologically and uses labels "Newest," "Newer," "Older," and "Oldest" by default (a). When users change the sorting order, they reverse the order of the labels (b).

Related design patterns

An alternative to PAGINATION is CONTINUOUS SCROLLING, which allows users to view all items in the search results as a scrolling list.

CONTINUOUS SCROLLING

Problem

Although pagination is a commonly used technique to navigate a large number of search results, users' interaction experience is not continuous since users have to wait for the page to refresh before seeing the next set of results.

Solution

Allow users to scroll through results in a large scrolling list. Like pagination, show users only a subset of data at a time. Request additional data in real time from the server using Rich Internet Application (RIA) technologies such as Ajax and show users the next set of search results as they reach the bottom of the current list without page refreshes (Figure 6.37).

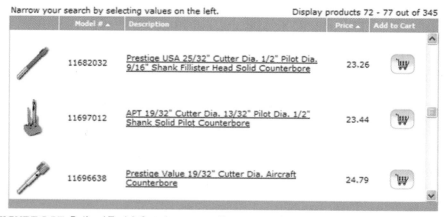

FIGURE 6.37 Rutland Tool & Supply uses continuous scrolling to show users items in a product list.

Why

Pagination requires users to switch attention between navigating pages and reviewing search results. In addition, with pagination, interaction is challenging when users want to select items from different pages before applying an action (e.g., when users want to compare items that are not all on the same page). In such instances it's often unclear to users whether their selections on other "pages" were retained as they paged through search results and selected items. In addition, pagination requires important screen real estate, often pushing content down the page. The continuous-scrolling approach solves these issues by showing the items in a scrolling list and retrieving the next set of items only when users reach the bottom of the list.

At this time, the evidence favoring continuous scrolling over pagination is inconclusive. As mentioned before, Bernard et al. (2002) found that users took longer and had a lower preference for search results pages with 100 items when compared with 10 items or 50 items per page. However, this research was based on paginated results and did not introduce continuous scrolling. Since interactions such as comparison and selection become easier with continuous scrolling, the approach should not be discounted.

How

Show users search results in a list with a subset of items exposed. As users scroll down and reach the bottom of the current list, fetch new data and show users the next set of items. To make scrolling appear smooth and continuous, prefetch and store the next few sets of data and request additional data as users scroll. If users have to wait for data to load, show a "please wait …" indicator so users know that additional data are being retrieved (Figure 6.38).

INDICATE TO USERS THE SUBSET OF ITEMS THEY ARE VIEWING

Like the pagination pattern, show which items users are currently viewing along with the total number of items in the search results (Figure 6.39).

FIGURE 6.38 DZone.net shows an animated "LOADING" icon when it's fetching additional data from the server.

FIGURE 6.39
MSN's "Live Search," which employs continuous-scrolling approach, indicates the result set users are viewing—"29–40 of 13,900,000" in this example.

Related design patterns

CONTINUOUS SCROLLING is inappropriate when users are likely to bookmark search results. For datasets with predictable patterns (e.g., alphabetical and chronological), PAGINATION is a better choice because it allows users to jump to a specific page or the last page without waiting for each intervening dataset to load.

FILTERING

Problem

Often, users' search criteria are too broad, resulting in a very large number of results for them to wade through and identify results that match their needs. Although users can redo searches by making search criteria more specific, they may still end up with a large number of results.

Solution

Allow users to narrow down their list of search results by applying filters on one or more data attributes (Figure 6.40).

Why

When faced with a large number of search results, filtering is an effective method to narrow them down to a manageable set. It also permits users to

FIGURE 6.40 Download.com allows users to filter the list of downloadable software by operating system, license type, file size, and categories.

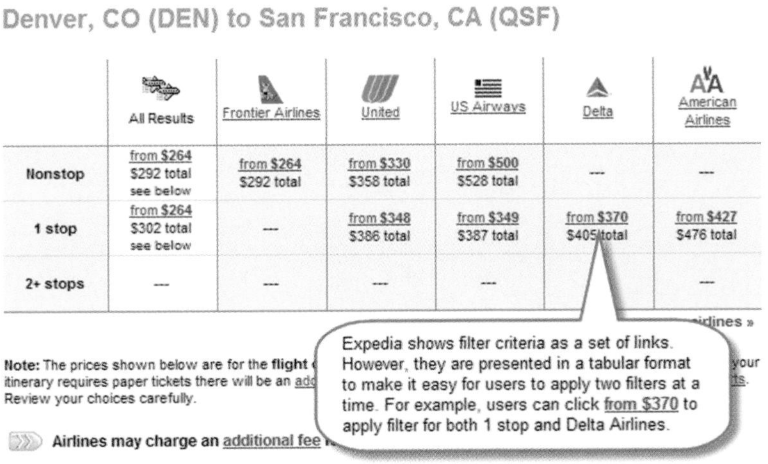

FIGURE 6.41 Expedia allows users to filter search results by airlines and shows filtering options as links.

start searching with broader search criteria and later become more specific as they learn more about the search result set and the available filtering attributes. Allowing users to filter is similar to incorporating some of the advanced search or parametric search functionalities on the search results page.

How

On the search results page, filters are usually shown as dropdown lists, a set of radio buttons, or links (Figure 6.41). As users filter by different attributes, the remaining filtering options are not updated to reflect the attributes available in the remaining search results because they would be in a FACETED SEARCH (see the following pattern). As a result, users could see "zero" items in the search results for certain combination of filtering options. However, it is easy for users to change or clear their filter criteria and return to the previous state and manipulate search results by applying a different set of filters.

Related design patterns

FILTERING in traditional applications can become slow because applying filtering criteria would require a page refresh. Therefore, consider using DYNAMIC QUERYING (see Chapter 8), which updates search results as users make filtering choices and affords a richer interactive experience to users. Using FACETED SEARCH should also be considered as an alternative to filtering, because it allows users to iteratively narrow down to the desired item(s) and eliminates the possibility of a "zero" result set. In addition, when search results are presented as TABULAR LISTS, users may place filtering options in individual columns (see Chapter 7).

FACETED SEARCH

Problem

When presented with a large number of search results, users may find it difficult to locate the desired item(s). Although they can apply filters to their search result set, the possibility of an empty list of results with certain filtering options cannot be avoided.

Solution

Allow users to narrow down the number of items in the search results based on the relevant item attributes (i.e., facets) (Figure 6.42). Narrowing search results by selecting a facet essentially makes search criteria more precise, which can be used to search within results to refine them. With each refinement to the result set, narrowing facets are updated to reflect attributes that are available in the updated search result set. Users can then use the updated facets to further narrow down results to a manageable, browsable set.

Why

Faceted search allows users to reduce the number of search results quickly to get to the desired item(s). Showing narrowing options (facets) is easier for users because they don't have to know the syntax necessary to specify their search precisely. Because narrowing attributes are derived from the search result set, users are never left with an empty result set. In addition, being able to see all available options, users can better understand how data are structured and perhaps use that information to specify better searches in the future.

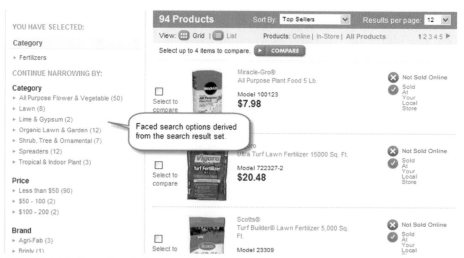

FIGURE 6.42 Home Depot allows users to narrow search results using facets such as "Category," "Price," "Brand," and others.

How

Along with the search results, show users relevant facets with which to narrow down their search results set. For each narrowing facet, show the corresponding number of search results so users can easily judge the extent to which their search results set will narrow when choosing that facet. As users make their choices, update the set of narrowing facets based on the new set of search results. Doing so allows users to iteratively refine their search results and quickly reduce them (Figure 6.43).

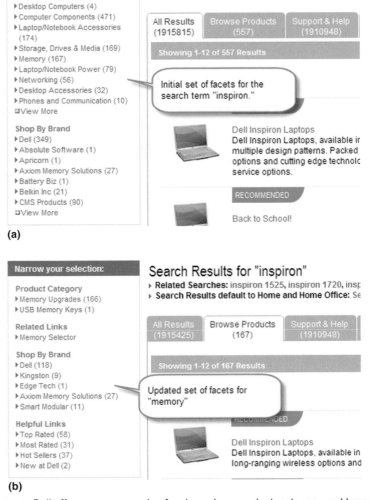

FIGURE 6.43 Dell offers users narrowing facets such as product, category, and brand (a). For each narrowing facet, users are shown the corresponding number of search results. As users select a narrowing facet, the number of results is updated along with a set of facets (b).

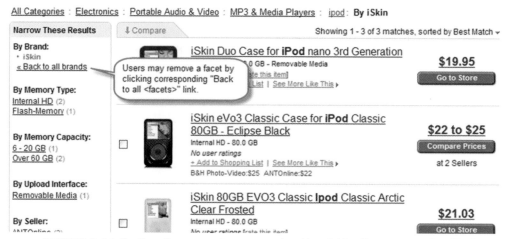

All Categories : Electronics : Portable Audio & Video : MP3 & Media Players : ipod : By iSkin

FIGURE 6.44 NexTag allows users to remove a facet by clicking the corresponding "Back to all …" link in the "Narrow These Results" section.

ALLOW USERS TO REMOVE NARROWING FACETS

Show users their chosen narrowing facets and allow them to remove them as necessary, to make it possible for them to backtrack and choose other facets to narrow down results (Figure 6.44).

Related design patterns

Like FILTERING, faceted search assumes page refreshes with user selection of a narrowing option. Using DYNAMIC QUERYING is another option available when using rich Internet applications where selecting a facet updates the result set without page refreshes. FACETED NAVIGATION also typically accompanies faceted search. The main difference between them is that the former focuses strictly on users browsing the information space, whereas the latter is initiated with a user search.

SAVED SEARCHES

Problem

Users may want to rerun one or more of their searches in the future. Specifying the same search criteria over and over again is inefficient and error-prone, as users may forget to include one or more criteria for complex searches.

Solution

Allow users to save their ad hoc search queries and resubmit them as needed. In addition, consider allowing users to set alerts so they can be kept informed of new items that match their search criteria (Figure 6.45).

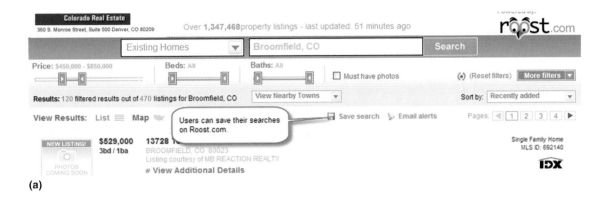

(a)

(b)

FIGURE 6.45 Roost allows users to save searches (a). When saving searches, users may specify the frequency with which they want to be alerted of any new matches based on their search criteria (b).

Why

The ability to save searches can save users time, especially when searches are complex and involve a combination of filtering, sorting, and customization options. Even when searches are not complex, allowing users to save searches makes it easy for them to remember past searches and share them with others. Furthermore, allowing users to set notification alerts for their saved searches makes the application more useful because users don't have to regularly run their saved searches and identify changed items.

How

On the search results page, offer users an option to save their searches (Figure 6.46). Place the "Save Search" action close to the search criteria so users can clearly see the parameters on which they searched.

MAKE IT EASY FOR USERS TO RERUN THEIR SEARCHES

It is important that users be allowed to rerun their saved searches easily. If saved searches are going to be accessed often, make them available and easily

FIGURE 6.46 Monster, a job-posting and -searching application, offers users the opportunity to save their searches on the "Job Search Results" page next to the search criteria.

FIGURE 6.47 Roost allows users to access their saved searches by showing them as a dropdown list. The "My Saved Searches" option is part of the utility navigation in the page header.

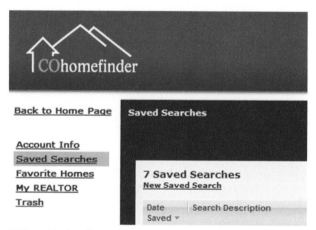

FIGURE 6.48 COHomeFinder allows users to manage their saved searches in their "My Account" section.

accessible on the main page (Figure 6.47) or include them in the utility navigation in the page header region. Also, consider making them available in the "Your Account" section, where it would be easier for users to manage their list of saved searches (Figure 6.48).

Save Search / Create Job Alert

Name This Search

Name

user interface designer

Create a Job Alert (optional)

How often should alerts be sent?

Daily

How would you like alerts to be delivered?

☑ ✉ Email HTML ▾   ☐ ☺ Yahoo! Messenger

  ◉ pawanvora@yahoo.com   pawanvora

  ○ pawan.vora@gmail.com

Add an email address

Cancel   Save

FIGURE 6.49 When saving search results, Yahoo! Jobs offers users the option to set up necessary alert/notification options. Users can specify both the notification method (e.g., mail or Yahoo! Instant Messenger) and its frequency.

(a)

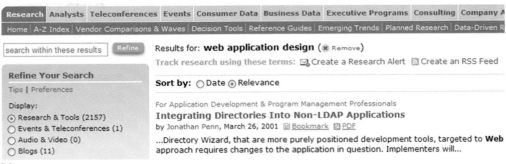

(b)

FIGURE 6.50 Both Indeed (a) and Forrester Research (b) allow users to save their searches either as an email alert or an RSS feed.

CONSIDER OFFERING NOTIFICATION OPTIONS

Asking users to save their searches may not be enough, because users may not remember to check their saved searches regularly and review updates. Even when they do rerun their searches, they may find it difficult to identify changed items. Make saved searches more useful by offering users the option to create alerts and set up notification so they can be informed of changes (Figure 6.49).

A more recent trend is to allow users to save their searches as email alerts or subscribe to Really Simple Syndication (RSS) feeds (Figure 6.50). Once subscribed, users can use an RSS reader software to monitor the feeds for updates. This eliminates the need for users to sign in to the application to access their saved searches.

Related design patterns

If two or more users have the need to perform the same search, allow users to share their saved searches with other members in their group (see the SHARING pattern in Chapter 9).

CHAPTER 7
Lists

INTRODUCTION

Lists are common in web applications for displaying a collection of items. However, the approach used to present lists depends on the nature of items in the collection. A SIMPLE LIST is typically used to present a collection of items with only one or two attributes. It may be used for multiattribute items, if additional attributes are not going to be referenced by users for comparing or sorting. Presenting multiattribute items for which sorting and comparing are important is best accomplished using a TABULAR LIST.

When list items need to show a parent–child relationship, a HIERARCHICAL LIST is most appropriate. Items in a hierarchical list often revert to a TABULAR LIST when resorted as parent–child relationships may no longer be appropriate with the changed order of the list items.

An EVENTS LIST and TIMELINES are used for lists containing items with time-based information. An EVENT LIST is appropriate when showing future events and TIMELINES are suitable for showing historical events.

With increasing multimedia content, textual lists are giving way to IMAGE LISTS/GRIDS, where items are shown as image thumbnails. Images are now being considered even for items that have traditionally been shown as textual lists—especially for search results. With geographical map information being easily accessible through open application programming interfaces (APIs), map-based interaction is also becoming commonplace and item lists with geographical (or spatial) attributes are often complemented by MAPS.

In web applications, users do not simply view list items but take actions either on individual items (e.g., edit, remove, copy, etc.) or on multiple items (e.g., compare, move, delete, etc.). These LIST ACTIONS affect items in one or more ways. There are a set of actions, however, that do not change the items and, instead, facilitate sharing, printing, and analysis by exporting data in other formats (LIST UTILITY FUNCTIONS).

Default message categories

These are the message categories that every new project starts with.

- Assets 🗑
- Code 🗑
- Copywriting 🗑
- Design 🗑
- Miscellaneous 🗑
- Transcripts 🗑

Add a new default message category: [   ] [Add category]

FIGURE 7.1 Basecamp shows message categories as a simple list with a "delete" action associated with each item.

SIMPLE LIST

Problem

Users need to be presented with a list of items with one to a few attributes, and each item could be associated with one or more actions. In addition, the items to be presented do not need to be sorted or compared on any of the attributes.

Solution

Show users a simple list of items with associated actions (Figure 7.1).

Why

Users' familiarity with lists makes it a very effective design approach to present a set of items, especially when items are primarily text based and have basic actions associated with them. For example, lists are commonly used on dashboards and portals (see Chapter 4), where users are shown a list of items such as to-dos, top referrer web sites, most popular products, and so forth (Few, 2006). Users can then click on a list item to navigate to view its details.

How

Show simple lists as either numbered or nonnumbered lists. Numbered lists are especially useful when numbers represent the item's rank order, such as in the top 10 movies of the week or the top 10 news stories (Figure 7.2).

Consider using icons or other symbols with nonnumbered lists to improve the list's visual impact or to indicate the type of item. In addition, lists may use alternate shades of background color or a line separator to improve readability of closely spaced list items (Figure 7.3).

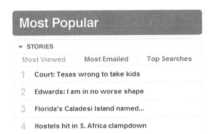

FIGURE 7.2 CNN shows the most popular stories as a numbered list.

FIGURE 7.3 The "Movie Showtimes in Denver" list uses an icon to identify a list item as a movie and alternate shades of background color to improve readability.

Although most simple lists show items with only one or two attributes, some lists may contain more. For example, search results often show page title, a brief description, web site address, and other information in a simple list format. When users do not need to sort the multiattribute list and compare items of those attributes, using a simple list is often a better alternative than a

TABULAR LIST (see the next pattern). However, when showing simple lists with multiple attributes, facilitate quick scanning by making the most important attribute in the list salient and by placing it before other attributes (Figure 7.4).

CONSIDER SHOWING SECONDARY ACTIONS ON HOVER

Items in simple lists may have one or more actions associated with them. To minimize visual clutter, limit actions that are visible for each list item by showing additional actions on-hover (Figure 7.5).

FIGURE 7.4 When showing a list of files, Basecamp shows file names in a larger font and darker color than the file description, username, file size, and other actions to improve scannability.

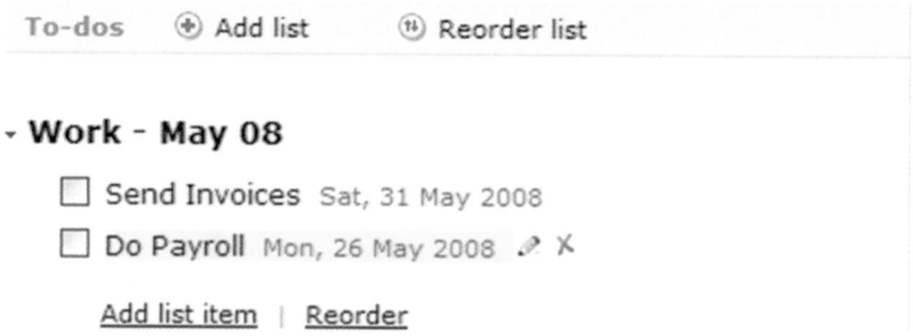

FIGURE 7.5 Zoho Planner shows only the checkboxes for to-do items by default. This makes the most common action of completing a to-do item visible and obvious. Not-so-common actions, such as edit and delete, are shown to users on hover.

Related design patterns

Although a SIMPLE LIST may be acceptable for showing items with multiple attributes, consider a TABULAR LIST if the list needs to be sorted or list items compared based on one or more of the attributes and as a way to minimize the space required for multiattribute lists.

TABULAR LIST

Problem

Users need to be presented a collection of items with several attributes so that they can clearly associate each item with its attributes as well as compare items to each other based on those attributes. In addition, they may want to sort the list based on one or more attributes.

Solution

Show users the list in a tabular format, where items are listed in rows and their attributes are shown in columns (Figure 7.6).

Why

Multiattribute information is best presented in tables because it provides structure to data. For example, column headers can identify the attributes for items presented in rows. In addition, presenting information in a tabular format makes it easy for users to compare items and, when supported, sort them in the desired order. Most important, users' familiarity with tabular arrangement of data into rows and columns makes it a useful approach to present multiattribute data.

How

Tabular data are generally read in rows with items in rows and attribute values in columns. Show attribute names in the table headers, unless they are implied by the data. For effective design, it's important that the table design

Top 100 Blockbuster Online Rentals

	MOVIE	RELEASE DATE	MPAA	AVG. RATING
1.	ADD Shooter	2007	R	★★★★☆
2.	ADD Premonition	2007	PG13	★★★☆☆
3.	ADD Ghost Rider	2007	PG13	★★★☆☆
4.	ADD Fracture	2007	R	★★★★☆
5.	ADD Transformers	2007	PG13	★★★★☆

1 | 2 | 3 | 4   DISPLAY OPTIONS: ▦ ▤   Results Per Page: 25

FIGURE 7.6 This list of "Top 100 Blockbuster Online Rentals" shows movies and their corresponding attributes, such as rank, release date, MPAA (Motion Picture Association of America), and the average user rating, in a tabular format.

		Symbol∨	News	Chart	Message board	Last	High target	Low target	Change	Shares	Market value	Today's change	StockScouter rating	
My Watchlist														
≫		$COMPX		⌁		2,464.58	0	0	16.31	NA	0.00	0.00	NA	×
≫		$INDU		⌁		12,625.62	0	0	24.43	NA	0.00	0.00	NA	×
≫		$INX		⌁		1,394.35	0	0	3.64	NA	0.00	0.00	NA	×
≫	▽	GOOG	▦	⌁	▤	549.46	700	500	-0.53	▦	27,473.00	-26.50	7	×
≫	▽	JAVA	▦	⌁		13.14	20	10	0.01	200	2,628.00	2.00	4	×
≫	▽	MSFT	▦	⌁	▤	28.47	30	25	0.22	100	2,847.00	22.00	8	×
		Total:									$32,948.00	-$2.50		

Quote watchlist — Update quotes | Manage accounts ∨ | Customize view ∨

Total: **$32,948.00** Today's change: -$2.50

Quotes delayed at least 15 min. 5:05 PM Eastern Time

FIGURE 7.7 This "Quote watchlist" from MSN Money shows a list of investments (as a stock symbol) along with several attributes, including user-entered attributes such as high target, low target, and shares. Users are likely to use this list to understand market values of their investments and determine the extent to which they have changed and the reasons for the change. This design supports these user goals by showing market value and changes both individually and in aggregate.

match its intended use rather than relying on users to do additional analysis (Figure 7.7).

MAKE TABULAR DATA READABLE BOTH BY ROWS AND COLUMNS

The readability of tabular data is affected by the readability of rows as well as columns. Improve the readability of rows by either adding a separator line for each row or using a different shade of color for alternate rows, known as *row striping* or *zebra striping* (Figure 7.8). Both approaches help create a visual grouping of items for rows and are particularly important for data tables with many columns (or wide columns), where users may find tracing data in each row difficult. A study by Enders (2008) concluded that zebra striping led to better task performance (at least not worse) and had a higher preference when compared with other styles such as plain, lined, two-color row striping, double striped, and triple striped.

In addition, improve the readability of columns by aligning attribute values in columns based on table cell contents (Figure 7.9). Follow these rules to align data (Galitz, 2002; Mayhew, 1992):

- Use right alignment for columns containing whole numbers (not "text" numbers such as a person's identifier).
- Use a decimal point and right alignment for numbers with decimal fractions; negative numbers may be shown in red and or enclosed within parentheses.

North America - Click an index for a detailed quote:

Symbol ▽	Name	Last	Change	%	Date/Time
.XOI	OIL INDEX	1,599.01	↑ 41.81	2.68%	May 16 4:48:23pm
.XMI	AMEX MAJOR MARKET INDEX	1,348.96	↑ 2.30	0.17%	May 16 4:48:23pm
.XAX	AMERICAN SE AMEX COMPOSITE INDX	2,375.72	↑ 29.14	1.24%	May 16 4:48:23pm
.XAU	PHLX GOLD SILVER INDEX CAPITAL-WEIGHT	187.87	↑ 5.54	3.04%	May 16 4:03:59pm
.VIX	CBOE JUMBO VOLATILITY INDEX	16.47	↑ 0.17	1.04%	May 16 4:14:56pm

(a)

Related Companies

Name	Exchange	Symbol	Last Trade	Change	Mkt Cap
Microsoft Corporation	NASDAQ	MSFT	29.99	-0.46 (-1.51%)	279.31B
Yahoo! Inc.	NASDAQ	YHOO	27.66	-0.09 (-0.32%)	38.06B
Baidu.com, Inc. (ADR)	NASDAQ	BIDU	364.59	+0.32 (0.09%)	12.47B
QuickLogic Corporation	NASDAQ	QUIK	1.89	+0.09 (5.00%)	55.63M
Time Warner Inc.	NYSE	TWX	16.47	-0.04 (-0.24%)	58.94B

(b)

FIGURE 7.8 Common approaches to improve the readability of rows are separating each row with a line, as shown in the Fidelity example (a), and alternating row colors, as shown in the "Related Companies" tabular list from Google Finance (b).

	Merchant	Category	Amount	Date ▼
☐	Audible.com 🔍	Books 🔍	($14.95)	May 20
☐	Blockbuster	Movies & DVDs	($18.39)	May 20
☐	Computer Received Tha	Credit Card Payment	$872.03	May 18
☐	Domino's Pizza	Fast Food	($23.00)	May 16
☐	Adt Security Service	Home	($37.24)	May 15

FIGURE 7.9 The transactions table on Mint.com uses correct alignment for each column: checkboxes are center aligned; "Merchant," "Category," and "Date" are left aligned; and "Amount" is decimal point and right aligned.

- Use left alignment for columns that contain text (including date and time).
- Use center alignment for columns that contain short words or status information (e.g., active, inactive).

An important exception is when numbers in a column do not share the same unit of measure, in which case use left alignment so that users do not compare the numbers.

	☆	Name ↑	Folders / Sharing	Date
☐	☆	📗 11.17 Open Items	me	Nov 11 me
☐	☆	📗 11.17 open items	me	Nov 12
☐	☆	📗 11.17 Open Items -	me	Nov 13 me
☐	☆	📗 9.08 Release - Open Items	me	Sep 5 me

FIGURE 7.10 Google Documents allows users to sort documents by columns and uses an arrow to indicate how a column is sorted. In addition, a slight gradient in the column headers is used to suggest that they are clickable.

ALLOW USERS TO SORT DATA COLUMNS

Sorting long data lists by columns helps users find desired items quickly and analyze them for specific types or statuses. Like its desktop counterpart, a common interaction approach for sorting tabular data is to let users click a column heading to sort by that column (Figure 7.10) and a second click to reverse the sort order (ascending or descending).

Indicate the column attribute by which the tabular data are sorted by placing an arrow icon next to the corresponding column heading to indicate whether data are sorted in an ascending (up arrow) or descending (down arrow) order. Sorting the data by columns and showing a sort indicator by default also suggests to users that the table can be sorted.

Sorting by column headings is appropriate when all possible ways users might sort data are available in columns. In instances where this is not possible, show sort options explicitly either as a dropdown list or a set of links (Figure 7.11).

For applications that require multiple levels of sorting (e.g., reporting), provide the functionality separately, where users can select more than one level of sorting, and for each sort can indicate if sorting should be ascending or descending (Figure 7.12). For multilevel sorting, three levels are usually sufficient.

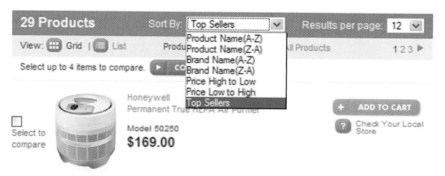

FIGURE 7.11 Home Depot does not use column headings for data because all of the information—brand, product name, and price—is in the same column. Therefore, it offers a "Sort By" dropdown menu that allows users to sort the data.

FIGURE 7.12 This design shows how users can be offered the option to sort on multiple attribute levels.

ALLOW USERS TO FILTER LARGE LISTS

Filters help users narrow a large number of items in a list to a manageable set (see the FILTERING pattern in Chapter 6). If narrowing options are attributes contained in the list and users are likely to narrow down by only one of them at a time, filters may be embedded in the tabular list itself (Figure 7.13).

On the other hand, if not all of the filtering options are available in the list and users are likely to filter by more than one option at a time, show filtering options separately above the list (Figure 7.14).

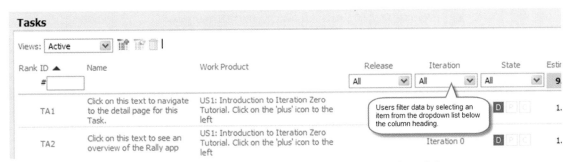

FIGURE 7.13 Rally allows users to filter data by selecting an item from the dropdown list below the column heading.

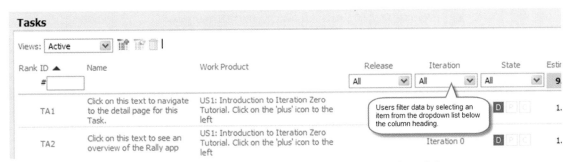

FIGURE 7.14 Blinksale shows the filtering options separate from the list, since they allow users to select more than one status and specify a date range, which would be difficult to show using list column headings.

	United Airlines	US Airways	Frontier Airlines	Continental Airlines	Airtran Airways	American Airlines
Lowest Price Flights ▸	**$312** total $353	**$312** total $353	**$369** total $400	**$380** total $421	**$406** total $448	**$465** total $507
Non-Stop Flights ▸	**$488** total $509	N/A	**$488** total $509	N/A	N/A	N/A
ON SALE Flight + Hotel Packages ▸	Buy Flight + Hotel and Save up to $325					

Total prices are for e-tickets and include taxes and fees. Extra fees* apply for paper tickets.   Showing 1-6 of 8 Airlines | See more airlines»

FIGURE 7.15 Expedia summarizes air fares in a summary view above the flight list. Users can click a link in the summary view to filter the flight list either by airline, price, nonstop flights, airline and price combination, and so forth.

In addition, consider a matrix view when data can be filtered by row and column attributes individually and combined (Figure 7.15).

ALLOW USERS TO SEE ALTERNATE VIEWS OF TABULAR DATA

Offer alternative views of tabular data when they help users understand data better and/or make it easier for them to find desired items. For example, when viewing reports on e-commerce applications, it's common to allow users to switch between textual and graphical views (Figures 7.16 and 7.17).

IMPROVE THE ACCESSIBILITY OF TABULAR DATA

Improve the accessibility of tabular information by including the following in the HTML markup (see also the ACCESSIBLE TABLES pattern in Chapter 11):

1. Describe the table's content using the **<CAPTION>** tag and the **<SUMMARY>** attribute. Within the **<CAPTION>** tag, include a short title describing the table's content. Unlike the **<CAPTION>** tag, the content of which is visible to users, the content within the SUMMARY attribute is not rendered on the page but provides a more detailed description of the table's content to those using alternate browsers.

2. Describe the relationship between column or row headings and the corresponding data by using the **SCOPE** attribute in the **<TH>** tag, which helps users establish context for the table's data.

Related design patterns

Most large lists need to be filtered; see the FILTERING pattern in Chapter 6 and the DYNAMIC QUERYING pattern in Chapter 8 for the choices available to designers for narrowing large lists. Large lists also typically cannot show all items on the same page, so PAGINATION is often an integral part of tabular lists; consider CONTINUOUS SCROLLING as an option as well (see Chapter 6).

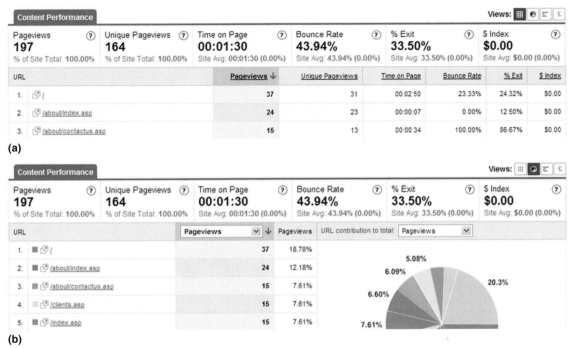

FIGURE 7.16 Google Analytics allows users to switch among several views: list (a), pie chart (b), bar chart, and a comparison to the site's average.

FIGURE 7.17 Home Depot offers users a grid view (a) and a list view (b) when showing items.

HIERARCHICAL LIST

Problem

Items in the list relate to each other in a hierarchical manner such that each list item may have one or more subitems with a parent–child type relationship (e.g., category–subcategory).

FIGURE 7.18 Digg shows comments as a threaded discussion. When users click "*n* Replies," replies are shown indented in a treelike structure.

Solution

Show list items as a "tree" of items, which clearly illustrates the relationship between parent and child item(s) (Figure 7.18). List items at the parent level (i.e., a group node or a parent item) may contain other groups (i.e., parents) and/or individual items (i.e., a leaf node or a child item) and can be expanded and collapsed to view its contents.

Why

For many lists, especially in emails and forums that have several participants and topics, it's important to show how items relate to each other. Showing items in a hierarchical list makes it easier for users to follow the thread of a discussion or conversation. In addition, it makes it easier to trace the discussion's history.

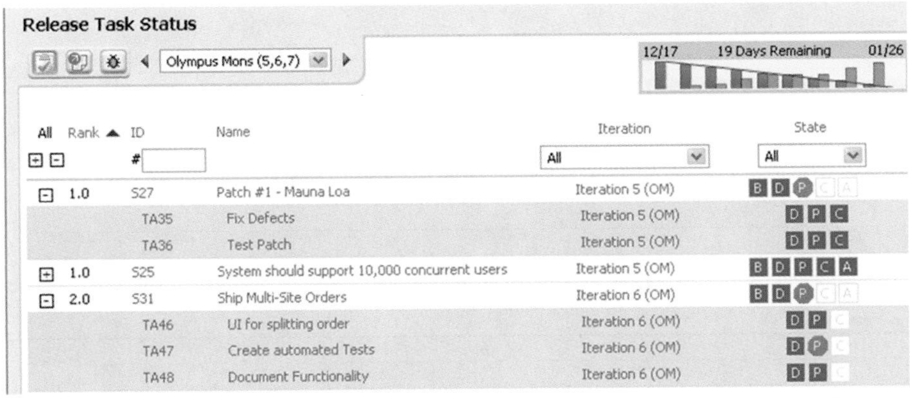

FIGURE 7.19 Rally shows a "Release Task Status" list in a hierarchical order by indenting subtasks below parent tasks. It does the same in the "State" column as well.

How

Make the list items' hierarchy clear by depicting the relationship between items at the parent and child levels. In addition, include expand and collapse controls for items at the parent level in the first column (Figure 7.19).

Indentation is the preferred method to indicate parent–child relationships among items in a multilevel hierarchical list. However, for single-level hierarchies—mainly used for grouping of information—some form of visual indication that emphasizes the item at the parent level is usually sufficient to show the hierarchical relationship (Figure 7.20).

WHERE APPROPRIATE, OFFER A NONHIERARCHICAL VIEW

For hierarchical lists, the default organization (sorting method) is the tree structure that shows parent–child relationships. For multicolumn (i.e., multi-attribute) lists, however, users may want to sort data by another attribute. For example, in discussion groups, users may want to view messages in a chronological order rather than the default hierarchical order of threaded discussions. When users can sort the columns, it may become necessary to switch to a non-hierarchical list; however, ensure that users are able to return to the original hierarchical view (Figure 7.21).

BE CAREFUL WHEN ALLOWING USERS TO DELETE PARENT ITEMS

Deleting an item at the parent level would cause all the child items, including other parent items within it, to be deleted. Therefore, when offering the "delete" option, make users aware of the action's consequences. If the "delete" action could inadvertently cause substantial data loss, restrict users to deletion

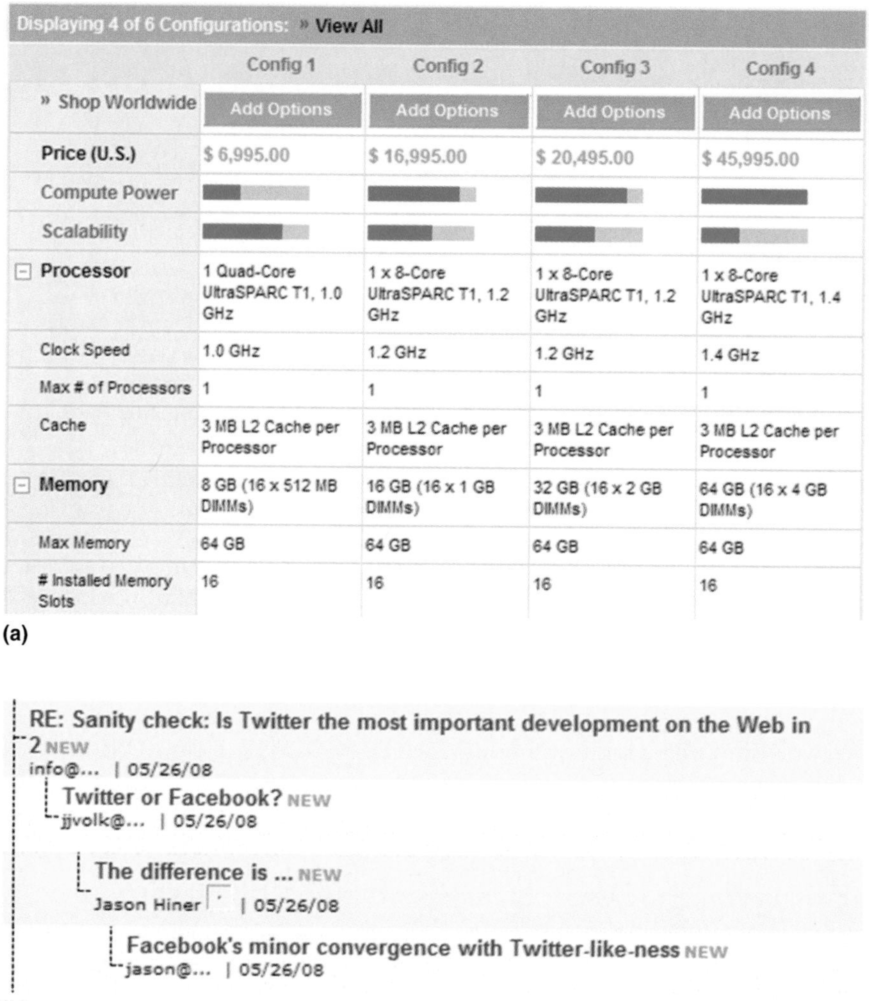

(a)

(b)

FIGURE 7.20 Sun shows server configuration comparison by making server parameters at a summary level bolder and in larger font (a). TechRepublic, on the other hand, indents items to indicate parent–child relationships between comments (b).

of only "empty" parent items. In addition, if necessary, only allow the item creator to delete a parent item (Figure 7.22).

Related design patterns

When sorted, HIERARCHICAL LISTS need to be presented as nonhierarchical lists, which may be either SIMPLE LISTS or TABULAR LISTS. In addition, users may want to sort hierarchical lists (SORTING; see Chapter 6).

Nabble | Computer Security » SSH (Secure Shell)   Login : Register

ssh security question

View: [Threaded ▾] New views   8 Messages — Rating Filter: [2 ▾] Alert me

⊟ ▶ ssh security question - Richard-23 May 02, 2008; 07:55am ☆☆☆
    ⊟   RE: ssh security question - Stawnyczy, Evan May 02, 2008; 10:16am ☆☆☆
         Re: ssh security question - Richard-23 May 03, 2008; 01:00am ☆☆☆
    ⊟   Re: ssh security question - Antonio A Hilario [c] May 02, 2008; 10:34am ☆☆☆
         Re: ssh security question - Remo Mattei May 02, 2008; 10:19pm ☆☆☆
     Re: ssh security question - Antonio A Hilario [c] May 02, 2008; 10:43am ☆☆☆
     Re: ssh security question - Tim Shubitz May 02, 2008; 10:39am ☆☆☆
     RE: ssh security question - Marc Serra-5 May 02, 2008; 10:26am ☆☆☆

« Return to forum

(a)

Nabble | Computer Security » SSH (Secure Shell)   Login : Register

ssh security question

View: [Chronologically ▾] New views   8 Messages — Rating Filter: [2 ▾] Alert me

Subject	Author	Date	Rating
▶ ssh security question	Richard-23	May 02, 2008; 07:55am	☆☆☆
RE: ssh security question	Stawnyczy, Evan	May 02, 2008; 10:16am	☆☆☆
RE: ssh security question	Marc Serra-5	May 02, 2008; 10:26am	☆☆☆
Re: ssh security question	Antonio A Hilario [c]	May 02, 2008; 10:34am	☆☆☆
Re: ssh security question	Tim Shubitz	May 02, 2008; 10:39am	☆☆☆
Re: ssh security question	Antonio A Hilario [c]	May 02, 2008; 10:43am	☆☆☆
Re: ssh security question	Remo Mattei	May 02, 2008; 10:19pm	☆☆☆
Re: ssh security question	Richard-23	May 03, 2008; 01:00am	☆☆☆

« Return to forum

(b)

FIGURE 7.21 Nabble offers users a feature to switch from a threaded view (a) to a chronological view (b) by selecting a different view from the "View" dropdown menu.

FIGURE 7.22 Nabble allows only the post's owner to delete the post permanently. The "Delete post permanently" option is not offered to other users.

EVENT LIST

Problem

Items to be shown to users involve date and time, or both—for example, schedules or planned events. Although users may want to see past events, their main focus is on upcoming or future events.

FIGURE 7.23 When users click "Calendar," Clemson University's web site shows users a monthly events view by default (a) and allows them to switch to a weekly view or a daily view (b). In all views, users may navigate to another month or day using the calendar control or "previous" and "next" pagination controls.

Solution

Use a calendar-like format to present items. In addition, consider showing items in a list view as well and allow users to switch between them (Figure 7.23).

Why

Users generally know how to interact with calendars because of their familiarity with desktop applications such as Outlook, Entourage, iCal, and so forth. In addition, using a calendar view makes it easy for users to see scheduled events and helps them with planning because they can clearly see available and busy time slots.

How

Show users a calendar with an appropriate default view—for example, calendars for personal or business use typically show a weekly view by default. However, allow them to change it to a different view per their preference (Figure 7.24).

(a)

(b)

FIGURE 7.24 Google Calendar shows users a weekly view by default (a), but allows them to change it on the "Settings" page (b).

FIGURE 7.25 Yahoo! Calendar highlights dates with entries by making them bold.

When using a calendar control for navigation, highlight days with one or more scheduled events to prevent unnecessary navigation (Figure 7.25).

ALLOW USERS TO SWITCH BETWEEN CALENDAR AND LIST VIEWS

Although events are typically shown in calendars because users may want to print the events list for reference, offer users both a list view and a calendar view (Figure 7.26). In the list view, order events chronologically.

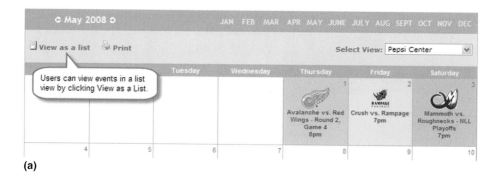

FIGURE 7.26 Pepsi Center shows scheduled sporting events in both (a) calendar view and (b) list view.

If event information includes both location and schedule information, consider showing users a location view as well. Although locations are often effective as maps (see the MAPS pattern later in this chapter), a list view may be more suitable if many events are scheduled for the same location, which may appear cluttered on maps (Figure 7.27).

ALLOW USERS TO SEARCH CALENDAR ENTRIES

When the total number of events is too large to be reasonably shown in a calendar view, allow users to search calendar entries (Figure 7.28).

RELATED DESIGN PATTERNS

When showing events in a list format, instead of a calendar format, use either the SIMPLE LIST or TABULAR LIST pattern depending on the number of attributes that need to be shown to users. In addition, use the SEARCH RESULTS pattern (see Chapter 6) when showing the results of event searches.

TIMELINES

Problem

Users need to be presented with time-based historical information (hours/minutes in a day, days of the week, months, years, etc.) to enable them to see trends and/or the evolution of an event.

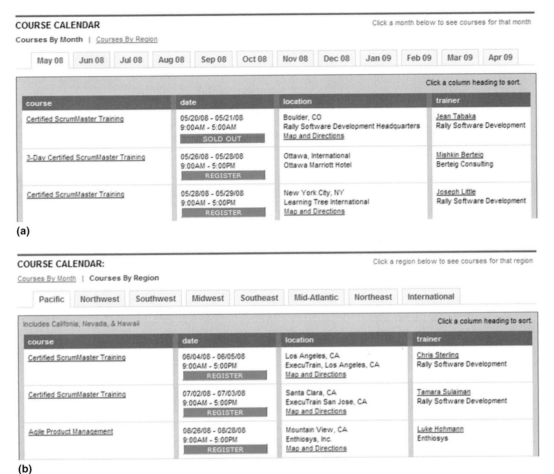

FIGURE 7.27 Agile University shows the course calendar using lists (a) but allows users to view them by months as well as regions (b).

FIGURE 7.28
SanDiego.org allows users to search by date range, event type, and keywords.

Solution

Show historical information as a timeline (Figure 7.29).

Why

Timelines are appropriate for presenting time-based data because they allow users to see relationships between events and facilitate comparison. They can also help users see the historical context or rationale, if any, for the current state.

FIGURE 7.29 *National Geographic* uses a timeline to help users navigate space travel content. The design also incorporates a CAROUSEL pattern (see Chapter 8) to allow users to navigate the timeline.

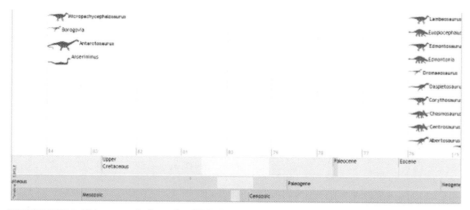

FIGURE 7.30 This example from the SIMILE Timeline project from MIT shows dinosaurs along the geological scale. Users can pan the timeline by dragging horizontally and access information not visible in the available viewport.

How

Show time along the horizontal axis and the data or event information along the vertical axis. When available screen real estate is limited, allow users to scroll or pan the timeline (Figure 7.30) or compress the timeline and allow them to zoom in and out as desired (Figure 7.31).

ALLOW USERS TO ACCESS EVENT DETAILS

Because a lot of information may be compressed in a small area, it may be difficult to show details on a timeline. Therefore, allow users to hover over or click on an event (or a data point) in the timeline to view its details (Figure 7.32).

FIGURE 7.31 Google Finance shows historical stock price information in two separate timelines, making the most of limited screen real estate. The timeline in the bottom frame (shown in gray) is the entire timeline for which the stock price was available. The timeline in the top frame shows details of the selected timeline segment. Users can select a timeline segment they want to view by manipulating the slider in the bottom frame.

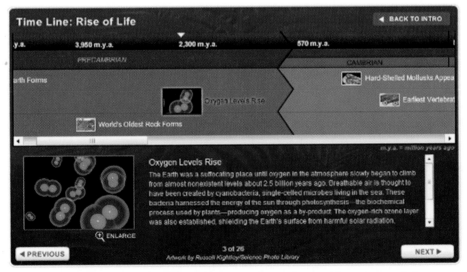

FIGURE 7.32 In this "Rise of Life" timeline from *National Geographic*, users can click on an event in the timeline to view its details in the bottom pane.

Related design patterns

Large TIMELINES that don't fit within the available screen space often incorporate the OVERVIEW-PLUS-DETAIL pattern (see Chapter 8) to allow users to zoom in and out to view details.

IMAGE LISTS/GRIDS

Problem

Items presented to users are visual in nature, and presenting them using only their textual description may make it difficult for users to recognize and locate desired items. In addition, users may be able to recognize an item by its image but may be unfamiliar with the item's name.

Solution

Show users items as image grids or image lists rather than a textual list. However, complement images with a textual description (Figure 7.33).

Why

> A picture is worth a thousand words.   –A proverb

Humans are able to recognize and recall images better than words (Paivio et al., 1968). Therefore, when showing multimedia content, such as photos, movies, music, and so forth, it's easier for users to scan and find the desired item when all items are presented as images rather than just in a textual list. The advantage of images over textual information—commonly referred to as Picture Superiority Effect (Lidwell et al., 2003)—is particularly evident in situations where users may have been casually exposed to the image before or know what the "prototypical" image they are searching for looks like. For example, if users are looking for a photo, an artist, an album, or a video that they have seen before or remember one or more elements of, it'd be faster for them to find it using images rather than text. Because memory for images and text together is generally better than text or images by themselves, consider

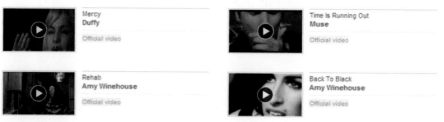

FIGURE 7.33 Last.fm shows top videos as an image grid and includes brief textual information about the videos.

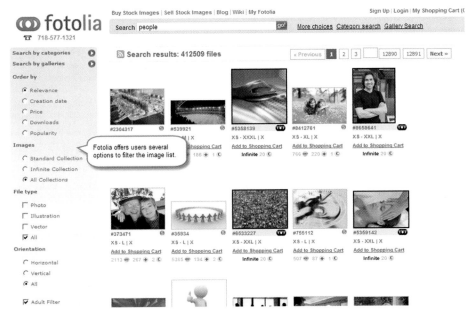

FIGURE 7.34 Fotolia offers users several options to filter the image list, including by categories, image orientation, file type, and so forth.

complementing images with textual description (Childers and Houston, 1984; Paivio et al., 1968).

In the early days of the Web, bandwidth was a limiting factor, and the focus was on sharing textual information. With broadband becoming commonplace, user interaction is changing, as users are not only viewing and uploading photos, music, and videos, but also sharing them. This has made the use of image lists quite commonplace.

How

Facilitate the quick scanning of items by showing item thumbnails in an image grid. Like other lists, consider providing users with necessary list pagination, sorting, and filtering options (Figure 7.34; see also the PAGINATION, SORTING, and FILTERING patterns in Chapter 6).

When space is limited, image lists may be implemented using the CAROUSEL pattern, where users are shown fewer items at a time, but they can use navigation controls to view images hidden from their view (Figure 7.35; see also the CAROUSEL pattern in Chapter 8).

SHOW USERS A PREVIEW OF THE IMAGES

When thumbnails are used to represent actual images, consider showing users a preview of the larger image on hover to minimize unnecessary navigation (Figure 7.36).

FIGURE 7.35 Yahoo! TV uses a carousel for its image lists.

FIGURE 7.36 iStockphoto shows users image (or video) previews in a hover style.

Image previews can also be integrated when an image list is part of a slideshow. Although the detailed image does not require navigating to another page, showing a preview makes it easy for users to distinguish between similar images, especially when thumbnails are relatively small in size (Figure 7.37).

EXPLORE USING AN IMAGE LIST AS AN ALTERNATIVE FOR OTHER LISTS

Increasingly, interaction with the Web is becoming visual. The assumption is that users would be more efficient and effective in their interaction if they can

FIGURE 7.37 This example from Vertigo SlideShow illustrates a thumbnail gallery to navigate images. It also provides image previews when users hover over a thumbnail.

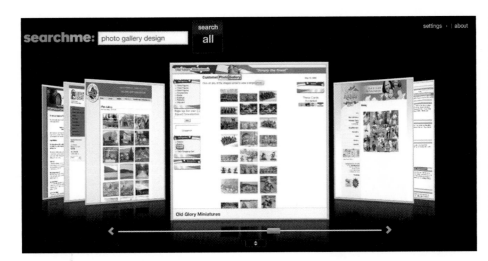

FIGURE 7.38 SearchMe shows search results primarily as a series of thumbnails of web pages that users can flip through to find the desired page. In addition, if they had previously accessed a useful one (or not useful enough), it's easier to visually recognize it when they see the image rather than just its title.

FIGURE 7.39 Viewzi, a search engine, groups results in several categories and uses various types of image lists for different search result groups; the shopping view is shown here.

view (or preview) content before navigating. Newer search engines have started exploring use of images to show search results (Figures 7.38 and 7.39).

Related design patterns

Unlike lists, especially tabular lists, which can be quite compact, IMAGE LISTS/ GRIDS usually require more space. When screen space is limited, consider using the CAROUSEL pattern to accommodate more items (see Chapter 8).

MAPS

Problem

Items to be presented to users contain spatial information that refers to either geographical (e.g., location of restaurants on a map) or physical locations (e.g., seating in an aircraft, a concert hall, or a stadium). In addition, for users, it's important to know the item's location in a geographical or physical space as well as its relation to other items in the same space.

Solution

Show items on either the map of a region or space in question (Figure 7.40).

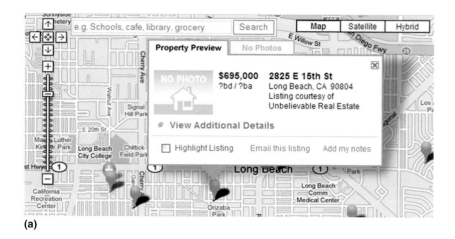

(a)

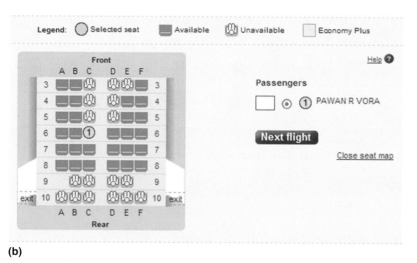

(b)

FIGURE 7.40 Roost shows location of homes on a map (a), and United Airlines allows users to choose their seat by showing a seating map (b).

Why

Because users are presented with spatial information, showing them on a map of the physical space eliminates the need for users to visualize its location. It also makes information more meaningful and relevant to user goals, such as finding a location, navigating to and from a location, and relating data to the targeted region.

How

Maps are typically used as a background image on which geographical, physical, and statistical information are superimposed. Depending on users' needs, maps may be represented as illustrations (using points, lines, and polygons), photographic or satellite images, text, or a combination (Figure 7.41).

SHOW DETAILED INFORMATION ON DEMAND

When showing several locations on a map, providing details of all of them at the same time could clutter the map and may make it difficult for users to parse relevant information. In addition, users may be interested in seeing details of only a few locations. To minimize complexity, a common approach is to provide users necessary details when they hover over or click on map markers. Detailed information can then be presented as hovertips or pop-ups.

Hovertips are typically used when details are not extensive, are purely informational in nature, and do not require users to take an action on the presented information, whereas pop-ups are used when users can take actions such as find directions (Figure 7.42). Another alternative is to show the pop-up after a few seconds' delay to support relatively new users who may not know what actions are available on the map markers (e.g., Microsoft's Live Maps).

FOR LARGE MAPS, PROVIDE USERS CONTEXT BY SHOWING OVERVIEWS

When panning and zooming large maps, it is important that users do not feel lost and are able to maintain their sense of location. Overviews within the map help provide such context (Figure 7.43). Most map overviews support panning within them, allowing users to move the "region" box inside the overview, thus affecting the map being viewed.

Some map overviews support zooming as well. However, using overviews for panning and zooming is generally not as efficient as panning and zooming on the main map (Hornbæk et al., 2002) (see also the OVERVIEW-PLUS-DETAIL pattern in Chapter 8).

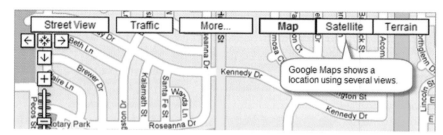

FIGURE 7.41 Google Maps shows a location using a map, satellite, terrain, and street views.

FIGURE 7.42 Zillow provides details about a location when clicked, as users may take follow-up actions to view home information and comparable homes in that area.

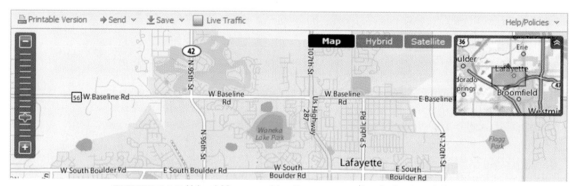

FIGURE 7.43 Yahoo! Maps provides the map overview in the top-right corner. The overview box not only provides context to users but also allows users to move the context rectangle within it.

CONSIDER USE OF SYMBOLS FOR SHOWING LOCATION TYPES

Maps may have to show more than one type of location—for example, a map may show restaurants, gas stations, lodging facilities, and so forth. Use one or more of the following approaches to indicate different location types:

Colors and shapes. Use of distinct colors and shapes is helpful when showing two to three location types on the map. Include a legend so that users can associate colors and shapes to location types. In addition, to not disadvantage users with color vision deficiencies, use colored markers in combination with unique shapes.

Pictographic symbols. Use recognizable pictographic symbols to identify types of locations such as restaurants, restrooms, gas stations, trail symbols, and so forth (Figure 7.44).

Although not used to indicate a location type per se, using thumbnails of actual photographs to identify a location is becoming a popular way to indicate a location on a map (Figure 7.45).

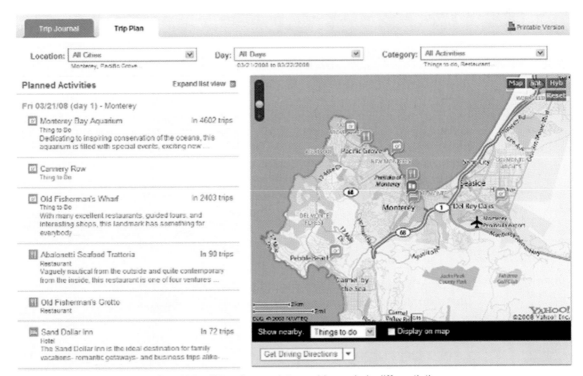

FIGURE 7.44 This trip plan from Yahoo! Travel uses pictographic symbols differentiating between places to visit, restaurants, hotels, and so forth.

FIGURE 7.45 This map view from Google Maps shows photographs for locations around San Francisco.

COMPLEMENT MAP VIEWS WITH A LIST, OR TABULAR VIEW, OF ITEMS

Although a map view is useful for showing location information, the location itself may have other attributes that are better represented in a list format. In addition, when users are interested in comparing attributes of items other than their location, tabular lists are more useful—for example, when comparing prices of homes shown on a map. Enable such comparison by offering users a list view of items in addition to the map view (Figure 7.46; see also TABULAR LISTS pattern earlier in this chapter).

For data with just a few attributes, it may help to show the list and map views side by side to make it easy for users to either select a location from the list and see it on a map or select a location on the map and see it on the list with all its attributes (Figure 7.47).

USE MAPS TO SHOW STATUS INFORMATION

Maps are also useful for showing status information on dashboards. For example, ShipCompliant for Six88 uses the U.S. map to show wineries their shipping compliance information (Figure 7.48).

USE MAPS TO SHOW REAL-TIME INFORMATION ABOUT MOVING OBJECTS

Maps may also be used to show real-time information about the location of objects in transit (e.g., trucks, trains, airplanes, and so forth). Once equipped

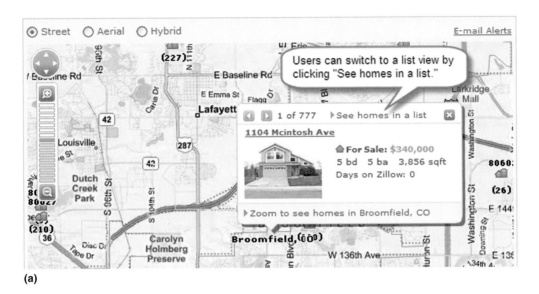

(a)

(b)

FIGURE 7.46 By default, Zillow shows users search results in a map view (a). However, it allows users to click "See homes in a list" to change to a list view (b).

with global positioning system (GPS) devices, an object's current position can be overlaid on the map to show its current location. This is useful for tracking locations of a fleet or figuring out the current location of a train, for example (Figure 7.49).

Related design patterns

Large maps typically don't fit within the available screen space and often use the OVERVIEW-PLUS-DETAIL pattern to allow users to maintain their context. In addition, maps use DRAG-AND-DROP for panning. See Chapter 8 for more information.

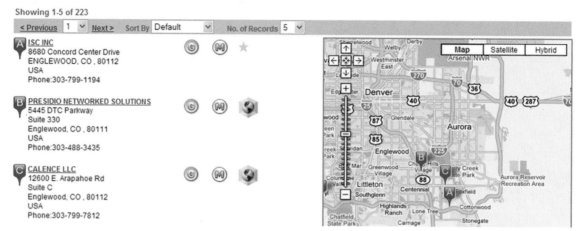

FIGURE 7.47 Cisco shows users the list view and map view side by side when showing partner search results.

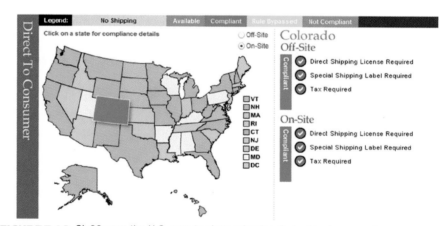

FIGURE 7.48 Six88 uses the U.S. map to show wineries their shipping compliance information. When users hover over a state, they are also shown their off-site and on-site shipping compliance record.

LIST ACTIONS

Problem

For items in lists, users may want to take one or more actions such as editing, deleting, comparing, and so forth. Desired actions may apply to an individual item or may require users to select two or more items.

Solution

For actions such as edit, delete, copy, and so forth that apply to individual items, clearly associate and show actions for each item. For actions that require

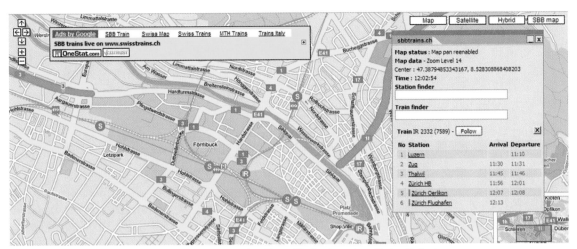

FIGURE 7.49 This train map shows the current location of trains based on Swiss Trains' timetable. Although it does not yet show actual train GPS positions, the site claims that the positions of trains is accurate.

FIGURE 7.50 PriceGrabber shows "Compare Prices," an action associated with each item, for every item in a product list. It also offers checkboxes in front of each item so that users can select two or more items and select "Compare" to get a side-by-side feature comparison of selected items.

selection of two or more items, show checkboxes for each item in the list and corresponding actions outside the list (Figure 7.50). Baxley (2003) referred to list actions such as *dedicated actions* and *shared actions,* respectively.

Why

By selecting a dedicated action for an item, users are implicitly choosing the item. Therefore, asking users to select the item before the action is an unnecessary step. In addition, long lists may require users to select an item and then scroll up or down to apply the action, further making the interaction inefficient.

For lists that support both dedicated and shared actions (see Figure 7.50), if not separated, clearly indicating which actions apply to individual items and which apply to multiple items would be a design challenge as well.

How

Place dedicated actions in the same row as the list item and repeat them for each item in the list, and place shared actions outside the list. If users may select one or more items, like in many web-based email applications, placing both dedicated and shared actions outside the list is acceptable when it helps reduce visual clutter (Figure 7.51). However, to minimize errors, consider disabling dedicated actions when users have selected more than one item in the list.

HIGHLIGHT THE ROW CORRESPONDING TO THE SELECTED ITEM

Showing selected items with only checkboxes often doesn't give enough visual indication about their selected states. A common approach to make selected items salient is to highlight corresponding rows by changing their background colors (Figure 7.52; see also the HIGHLIGHT pattern in Chapter 12).

		From	Subject	Date ↓	Size
	☐	Sample Bullentin	RE: Brand name samples you know and trust	5/15/08	6 KB
	☐	xatezadi58017	We carry on the best Replica's	5/14/08	2 KB
	☐	myxyhydy67763	All the best brands	5/13/08	2 KB
	☐	mexelily67407	XYNERGY CORP - With OIL prices near $125 a barrel, an ENERGY play under a .01 is a GIFT!	5/12/08	5 KB
	☐	havebuvusuf47	Get the Finest Replica!	5/10/08	2 KB
	☐	risirabu15460	Get the Finest Replica!	5/07/08	2 KB

New   Delete   Not junk   Report phishing scam   Mark as unread   Move to   Options
6 messages   Page 1
6 messages   Page 1

FIGURE 7.51 For actions that may be applied to one or more items, like in this Hotmail example, it's acceptable to group together all controls and have users select one or more items using checkboxes.

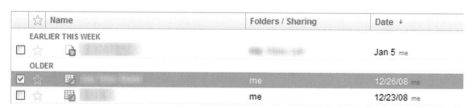

FIGURE 7.52 Google Docs highlights selected items by changing the corresponding row's background color.

Recent order history from the last 9 months.

order date	order #	preview	total	status		
11/29/2007	36551483	⌕	$30.00	Complete	Track	Return
11/28/2007	36497544	⌕	$39.72	Complete	Track	Return
11/5/2007	35893093	⌕	$54.99	Complete	Track	Return
6/20/2007	34058156	⌕	$80.19	Complete	Track	Return
2/21/2007	32494644	⌕	$499.00	Complete	Track	Return

(a)

Saved Meals

Saved As	Meal Details	
Family	1 Medium(12") Thin Pizza, 1 Medium(12") Thin Pizza, 1 Medium(12") Thin Pizza	Remove
Weekday Special	1 Medium(12") Thin Pizza, 1 Medium(12") Thin Pizza	Remove
Friday Order	1 Medium(12") Thin Pizza, 1 Medium(12") Thin Pizza	Remove

(b)

		per-package basis	Orders									
⊞	TC20	Purchase One Item	530: Purchase Your Items	Acceptance	Important	test3	Shopping	Manual	Fail	114	01/04/2008	⚏⚏⚏
⊞	TC21	Purchase Multiple Items	530: Purchase Your Items	Acceptance	Important	pm	Shopping	Manual	Fail	114	01/04/2008	⚏⚏⚏
⊞	TC22	Purchase MAX Items	530: Purchase Your Items	Acceptance	Important	pm	Shopping	Manual	Fail	118	01/05/2008	⚏⚏⚏
⊞	TC23	Select MAX+1 Items	530: Purchase Your Items	Acceptance	Important	guest	Shopping	Manual	Fail	118	01/05/2008	⚏⚏⚏
⊞	TC27	Default Shipping - Ground		Acceptance	Useful	test1	Shipping	Manual	Fail	118	01/05/2008	⚏⚏⚏
⊞	TC28	Promo Code GUI	540: Payment - Promotional Codes	Acceptance	Important	test2	Shopping	Manual	Fail	115	01/05/2008	⚏⚏⚏

(c)

FIGURE 7.53 Examples of lists with (a) dedicated actions as links, (b) as buttons on the "Your Account" page of Dominos, and (c) as icons.

CONSIDER USE OF ICONS AND ACTION LISTS FOR DEDICATED ACTIONS

Dedicated actions can be shown as a set of links, buttons, or icons (Figure 7.53). However, because dedicated actions are repeated for each list item, having several actions in the same row as links or buttons may require additional screen real estate and can add to the visual clutter. In such situations, consider using action menus (Figure 7.54).

Another design option to allow dedicated actions in a limited space is to move less-common actions to the item's "details" page or show them on hover (Figure 7.55). Although this approach hides some actions, it may help simplify the user interface.

FOR LONG LISTS, REPEAT SHARED ACTIONS

For long lists requiring scrolling, repeat shared actions above and below the list. This will either eliminate the need for scrolling, as users will have one set of shared actions always visible or at least minimize scrolling to initiate an action after they have selected items.

FIGURE 7.54 Box.net offers an action menu for each item in both (a) list view and (b) icon view.

FIGURE 7.55 TO DO list in Basecamp shows only one important action for each to-do item—a checkbox to indicate task completion. Other actions for editing, deleting, and moving the TO DO items are shown only on hover.

FOR MULTISELECT LISTS, ALLOW USERS TO SELECT (UNSELECT) ALL ITEMS

When users are likely to select many or all of the items in a list, allow them to select or unselect all list items (Figure 7.56). There is one exception to this rule, however. For actions such as "compare," where users would benefit from selecting fewer items, it's better to not offer them the "Select All" option

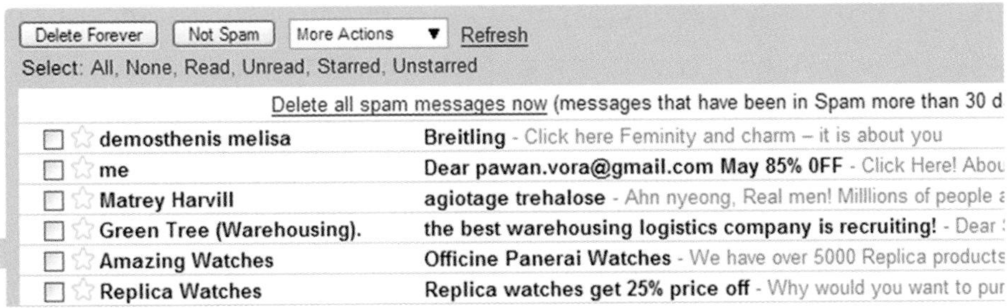

FIGURE 7.56 Gmail allows users to select all (or none) emails. In addition, users have the option to select email based on other characteristics: read, unread, starred, and unstarred.

since selecting many items would make it difficult to show all items on the comparison.

DESIGN TO PREVENT SELECTION ERRORS

In instances where users' selections are constrained either by the number of items they can select or the specific items they can select, design the interface to prevent selection errors. For example, if users cannot select more than 4 items from a list of 10 items, as soon as users have selected 4 items, disable the checkboxes for other items. Or if there are dependencies on what users may select, enable or disable options based on their selections (Figure 7.57).

SHOW CONFIRMATION AND ACKNOWLEDGMENT MESSAGES AS APPROPRIATE

List actions affect the list items in one of the following ways:

1. They immediately apply the action to selected items and show users the result. The result may be shown on the same page or on a separate page. For example, actions, such as "update cart," keep users on the same page, whereas actions, such as "compare," take users to a separate page.

2. They ask users for additional information by showing a dialog or taking them to a separate page. Once users have provided additional information and submitted the request, they are returned to the list page, where they can see the results of the selected action. The actions in this category include "new," "edit," "copy," "email to a friend," and so forth.

3. They confirm user intent by requiring them to respond affirmatively to the selected action—for example, "Are you sure you want to delete . . . ?" (Figure 7.58). Requiring users to confirm their intent is important for actions that lead to unrecoverable data loss (e.g., "delete").

   It's important to remember that not all "delete" actions require a confirmation message; only those actions with unrecoverable outcomes should require user confirmation. For example, deleting an item from a shopping cart should not require confirmation, as it's relatively easy to add it back.

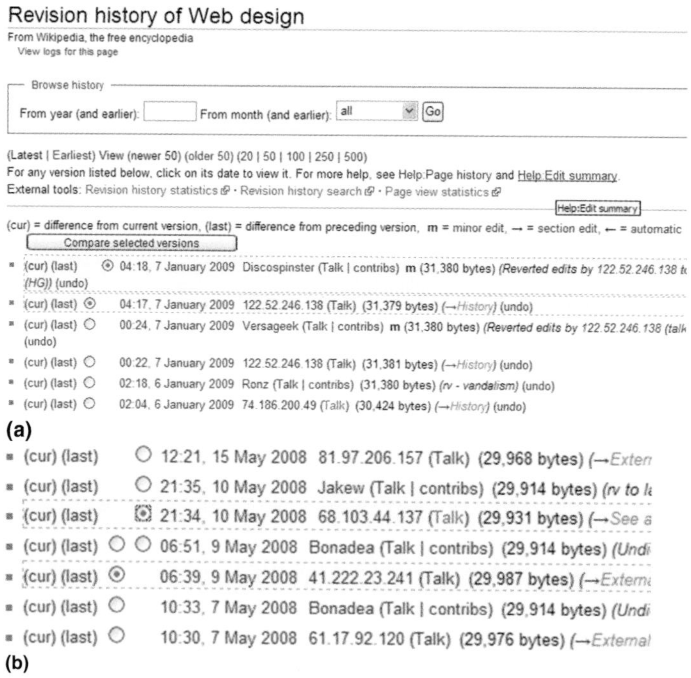

FIGURE 7.57 Wikipedia allows users to select two article versions for comparison on the history page. To compare two versions, users select the left-column radio button of an older version, select the right-column radio button of a newer version, and then click "Compare selected versions." Selection choices update dynamically to prevent selection of incorrect versions. By default, the last two versions are selected for comparison (a). As soon as users select another version in a column, the radio buttons in the other column are automatically updated to offer only valid choices (b). This design prevents selection of the same version for comparison or selection of an older version of a more recent document and a newer version of an older document.

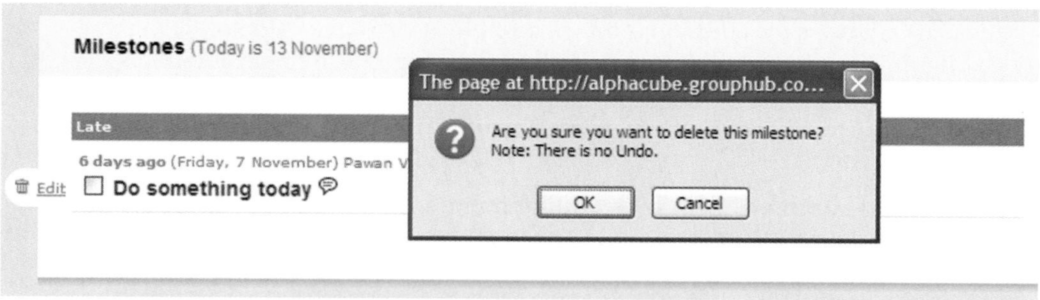

FIGURE 7.58 When deleting a milestone, Basecamp asks users to confirm that they want to delete it. The site also advises that the milestone being deleted will not be recoverable.

FIGURE 7.59 When applying the "delete" action, Gmail immediately moves the item to trash but offers users an "undo" option to recover the deleted item.

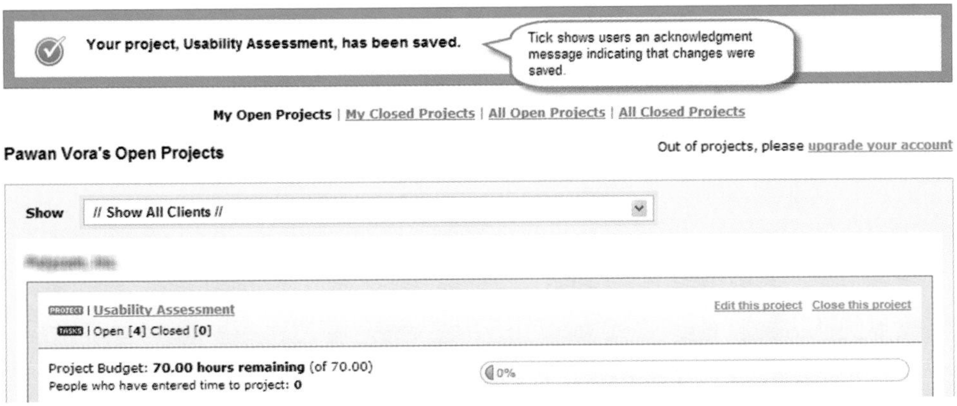

![Tick project saved acknowledgment interface]

Your project, Usability Assessment, has been saved.

Tick shows users an acknowledgment message indicating that changes were saved.

My Open Projects | My Closed Projects | All Open Projects | All Closed Projects

Pawan Vora's Open Projects   Out of projects, please upgrade your account

Show   // Show All Clients //   ▼

PROJECT | Usability Assessment   Edit this project   Close this project
TASKS | Open [4] Closed [0]

Project Budget: **70.00 hours remaining** (of 70.00)   0%
People who have entered time to project: **0**

FIGURE 7.60 After saving changes to a project, Tick presents an acknowledgment message indicating that the changes were saved.

In addition, for "delete" actions that are frequent and may annoy users if prompted to confirm every time, a more recent trend is to forego the confirmation message; instead, users are offered an "undo" option so that they can reverse their action (Raskin, 2007). This approach is becoming common in applications (e.g., emails), where the "delete" action does not prompt a user confirmation but offers "undo" (Figure 7.59). The applications may allow users to undo only the last action, or they may allow several levels of undo similar to desktop applications. Plus, the applications may support a "redo" function as well.

For list actions, where it may not be immediately clear to users that the action was completed successfully, it's important that they be presented with a message acknowledging a successful outcome (Figure 7.60). Conversely, if an action couldn't be completed successfully, users should be shown an appropriate error message indicating the reasons for failure and remedial user actions, if any.

Related design patterns

In addition to list actions, users may need to be presented with utility functions that apply to the list as a whole (see the next section for the LIST UTILITY FUNCTIONS pattern).

LIST UTILITY FUNCTIONS

Problem

Certain actions users might take do not require them to select specific items but rather apply to the list as a whole—for example, printing, downloading, emailing, and so forth.

Solution

Similar to shared list actions, LIST UTILITY shows functions (e.g., email, export, and so forth) outside the item list (Figure 7.61).

Why

The list view as shown may not be sufficient for users' needs. They may want to use information in their own analysis using their own tools. In addition, they may want to share information with others who may not have direct access to the data. Utility functions can help users in performing such analyses and facilitate sharing.

How

First, distinguish utility functions from shared list actions. Because utility functions apply to the list as a whole and not individual items, it's important they be shown outside the list and are presented separately from the shared list actions. The latter requires selecting items from the list, whereas the former does not.

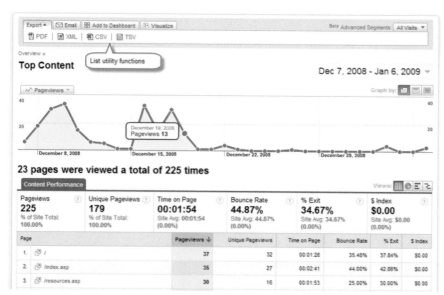

FIGURE 7.61 Google Analytics offers the utility functions "Export," "Email," and "Add to Dashboard."

The most common export/download formats include Adobe PDF, Excel, CSV (comma-separated values), TSV (tab-separated values), and XML (eXtensible Markup Language), because they allow users to import data to a preferred spreadsheet or database application and manipulate or view the data as necessary. The XML data format is also useful when data may be used as input to other applications and/or converted to other formats such as HTML (HyperText Markup Language) or SVG (Scalable Vector Graphics) for presentation purposes. Adobe PDF is useful when it's important to maintain the visual look of data being exported.

Another commonly used utility function is "Print." This may be implemented as simply a "printer-friendly" version of the page that users can print on standard printers, by removing banners, advertisements, navigation, and other branding information and resizing it to fit. Resizing the page for printing is particularly important with FIXED-WIDTH LAYOUTS (see Chapter 12), which may cut off text on the right when pages are printed in a portrait layout mode (instead of landscape). When printing lists, it may help to ask users if they want to include details in the printed report (Figure 7.62).

SHOW USERS A PAGE PREVIEW BEFORE PRINTING

Because it may not be clear to users what they are printing, show users a preview and offer a print action (Figure 7.63).

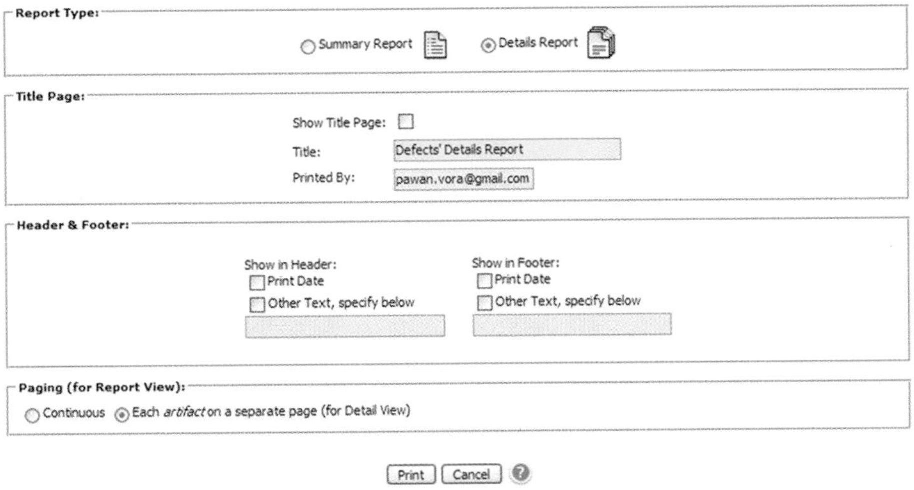

FIGURE 7.62 Rally offers users elaborate options for printing. It allows them to get either a summary or a detailed report with options to customize the header, footer, and title page. In addition, for a detailed report, it allows users to print each artifact ("defect" in this example) to start on a separate page or continuously without any page breaks. These features are especially helpful in team environments and show the web application striving to meet users' offline needs.

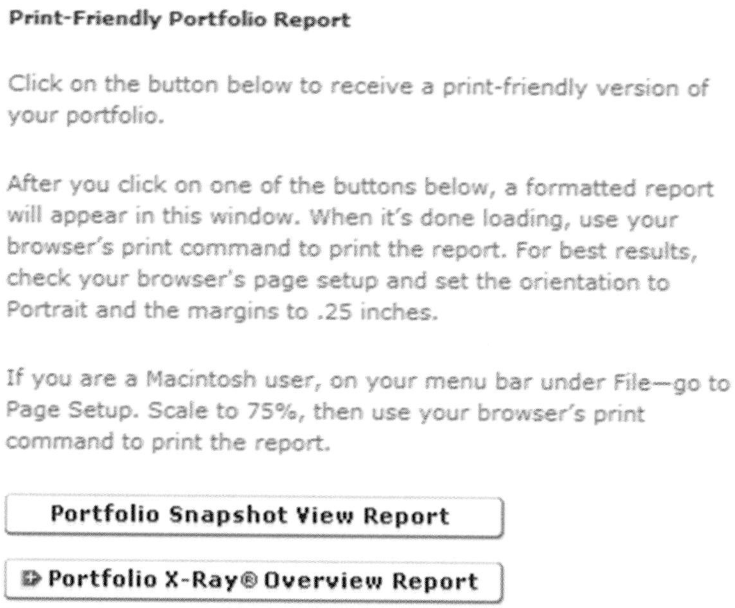

Print-Friendly Portfolio Report

Click on the button below to receive a print-friendly version of your portfolio.

After you click on one of the buttons below, a formatted report will appear in this window. When it's done loading, use your browser's print command to print the report. For best results, check your browser's page setup and set the orientation to Portrait and the margins to .25 inches.

If you are a Macintosh user, on your menu bar under File—go to Page Setup. Scale to 75%, then use your browser's print command to print the report.

Portfolio Snapshot View Report

⯈ Portfolio X-Ray® Overview Report

(a)

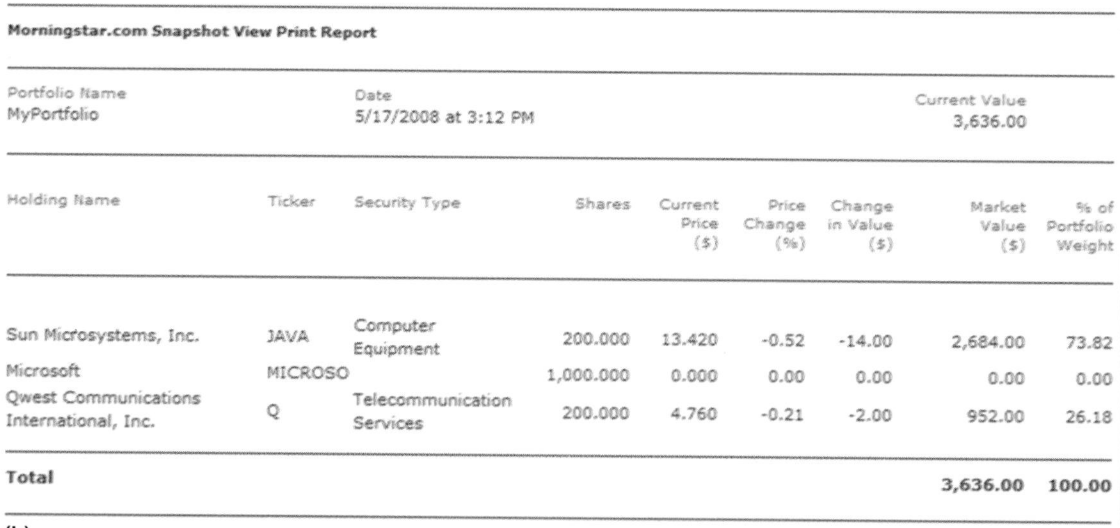

Morningstar.com Snapshot View Print Report

Portfolio Name	Date	Current Value
MyPortfolio	5/17/2008 at 3:12 PM	3,636.00

Holding Name	Ticker	Security Type	Shares	Current Price ($)	Price Change (%)	Change in Value ($)	Market Value ($)	% of Portfolio Weight
Sun Microsystems, Inc.	JAVA	Computer Equipment	200.000	13.420	-0.52	-14.00	2,684.00	73.82
Microsoft	MICROSO		1,000.000	0.000	0.00	0.00	0.00	0.00
Qwest Communications International, Inc.	Q	Telecommunication Services	200.000	4.760	-0.21	-2.00	952.00	26.18
Total							**3,636.00**	**100.00**

(b)

FIGURE 7.63 When printing a Morningstar portfolio, users are first shown print options and instructions to use the browser's print action (a) and then are shown a preview of the report (b).

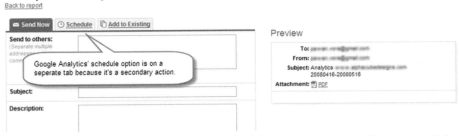

FIGURE 7.64 When emailing a report, Google Analytics offers users the option to schedule it. Because it's a secondary action, it puts the option in a separate tab.

FOR REPETITIVE ACTIONS, ALLOW USERS TO SET UP ALERTS AND/OR SCHEDULES

If a utility function is likely to be repeated in the future or on a regular basis (e.g., email), allow users to either set up an alert or schedule the function to repeat at regular intervals (Figure 7.64).

Related design patterns

List utility functions are similar to LIST ACTIONS and require that users are shown appropriate acknowledgment messages after successful task completion.

CHAPTER 8
Rich Internet Applications

INTRODUCTION

As discussed in Chapter 1, Rich Internet Applications (RIAs) can deliver responsiveness and interactivity comparable to desktop applications. With RIAs, the interaction seems continuous and dynamic because users do not have to wait for pages to refresh for basic data and layout updates and can immediately see the results of their actions.

Perhaps the earliest rich interaction in web applications was a RICH-TEXT EDITOR, which enabled users to include formatted text on web pages without knowing the underlying HTML (HyperText Markup Language). With the advent of technologies such as Flash and Ajax (Asynchronous JavaScript and XML), richer interactions have become possible because they allow communications with web servers without explicit "submit" actions. Their initial use, therefore, has been to replace the interactions that require users to wait for results to be processed by web servers and returned to them with a page refresh. These include validating user input and providing necessary feedback to users when filling out forms (RICH FORM); offering valid choices for data input (AUTOSUGGEST/AUTOCOMPLETION); allowing users to edit information in the same location it's being viewed (EDIT-IN-PLACE); panning and zooming around the information space (OVERVIEW-PLUS-DETAIL); sorting and filtering information in real time (DYNAMIC QUERYING); and previewing the effects of user changes (LIVE PREVIEW). Enabling such richer interactions requires use of direct manipulation techniques common in desktop applications such as DRAG-AND-DROP and interactive controls such as SLIDERS.

In addition, to communicate changes effected on the page and help users maintain their visual context, designers have started relying on visual effects (ANIMATIONS/TRANSITIONS). Popular techniques include showing delays and progress in retrieving data (DELAY/PROGRESS INDICATOR); briefly highlighting changed information on a page (SPOTLIGHT/YELLOW-FADE); and allowing users to browse through a large set of items in a limited space

(CAROUSEL). By combining real-time aspects of data update with relevant visual effects, RIAs tend to make web application interactions efficient, effective, and pleasurable.

RICH-TEXT EDITOR

Problem

Information entered by users may benefit from richer formatting, such as bold, underline, italic, and bulleted list. In addition, the information may be better presented using colors, tables, images, and hyperlinks. Although this can be achieved with HTML, users cannot be expected to know HTML, and even if they do, they cannot be expected to provide valid HTML. In some instances, allowing users to directly enter HTML (or JavaScript) may lead to security breaches as well.

Solution

Allow users to enter information using rich-text editors with necessary controls for formatting and inserting images and hypertext links (Figure 8.1).

Why

Plain text can go only so far. In applications where information is targeted to be used by others, such as email and blogs, it is important for users to emphasize certain information by making it bold, underlined, italicized, or presented with a different color. In some instances (e.g., blogs, job sites), it may also be important to provide supporting information such as tables, images, and links to other web pages. Although this is possible by allowing users to enter their information in snippets of HTML, they cannot be expected to be familiar with it. Allowing users to enter HTML may take more development effort to ensure that user-entered HTML is valid and that it doesn't break the presentation of the rest of the page.

Rich-text editors, because of their WYSIWYG (What You See Is What You Get) nature, are easier ways to format text and can be converted to HTML both for storage and to allow users to see the effects of their selections immediately. Moreover, rich-text editors are easy for users who are likely to be familiar with similar interactions in office-productivity applications such as Microsoft Office, Corel WordPerfect Suite, OpenOffice, and so forth.

FIGURE 8.1 Yahoo! Mail offers users a rich-text editor for composing emails. Note that it also offers the option of inserting emoticons (i.e., "smileys").

How

Rich-text editors are typically used as part of a larger application and for specific data-entry tasks such as composing an email or creating a blog entry. So, it's important to show users the text-entry areas that can be formatted using rich-text controls and the formatting options that are available (e.g., bold, underline, italic, bulleted list, hyperlink, images, etc.).

OFFER USERS ALTERNATIVE TEXT INPUT OPTIONS

Some users may not want to use rich-text options. When feasible, offer alternative text-input options such as plain text or HTML. In email applications, for example, consider providing a text option (Figure 8.2). In blogs, on the other hand, offer the option to enter HTML directly (Figure 8.3). Ensure that user-entered scripts (e.g., JavaScript) in HTML code are removed before saving the information to prevent security breaches.

OFFER ONLY RELEVANT RICH-TEXT FORMATTING CONTROLS

It is not necessary to offer all possible controls to users, just those most users are likely to use. For example, Gmail does not offer any controls for creating

FIGURE 8.2 Gmail offers users the option to switch the email text from rich text to plain text.

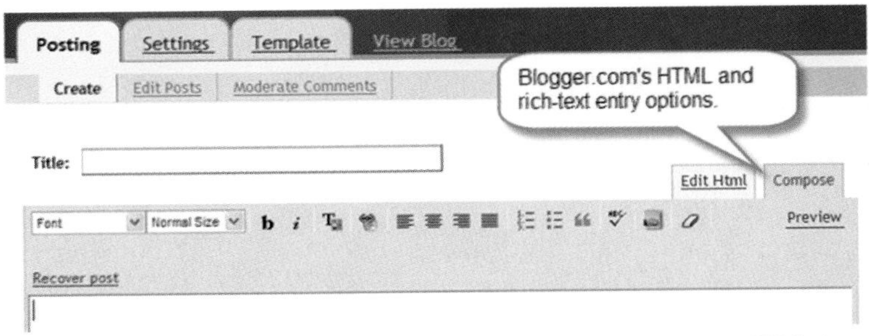

FIGURE 8.3 Blogger invites users to enter their posts in either rich-text or HTML format.

tables when composing an email (Figure 8.4). This does not mean that emails using rich-text editors should never offer users the option to create tables, but it is acceptable to restrict the set of rich-text controls.

ALLOW USERS TO ENLARGE THE TEXT-INPUT AREA

When users' text input is lengthy, viewing the composed text in the available area may be difficult. In such cases, allow users to enlarge text-input areas and/ or preview messages before posting. For example, Gmail (see Figure 8.4) and Yahoo! Mail (see Figure 8.1) both offer users the option to enlarge the text-input area, which launches the editor in a separate window so it can be enlarged as necessary (Figure 8.5).

FIGURE 8.4 Gmail does not offer users any controls to create tables when composing an email.

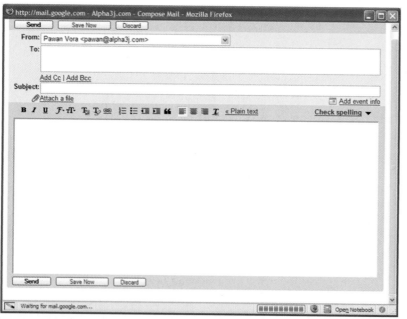

FIGURE 8.5 By launching the email editor in a separate window and allowing it to be resized as necessary, Gmail offers users a way to view larger amounts of information.

Related design patterns

RICH-TEXT EDITORS are comparable to LIVE PREVIEW—both are WYSIWYG tools. While RICH-TEXT EDITORS reflect the effects of the changes, LIVE PREVIEW allows users to view the effects of their configuration choices on an item or the interface itself.

RICH FORM

Problem

Some of the inefficiencies in filling out forms are caused by the need for users to wait after submitting the form for it to be validated. Fixing validation errors requires the form to be resubmitted and revalidated. In some instances, users have to be asked to fill out forms in short chunks because the dependencies in user choices can only be determined after the submitted form has been subjected to necessary business rules—for example, offering users a choice for a purchase order or credit card information based on their choice of billing.

Solution

In addition to patterns discussed in Chapter 2, such as FORGIVING FORMAT, INPUT HINTS/PROMPTS, SMART DEFAULTS, and REQUIRED FIELD INDICA-TORS, use interactive forms that validate users' input as it is entered, preventing errors by offering users only valid choices. In addition, wherever possible, show dependent or subordinate choices closer to the parent selection (Figure 8.6).

Why

A non–rich form requires users to enter data and submit the form to the server for validation or send bits of selections to the server to show dependent choices. The user is then presented with either the "success" page or errors to be corrected with an accompanying page refresh. Using a rich form not only eliminates page refreshes but also can possibly prevent them altogether by identifying errors at the source. Users also feel in control as errors and prompts are now well integrated with the form.

How

Design the form so that user input is validated either as it is being entered or when the user moves to the next form element (or the focus is removed from the current form element). If the data input or selection is invalid, present appropriate prompts or messages so that users can correct errors immediately (Figure 8.7).

DESIGN THE FORM TO MINIMIZE ERRORS

Not only can rich forms validate user input as users are filling out the form, they can also help minimize errors in the first place. For example, as shown in Figure 8.6, the AUTOSUGGEST/AUTOCOMPLETION pattern can offer users valid options while entering data; effective calendar controls can ensure valid

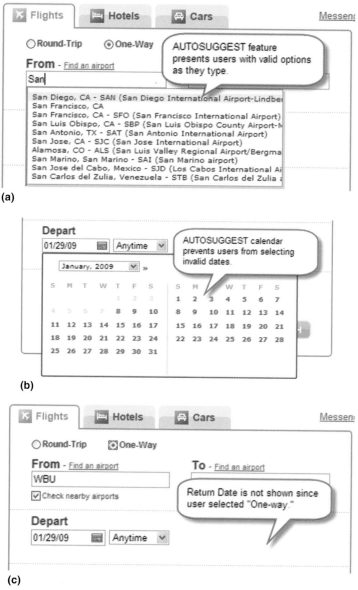

FIGURE 8.6 Yahoo! FareChase uses a combination of RIA technologies to make this form "rich": (a) the AUTOCOMPLETE pattern for "From" and "To" fields, (b) showing only valid dates for departure and arrival dates by disabling invalid dates, and (c) hiding the "Return" date when users indicate a one-way flight.

date selections; and enabling or disabling appropriate controls as per user selections can minimize incorrect data entry. Other common design elements include "drilldown" approaches to ensure that users see only correct dependent options (Figure 8.8) and password strength meters to ensure that users select secure passwords (Figure 8.9).

FIGURE 8.7
When registering, Picnik validates information as soon as it is entered. Once validated, form elements are supplemented with appropriate icons to indicate if entered information is valid.

FIGURE 8.8
As users select a make, Kelly's Blue Book updates the "All Models" dropdown menu by offering them only valid choices.

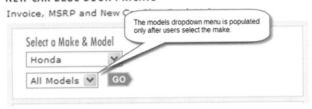

FIGURE 8.9 As users enter passwords, a password strength meter rates the password from weak to strong, enabling users to choose better passwords.

Related design patterns

As shown in the examples, richness in forms is achieved by patterns such as AUTOSUGGEST/AUTOCOMPLETION as they respond to users' input to show only valid choices to prevent errors. A SLIDER pattern (aiding user entry for data ranges) and DELAY/PROGRESS INDICATORS (communicating progress during user waiting periods) are also common with RICH FORMS.

AUTOSUGGEST/AUTOCOMPLETION

Problem

Because the total number of possible items at the outset is fairly large, presenting users a standard dropdown list is not feasible when users enter data such

FIGURE 8.10 Google combines AUTOSUGGEST options with search results. As users enter a term, they see a menu showing potential search terms along with the total number of matched results. Users can click the desired suggestion in the menu or navigate to it using the up and down arrow keys.

as dates, email addresses, search terms, and so forth. However, it is possible to predict these data based on task context or partial user input. In addition, text being entered may be lengthy or difficult to remember, making errors likely and resulting in suboptimal user experience.

Solution

Suggest possible alternatives as users enter data and allow them to select one of the suggested alternatives (Figure 8.10).

Why

By suggesting matches and allowing users to select from a list, not only is the interaction made more efficient, since users can quickly focus on the correct choice, but the potential for errors is minimized as well. Because *recognition is easier than recall*, it is easier for users to recognize the correct syntax or format of information from available choices than recall it—for example, it's easier to pick San Antonio (SAT) from a list of airports than to remember the code for it.

How

The user interface element for this pattern is a text box that allows free-form data entry. As users type, they are shown a list of items (below the text box) that closely match what has been typed so far. As users continue to type, the list continues to narrow down until the desired item is suggested or no matching items are found. In cases where related information is available for suggested

> **NOTE**
>
> For non-RIA applications, where potential choices for users are finite, users would typically be offered a "Select" button next to the text field. Clicking "Select" would open a pop-up window (or take users to another page) to allow users to select the desired item from a paginated or scrolling list; users may be offered a search mechanism as well.

FIGURE 8.11
Yahoo! Mail shows both matching names and email addresses when users enter a recipient's email address.

FIGURE 8.12 Kayak shows both city and airport codes when users specify departure and arrival locations.

items and could help users make a correct choice, include it as well. For example, when entering an email address, show both the address and name (Figure 8.11), or when entering the city in an air travel–reservation application, show both the city and airport code (Figure 8.12). Another example is to indicate the total number of matches for a given search query, as done by Google Suggest (see Figure 8.10).

ENABLE KEYBOARD ACCESS TO SELECT AN ITEM IN THE SUGGESTED LIST

Asking users to take their hands off the keyboard and use the mouse to select an item from the suggested list would be inefficient. Therefore, allow users to navigate within the suggested list of items using the up and down arrow keys, and select highlighted items using either the "Enter" or "Tab" key. For search applications, the "Enter" key can take users directly to the search results page and for web applications that have additional fields, move the focus to the next logical form element.

HIGHLIGHT THE FIRST MATCH IN THE SUGGESTED LIST

Highlight the very first match in the suggested list (see Figures 8.11 and 8.12) and allow users to select it by pressing the "Tab" or "Enter" key. The application should then populate the text field with the highlighted item. However, it is important that users indicate their intent by pressing the "Tab" or "Enter" key and that the application not infer users' intent and type the rest of the text for them.

Related design patterns

The AUTOSUGGEST/AUTOCOMPLETION pattern is typically used in RICH FORMS and DYNAMIC QUERYING to restrict users' input to valid choices and thus prevent errors.

EDIT-IN-PLACE

Problem

When users are creating or editing items with just a few properties (no more than three or four), showing a pop-up window, or taking users to a separate "editor" page makes the interaction inefficient. This is because users have to launch the editor, make changes, save those changes, and wait for the page to refresh to see updated information.

Solution

Allow users to create a new item or make changes to the properties of an existing item "in place" using a lightweight editor (Figure 8.13). In some instances, it is better to offer users the "edit-in-place" option only for editing a few chunks of information of existing items but not for creating new items. For example, in a bug-tracking application, changing an existing bug's status is more suitable for edit-in-place, but creating a new bug entry may not be beneficial with

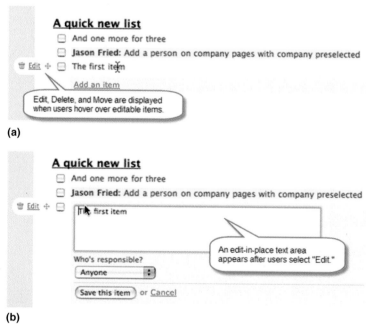

FIGURE 8.13 When users hover over an editable to-do item, Basecamp shows "Edit," "Delete," and "Move" options (a). When they click "Edit," they are shown the to-do item editor with the "Save this item" and "Cancel" options (b).

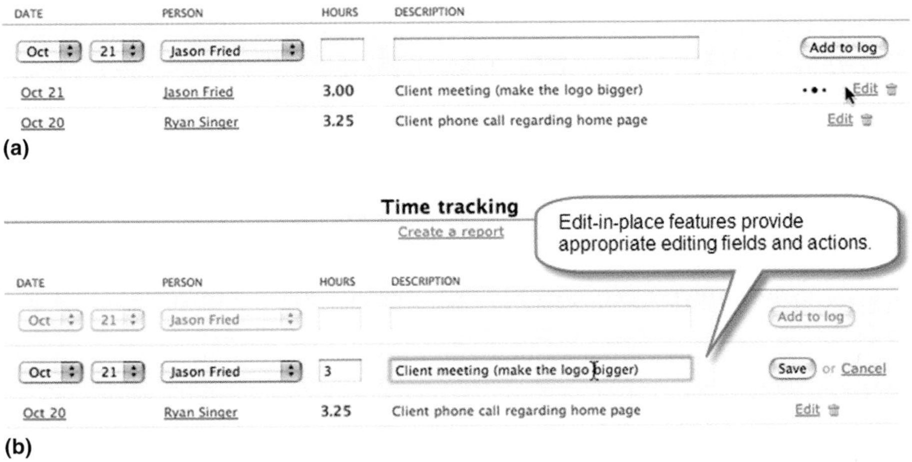

FIGURE 8.14
In Basecamp, users can edit a time-tracking item in-line. When a user clicks "Edit" next to a list item (a), the item becomes editable and "Edit" and "Delete" options are replaced by "Save" and "Cancel" (b).

edit-in-place, since entering a bug requires entering several pieces of information such as a brief title, description, steps to recreate the bug, and so forth.

Why

Allowing users to change an item's properties in its original context, without popping up a separate window or going to a new page, is a far easier way to provide or change a few snippets of data. Requiring users to go to a separate page makes the interaction discontinuous because users have to wait for the editor to load and then switch their attention to a new context.

How

When users activate an edit feature, put the item in the "edit" mode by showing its properties in editable fields (i.e., text boxes, dropdown buttons, or other form controls as necessary). Users can then make necessary changes and either save or cancel their changes to return to the "read" mode (Figure 8.14).

If necessary, use more space for the "edit" mode. In addition, since being able to edit text may be a new experience for web users, provide necessary prompts or instructions to let users know how the feature works; providing instructions and/or actions when users hover over an editable item is a common way to inform users.

SELECT THE TEXT FOR ITEMS WITH ONLY ONE EDITABLE PROPERTY

If the item being changed has only one editable property (e.g., name or title), select the item's text so that users can simply overwrite existing text (Figure 8.15).

Related design patterns

When edited information is being saved, it's often useful to show a DELAY/ PROGRESS INDICATOR to confirm the "save" action's progress. When using

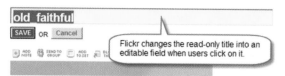

FIGURE 8.15 Flickr allows users to edit a photo's title by clicking on it. When users click the title, the text of the title is selected by default, allowing them to overwrite it.

EDIT-IN-PLACE for a new item, a SPOTLIGHT/YELLOW-FADE technique may be used to indicate the addition of items.

OVERVIEW-PLUS-DETAIL

Problem

When presented with a large dataset, users may want to zoom in to different areas of the dataset to access detailed information. At other times, users may want to zoom out to a higher "overview" level to get reoriented. Requiring users to go back and forth between an overview and a detail view makes navigating the information space extremely inefficient.

Solution

Show users both the overview and detail view panes with a movable viewport in the overview pane that shows the zoomed-in area (Figure 8.16).

Why

When working with information spaces that are too large to fit on screens, users have to access information by zooming in and out to view the desired detail.

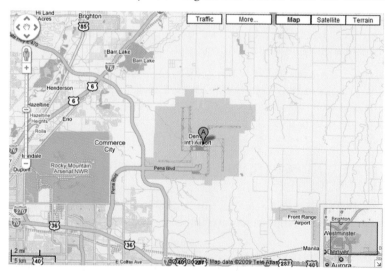

FIGURE 8.16 Google Maps show the overview pane in the bottom-right corner with a viewport highlighting the currently zoomed-in area.

By allowing users to view details of the areas of interest while simultaneously seeing the overview (albeit in a much coarser resolution), the need to zoom out to access other areas of the information space is eliminated. Allowing users to move or manipulate viewports also makes it easy to quickly navigate the information space without losing context. Moreover, showing viewports in the overview pane provides a sense of where the user is in the information space; in essence, it answers the common orientation-related question: Where am I?

This pattern is based on one of the basic principles of information visualization: focus plus context.

> First, the user needs both overview (context) and detail information (focus) simultaneously. Second, information needed in the overview may be different from that needed in detail. Third, these two types of information can be combined within a single (dynamic) display, much as in human vision. (Card et al., 1999, p. 307)

The main design implication of this principle is to show selected regions of interest in greater detail (i.e., focus) and to preserve a global view at reduced detail (i.e., context) in such a way that all information is visible simultaneously.

How

Make the overview pane available to users at all times. It can be positioned as an inset pane within the detail pane (see Figure 8.16) or positioned next to the detail pane (Figure 8.17).

Show the viewport within the overview, highlighting the currently zoomed-in portion of the detail pane. Allow users to drag the viewport within the overview pane to zoom in to different areas within the overview. If users can pan information in the detail pane, move the viewport in the overview pane along with it. If feasible, allow users to adjust the viewport size to change the dataset's

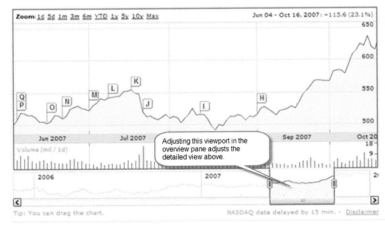

FIGURE 8.17 Google Finance positions the overview and detail panes, one above the other, and allows users to see detailed price trends for a stock by letting them adjust the viewport size in the overview pane.

scale in the detail pane. For example, Google Finance allows users to change the viewport size so they can zoom in or out of the date range for the stock price–trend chart (see Figure 8.17).

Related design patterns

When zooming and panning the detail area or moving and/or resizing the viewport, using DRAG-AND-DROP is necessary. Additionally, some type of visual effects (ANIMATION/TRANSITIONS) may be employed to allow users to maintain the visual continuity between states.

DYNAMIC QUERYING

Problem

When presented with a large number of items, users may want to "tune" their criteria to reduce the number of items to a manageable set. Although traditional filtering mechanisms address the problem (see the FILTERING pattern in Chapter 6), user interaction can become cumbersome, since with every filtering choice users need to "submit" their criteria and wait for the page to refresh to see an updated item list.

Solution

Allow users to filter items using a set of interactive controls (i.e., sliders, checkboxes, radio buttons, and so forth) so that with each selection, they can see updated results without having to wait for the page to refresh (Figure 8.18).

Why

In traditional web applications, filtering requires users to make narrowing selections, submit them to the server, and wait to view the updated result set after a refresh. With every filtering choice, users go through the same process, leading to an interrupted experience. RIAs eliminate the explicit "submit" action and accompanying page refreshes, thus providing a more fluid and interactive experience.

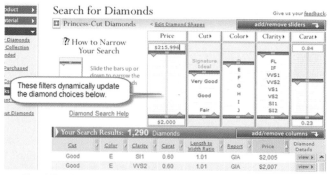

FIGURE 8.18 Blue Nile allows users to narrow diamond choices by allowing them to filter by price, cut, color, clarity, and carat. The range for each choice is selected by users using sliders.

How

Show criteria to users as a set of checkboxes, sliders, radio buttons, and links along with results. As users make different selections, narrow or expand the results set without any page refreshes, enabling users to immediately see the effects of their choices (Figure 8.19).

To the extent possible, make all choices visible to users and minimize the use of dropdown lists or hidden (cascading) options.

Related design patterns

Although DYNAMIC QUERYING is a powerful way to show users a filtered dataset in almost real time, processing delays are inevitable. Therefore, the DELAY/PROCESS INDICATORS pattern commonly accompanies this pattern.

LIVE PREVIEW

Problem

Unlike off-the-shelf, mass-produced products, many new products can be customized to users' preferences along one or more product attributes. For example, when purchasing a car, users may customize its color, trim, and other options and accessories. However, not being able to see the effect of their choices can leave users unsure about their selections and prevent them from exploring other possibilities. In addition, asking users to wait to see the effect of their changes after every selection can become tiresome.

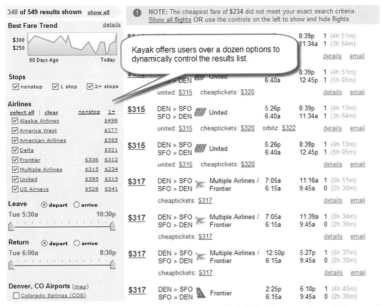

FIGURE 8.19 Kayak allows users to filter matching flights by the number of stops, airline, arrival and departure times, arrival and departure airports, and several other options.

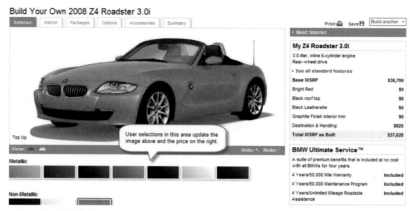

FIGURE 8.20 BMW allows users to customize their vehicles by allowing them to select exterior and interior colors (among other options). As users make selections, their choices are immediately reflected in the image and in price. BMW also offers "Undo" and "Redo" options, making it easy for users to return to their previous choices.

Solution

Show users a preview of the item with their selections immediately without having to "submit" their choices and waiting for the page to refresh (Figure 8.20).

Why

Allowing users to preview the results of their selections makes it easier for them to decide whether they want to keep, change, or discard their choices. Also, by offering immediate feedback, live preview invites exploration not possible with traditional web applications, which require users to make selections, request a preview, and wait for the application to show the effects of their choices.

This is similar to the RICH-TEXT EDITOR pattern where users customize text in terms of color and formatting and can see the results immediately in a WYSIWYG fashion.

How

Offer users customization options along with an image of the actual item. As users choose different options, update the item's image to reflect their choices.

CONSIDER SHOWING MULTIPLE VIEWS OF THE CUSTOMIZED ITEM

For three-dimensional items or items with multiple surfaces, consider showing users multiple views of the customized item so that they clearly understand the impact of their choices. For example, Nike allows users to view the customized shoe from a variety of angles such as top view, side view, front view, and so forth (Figure 8.21). Similarly, BMW allows users to switch between the front and back views to customize the exterior (see Figure 8.20) and between the driver's view and dashboard view to customize the interior (see Figure 8.22).

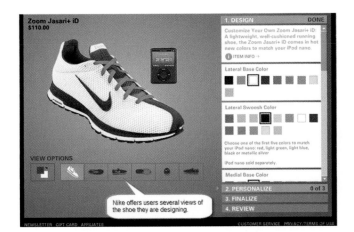

FIGURE 8.21 NIKEiD presents users a customized view from a variety of angles.

FIGURE 8.22 BMW offers users the driver's side view and dashboard view when they are customizing the car's interior.

Lands End, on the other hand, offers not only the front and back view but also a view showing a model wearing the customized item (Figure 8.23).

Related design patterns

As mentioned, the LIVE PREVIEW pattern is similar to the RICH-TEXT EDITOR pattern in that it attempts to provide a WYSIWYG view of users' selections as they are made. In addition, preview is useful when users are customizing the interface; CUSTOMIZATION is a relevant pattern as well (see Chapter 4).

DRAG-AND-DROP

Problem

Traditional web applications require indirect methods for rearranging or reordering data items. For example, users can reorder a list of items in one of two ways: select the desired item and choose up or down actions or enter the

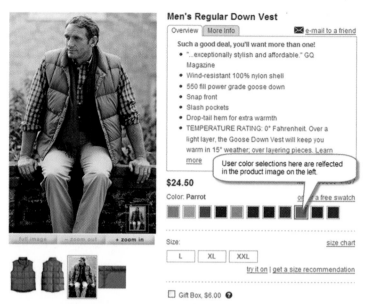

FIGURE 8.23 Lands End shows a model wearing the customized clothing.

FIGURE 8.24
My MSN allows users to drag-and-drop columns to customize column order.

desired order of items in text fields and select a "reorder" action. Although both these approaches are reasonable, they do not provide users immediate feedback of their actions and can be cumbersome for even relatively short lists.

Solution

Allow users to directly manipulate data items and/or page components using a drag-and-drop interaction style (Figure 8.24).

Why

In non-RIA web applications, moving or rearranging of data items typically requires taking users to another page, where the effects of the changes are not visible until the desired rearrangement is submitted to the server and the original page is updated to reflect the new order or layout. Employing direct-manipulation methods similar to those common in most desktop applications (e.g., deleting a document by dragging it to the trash) can make the interaction efficient and encourage exploration.

How

Allow users to drag data items (or components) from their current place, move them to a new location and place, and drop them there. Drag-and-drop may be used for the following:

- Rearranging items on a list (Figure 8.25).
- Moving overlaying pop-ups from one location to another (Figure 8.26).
- Building lists such as adding an item to the shopping cart (Figure 8.27).
- Indicating an action (Figure 8.28).
- Resizing an object (Figure 8.29).

When supporting drag-and-drop, it is important that the user interface is responsive and changes are shown instantly without any delays.

Home Projects

- Clean garage
- Hang pictures
- Create home inventory

FIGURE 8.25 Ta-Da Lists allows users to reorder items in their list using a drag-and-drop mechanism.

FIGURE 8.26 Live Maps from Microsoft allows users to move the scratch pad pop-up using drag-and-drop. It also increases the transparency of the scratch pad, allowing users to see the map and to indicate the "dragging" mode.

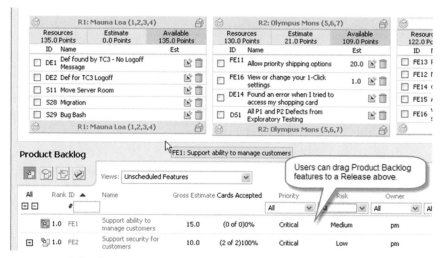

FIGURE 8.27 Rally allows users to move items from the Product Backlog to a Release, which aids planning and developing high-level estimates.

FIGURE 8.28 iGoogle allows users to drop a "portlet" onto a tab, which indicates the action of moving it to that tab. This example shows the "Stock Market" portlet being dragged from the "Home" tab to the "Finance" tab.

FIGURE 8.29
Picnik allows users to
resize an image using
drag-and-drop.

OFFER NECESSARY AFFORDANCE FOR DRAG-AND-DROP AREAS

It is important that the user interface clearly indicate what is (and is not) "draggable," and which areas are (and are not) valid "drop" zones. This can be accomplished by:

- Showing clear handles for dragging.
- Changing the cursor to a "move" icon (✥) when it hovers over "draggable" items by setting the CSS **cursor** property to **move**. When using drag-and-drop

for resizing, use the "resize" icon (⬉) by setting the CSS **cursor** property to **nw-resize**, **sw-resize**, **w-resize**, and so on, as appropriate.
- Highlighting drop zones when an item is dragged over it.
- Not highlighting nondrop zones, which should show a "not allowed" icon (⊘), by setting the CSS **cursor** property to **not-allowed**.

> **NOTE**
>
> Drag-and-drop is not accessible to users with visual and/or motor disabilities. Therefore, the interface should always use drag-and-drop interaction redundantly and offer other more accessible ways to allow rearrangement of data items. See Chapter 11 for more information on accessibility.

Related design patterns

The DRAG-AND-DROP pattern is also used to make selections using SLIDERS in DYNAMIC QUERYING and moving or adjusting viewport sizes in OVERVIEW-PLUS-DETAIL.

SLIDER

Problem

Specifying one or more values between a range of values is error-prone, as users have to know valid values. In addition, they also need to know the precision of the desired input (e.g., 10 versus 10.1 versus 10.12). Although such information can be included in the page design, the page may get cluttered as the number of form elements requiring such data input increase.

Solution

Offer users a slider control specifying an acceptable range of values. Users can then drag the slider(s) to set a value (Figure 8.30) or a range of values (Figure 8.31).

Why

For traditional web applications, because of a lack of native support for the slider control in the current version of HTML, users are offered a text field, a set of radio

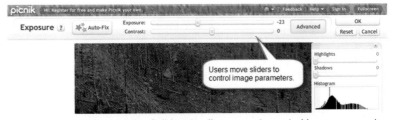

FIGURE 8.30 Picnik uses a variety of sliders to allow users to control image parameters such as highlights, shadows, histogram, exposure, contrast, and so on.

FIGURE 8.31 Kayak uses two handles for each "Flight Times" slider to allow users to set a range for "Leave" and "Return" times.

buttons, or dropdown lists to specify one or more values within a range. However, sliders provide an easier and more direct method of selecting a value within a range (Galitz, 2002). In addition, they prevent user errors when compared with entering values in text fields. Another important advantage of sliders is that the data range can be continuous as well as discrete, and the design of the slider can convey the appropriate precision of user input. It is also faster to select values using sliders when compared to a selection involving a text-input field or radio buttons.

How

Allow users to set one value or a range of values by dragging and dropping the slider(s) in the slider control. In addition to drag-and-drop, enable users to click directly on the arm to move the slider to the clicked location. Allow users to control the slider using the left, right, up, and down arrow keys on the keyboard as well. It is important that the arrow keys match the orientation of the slider—that is, left and right arrow keys should work for horizontal sliders and up and down arrow keys should work for vertical sliders. However, it is good practice to have the other set of arrow keys work as well. Finally, where feasible, allow users to simply enter the value in a text field (Figure 8.32).

FIGURE 8.32 Splashup (from Faux Labs) allows users to specify colors by entering RGB (red, green, blue) values or the corresponding hexadecimal values. Because of the context and users' familiarity with color selection in other desktop-based image-editing applications, providing verbal descriptors for the sliders is not necessary.

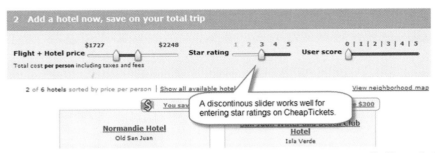

FIGURE 8.33 CheapTickets uses a discontinuous slider to allow users to specify filter criteria for hotels' star rating and user score.

Most slider implementations are for selecting a value on a continuous scale within a range of available values. However, when users may only select discrete values within a given range, use a discontinuous slider that, when dragged, jumps from one value to another to prevent users from considering a value between two discrete values (Figure 8.33). Users should be able to click on any discrete value to have the slider jump to that value.

USE DESCRIPTIVE ANCHORS FOR SLIDER ARM VALUES

When using sliders for continuous values, use anchor labels (i.e., descriptors or icons) at the end of the slider arm (see Figure 8.33). For sliders with discrete values, use labels at each end as well as for each major value on the slider arm (see Figure 8.33). For sliders conveying colors or other multiattribute values, labels may not be necessary; however, show all attribute values such as RGB or hexadecimal values for colors (see Figure 8.32).

INFORM USERS OF THE SELECTED VALUE(S)

For both continuous- and discrete-value sliders, users should always know the value(s) they have selected. In addition, when selected values affect more than one value (e.g., specifying a color using RGB, CMYK [cyan, magenta, yellow, black], or hexadecimal values), show users all the values (see Figure 8.32).

Related design patterns

The DRAG-AND-DROP pattern is essential to make slider controls work because users drag the slider to indicate their selections. Slider controls are also commonly used in DYNAMIC QUERYING and may be applicable in RICH FORMS to specify one or more values within a range.

ANIMATIONS/TRANSITIONS
Problem

An important usability heuristic is to "keep users informed" of changes in the interface (Nielsen and Molich, 1990). When using RIAs, often only a part of the

FIGURE 8.34 When an item is added to the shopping cart, Gap slides the shopping cart down on the same page to indicate that the selected item was added to the cart. This eliminates the need to take users to the shopping cart page and have a "Continue Shopping" button, an interaction approach commonly followed on most non-RIA e-commerce sites.

interface is changing, and it is quite likely that users will be unaware of those changes because they are focusing on other interface areas. In addition, when users are interacting with the application causing the page's state to change—for example, showing the next set of photos when using the CAROUSEL pattern or zooming in and out of an image—showing users just the final state without showing intermediate states can be abrupt and disorienting, since they may find it difficult to understand the relationship between the initial and final states.

Solution

Use appropriate visual effects (i.e., transitions and animations) to direct users' attention to page changes (Figure 8.34).

Why

Because our peripheral vision is attuned to detect movement (Faraday and Sutcliffe 1997; Peterson and Dugas, 1972), using animation to direct users' attention to changes on the page is a useful and effective technique, especially for RIAs, where the page does not refresh with changes in the page's content.

Animations and transitions also have an aesthetic value that cannot be ignored. They make web applications appear interactive and dynamic and contribute to the characterization of RIAs as "cool," an attribute commonly lacking in traditional web applications, which are limited to relatively static images and layouts in their visual designs.

How

For RIAs, use animation when page elements change appearance but not position (Figure 8.35; see also Figure 8.46 later in the chapter) or when they move from one position to another but not necessarily change appearance (see Figure 8.34).

(a)

(b)

FIGURE 8.35 When users hover over the Amazon's logo (a), its appearance changes (b), making it look like a button. It is the most basic type of animation.

FIGURE 8.36 A commonly used "please wait" animated icon for RIAs.

Users may be shown a very simple animation to demonstrate that the system is busy loading information or saving data (Figure 8.36; see also the ICONS pattern in Chapter 12).

In some instances, a similar animation may be used to force a delay, indicating to users that their request was received. When the animation disappears, they know that the request was processed and they can resume; an animated progress bar may be used for longer wait times (see the DELAY/PROGRESS INDICATOR pattern next). Upon successfully processing user requests, the updated element's background can be faded out to subtly indicate the change on the page (see the SPOTLIGHT/YELLOW-FADE pattern later in this chapter).

USE TRANSITIONS WHEN INTRODUCING OR REMOVING CONTENT ON A PAGE

When showing new page content (or exposing hidden content), use appropriate transition effects. For example, when showing new content, consider using a slide-down (or slide-up, slide-left, or slide-right) transition effect (Figure 8.37).

Slide-up and slide-down transition effects are most common for expand and collapse actions, respectively, in treelike structures or when using accordion controls for menus.

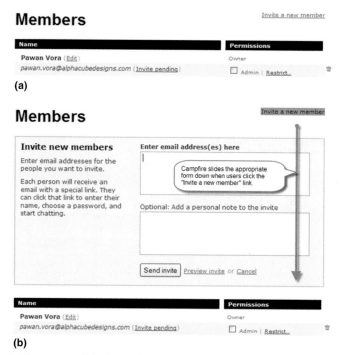

(a)

(b)

FIGURE 8.37 When users click the "Invite a new member" link (a), Campfire uses a slide-down transition to show the "Invite new members" editor (b).

FIGURE 8.38 When users click on the "next" or "back" arrow buttons, Hulu uses slide-left and slide-right transitions, respectively, to show the next or previous episode feature.

Match the transition direction to the direction implied in the user action. For example, if users click the "next" button, use the slide-left transition; conversely, use the slide-right transition when users click the "back" button (Figure 8.38; see also the CAROUSEL pattern later in this chapter).

PLAY ANIMATIONS BRIEFLY

The goal of animation should be to attract users' attention and inform them about something. Once that's done, the animation should either remain static or disappear; it should not loop endlessly.

AVOID GRATUITOUS ANIMATIONS

Animation is an effective tool only when it serves a specific purpose such as communicating state changes and/or improving interaction.

Because animated elements of a page draw users' eyes, frivolous animations divert users' focus from valuable page information. Therefore, do not use animation gratuitously—all it does is distract. Gratuitous animations that do not communicate include visual effects such as using a marquee (of course, it is acceptable when showing a stock ticker tape).

Related design patterns

Another way to keep users informed of changes in the interface is to use the DELAY/PROGRESS INDICATORS and SPOTLIGHT/YELLOW-FADE patterns.

DELAY/PROGRESS INDICATORS

Problem

Even though RIAs strive to provide real-time feedback, users often face noticeable server or processing delays before processing is complete and new information is presented.

Solution

Show users either a delay indicator to suggest the system is busy processing the request (Figure 8.39) or a progress indicator not only to indicate that the system is busy but also to indicate progress in terms of percentage complete, stage of processing, time remaining, or a combination thereof (Figure 8.40).

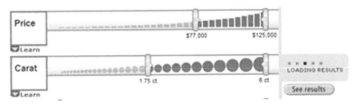

FIGURE 8.39 Amazon's progress indicator for diamond search (short delay).

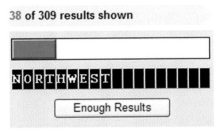

FIGURE 8.40 Kayak uses a progress bar when retrieving matching flight information (long delay).

Why

Showing wait/progress indicators serves two purposes:

1. They let users know the application has received their request and is working on it.
2. They keep users informed about where the application is in terms of processing the request.

Users can use this information to anticipate the amount of time they have to wait and can opt to cancel the operation. Like the ANIMATIONS/TRANSITIONS pattern, progress indicators provide necessary feedback to users and keep them informed of the system status (Galitz, 2002; Nielsen and Molich, 1990).

How

Different approaches may be used to indicate progress depending on the length of the delay. For shorter delays (less than 10–15 seconds), progress indicators may take the form of:

- A text message such as "loading" or "please wait …" (Figure 8.41).
- An animated icon (e.g., an hour-glass) (see Figure 8.36).

For longer delays (more than 10–15 seconds), use a progress bar that shows the extent of progress and that indicates the status and/or an estimate of remaining time. If completing an action is going to take a long time, let users cancel the operation at any time (Figure 8.42).

FIGURE 8.41 Kayak uses an "Updating results" message for shorter-duration delays.

FIGURE 8.42
When loading a photo, Picnik uses a progress bar that shows the extent of progress. Users are also offered the option to cancel the upload process at any time.

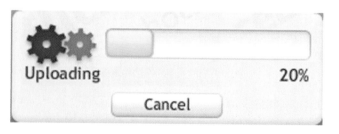

FIGURE 8.43 Picnik uses interesting progress bar messages (e.g., "Fluffing clouds" or "Sprinkling dew") while loading the application.

For really long delays, show status information or other engaging content to shorten the perception of the delay (Figure 8.43).

Related design patterns

Processing delays, usually shorter ones, are quite common in DYNAMIC QUERYING and EDIT-IN-PLACE implementations. If users need to be informed about any page changes when processing is complete, the SPOTLIGHT/YELLOW-FADE pattern may be useful.

SPOTLIGHT/YELLOW-FADE

Problem

Often, it is important to direct user attention to a specific page change either caused by a user action or initiated by the system. Because the change is not significant enough to keep the updated information highlighted (see the HIGHLIGHT pattern in Chapter 12) and because several elements on the page could change over a period of time, permanently highlighting may make the interface appear cluttered. Offering messages that inform users of changes for monitoring-type applications that show live data, such as stock quotes or sports scores, may make the interface jumpy and distracting, as values on such interfaces keep changing frequently.

Solution

Highlight the changed area for a very brief period—like a spotlight—to create an animation-type effect that grabs user attention. This approach is a generic version of the yellow-fade technique proposed by Linderman (2004) to subtly spotlight a recently changed area on a page (Figure 8.44).

Why

This brief highlighting approach helps provide sufficient animated effect to get users to quickly attend to the change when relatively small changes are happening on the page. Additionally, because the effect is transient, users not only are not distracted by the highlight and can return to the task at hand, but the interface remains uncluttered as well.

How

Highlight changed content briefly (no more than a few seconds) to create an animation-like effect. Choose an unsaturated highlight color that provides a noticeable contrast from the rest of the background (Figure 8.45).

(a)

(b)

(c)

FIGURE 8.44 When users return to a page with a recent change, the changed area is highlighted (a). After a few seconds it gradually fades out (b) to return to the normal background (c). The change is thus communicated to the user without cluttering the interface. (*Source:* Linderman, 2004.)

Related design patterns

Use of the SPOTLIGHT/YELLOW-FADE pattern is quite common in EDIT-IN-PLACE implementations and PORTALS with portlets that provide live data updates (see Chapter 4).

(a) (b) (c)

FIGURE 8.45 Picnik uses the spotlight technique when applying the "Exposure > Autofix." Using this approach eliminates the need for dedicating a certain interface area for such messaging. Also, because the message fades out within a few seconds, users do not have to dismiss it and can continue working with the image.

CAROUSEL

Problem

The total number of items (either images or a combination of images and text) to be presented to users cannot be accommodated in the available space.

Solution

Show items as a "carousel" to allow users to browse through them quickly. Although the notion of a carousel conjures up a circular structure to facilitate navigation both forward and backward, many implementations of the carousel are linear and work as viewports that allow users to view a few items at a time, and go forward and backward to access remaining items (Figure 8.46).

Why

A carousel allows users access to several items in a relatively small amount of screen real estate and allows designers to allocate more space per item. Using circular carousels also enables users to access items by clicking on either left or right arrows. Carousels are most commonly used for images; for example, when browsing through photo albums (*www.flickr.com*); movies, music, or book listings (*movies.yahoo.com, www.amazon.com*); or real estate listings (*www. zillow.com, www.funda.nl*).

How

Present items in carousels either vertically or horizontally as a "strip" with navigation buttons (usually arrows) at each end of the strip (Figure 8.47). In designs where a carousel is implemented as a slideshow, highlight the item currently being viewed (see Figure 8.46). In addition, use a "slide" transition effect when one set of items in the carousel is replaced by the next set to indicate the relationship among the items.

INFORM USERS OF THE PRESENCE, OR ABSENCE, OF ADDITIONAL ITEMS

When using linear carousels, let users know whether additional items are available by enabling or disabling left and right arrows as appropriate. For example,

FIGURE 8.46
Flickr uses a carousel
approach in their
slideshow.

FIGURE 8.47 Amazon presents items in the carousel horizontally with prominent buttons at each side.

when users reach the end of the carousel, disable the right arrow, and when users revert to the first item, disable the left arrow. Pagination cues may also be used to indicate that users have reached the first or last item in the set (Figure 8.48). Additionally, a partial image of the previous or next item in the carousel may be shown (Figure 8.49).

Related design patterns

CAROUSELS use visual effects (ANIMATIONS/TRANSITIONS), such as slide-left, slide-right, slide-up, and slide-down, to allow users to maintain visual context between items in the carousel. For linear carousels, use PAGINATION indicators to show users' location within the carousel (see Chapter 6).

USABILITY ISSUES INHERENT WITH RIAS

Like any other web application, poorly designed RIAs can undermine usability and must be tested for usability. In fact, there are a few inherent usability issues with RIAs designers must be aware of. These issues relate to the use of the "back" button and bookmarking (or favorites) functionality.

The "back" button problem

Users who are not used to RIA-style web applications may not be aware that it is possible for part of a page to update, so when they see a piece of a web page

FIGURE 8.48 Yahoo! Food uses left and right navigation arrows for browsing. Also, because it uses a linear carousel, it uses pagination-like indicators (as dots) to indicate which "section" the user is viewing.

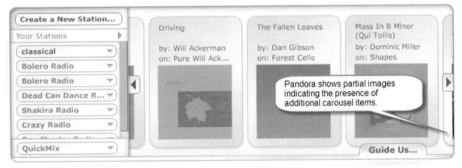

FIGURE 8.49 Pandora shows partial images of previous and next songs to indicate the presence of additional carousel items.

change, they may think they have navigated to a new page. They may then try to click the browser's "back" button to return to the previous state of the application, which takes them to the previous page in the browser's history instead of the previous state of the application. Although users are trying to undo a previous action, they typically find themselves completely out of their task context and could potentially lose data.

A common solution to this problem is to allow users to undo their actions on the same page. However, it is more important to understand users' natural behavior with the application and determine if the RIA approach is appropriate for the task at hand. A good example is Gmail, which uses RIA for lists or emails (i.e., "Inbox," "Starred," "Sent Mail," etc.) and when viewing conversations (i.e., chronological thread of email exchanges) but allows users to use the browser's "back" button to return from the conversation page to the list page (Figure 8.50).

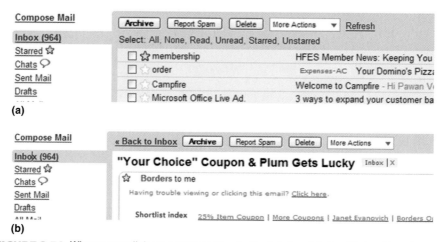

FIGURE 8.50 When users click on a conversation in the list view (a), Gmail takes them to a separate page (b). This allows users to click the browser's "Back" button to return to the list page from the conversation page.

The bookmarking problem

Because the browser's location/address bar stays exactly the same when users select functions and change the application's state, turning bookmarking into specific application views is impossible. Although some clever approaches are available to address the bookmarking problem by rewriting URLs, it is typically not a big issue for web applications because users do not need to bookmark specific states. For more information on URL rewriting, see AJAX: How to Handle Bookmarks and Back Buttons, Brad Neuberg (2005) at *www.onjava. com/pub/a/onjava/2005/10/26/ajax-handling-bookmarks-and-back-button.html*

CHAPTER 9

Social Applications

INTRODUCTION

Increasingly, web applications are designed to encourage user participation and sharing. User participation is typically in the form of user-contributed content, where users add their own content to the application (ADD/UPLOAD CONTENT) and describe it using tags (TAGGING). Other ways for users to participate is by providing RATINGS and REVIEWS of content offered by the application. Many applications also involve users in promoting items by letting them vote for their usefulness and relevance (VOTE TO PROMOTE).

To ensure that user participation leads to a trusted online community, users have to establish an account with the application and create a USER PROFILE. Although for products and services, trust may be established through RATINGS and REVIEWS, for users it's important that they achieve a high REPUTATION, especially if they want to transact online or gain respect of other online community members. One aspect of reputation is based on the size of users' social networks. Social applications, therefore, facilitate users to connect with others with shared interests, backgrounds, and experiences (DISCOVER NETWORK MEMBERS). Once discovered, not only can they "friend" them (FRIEND LIST) and/or "follow" their activities online, but they can also create groups to discuss and share common interests (GROUPS/SPECIAL-INTEREST COMMUNITIES). Social applications also facilitate interaction among friends by allowing them to chat in real time, send messages to each other, and write comments in shared areas (MESSAGING); for encouraging real-time messaging it's also important to convey users' online status (PRESENCE INDICATOR).

Participation and interaction are further enhanced when users can share photos, news stories, videos, bookmarks, and other content—commonly referred to as *social objects*—with their friends and trusted colleagues (SHARING) or work together to coordinate activities and events or co-create content (COLLABORATION).

ADD/UPLOAD CONTENT

Problem

Users need to transfer content files, such as music, photos, presentations, and so forth, from their own computers to those of the application providers to share them with other users.

Solution

Provide users a way to upload one or more content files. In addition, if appropriate, allow users to describe (and tag) the content and indicate their preferences for who can view it (Figure 9.1).

Why

Making uploading of files easier is essential for web applications that rely on users to provide content. Furthermore, to make it easy for users to find their uploaded content, allow them to tag it (see the TAGGING pattern next).

How

In most cases, users will have the content files on their computer. Therefore, make it easy for them to upload them from their computer. When users are likely to upload several files at a time, such as when uploading photos, allow them to select multiple files and upload them all together (Figure 9.2).

ALLOW USERS TO COPY FILES FROM OTHER ONLINE SOURCES

In cases where users may already have uploaded their files (e.g., photos) on sites such as Picasa or Flickr, make it easy for them to transfer files directly from

FIGURE 9.1 SlideShare allows users to upload content (i.e., presentations) as well as provides a way to describe and label it to make it easy to find and share. In addition, to facilitate uploading of content, SlideShare offers several upload options: bulk upload, single upload, URL upload, email upload, and browser plug-in.

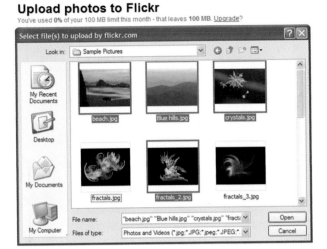

FIGURE 9.2 Flickr allows users to select and upload multiple photos at the same time.

FIGURE 9.3 MyFolia allows users to import photos from their Flickr, Picasa, or Gravatar accounts.

those accounts (Figure 9.3) rather than make them search for the files on their computers or download them from the original site to their computers before uploading them again.

ALLOW USERS TO REMOVE SELECTED CONTENT FILES FOR UPLOAD

It is possible for users to select incorrect files to upload or change their minds about certain files after they have selected them. Allow them to remove such files (Figure 9.4).

File
Size
Remove?
P1000020.JPG
2.41 MB
Blue hills.jpg
crystals.jpg
Users can remove a photo selected for upload.

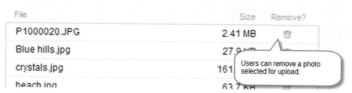

FIGURE 9.4 Flickr allows users to remove files selected for upload.

ALLOW USERS TO SET PRIVACY PREFERENCES

Users may not want to share uploaded content or may want to limit sharing to certain users. Offer them options to specify such privacy and sharing preferences (Figure 9.5).

KEEP USERS INFORMED ABOUT THE UPLOAD PROGRESS

Allow users to monitor the progress of content uploading by providing a progress indicator (see the DELAY/PROGRESS INDICATOR pattern in Chapter 8). This makes it easier for them to judge the time it will take to upload the files. In addition, users can interrupt the upload if they feel that it may take longer than they had anticipated or they realize that they selected an incorrect file to upload.

CONFIRM SUCCESSFUL UPLOAD OF CONTENT FILES

Acknowledge to users a successful upload of files. Once files have completed uploading, either take users to the page where they can manage the uploaded

FIGURE 9.5 Flickr allows users to define privacy settings for uploaded photos.

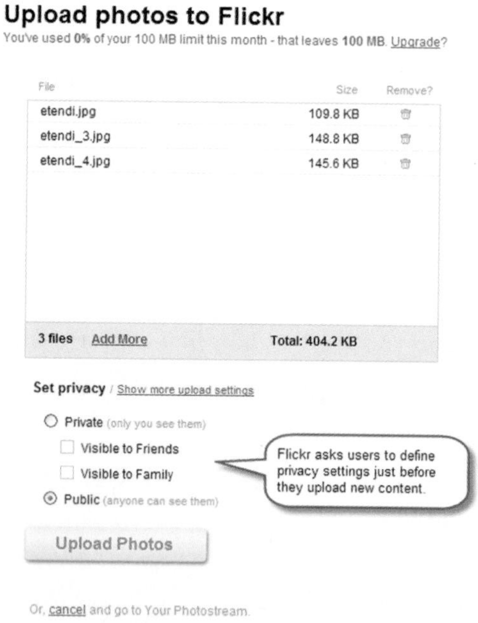

Upload photos to Flickr
You've used 0% of your 100 MB limit this month - that leaves 100 MB. Upgrade?
File
Size
Remove?
etendi.jpg
109.8 KB
etendi_3.jpg
148.8 KB
etendi_4.jpg
145.6 KB
3 files
Add More
Total: 404.2 KB
Set privacy / Show more upload settings
Private (only you see them)
Visible to Friends
Visible to Family
Public (anyone can see them)
Flickr asks users to define privacy settings just before they upload new content.
Upload Photos
Or, cancel and go to Your Photostream.

files or keep them on the same page with the option to upload more files. If users would benefit by tagging content or providing descriptions, suggest appropriate next steps to them.

Related design patterns

Because uploaded files may be large, especially when adding media files, use of the DELAY/PROGRESS INDICATORS (see Chapter 8) pattern is relevant and should be considered. In addition, most applications that support user-generated content require that users describe them using tags (TAGGING).

TAGGING

Problem

Web applications that allow users to add content (e.g., bookmarks, photos, music, videos, and so forth) may also want to allow them to categorize or label their uploaded content to make it easier to find later. However, with all the different ways users may want to label content, it may be impossible to anticipate and make available all potential labels and variations (or categories and subcategories). For example, users may want to label personal photos with labels such as the names of people, occasions, locations, ages, emotions, and so forth.

Solution

Allow users to label (i.e., *tag*) content with any descriptive information they desire so as to make it easy for them to find it later (Figure 9.6). The labels used for tagging content should not be restrictive except when they might be offensive to other users of the application; for example, an application might not want to include profanity in labels.

Why

The use of open-ended tags encourages a personally meaningful and natural vocabulary. This makes it easy for users to find items later and allows them

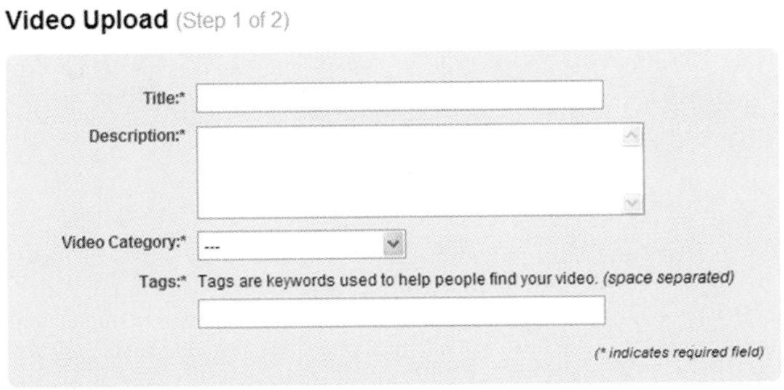

Video Upload (Step 1 of 2)

Title:*

Description:*

Video Category:* ---

Tags:* Tags are keywords used to help people find your video. *(space separated)*

(* indicates required field)

FIGURE 9.6
YouTube asks users to add tags when uploading videos.

to explore and interact with content in a myriad ways (Marlow et al., 2006). For example, by allowing users to label emails (and add multiple labels to the same email), Gmail permits users to not only use tags that describe the content of the email but also to describe actions and priorities (e.g., "to do," "important," "urgent," and so forth). In addition, users don't have to force-fit items into a category/subcategory combination; they can place them in many virtual categories at once.

Application developers also benefit from tagging because they do not have to address the whole categorization scheme (i.e., taxonomy) in advance. They can rely on users' tags to continually create a dynamic, evolving taxonomy (also referred to as *folksonomy*)[1] and use it to supplement the high-level taxonomy to facilitate navigation.

Finally, tagging can encourage user participation and sharing since it can help create communities with shared interests and allow users to explore content that is tagged similar to theirs.

How

Adding tags to a content item should be straightforward. To tag an item, let users enter keywords separated by a space or a comma (or another delimiter) in a text field. Using space as a delimiter may be problematic when users want to enter multiword tags. Therefore, consider use of commas, semicolons, or other special characters as delimiters. In addition, allow users to tag both the content they are adding and the content that already exists (Figure 9.7).

FIGURE 9.7
Flickr allows users to add tags to photos they upload.

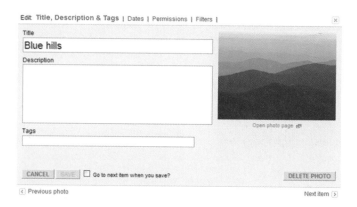

---

[1]Thomas Vander Wal (2007) coined the term *folksonomy* and described it as follows: "Folksonomy is the result of personal free tagging of information and objects (anything with a URL) for one's own retrieval. The tagging is done in a social environment (usually shared and open to others). Folksonomy is created from the act of tagging by the person consuming the information."

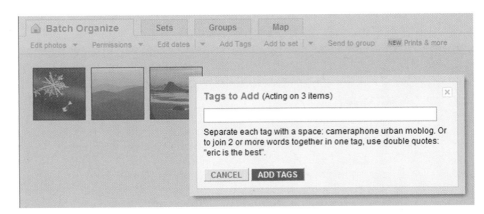

FIGURE 9.8
Flickr allows users to apply tags in a "batch" mode. Users can batch photos that they want to tag and then click "Add Tags" to add descriptions to all the items in the batch.

KEEP TAGGING OPTIONAL

The main purpose of tagging is to allow users to provide some descriptive information about content to facilitate finding it in the future. Because the primary user task is to add content, tagging (or providing other descriptive information) should be optional. However, users should be permitted to add tags later.

ALLOW USERS TO TAG SEVERAL ITEMS TOGETHER

For content such as photos, users may want to add the same tags to several items. Allow them to select items that will share the same tags and apply tags to them in "bulk" or "batch" mode (Figure 9.8).

SUGGEST TAGS TO MINIMIZE VARIABILITY

One of the problems with tagging is that items may be tagged using seemingly similar labels caused by typos, plurals, or minor differences in spellings (e.g., color versus colour). For example, one user may label an item as "web site," another as "website," and yet another as "web_site" or "websites." By suggesting tags and letting users pick from them, the application can minimize redundancy and unnecessary distinctions in tags.

In addition, suggesting tags may also make users consider alternative ways to describe content and avoid conservative labels from users new to tagging. Suggestions may be in the form of the following (Smith, 2007):

- *Previously used tags.* Tags that the user has entered already.
- *Popular tags.* Tags that have been used frequently by others.
- *Recommended tags.* Tags the user should consider based on popular tags, recently used tags, and other factors.

To make it easy to add suggested tags, allow users to select from a list (Figure 9.9). In addition, while entering tags, suggest tags using the AUTOSUGGEST/AUTOCOMPLETION rich-interaction pattern (see Chapter 8).

FIGURE 9.9 Delicious both recommends tags and lists popular ones for users to consider when adding a bookmark and tagging it. To use one or more tags, users just have to click on them, and those tags are populated in the "tags" text field.

ALLOW USERS TO CHANGE AND DELETE THEIR TAGS

Users may want to change their tags because they made a mistake or have found other tags that better describe the content. Also, if users have tagged a content item to describe an action they are going to take (e.g., labeling an item "to do" or "urgent" in Gmail), they may want to remove those tags if they are no longer relevant. To accommodate such needs, allow users to remove, change, or add tags to an existing item (Figure 9.10).

Managing tags should be possible in batch mode as well—that is, users should be able to change or delete tags for multiple items at the same time. If it would help users, allow them to replace one tag with one or more tags as well.

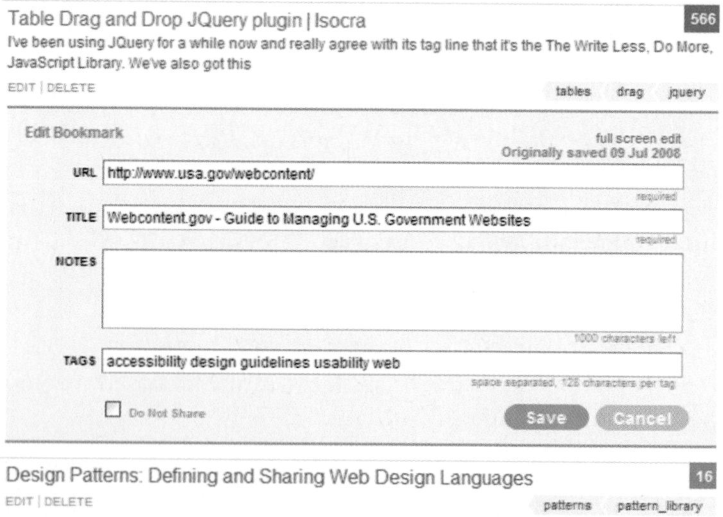

FIGURE 9.10 Delicious allows users to change or delete tags by clicking "edit" next to the bookmarked item.

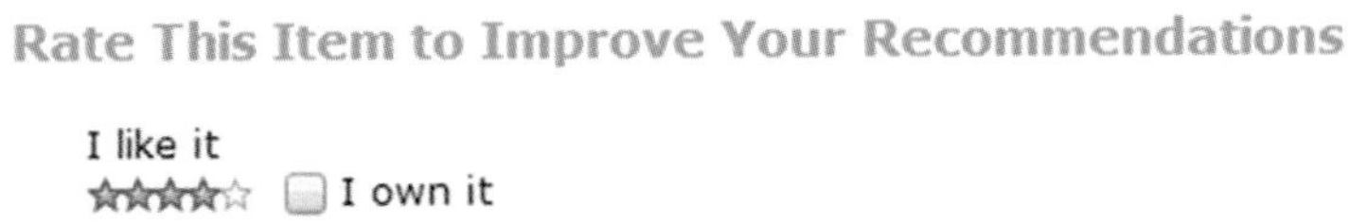

Rate This Item to Improve Your Recommendations

I like it
★★★★☆ ☐ I own it

FIGURE 9.11 Amazon allows users to rate items using a five-star rating system. They also make it clear that rating the item will help Amazon provide better recommendations.

Related design patterns

When tags are used for labeling items, TAG CLOUDS are usually offered as a way to navigate and explore content (see Chapter 5).

RATINGS

Problem

With an abundance of content accessible on the Web, users are faced with the problem of identifying relevant and useful content; this is made even more difficult with user-contributed content that has not been reviewed or edited for quality. Applications also face a similar problem because their personalization and recommendation algorithms often rely on user interests that are the same when they try suggesting content to users.

Solution

Allow users to indicate their likes and dislikes by rating items (e.g., movies, music, videos, restaurants, hotels, and so forth; Figure 9.11). Ensure that rating an item is quick and does not take too long or interrupt users' main task.

Why

It is impossible for users to weed through all the available content to separate useful and relevant content. In addition, when buying products and services, deciding among the available options can be paralyzing (Schwartz, 2004). Therefore, to help make decisions, users typically depend on others' experiences, which are conveyed through ratings and reviews (see the REVIEWS pattern that follows).

Ratings in the form of star ratings are useful for two reasons: (1) providing ratings is relatively straightforward; and (2) they provide quick, at-a-glance information about the usefulness or quality of products, services, content, and other items as judged by other users. This makes it easy for users to at least filter out content at a gross level. Ratings can be used in a variety of ways. For example,

- eBay, a marketplace for buying and selling products, uses ratings to create a detailed feedback profile of sellers.
- Amazon, an online retailer and marketplace, uses ratings for its products as well as its sellers.
- NexTag, a comparison-shopping application, uses ratings to show the quality of products as well as the reliability of sellers.

An indirect measure often used to judge items is its popularity based on the number of purchases, downloads, wish list additions, and so forth. However, this method indicates users' actions and behaviors, but not their satisfaction and experience with the product or service after they have purchased or experienced it. Popularity and quality are not the same. For example, a best-selling author may sell many copies of a newly published or to-be-published book even before anyone has had an opportunity to read and review it. In addition, the ratings and reviews obtained from other users of a product have been found to be useful and trustworthy to help users make purchase decisions. Gauri et al. (2008) concluded:

> It is interesting that of all the attributes, positive customer reviews have the greatest impact on repurchase intention. This is consistent across all categories (i.e., books and magazines; DVDs and videos; and flowers and food). Even more impressive is the finding that number of years on the Web has the least impact on repurchase intention. It suggests that stores would attract more customers by having positive customer reviews. Another interesting finding is that it is not the total number of reviews that influences customer repurchase intention, but the percentage of positive reviews.

How

Web applications that attempt to capture users' feedback relatively quickly employ a star-rating approach with one star representing the lowest rating and five stars representing the highest rating; some applications allow increments of half stars, thus increasing the range of the scale.

Two types of interaction approaches are commonly used when using star ratings:

1. *Separating the user's ratings from the average rating.* With this approach, users are shown an item's average rating separately from their own rating. To rate an item, users are shown a set of five "empty" stars. As users hover over the stars, stars reflecting the corresponding rating are highlighted. Users then click to assign and save a rating. Users are then shown their ratings in a different color from the average rating (Figure 9.12); they are also offered an option to either remove their ratings or change previously assigned ratings.

2. *Combining the average rating with the user's ratings.* By default, users are shown stars in red to indicate the current average item rating. As users hover over the stars, the red stars are replaced by yellow stars (or another color). As users click to assign and save a rating, the stars are shown in the yellow state to indicate that the item has been rated by the user (Figure 9.13).

Although it makes intuitive sense to separate the current rating from the users' ratings, both of these approaches are widely used. In some instances, both approaches are used within the same application. For example, Blockbuster separates the aggregated average rating from the users' rating on the movie

(a)

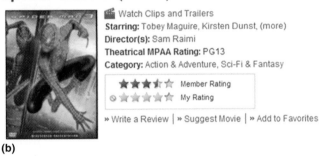

(b)

FIGURE 9.12 Blockbuster shows users "empty" stars before they have rated an item (a) and then in color after they have entered their rating (b).

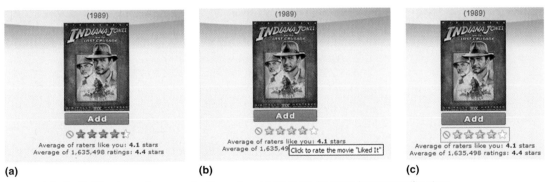

(a)   **(b)**   **(c)**

FIGURE 9.13 Netflix shows the current rating using red stars (a). As users hover over the stars, the fill color changes to yellow to indicate their rating (b). Once a desired rating is noted, the stars are filled yellow to indicate that users have rated the item (c).

details page but combines them on other listing pages; it may be using the "combined" approach on listing pages to save space and minimize clutter.

ANCHOR THE RATINGS

Anchor each rating with a verbal descriptor to clarify to users what each star rating means (Figure 9.14).

FIGURE 9.14
Hulu, an application for watching TV episodes and movies, anchors each star rating with a verbal descriptor.

FIGURE 9.15 Netflix shows the user's star ratings in yellow and aggregated average ratings (that users have not rated) in red.

INDICATE TO USERS IF THEY HAVE ALREADY RATED AN ITEM

To ensure that users don't waste time rerating an item, let users know if they have already rated it (Figure 9.15). Although users should be allowed to change their mind and remove their ratings, to prevent abuse, they should not be allowed to rate the same item more than once.

SHOW USERS A BREAKDOWN OF THE RATINGS

Average ratings are typically used to show an item's rating. However, when an item has received fewer ratings, the average rating is not very reliable. For example, if an item has received a rating of five stars, four stars, and one star, when showing the rating, it will display the average rating of three stars—not a true reflection of user preference. To ensure that the item's quality is judged more accurately, show users a breakdown of the ratings (Figure 9.16).

ALLOW USERS TO RATE AN ITEM USING MULTIPLE CRITERIA

When an item may be judged on several criteria (e.g., ambience, quality of service), offer users additional evaluation criteria to encourage more precise evaluations (Figure 9.17). Providing additional rating criteria may also identify specific aspects of an item that users favored (or did not favor).

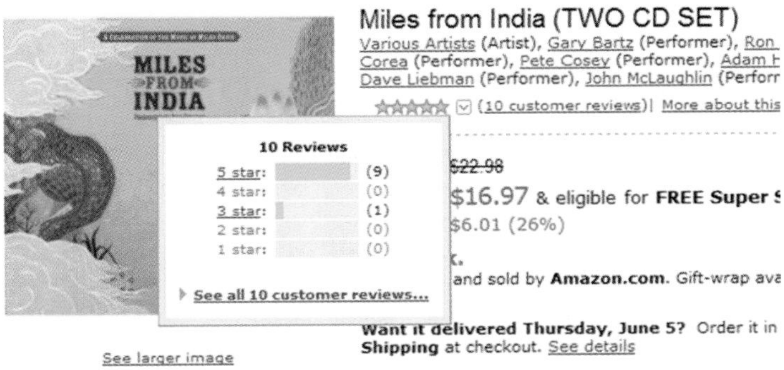

FIGURE 9.16 Amazon shows the rating distribution when users hover over the average rating. In addition, to make it easy for users to get to the reviews, it links ratings to corresponding reviews.

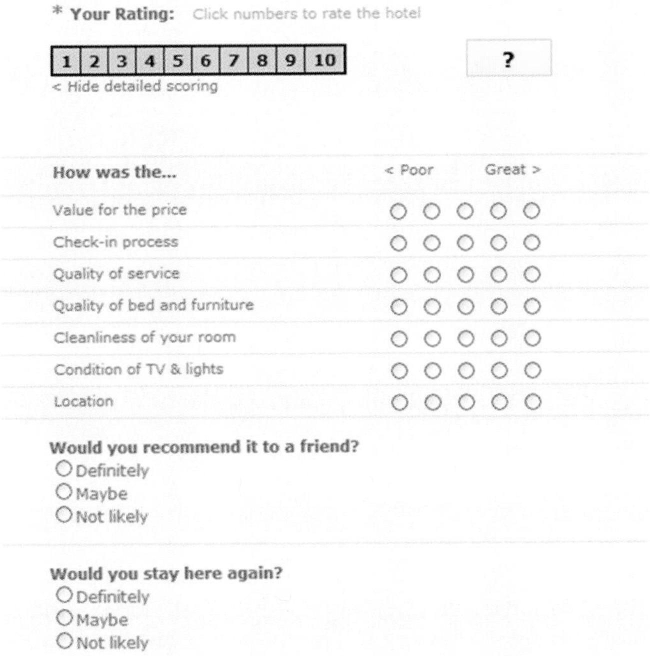

FIGURE 9.17 In addition to asking users to provide an overall rating, TravelPost offers them the option to provide a detailed rating using several evaluation criteria.

Related design patterns

To get a rationale for users' ratings and encourage participation, consider complementing ratings with REVIEWS. The PERSONALIZATION pattern is also relevant for user ratings, as applications using personalization often rely on user feedback to recommend relevant and useful content (see Chapter 4).

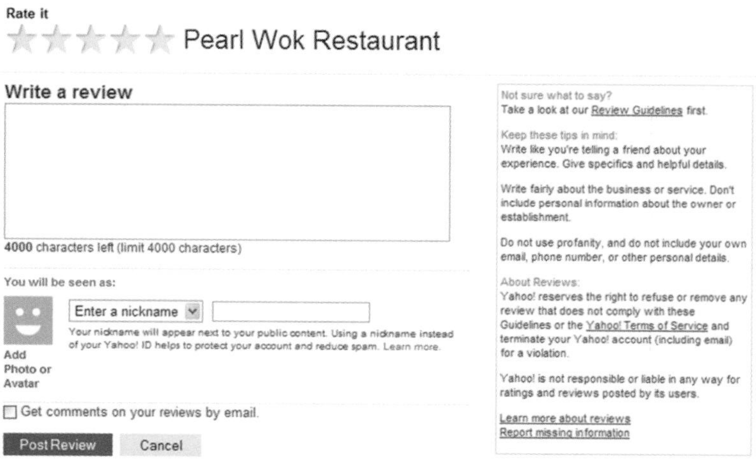

FIGURE 9.18 Yahoo! Local allows users to both rate restaurants and write reviews.

REVIEWS

Problem

Although ratings are useful, they do not provide insights in to the reasons for a higher or lower rating. In addition, users rating an item may want to share the reasons behind their opinions about the quality of an item, satisfaction with a transaction, or experience at a location. Showing a simple rating system may be limiting because users won't be able to elaborate on their reasoning.

Solution

In addition to providing a rating, allow users to write a review that expresses their opinions and reasons for the quality of an item or satisfaction with their transactions (Figure 9.18).

Why

Users invariably trust reviews by other like-minded and "unbiased" users over the claims made by the product's seller (Gauri et al., 2008). Edelman's Trust Barometer (2008) found that about 60 percent of people tended to trust people like them—that is, those who shared their interests and held similar beliefs. In addition, understanding a range of experiences from different viewpoints can help users judge how well an item's attributes match their needs, and thus they can make better informed decisions.

How

Offer users an option to write a review in addition to rating an item. If an item has not received any ratings or reviews, encourage users to be the first to write a review (Figure 9.19).

(a)

(b)

FIGURE 9.19 For unreviewed products, HP asks users to be the first to review them (a). Yelp encourages users to review items quickly by recognizing the first reviewer (b).

ALLOW USERS TO JUDGE USEFULNESS OF EXISTING REVIEWS

To encourage users to write quality reviews and to minimize abuse, allow other users to vote on the usefulness of reviews (Figure 9.20).

ALLOW USERS TO SORT REVIEWS

To prevent giving undue emphasis to high or low ratings, show reviews in reverse chronological order by default. However, users may prefer to sort reviews by high ratings or low ratings (Porter, 2008). Therefore, allow them to sort reviews on the ratings and date posted.

Related design patterns

Reviews usually go hand-in-hand with RATINGS because users are generally asked to supplement their ratings with reviews. To improve the quality and usefulness of reviews, consider asking other users to indicate whether a review was useful and use that information to compute users' REPUTATION. In addition,

FIGURE 9.20
Yelp allows users
to rate reviews as
"Useful," "Funny,"
or "Cool."

ask users to LOG IN before allowing them to write reviews to minimize abuse and biases (see Chapter 3).

VOTE TO PROMOTE

Problem

Web applications driven by user-generated or user-contributed content[2] need a way to determine the most useful or interesting content and make it available to the rest of the community.

Solution

Allow community users to vote in favor of or against submitted items based on their usefulness, quality, or "interestingness," and promote items with the most votes (Figure 9.21).

Why

In applications with an active user community, the total number of submitted items can be so large that identifying content that users will find useful

FIGURE 9.21 In the "New Links" tab, DZone.com allows users to vote a story up or down (1). The stories that receive the largest number of votes then get promoted to the "Popular Links" tab (2).

---

[2]User-contributed content includes pointers to existing resources such as interesting news, video, photos, and so forth.

(a)

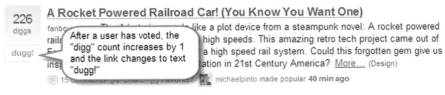

(b)

FIGURE 9.22 When a user "diggs" a story on Digg (a), the total number of diggs increases by one and the "digg it" link label changes to text "dugg!" to prevent additional votes by the same user.

and interesting can be extremely difficult. Designating a few people to identify useful stories for the rest of the community would be neither feasible nor practical. In addition, if items submitted by users are time sensitive (e.g., news stories), delays in surfacing relevant items may compromise the usefulness of the application itself.

Using a democratic voting process to identify items that deserve to be promoted and shared with other users is perhaps the most optimal way to make the application useful. Further, asking users to vote on items they find valuable also increases their involvement and participation.

This voting approach to promote a story has its downsides, however. Because voting is based more on what a user finds interesting, rather than the voted item's quality and verifiability (especially if it's a news story), often sensational stories are surfaced, leaving useful content at the bottom.

How

Show users submitted items and allow them to vote for or against them. As they cast their vote, increase or decrease the vote count and acknowledge that they have voted on the item (Figure 9.22).

ALLOW USERS TO "UNVOTE"

Users should be able to change their minds—"unvote" an item—if they believe they made a mistake. Therefore, ensure that users can change votes (Figure 9.23).

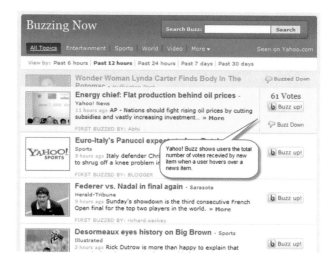

FIGURE 9.23 Digg allows users to "undigg" a story on the users' profile pages within 15 minutes of "digging" a story.

FIGURE 9.24
Yahoo! Buzz shows users the total number of votes received by a news item when a user hovers over an item.

SHOW THE NUMBER OF VOTES FOR ITEMS

Show the number of votes received by items so users can determine the popularity of an item in comparison to others (Figure 9.24).

TAKE STEPS TO MINIMIZE ABUSE

Users may have reasons to promote specific items or demote other items and may adopt practices to manipulate the voting system. To minimize such abuse, consider incorporating one or more of the following:

1. Allow only logged-in users to vote on items. This prevents abuse by not letting a few users to artificially promote an item up or down.
2. Limit the number of items users can vote for or against within a certain time period.
3. Restrict the rate at which an item can be voted up or down.
4. Include criteria other than the total number of votes in computing an item's popularity score. For example, Digg considers the source of the story, user history, traffic in the category to which the items belong, and so forth to calculate an item's "interestingness."

ALLOW VOTING TO BE INITIATED FROM ANOTHER SITE

To make it easy to promote an item, many social applications provide the means (i.e., widgets) to be placed on other web sites. Once placed on a web

FIGURE 9.25
YouTube offers users several options to promote a video on applications such as Digg and Reddit.

page, users can promote content directly from another web site rather than visiting the application that shows "promoted" content (Figure 9.25).

Related design patterns

To allow voting to be initiated from other sites, it's important that the application supports SHARING.

USER PROFILE

Problem

Web applications that require users to log in typically store user information. Users need easy access to this information so they can manage (i.e., add, update, and remove) it and keep it up to date. In most applications, such information is private and accessible only to the account owner. Social applications, however allow users to make some or all information public. Typically labeled as User Profile, user account information on such applications is quite detailed and may never be completely filled out.

Solution

Allow users to manage their profiles and keep all or part of them private. In addition, for social networking applications, extend the User Profile to include users' connections and interactions with their online community (Figure 9.26).

Why

For online community–based applications and social networking applications, users' identities are revealed through their profiles. The more detailed a user's profile, the easier it is for other users (and the application) to decide whether they share similar interests and whether they can trust him or her before connecting (or "friending") them.

This is not to downplay the fact that users' profiles may contain "made-up" information when they believe it will improve their appeal to other users—for example, in matchmaking applications and online marketplaces. However, part of users' identities are also established by what others say about them—their ratings, recommendations, testimonials, and so forth—and can help, at least to a certain extent, to mitigate fraud and misrepresentation.

FIGURE 9.26
Facebook allows users to manage their profiles and also to indicate how they want to share personal information.

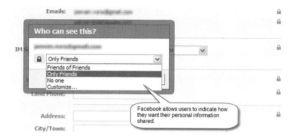

How

At the most basic level, user profiles include a name and photo; although the latter is usually optional. Any additional profile information should match the purpose of the application. For example, Google Health asks for users' demographic information, medications, allergies, immunizations, and so forth, whereas Match.com, a matchmaking application, asks for information about physical and social characteristics and those users prefer for a partner (Figure 9.27).

FIGURE 9.27 Google Health's profiles include users' demographic and medical information (a), whereas Match.com's profiles include physical and social characteristics of users and desired partners (b).

SUPPORT UNIVERSAL IDENTITY OPTIONS SUCH AS OPENID

Users may be hesitant when signing up for an application if they feel they may have to reenter all their personal information. To facilitate the transfer of such information, consider using universal identity options such as OpenID (see the REGISTRATION pattern in Chapter 3).

MAKE IT EASY TO CONNECT TO KNOWN USERS

Social networking applications rely considerably on users' network of friends, family, and colleagues to improve their experience. However, transferring tens or hundreds of contacts can be time consuming. To facilitate the process, social networking applications typically offer an import feature from popular email applications and use that information to determine which users' friends already use the application to help them connect with each other (Figure 9.28).

LET USERS BUILD THEIR PROFILES GRADUALLY

Users typically don't like to provide detailed personal information when signing up (see the REGISTRATION pattern in Chapter 3). However, to provide

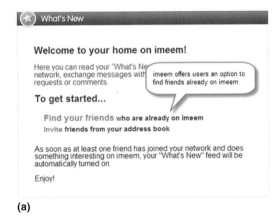

FIGURE 9.28 imeem, a social networking site for media professionals, offers users an option to find friends already on imeem (a) using their existing online address books (b).

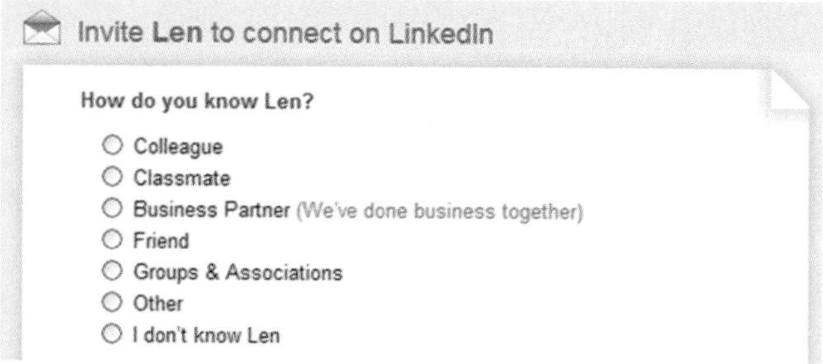

FIGURE 9.29 LinkedIn asks users how they know others when they are trying to connect with them. When they respond to the question, their profiles are updated accordingly.

useful recommendations and to offer ways to connect them with other users with similar interests, it's important that users' profiles be as complete as possible. To support such opposing user goals and application needs, allow users to build users profiles gradually. A common approach to effectively building a profile is to trigger relevant profile-related questions when users take certain actions. For example, LinkedIn asks users profile-related questions when they are requesting to connect with another user or accepting another user's request to connect (Figure 9.29).

GIVE USERS AN INCENTIVE TO UPDATE THEIR PROFILES

On social networking sites, the value of the application to users grows as they increase their connections. In such cases, offering an incentive, monetary or otherwise, can encourage people to update their profiles; this also benefits application providers, as more users may sign up for their service.

INDICATE TO USERS THE EXTENT TO WHICH THEIR PROFILES ARE COMPLETE

To encourage users to complete their profiles, indicate the extent to which they are complete. In addition, offer suggestions as to the actions they can take to improve the completeness of their profiles (Figure 9.30).

ALLOW USERS TO MAKE ALL OR PART OF THEIR INFORMATION PRIVATE

Profile pages usually help in three ways:

1. They make it easy for users of the application to find others and learn about them, as well as connect with them.
2. They help personalize the application for its users.
3. They help users maintain relevant information about themselves in one place.

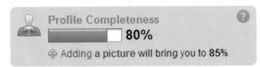

FIGURE 9.30 LinkedIn shows users to what extent their profiles are complete. They also suggest that adding a picture will increase profile completeness to 85 percent.

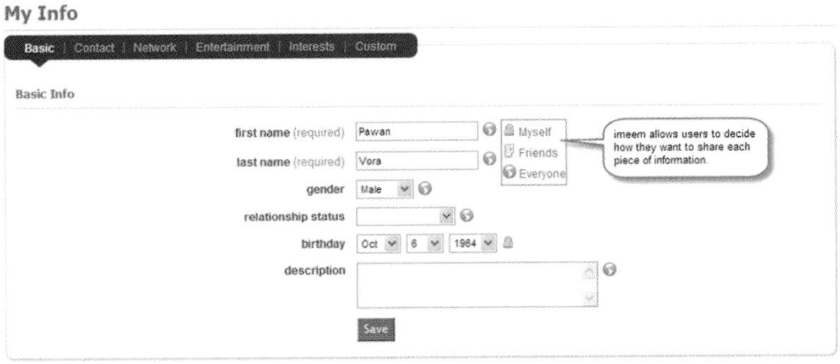

FIGURE 9.31 For each individual piece of information in the profile, imeem let's users decide whether they want to keep that information private (i.e., "Myself"), share it with users in the network (i.e., "Friends"), or share it with all imeem users (i.e., "Everyone").

Users should ultimately decide which information they want to keep private, even though the more users are willing to share information, the more useful the application can be made (Figure 9.31).

ALLOW USERS TO USE PSEUDONYMS AND AVATARS

In addition to allowing users to indicate which information they prefer to share (and not share), allow users to use a pseudonym and an avatar[3] for themselves; they are also referred to as *handles*. Avatars have been particularly popular in forums and gaming applications where users may prefer to take on different personas (Figure 9.32).

Because pseudonyms and avatars are how users "recognize" each other in social applications (because many of them may not have met in person), it is a common practice to restrict how often they can be changed. Many applications penalize users if they change their pseudonyms and avatars too often, and some of them may allow changing only the avatar image but not the pseudonym. In addition, to encourage "good" behavior, online communities may restrict access to those who are unwilling to divulge their true identities (e.g., matchmaking applications).

---

[3]An *avatar* is a textual or graphical representation of a user in an online application.

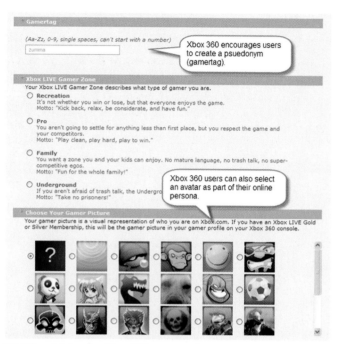

FIGURE 9.32 When joining the Xbox 360 community, users can choose a pseudonym (i.e., "Gamertag") and their avatar image (i.e., "Gamer Picture").

MAKE USER PROFILES DYNAMIC

For social applications, the user profile, in terms of information about users themselves, does not change enough and may become uninteresting for their network friends. To make it more relevant and more interesting, and to communicate what is happening in one's life, make the profile dynamic by doing one or more of the following (Porter, 2008):

- Show new friends, connections, and groups that a user has joined.
- Show a list of public comments (i.e., scraps, pokes, wall comments, etc.).
- Show users' status and mood information.
- Show any recent activities in their applications that they have subscribed to (e.g., books they have read, movies they have watched, etc.)

Showing such information makes users' profiles seem more "alive" and useful for their friends.

Related design patterns

Because users have to register to set up their account and USER PROFILE, consider the best practices identified in the REGISTRATION pattern (see Chapter 3). In addition, because users may be interacting with others with whom they have no prior experience, they need a way to determine their trustworthiness, which may be established through their REPUTATION.

REPUTATION

Problem

In many community-based web applications, it's important that users feel comfortable interacting or transacting with others with whom they have no prior experience. In addition, users may need some indicators to identify the trustworthiness or expertise of people who are offering suggestions, solutions, or products. Some common scenarios are choosing a seller from whom to purchase an item (e.g., eBay, Amazon Marketplace, NexTag), choosing a book to buy (e.g, Amazon), choosing a movie to rent (e.g., Netflix), choosing a restaurant to visit (e.g., Yelp), trusting a suggestion or an answer offered by a person (e.g., Yahoo! Answers), and so forth.

Solution

Enable some form of reputation system to help users identify those with high reputations. The reputation system must not only make it easy to identify and compare user reputations, but it should also have a consistent and reliable way for building reputations (Figure 9.33).

Why

Online interactions and transactions (monetary or otherwise) involve two types of users: *providers* (or sellers) and *receivers* (or consumers) of services, products, and information. In the absence of a face-to-face interaction, providers need a way to establish trust or a positive reputation with receivers. Designing a reputation system is then a way to establish criteria for determining trustworthiness of providers and receivers within the community. Having a reputation system in place, therefore, helps users to better anticipate the likelihood of the outcome when interacting or transacting with other community users.

Further, not all community users are equal—some are more experienced, reliable, and credible than others. Distinguishing them helps in determining how much weight to give their opinions and recommendations. Finally, using a reputation system is not just a way of establishing trust, but also a way for users to build their reputations and is an important motivation for users to participate in community-based applications (Porter, 2008).

FIGURE 9.33 eBay allows buyers to rate sellers on several criteria. Once sellers receive 98 percent positive feedback, they receive a Power Seller badge.

FIGURE 9.34 Yelp offers several ways for users to gain reputation: total number of friends, number of reviews, number of first reviews, number of fans, number of lists, number of compliments, and so forth.

How

Users' reputation is typically based on two criteria (Figure 9.34):

1. *A user's connections, actions, and history within the community.* This commonly includes how long a user has been an active community member, the total number of connections (or friends), the number of followers (or fans), the number of recommendations, the number of reviews, and so forth.

2. *The feedback from other community members.* In other words, what others who have no apparent interest in a user's reputation say about him or her (Crumlish, 2004; Porter, 2008). Therefore, a reputation system must include a feedback mechanism to judge the quality, timeliness, and accuracy of claims made about the products, services, and information. In addition, a reputation system should be robust enough to prevent abuse and manipulation by its users.

Having multiple ways to achieve a reputation is important because it allows users to gain reputations in ways that match their behaviors and personalities. Like *connectors* and *mavens* in Malcom Gladwell's *The Tipping Point* (2000), some can achieve a reputation by having a large network and others by writing useful and extensive reviews.

OFFER USERS A QUICK WAY TO JUDGE A REVIEW'S USEFULNESS

Web applications that allow users to submit reviews also allow readers of those reviews to judge their usefulness. Allowing all to see the usefulness of submitted reviews reduces the chances of bias and abuse and encourages reviewers to submit detailed and relevant information. In addition, the usefulness ratings can be used by other users to judge the reputation of the reviewer.

To make it easy to rate usefulness, ask users to simply indicate whether a review was helpful or useful without accompanying comments or ratings (Figure 9.35).

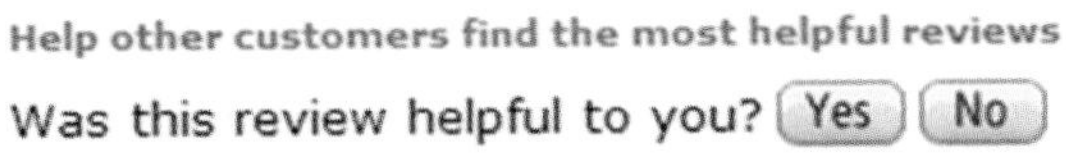

Help other customers find the most helpful reviews

Was this review helpful to you? (Yes) (No)

FIGURE 9.35 Amazon asks users whether a review was helpful to them with "Yes" and "No" options. It also clarifies why users should judge the review by prefacing the question with "Help other customers find the most helpful reviews."

RECOGNIZE ACHIEVEMENTS OF COMMUNITY MEMBERS

Like merit badges, recognizing achievement in communities helps distinguish performance, activity, and expertise levels among members. This may be as simple as achieving a Power Seller badge on eBay by maintaining a 98 percent positive feedback score and providing a high level of service to buyers. Achieving the Power Seller badge helps buyers know that they are working with an experienced eBay seller. It also helps sellers, since they may get more (and higher) bids as more buyers feel comfortable transacting with them.

Alternatively, the achievement may be in the form of ranked levels as on Amazon Web Services forum, where community members earn points by providing correct and helpful answers. By accumulating points, members achieve different score levels and receive associated merit icons (Figure 9.36).

ON COMPETITIVE SITES, SHOW USERS' RANKS

In web applications where users are competing with each other (e.g., Gaming), show their relative performance to help them understand where they rank relative to other users. This may be in the form of a leaderboard, which lets users see who the leading users (e.g., top players) are (Figure 9.37).

Use leaderboards with caution if they could lead to a perception of cheating. For example, Digg abandoned their Top Contributors page because it led to the perception of manipulation of the top stories (see *blog.digg.com/?p = 60*). And on Amazon, there is a backlash against the reviewer Harriet Klausner, as other reviewers feel that she cannot possibly read seven books a day and post reviews in order to be the top reviewer (see *Is Harriet Klausner for Real?*, available at *www.bokardo.com/archives/is-harriet-klausner-for-real/*).

Required Points	Amazon Web Services Score Level	Icon
2000	Ace	
750	Expert	
300	Guide	
50	Enthusiast	
5	Newbie	

FIGURE 9.36 Community members on the Amazon Web Services forum can receive merit badges (e.g., "Ace," "Expert," "Guide," etc.).

FIGURE 9.37
Kwanzoo, an entertainment trivia site, shows top players' ranks and points in a leaderboard format. It also shows whether a user moved up or down and by how much.

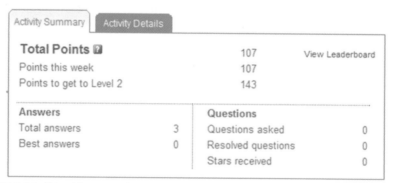

FIGURE 9.38 Yahoo! Answers shows users how many points they have accumulated and the number of points that they need to get to the next level.

CLEARLY INDICATE HOW USERS CAN REACH THE NEXT LEVEL

When using reputation levels, make it easy for users to determine how they can reach the next level. This keeps them interested and motivated to participate (Figure 9.38).

CONSIDER INCORPORATING PEER RECOMMENDATIONS

In the reputation systems discussed so far, users indirectly earn a reputation based on the swiftness of transactions, quality of the products delivered, usefulness of advice, and so forth. Many social networking applications, on the other hand, allow users to establish reputations through testimonials or recommendations that they receive. LinkedIn, for example, allows users to write recommendations for others. Users who get recommendations receive a thumbs-up icon on their profiles and an indication of how many people have recommended them.

Although it could be argued that peer recommendations are based on past interactions, transactions, or services provided, and there are other similar forms of reputation systems, an important difference is that the recommendation action is phrased more directly toward the person rather than the services offered or products sold by him or her—that is, "recommend this person," instead of "recommend services offered by this person."

Related design patterns

Both RATINGS and REVIEWS patterns may accompany REPUTATION because gaining reputation requires users to rate and review the transactions or activities they are involved with.

DISCOVER NETWORK MEMBERS

Problem

Users new to a social application may not know how to connect with others with similar interests or with whom they have lost touch. In addition, users who are part of other community-based applications may want to find out if anyone on their current "friends" list is already a member of the community they are joining.

Solution

Make it easy for users to discover network members based on common interests, past workplaces, other online communities, and contacts (i.e., email address books) (Figure 9.39). In addition, recommend friends based on users' profiles and stated interests to make it easy for users to find new "friends."

Why

Social networking or community-based applications revolve around connecting users with current, past, and potentially future friends and colleagues. Without an easy way to connect with them, the community aspect of the application disappears.

How

Social networking applications can help users discover friends in a myriad of ways: by email address books, instant messenger (IM) buddy lists, users' existing networks, recommendations, and searches. Having multiple ways to discover connections is important, since users may not have filled out their profiles completely and may use email addresses differently than those in their address books.

ALLOW DISCOVERY OF FRIENDS BY EMAIL ADDRESS BOOKS

Enable users to import their existing address books from popular email applications such as Outlook, Gmail, Yahoo! Mail, and so forth (Figure 9.40).

FIGURE 9.39 Facebook offers users several options to find friends: by email (uploading of contact files too); by schools, colleges, and work locations; and by IM buddy lists. The site also offers recommendations via "Discover People You May Know" based on profiles and current network.

FIGURE 9.40 When signing up, Yelp offers users an option to find existing friends by matching their contact lists on email systems such as Hotmail, Yahoo! Mail, AOL Mail, and Gmail.

Offer this as an option after users have signed up; it helps in the following ways:

1. To facilitate quick sign-up, users typically provide (or are asked to provide) very minimal information about themselves. This makes it difficult to connect them with people they already know in the community. By not getting a sense of community after signing up, users may question the usefulness of the application and may not return.

2. Accessing users' email address books is relatively straightforward once they have provided login credentials, which makes it easy for the application to help them find and connect with those already in their contact lists.

Find more people you know

50 new colleagues from **U S WEST**

13 new colleagues from **XOR**

4 new colleagues from **US WEST Information Technologies**

23 new classmates from **State University of New York at Buffalo**

FIGURE 9.41 Using past organizations and educational institutions in users' profiles, LinkedIn offers options to discover friends.

ALLOW DISCOVERY OF FRIENDS BASED ON USERS' PROFILES

Another option is to allow users to discover friends based on their profiles. Once users have completed at least part of their profiles with information about their workplace or educational institutions, inform them about users who match their information (Figure 9.41).

ALLOW DISCOVERY OF FRIENDS BASED ON EXISTING CONNECTIONS

Allow users to explore their friends' profiles and view friends' friends to make it possible for them to discover common friends they didn't know were part of the community. In addition, rather than making users actively browse friends' profiles to discover common friends, the application can periodically suggest friends from users' connections who they may know.

ALLOW USERS TO SEARCH OTHER COMMUNITY MEMBERS

Allow users to search for people (Figure 9.42) in addition to allowing them to discover members based on their profiles, address books, and buddy lists (see SAMPLE SEARCH and PARAMETRIC SEARCH in Chapter 6).

REQUIRE CONFIRMATION OF "FRIEND" REQUESTS

While it's easy to find network members with whom users may want to connect (i.e., a "friend"), it should not be an automatic process. It's important that requests to "friend" someone are acknowledged and confirmed before adding them to their friend lists. In addition, when accepting a request to become a friend, it helps to ask them to indicate the nature of their relationship. This information can be used to update profiles (and make them more complete) and further discover network members with whom users can connect.

SUPPORT THIRD-PARTY INTRODUCTIONS

Users may want to "friend" with users they do not know. Although users should be permitted to send direct requests to add them to their network, if there's a mutual friend that both users know, allow them to be introduced. This may help reduce hesitation on the part of both users in becoming friends.

ALLOW USERS TO "FOLLOW" OTHERS

Offer another recently popular "friending" approach called "following," where users can visit other users' profile pages and choose to "follow" their activities (or "status" in Twitter's case) (Figure 9.43).

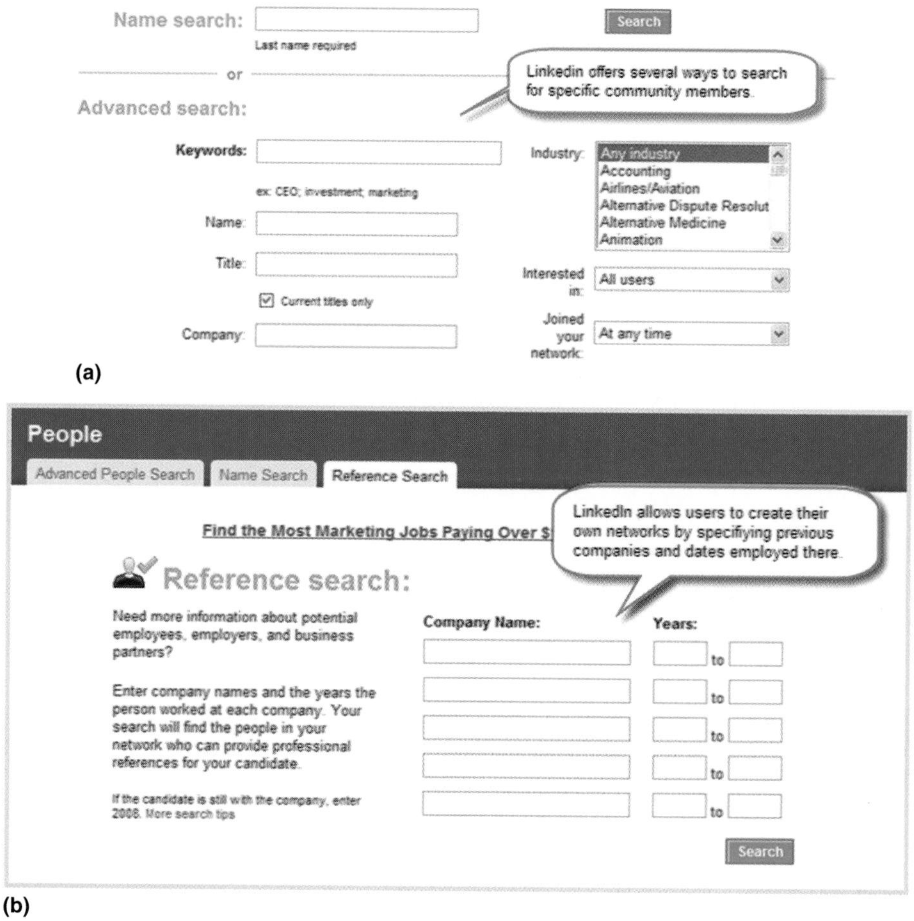

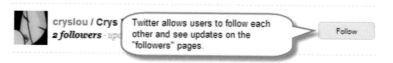

FIGURE 9.42 LinkedIn offers users several options to search their membership list (a). They also offer a reference search for finding people in one's network who may be able to provide references for a candidate (b).

FIGURE 9.43 Twitter allows users to follow other users; "followed" users' activities are then shown as updates on the "followers'" pages.

Related design patterns

As users add friends to their networks and indicate their relationship to their friends, it offers a good opportunity for the application to update their USER PROFILES. In addition, it is important to offer mechanisms for users to grow

FIGURE 9.44 MySpace allows users to view and manage their friend lists on the My Friends page. In addition, it allows users to group friends into separate categories. They can also indicate privacy settings in terms of who can view the categories they create.

their network, because the size of the network is an important factor that contributes to their REPUTATION.

FRIEND LIST

Problem

Users are likely to communicate with the same core group of people—friends, colleagues, family, and acquaintances. Requiring them to remember their information every time they want to contact someone would make the interaction inefficient.

Solution

Allow users to create and maintain a friend list (Figure 9.44); friend list is also referred to as a "buddy list." In addition, allow users to group their friends to make it easier to find them and communicate as a group.

Why

A friend list is similar to an address book and enables users to find their friends and their profile information quickly. In addition, like address books, many users of social networking applications have tens to hundreds of friends. If presented just as a simple list or paginated list, finding friends can become difficult. Therefore, it's important for users to be able to group their friends based on their relationship, how frequently they interact, how they were introduced, and so on. In essence, this helps users maintain, if they so desire, an accurate "social graph" of their friend list. Furthermore, this feature also allows them to tailor their privacy controls and send messages to them as a group instead of individually.

How

Update users' friend lists whenever they accept a request to become a friend or when their request to "friend" someone is accepted.

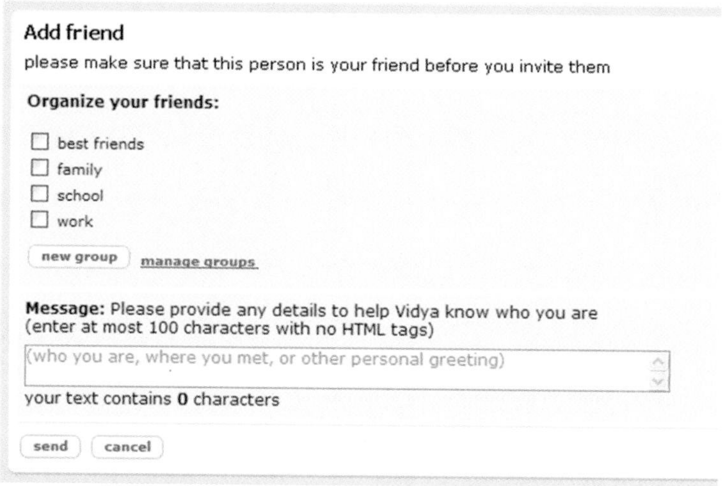

Add friend

please make sure that this person is your friend before you invite them

Organize your friends:

☐ best friends
☐ family
☐ school
☐ work

(new group) manage groups

Message: Please provide any details to help Vidya know who you are
(enter at most 100 characters with no HTML tags)

(who you are, where you met, or other personal greeting)

your text contains **0** characters

(send) (cancel)

FIGURE 9.45 Orkut allows users to group their friends into different categories. By default, they offer the groups "best friends," "family," "school," and "work"; users can also create their own groups and put the same friend in more than one group.

ALLOW USERS TO GROUP THEIR FRIENDS

Users may want to group their friends to make finding them easier—for example, they may want to group them based on the nature of their relationship or on the frequency of their interaction with them. To afford maximum flexibility on how they want to organize their friends, allow them to create their own groups. If users have created groups, make assigning friends to a group part of the accept (or "request to add") process (Figure 9.45).

MAKE THE FRIEND LIST EASILY ACCESSIBLE

Among the common reasons users visit social applications is to interact with their friends or see their status and history. To enable quick access to such information, make it easy for them to access their friend list. Most social applications allow users to see a list of friends on their home pages.

ALLOW USERS TO VIEW THEIR FRIENDS' ONLINE STATUS

An important reason to maintain a friend list is to enable messaging between friends (both synchronously and asynchronously). To initiate synchronous messaging (i.e., chats), it's important to know if a friend is online (Figure 9.46; see the MESSAGING and PRESENCE INDICATOR patterns later in this chapter).

Related design patterns

To promote communication with friends, both the MESSAGING and PRESENCE INDICATOR patterns usually accompany FRIEND LIST. In addition, to make it easy to find people, a friend list is often shown as an IMAGE GRID (see Chapter 7).

(a)   **(b)**

FIGURE 9.46 MySpace allows users to filter their friend list by who is online (a). Gmail, on the other hand, shows a green bullet in front of online users (b).

GROUPS AND SPECIAL-INTEREST COMMUNITIES

Problem

Users need a way to connect with those with similar interests and experiences so that they can learn, share their knowledge and opinions, build relationships, grow professionally, grow their networks, and so forth.

Solution

Allow users to join and create groups, also referred to as forums or online communities (Figure 9.47).

Why

One of the reasons users participate in community-based applications is to connect with those who share similar interests and experiences. Enabling users to create groups and connect with others is therefore essential because it contributes to a sense of community and encourages participation. For companies, forums and communities are also useful for customer support because they allow customers to help each other and, in the process, reduce support costs.

FIGURE 9.47 LearnHub, a site that supports educational communities, allows users to join existing ones or to start their own community.

FIGURE 9.48 43 Things creates groups dynamically based on tags.

FIGURE 9.49
Facebook allows
users to create their
own groups.

How

Groups or online communities are virtual places where users with like interests can share and connect with each other. Therefore, a community can be in the form of discussion groups around a topic (e.g., Usenet); groups created within a social networking application (e.g., Facebook); discussions around social objects such as photos, music, movies, books, and so forth (e.g., YouTube, Flickr); comments in response to a blog entry (e.g., blogger); or communities created by companies to support their customers (e.g., Dell Support Forums).

Groups can be derived dynamically by using shared tags (Figure 9.48), or users can create them explicitly based on their specific interests (Figure 9.49). Creating groups dynamically is a good way to discover people who share common interests. However, such implicitly created groups may not be sustainable because users have not chosen to be part of that group. Explicitly formed groups, on the other hand, require users to join them and may have better chances of surviving.

Groups may also be created around specific events by people attending, or those wishing to attend, an event. Events are just a type of group with location

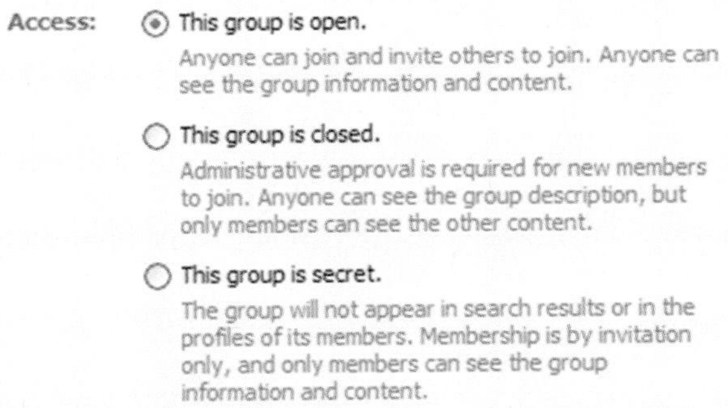

Access: ⦿ This group is open.
Anyone can join and invite others to join. Anyone can
see the group information and content.

○ This group is closed.
Administrative approval is required for new members
to join. Anyone can see the group description, but
only members can see the other content.

○ This group is secret.
The group will not appear in search results or in the
profiles of its members. Membership is by invitation
only, and only members can see the group
information and content.

FIGURE 9.50 Facebook categorizes groups into open, closed, and secret groups. Open groups are public groups, secret groups are private groups, and closed groups are semipublic, since they require approval of the group administrator to join.

and dates. A good example is SlideShare (*www.slideshare.net*), where users can create event-based groups. The advantage of event-based groups is that they can allow users to join groups for specific dates and locations.

ALLOW USERS TO MAKE GROUPS PUBLIC OR PRIVATE

Groups created by users can be either public or private (Figure 9.50). Public groups are helpful for general-interest subjects, such as cooking, hiking, politics, and so forth, that are likely to invite participation from many users. These public groups may spawn more specialized subcommunities as their users' interests demand. Private groups are typically created by users who have very specific goals or are dealing with topics that are sensitive in nature.

Public groups can be joined by anyone and may or may not require acceptance by the creator of the group. Private groups, on the other hand, are restricted to those invited by the creator of the group. Joining public groups is usually as easy as clicking "Join this group" and confirming the intent.

ENCOURAGE USERS TO JOIN AND PARTICIPATE

Users generally prefer to join groups or communities that are active. Therefore, it is important to show indicators of group activity such as number of users, number of posts, number of replies, recency of posts, and so forth (Figure 9.51).

It also helps to show a gallery of active group users. This may be done by showing users' avatars as part of the discussion and/or showing a gallery of new or active community members.

SHOW USERS THEIR FRIENDS' GROUPS

Because users share some commonality with their friends, they are more likely to join the groups to which their friends also belong. Therefore, it's important for users to see the groups their friends have joined.

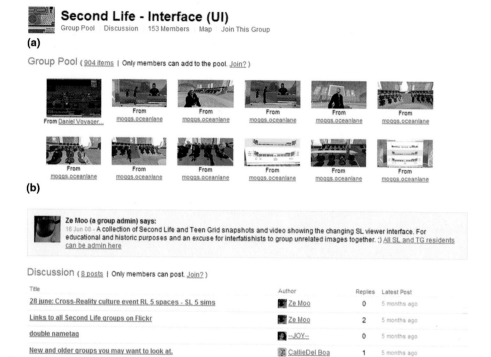

(a)

(b)

(c)

FIGURE 9.51 Flickr shows users the number of group members (a), the "photo pool" (b), and a list of ongoing discussions (c) to indicate activity and interest in the group.

FIGURE 9.52 Rally Software uses communities to support new and existing users, share their release backlog, invite users to request features, and so forth.

CREATE COMMUNITIES TO INVITE IDEAS AND SUGGESTIONS

It is not necessary to have communities started only by users. They may be started by companies to invite comments and feedback from customers (Figure 9.52).

Several companies have used communities to shape their products and service offerings. Salesforce.com uses the IdeaExchange community to invite ideas from users and ask them to promote or demote ideas on their product road-map (see *ideas.salesforce.com/popular/ideas_under_consideration*).

View Photos of Maya (1)

View Maya's Friends (123)

Send Maya a Gift

View Books (66)

Send Maya a Message

Poke Maya

Chat with Maya

FIGURE 9.53
Facebook offers users several messaging options: send an email, chat in real time (a green bullet indicates that the user is online), and poke (a nonverbal message).

Related design patterns

TAG CLOUDS are important navigation mechanisms for dynamically created groups because users can click relevant tags and navigate to the desired group (see Chapter 5). In addition, as users participate in communities, they may gain a REPUTATION based on the quality of their contribution.

MESSAGING

Problem

One of the reasons users participate in an online social community is to be able to communicate with one another. This may be in the form of a conversation (i.e., chat) or as a message that can be responded to later. Also, in some instances, users may want to send a broadcast message—that is, send a message to several people at once—and they may not necessarily need a response.

Solution

Enable users to communicate with each other synchronously (e.g., chat) or asynchronously (e.g., messages, pokes, scraps, etc.) (Figure 9.53).

Why

An important aspect of being in an online community and sustaining it is to encourage communication among its members. The easier it is for users to communicate with each other, the more likely that the community will thrive and be able to sustain itself.

How

Allow users to communicate with each other synchronously in real time using Instant Messaging (IM) features (e.g., chat), as well as asynchronously via sending messages to one another or posting messages on a shared public area. The most common asynchronous messaging options are to allow users to send private messages to an individual (Figure 9.54) or posting comments on shared areas (e.g., "walls" on Facebook).

TO FACILITATE CHATS, SHOW FRIENDS' ONLINE STATUS

Because synchronous messaging requires users to be online simultaneously to initiate conversation, indicate whether users are online (Figure 9.55; see also the PRESENCE INDICATOR pattern next for additional details).

FIGURE 9.54 LinkedIn allows users to communicate with each other using the "Send a Message" option.

FIGURE 9.55 Facebook shows users the number of their friends who are online.

FIGURE 9.56 Facebook allows users to post comments on their friends' "walls."

SUPPORT BROADCAST MESSAGES

Although one-to-one communication between users is effective via messaging options such as chat and email, users may want to write a message for everyone to see. It's a broadcast message rather than a message targeted to a specific person in the network. Several different terms are in use today to indicate this feature, such as *walls* (e.g., Facebook), *scraps* (e.g., Orkut), and *comments* (e.g., MySpace) (Figure 9.56).

ALLOW USERS TO INDICATE THEIR MESSAGING PREFERENCES

Because broadcast messages, such as comments and scraps, are part of a user's profile, they are visible to anyone who is granted access to profiles. However, allow users to manage permissions so that they can specify who can write and view comments (Figure 9.57). Once set, it's important that such preferences be clearly indicated on users' profile pages (Figure 9.58).

Related design patterns

To allow users to communicate synchronously (i.e., in real time), it's important that they know when their "friends" or "contacts" are online. Having a PRESENCE INDICATOR can help communicate users' online status and willingness to converse.

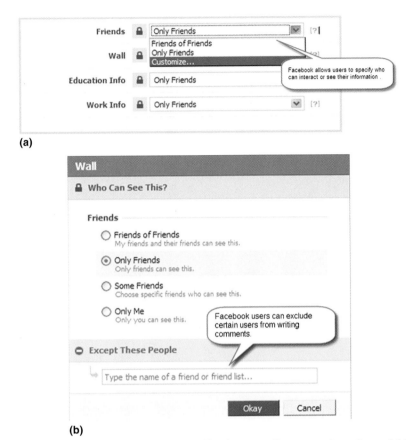

(a)

(b)

FIGURE 9.57 Facebook allows users to specify who can write comments on the wall (a). It also allows specific users to be excluded from writing comments (b).

FIGURE 9.58 Yahoo! Answers indicates users' communication preferences on their profile pages. In this example, the user has chosen to not communicate via either IM or email.

PRESENCE INDICATOR

Problem

In applications that allow users to interact with each other and maintain their friends (or contact) list, users may want to know whether they can initiate a real-time conversation with one or more friends.

FIGURE 9.59
Meebo, an online
IM aggregator,
shows users their
contacts and online
statuses. Like other
desktop-based
instant messaging
aggregators, it
groups offline
users separately
and distinguishes
contacts' IM account
types with icons.

Solution

Show users an indication of whether another user is online (Figure 9.59).
However, respect each users' privacy preferences and indicate their online
status accordingly.

Why

An important purpose of community-based applications is to promote interaction and communication among its members. Although this can be achieved
by offline messaging approaches such as email, allowing real-time communication promotes a better sense of community. Therefore, knowing whether a user
is online is important because it can suggest to others that they can initiate a
conversation.

How

Like instant messaging (IM) programs (e.g., AOL Instant Messenger, Yahoo!
Messenger, MSN Messenger), use a status image or some other marker to indicate whether a user is online.

ALLOW USERS TO INDICATE THEIR ACTIVITY STATUS

A recent trend is to allow users to indicate their activity status along with their
presence indicator (Figure 9.60). This approach is also referred to as *status
casting* (popularized by Twitter, which allows users to send short messages
informing others of what they are doing). Status casting is similar to status messages in IMs, where users indicate their current status such as "Busy,"

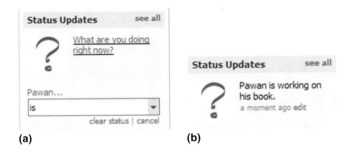

FIGURE 9.60
Facebook allows
users to indicate
what they are
working on (a). Once
they indicate their
status, it is shown to
other users (b).

"Out to lunch," "Be right back," and so forth, except that many of the IMs offer preset options for users to choose from in addition to allowing users to set their own messages.

ALLOW USERS TO SET THEIR STATUS PREFERENCES

For privacy, or other reasons, some users may choose not to display their online presence indicator and status to others. Or they may want (or not want) only certain users to see their online status. To accommodate such preferences, allow users to identify those who can (and cannot) view their status.

Related design patterns

Online presence indicators are useful not just for knowing if other users are online but also in deciding whether to initiate a conversation with them. Therefore, the PRESENCE INDICATOR pattern is usually accompanied by the MESSAGING pattern.

SHARING

Problem

Users may want to share content—photos, videos, news articles, and so forth—with others; the content being shared may or may not belong to the person sharing it.

Solution

Enable users to share content with others (Figure 9.61).

Why

There are several reasons why users may want to share information, including (Porter, 2008):

- To keep family and friends informed
- To share unique and enjoyable experiences
- To reciprocate
- To help answer others' questions or do research
- To introduce people to one another
- To share laughs

FIGURE 9.61
SlideShare offers several sharing options. When someone uploads a slideshow, it's automatically shared with others. In addition, users can click "Share this slideshow" to invite specific people to view it, or they can share it with the general population by adding the link to applications such as Digg, Reddit, and MySpace.

An interesting by-product of sharing is that it may help users increase their reputation within the community—by recognizing them as experts in some fields (see the REPUTATION pattern earlier in this chapter). In addition, sharing is the foundation of social interaction. For a community to thrive (and survive), whether online or offline, it's essential that it support sharing and improve participation and interaction among its community members.

How

Porter (2008) identified two forms of sharing: *implicit* and *explicit*. Implicit sharing occurs when content is shared by virtue of users' participation in a community. For example, when users bookmark a page on Delicious, upload photos to Flickr, or put videos on YouTube, the items are implicitly shared with the rest of the community, unless they are marked as private. Implicit sharing doesn't require any specific action from other users either. Items are shared with community users as soon as they are posted or made available to the application (Figure 9.62). Explicit sharing, on the other hand, requires users to send an explicit message, usually via an email, to access content on applications such as Google Docs, Zoho, Delicious, and others.

ALLOW USERS TO SHARE CONTENT VIA EMAIL

The most basic sharing feature is to allow users to send interesting content (e.g., news stories, recipes, photos, videos, travel plans, etc.) via email. Allow users to share content entering one or more recipient names and their email addresses (and their own information to let recipients know who is sending the information). The shared content may be part of the email or sent as a link

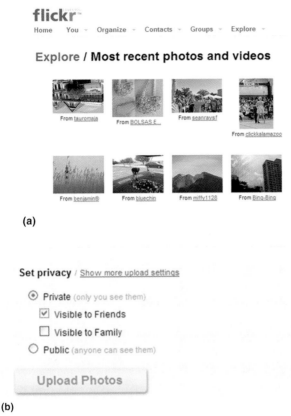

FIGURE 9.62 Users' photographs are shared with all the Flickr users (a), unless marked as private when uploaded (b).

depending on the nature and size of the content. For example, recipes may be included in the email itself, but photos and videos may require recipients to follow a link provided in the email.

To ensure that users who initiate sharing are human, consider using CAPTCHA (see Chapter 3). In addition, to quell users' concerns about the application provider's intent to harvest email addresses, include a link to the privacy policy.

ALLOW USERS TO POST CONTENT ON OTHER SITES

With increasing user participation, it's important to make sharing easier through third-party applications as well. Many applications and content sites now allow users to promote content on their applications through sites such as Digg, Facebook, Delicious, and so forth (Figure 9.63).

FIGURE 9.63
SlideShare allows users to share a presentation to a variety of web applications.

SET UP PERMALINKS

Permalinks are permanent URLs for web content and make it easy to link to a specific blog or forum post. Content that may move from its current location (e.g., home page or the front page of a blog) benefits from having a permalink because the link does not change and therefore makes it easy for other users to link to it.

For example, with blogs, the main blog page changes as new entries are posted. When a blog entry first appears, it may be at the top of the page and then moves down the page as more entries appear, eventually getting pushed to a different page. To make sure that users can access the entry any time in the future, allow users to access it using its permalink.

Permalinks are also useful when content is likely to be linked from sources other than the application providing the content. In addition, permalinks are typically designed to be easier to read compared to the original URL.

Using the format shown in the following Tip allows search engines to extract permalinks and establish the relationship between the documents rather than deciphering the relation from the anchor (i.e., <a>) tag.

TIP
Include the permalink of a page within the
HTML using rel="bookmark" as follows:
<link rel="bookmark" href="permalink URL" />

ALLOW CONTENT TO BE EMBEDDABLE

Allow content such as videos, music, threaded discussions, and so forth to be shared by making it embeddable in applications other than where the original content resides. Make embedding content easy by offering users the necessary HTML (or JavaScript) to copy and paste it on a web page of their choice (Figure 9.64).

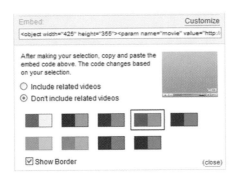

FIGURE 9.64
Not only does YouTube make it easy for users to embed a video on web pages of their choosing, but it also allows them a few customization options.

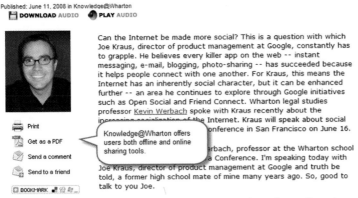

FIGURE 9.65 Knowledge@Wharton not only offers users the online options to read the article, listen to it, and share it with others, but it also promotes offline use by allowing the download of the audio and article's PDF version.

OFFER PRINTABLE VERSIONS OF THE PAGE

Not all sharing happens online. There are users who prefer to share printed materials. Offer them options to view a printer-friendly version of the page or a PDF (Figure 9.65). They can then print the page or share it offline. If they have Adobe Acrobat, users may find it easier to annotate the material as well.

Related design patterns

To prevent spam or submissions by automated web crawlers, CAPTCHA is often used when users share content with others (see Chapter 3). SHARING is also the first step for COLLABORATION.

COLLABORATION

Problem

When sharing, users may not want to just share information with others but also to work with them collaboratively so that all can contribute to the final result.

Solution

Enable collaboration such that the participants can work on the same item (e.g., documents, worksheets, etc.) at the same time or by taking turns (Figure 9.66).

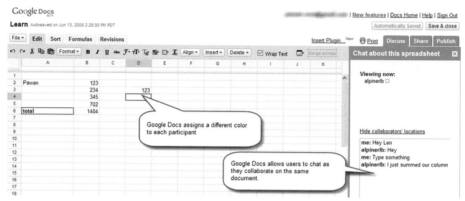

FIGURE 9.66 Google Docs allows multiple users to work on the same worksheet at the same time. To distinguish among participants, they are assigned different colors. It also allows them to chat while working on the same document, further facilitating collaboration.

Why

For their successful completion, many tasks require collaboration between two or more people. The nature of collaboration is often in real time, where all participants work (i.e., discuss, write, sketch, chat, etc.) simultaneously; or collaboration may be of a turn-taking nature, when only one person works on the item at a time and then sends it on to others.

How

Collaboration involves several activities: sharing information with others, coordinating and inviting others to participate, working together on shared documents, reviewing changes and updates, and, if necessary, reverting to older versions.

ALLOW USERS TO SPECIFY THE NATURE OF SHARING

As a first step in collaboration, users must share the item with others and specify how the item should be shared. The item's owner can determine whether the people with whom the item is shared can view the item, comment on it, and/or modify it (Figure 9.67).

FACILITATE SCHEDULING

Coordination is an important aspect of working together. An important task when working together is to determine a mutually convenient time for all participants. This can be done in several ways. One approach is to allow participants to share their schedules so that available times can be discerned by viewing them at the same time. Many calendar web applications allow users to share their calendars to help identify times that are open for scheduling (Figure 9.68).

When sharing calendars is not possible, a common approach is to have the team leader suggest a few times and let the rest of the team members vote on the preferred times (Figure 9.69).

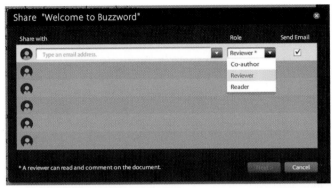

FIGURE 9.67 Buzzword (from Adobe) allows users to indicate the roles of users with whom the document is shared: "Co-author," "Reviewer," or "Reader." A reader can only view the document, a reviewer can read and comment on the document, and a co-author can read, comment, and modify the document.

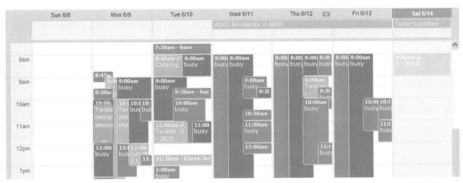

FIGURE 9.68 This example from Google Calendar shows four shared calendars. Once shared and overlaid on each other, it's easy to see that the only open time for all four users is on Tuesday from 12:00 to 12:30 P.M.

Enter your name in the text box below and cast your vote by selecting the corresponding fields. Click the "Participate" button to save the information.

	October 2008					November 2008	
	Thu 30		**Fri 31**			**Mon 3**	
	8:00 AM	10:00 AM	11:30 AM	3:00 PM	4:30 PM	11:00 AM	2:30 PM
Paul				OK		OK	
Your name	☐	☐	☐	☐	☐	☐	☐
Count	0	0	0	1	0	1	0

Participate

FIGURE 9.69 To find a mutually convenient time, Doodle.ch allows users to create a poll and have the rest of the team members respond by checking convenient times to hold a meeting or schedule an event.

Not all meetings can be scheduled. Often, when chatting or having a conversation, users may want to share a document or start a collaborative session. Allow users to have such impromptu meetings to improve collaboration (see the PRESENCE INDICATOR pattern earlier in this chapter).

ALLOW ADDITIONAL MODES OF INTERACTION

While working in real time, either on the same document or brainstorming using a whiteboard, improve collaboration by letting participants see each other, chat with each other, talk to each other, write notes, and so forth (Figure 9.70).

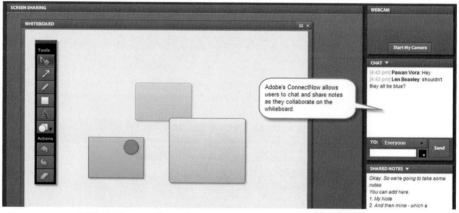

FIGURE 9.70 Adobe's ConnectNow allows users to chat, take notes, view each other on a web cam, talk, and so forth while having a meeting or collaborating on a whiteboard.

FIGURE 9.71
While showing users who is editing the document (a), Adobe Buzzword does not permit simultaneous changes. If users attempt to do so, a message indicating the reason they are "locked" from updating the document is shown (b).

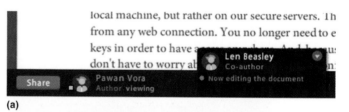

(a)

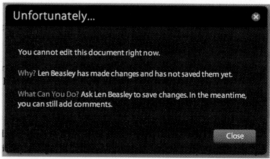

(b)

ALLOW USERS TO MANAGE REVISIONS

When working together on the same document, it's important that users are not overwriting one another's updates. The application should create necessary "locks" to make the interaction relatively seamless, rather than having users "check out" documents to make changes and then "check in" the updated documents (Figure 9.71).

When several participants work on a document, it's important to know what changes were made and who made them. Most applications allow users to select versions of the document and show a comparison by highlighting what was added, deleted, and changed (Figure 9.72).

Once users have identified the changes, if they do not agree with the changes or prefer a previous version of the document, they should be allowed to revert back to any of the previous versions (Figure 9.73). This is very common in

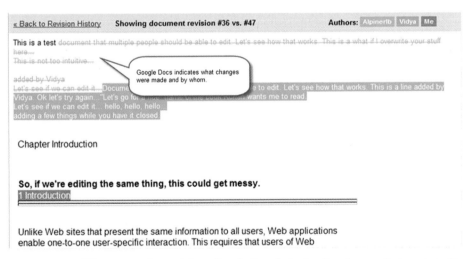

FIGURE 9.72 When comparing revisions, Google Docs indicates the changes that were made and who made them.

FIGURE 9.73 Zoho Writer shows users the documents' version in the "Show version" dropdown list. Users can view any version and then click "Revert" to return to that version of the document. Note that this feature is enabled for users regardless of whether they are collaborating.

wikis,[4] where pages can be added, edited, or deleted by any of the participants. Most wikis, therefore, allow users to roll back the pages to previous versions.

Related design patterns

The first step in COLLABORATION is SHARING documents or other artifacts; in addition, to facilitate collaboration, MESSAGING among users is essential.

---

[4]A wiki is a web application that allows users to collaboratively create, edit, and link web pages using a very simple markup method; more recently, wikis have provided rich-text editing capabilities as well.

CHAPTER 10

Internationalization

INTRODUCTION

Web applications designed for global audiences need to address two important issues in their design: *internationalization* and *localization* (Aykin, 2000):[1]

- *Internationalization* (I18N)[2] is the process of designing an application so that it can be adapted to various languages and regions without engineering changes.
- *Localization* (L10N) is the process of adapting an application for a specific region or language by adding locale-specific components and translating text.

Internationalizing web applications is an important step toward localization. Not only can it decrease the total effort of localization by half (Hurst, 2007), but it can also eliminate the need to develop region- and language-specific versions of the applications. The process of internationalization helps incorporate necessary flexibility and adaptability in web applications during the initial design (and not just during localization) and requires paying attention to cultural norms and preferences, color choices, image appropriateness, and so forth (EXTENSIBLE DESIGN). In addition to designing for extensibility, designers must ensure that formats used for dates (DATE FORMAT), times (TIME FORMAT), numbers (NUMBER FORMAT), and currencies (CURRENCY AND CURRENCY FORMAT) follow familiar conventions and do not require undue effort for their interpretation (see the Geolocation sidebar).

Once applications are localized, it's important for users to be easily able to navigate to desired local applications (GLOBAL GATEWAY) and/or change the language while interacting with an application (LANGUAGE SELECTOR).

---

[1] A related term is *globalization* (sometimes abbreviated as G11N), which refers to the process of preparing both the application and the business for international markets (Aykin, 2000).

[2] The terms *internationalization* and *localization* are sometimes abbreviated as I18N and L10N, respectively. The 18 in I18N refers to the number of letters between the *I* and *N* in the word *internationalization*; similarly, the 10 in L10N represents the number of letters between the *L* and *N* in the word *localization*.

GEOLOCATION

To present appropriate formats for date, time, number, and currency by default, many applications use the *geolocation* approach. Geolocation refers to identifying the geographic location of the computer on the Internet. Knowing the geographic location of the computer, and thus the location of its user, web applications can direct users to an appropriate region-specific version of the application. For example, users from India typing *www.google.com* can be directed to *www.google.co.in*, and those from Japan can be directed to *www.google.co.jp*. Geolocation can also be used to make a reasonable guess about users' date, time, number, and currency preferences. For example, users accessing the application from the United States can be shown prices in U.S. dollars ($), and for those accessing the application from Japan, they can be shown prices in yen (¥).

Although this chapter addresses a few of the important patterns, internationalization and localization are very rich topics. Readers are encouraged to consider the resources listed in the References at the end of the book, most specifically del Galdo et al. (1996), Aykin (2004, 2006), Yunkers (2002), and Ishida (2008).

EXTENSIBLE DESIGN

Problem

Although web applications are designed primarily for users in a region and for a language, designers may want to make them available in other regions and languages in the future.

Solution

Design web applications so that they do not favor any particular language or country and, when localized, they do not require a complete overhaul of the user interface or content, except for translation. This requires identifying and separating country- and language-specific application elements and its user interface and ensuring that none of the localizable elements are "hard-coded" in it.

Why

EXTENSIBLE DESIGN is the core of internationalization. It prepares web applications for localization and eliminates the need to create country- or language-specific versions. By having only one core version, not only does maintaining code become easier, but so does ensuring consistency in the user interface among language-specific instances of the application. Furthermore, by making web applications locale-independent and culture-neutral, extensible design avoids design elements that may be misinterpreted or offensive to other cultures.

An extensible design also helps make web applications more accessible to people with disabilities. For example, by designing the application such that it can accommodate expansion in text size when translated to other languages, it enables users with poor eyesight to enlarge text without affecting the page layout (see Chapter 11).

How

Extensible design encompasses all aspects of user interface design: markup, images, messaging, terminology, and so forth. Following are some of the best practices for developing an extensible design.

USE THE UTF-8 ENCODING FORMAT FOR WEB PAGES

Character encoding refers to mapping the characters (alphabets, numbers, punctuation marks, etc.) to a unique number (e.g., *A* is mapped to 65 in ASCII[3] encoding format). It helps web browsers determine the characters to display on a web page. Selecting the character-encoding method, therefore, determines the languages a web application may be able to support. Appropriate selection is also important for web applications that are designed to support users who may prefer languages other than English for inputting data.

The original encoding method, ASCII, is based on the English alphabet and supports 94 characters. ISO 8859-1, an extension of the ASCII encoding method, is based on a multinational character set and supports 191 characters from the Latin script. Although it supports English and several European languages, it doesn't support Asian language characters sets such as Chinese, Japanese, Indian, and several others. UTF-8 encoding method encodes all characters in the Unicode standard and thus supports the characters of most languages in the world. Therefore, to allow maximum coverage in terms of language support, use the UTF-8[4] encoding format.

Specifying the encoding method for web pages is pretty straightforward. Here are some examples:

- XHTML:

```
<meta http-equiv="content-type" content="text/html;
charset=utf-8" />
```

- JSP (Java Server Pages):

```
<%@ page contentType="text/html; charset=utf-8"
pageEncoding="utf-8" %>
```

[3]ASCII stands for American Standard Code for Information Interchange and is pronounced "æski."
[4]UTF-8 refers to Unicode Transformation Format-8-bit version.

> **NOTE**
>
> Semantic structure helps in improving accessibility as well. See the SEMANTIC MARKUP pattern in Chapter 11 for more information

For additional information on UTF-8 and Unicode standards, visit *www.utf-8. com/* and *www.unicode.org/faq/utf_bom.html.*

AVOID USING PRESENTATIONAL TAGS IN THE MARKUP

Instead of using tags such as <b> and <i> in the markup, use their semantically equivalent tags such as <strong> and <em>. Using presentational tags makes localization difficult because different languages have different approaches to emphasize text. For example, Japanese authors avoid emphasizing text by making it bold or italic because their characters are too complex for such text treatment (Ishida, 2008); instead, they use *wakiten* (boten marks) for emphasis (Figure 10.1).

ALLOW FOR TEXT EXPANSION

On average, non-English languages take up to 30 to 40 percent more space than English (Figure 10.2). This text expansion is commonly referred to as *text swell* and must be taken into account when localizing pages to European languages; localizing pages to Asian languages generally requires less space than English. To allow for text swell, design pages such that localizing to another

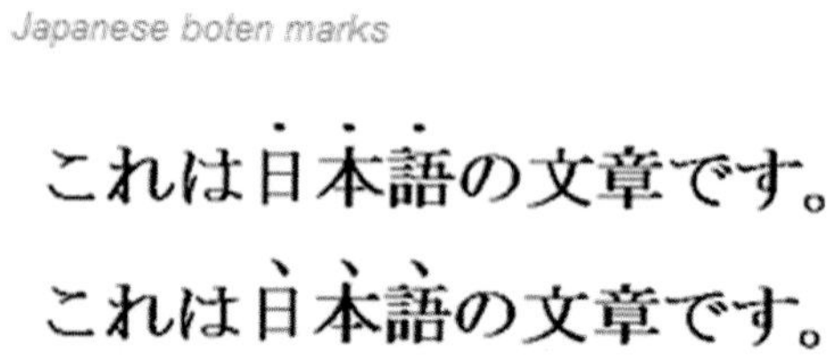

Japanese boten marks

これは日本語の文章です。

これは日本語の文章です。

FIGURE 10.1 Japanese authors prefer using boten marks for emphasis instead of making text bold or italic. The Cascading Style Sheets level 3 (CSS3) fonts module supports these native forms of emphasis (see CSS3 and International Text at *www. w3.org/International/articles/css3-text/#Slide0200.*)

English: Add Note
German: Addieren Sie Anmerkung
Spanish: Agregue La Nota
French: Ajoutez La Note

FIGURE 10.2 The phrase "Add Note" expands by 50 to 100 percent when translated to some European languages.

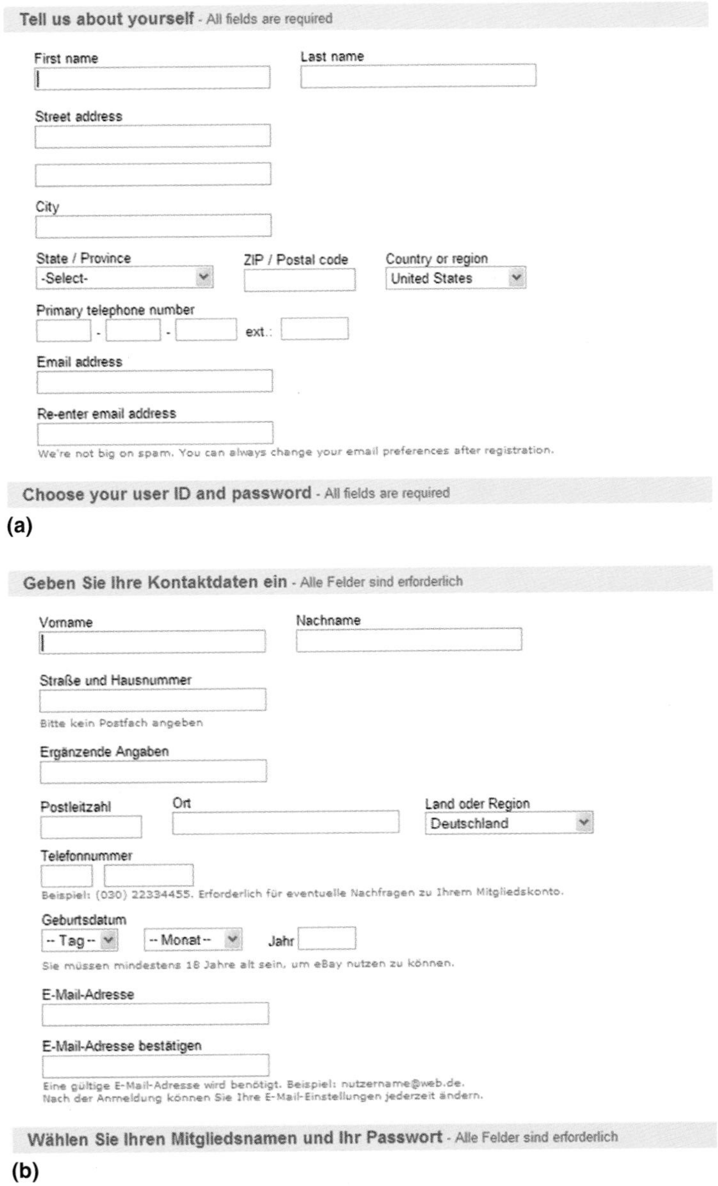

Tell us about yourself - All fields are required

First name

Last name

Street address

City

State / Province   ZIP / Postal code   Country or region
-Select-   United States

Primary telephone number
           -        -   ext.:

Email address

Re-enter email address

We're not big on spam. You can always change your email preferences after registration.

Choose your user ID and password - All fields are required

(a)

Geben Sie Ihre Kontaktdaten ein - Alle Felder sind erforderlich

Vorname

Nachname

Straße und Hausnummer

Bitte kein Postfach angeben

Ergänzende Angaben

Postleitzahl   Ort   Land oder Region
                       Deutschland

Telefonnummer

Beispiel: (030) 22334455. Erforderlich für eventuelle Nachfragen zu Ihrem Mitgliedskonto.

Geburtsdatum
-- Tag --   -- Monat --   Jahr

Sie müssen mindestens 18 Jahre alt sein, um eBay nutzen zu können.

E-Mail-Adresse

E-Mail-Adresse bestätigen

Eine gültige E-Mail-Adresse wird benötigt. Beispiel: nutzername@web.de.
Nach der Anmeldung können Sie Ihre E-Mail-Einstellungen jederzeit ändern.

Wählen Sie Ihren Mitgliedsnamen und Ihr Passwort - Alle Felder sind erforderlich

(b)

FIGURE 10.3 eBay's registration form places labels above the form controls (a). When the page is translated to German, the page layout remains unaffected (b).

language won't affect page layout. Some common approaches to allow for text expansion are:

- On pages with form elements, especially those that have multicolumn layouts, place labels above the form elements. Text swell caused by

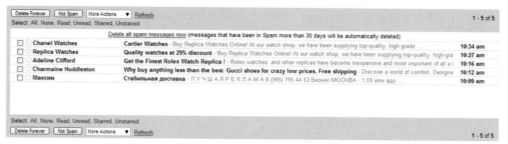

FIGURE 10.4 As the browser window expands, Gmail shows more text in message rows without affecting page layout. For narrower browser widths, Gmail truncates data and shows an ellipsis at the end.

translation then can be easily accommodated without affecting page layout (Figure 10.3).

- Do not force form elements or tabular data to fixed widths. Data in form elements such as buttons and dropdown lists may get clipped or appear in multiple lines, giving the page an unprofessional appearance. Similarly, translated data in narrower columns may cause information in a table cell to spill over to adjacent cells, or information may end up in several lines, making tabular data difficult to read. For secondary data, it may be acceptable to truncate or expand the data based on the browser window's width (Figure 10.4).

- Allow graphical elements to expand vertically and/or horizontally. Designing visual elements that allow for text swell makes their reuse possible, regardless of the language to which the application is localized (Figure 10.5).

- Allow sufficient space for icon labels. Because icons are not universally understood (see the ICONS pattern in Chapter 12), they are usually supplemented with a text label. Labels placement and icon design should also be accounted for with text expansion to avoid potential design issues during localization (Figure 10.6).

DESIGN MESSAGES TO ACCOMMODATE VARIABLE TEXT

Variable text, also referred to as *concatenated strings*, refers to text that is constructed using both static and variable text fragments and is usually presented in sentence form. For example, Figure 10.7(a) shows Google's search results page with the message "Results **1–10** of about **1,620,000,000** for **website.**" Variable texts in this message are the number of results being shown (1–10), the total number of search results (1,620,000,000), and the search query (web site). A similar message on Google India in Figure 10.7(b) has a different order of variables. It first displays the total number of search results (194,000), the number of results being shown (1–10), and the search query (वेबसाइट).Google Japan in Figure 10.7(c) has a different order of variable text starting with the

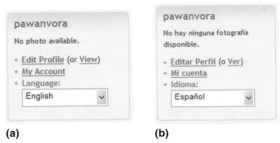

(a)   **(b)**

FIGURE 10.5 The "account" box on Blogger.com uses a box with rounded corners. When translating from English (a) to Spanish (b), more space is required to accommodate the translated information. Because of the box's extensible design, it can easily accommodate additional vertical space without affecting the layout.

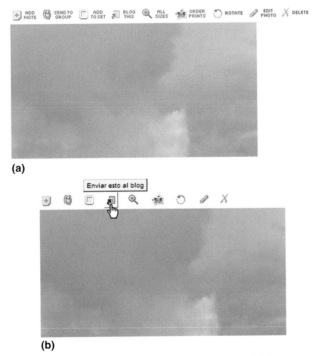

FIGURE 10.6 Flickr shows icon labels when a page is in English (a) but removes them when showing the page in other languages (b). Instead, they are shown as tooltips. This may be because the labels are embedded in the images requiring a different set of images for each language. In addition, because the translated labels require more space, it may be difficult to fit all the icons in the available space.

> **TIP**
> Allowing for text expansion is important even for web applications that are not going to be localized. When ignored, page design can break down or content may become difficult to read for users who prefer larger text.

FIGURE 10.7 Search results message on (a) Google United States, (b) Google India, and (c) Google Japan.

search query (web site), the total number of search results (1,150,000,000), and then the number of results being shown (1–10).

If messages are coded so that a variable text fragment is simply inserted in a static message, it would be almost impossible to localize the message. To make localization easier, therefore, it's important that code accommodates changing the sentence structure and reordering of the variables. Possible solutions are to either have the entire message translated or have a different way of presenting information, usually in a nonsentence form by separating the label and the variable text (e.g., Total number of search results: 200) (Hurst, 2007).

AVOID EMBEDDING TEXT IN IMAGES

Avoid including text in images. When text is embedded in images, localization requires a new image to be created with translated text. Instead, consider overlaying text on background images (Figure 10.8).

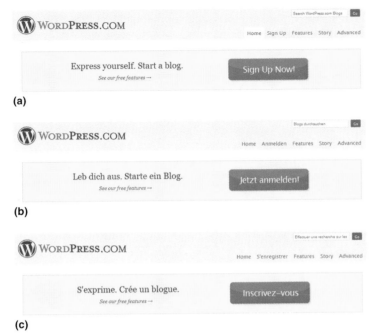

FIGURE 10.8 The "Sign Up Now!" button on WordPress.com is an overlay of the text "Sign Up Now!" on top of a button image (a), making it easy to reuse the button's original image as a background image and use translated text for other languages (b, c).

USE CULTURE-NEUTRAL IMAGES

When using images and icons, use universally recognized objects and avoid using images that are ethnocentric and/or may be considered offensive in other cultures. For example, to represent email, use an image of an envelope instead of a rural mailbox, which is readily understood only in the United States. In addition, avoid using hand gestures in icons and images, as they may be considered offensive in some cultures. For example, using an "okay" sign (index finger and thumb together forming a circle) is considered obscene in Brazil,[5] while the thumbs-up gesture (a sign of "all good" or "okay" in North America) is considered highly offensive in Iraq and other Islamic countries (Koerner, 2003).

Even symbols commonly considered to be "neutral" may not be so. The check symbol (a cross in a square box) means "correct" or "okay" in many countries. But in Japan and Korea, a circle is used instead of a check mark to mean "yes"; in fact, the checkmark indicates "no good" or "fail." Finally, avoid using maps that include controversial regional or national boundaries (e.g., showing national boundaries on maps of India and Pakistan).

[5]In Turkey it's a sign for something homosexual. In China, it can mean "zero" or the number three; in Japan and Korea, it can refer to the shape of a coin and means "money." For more information, see *The OK Hand Gesture Around the World—Learn the Meaning of Hand Gestures* (2008); *www.articlesbase.com/travel-tips-articles/the-ok-hand-gesture-around-the-world-learn-the-meaning-of-hand-gestures-624739.html.*

FIGURE 10.9 Amazon uses the label "basket" for its e-commerce site in the United Kingdom. (However, the icon still resembles a shopping cart.)

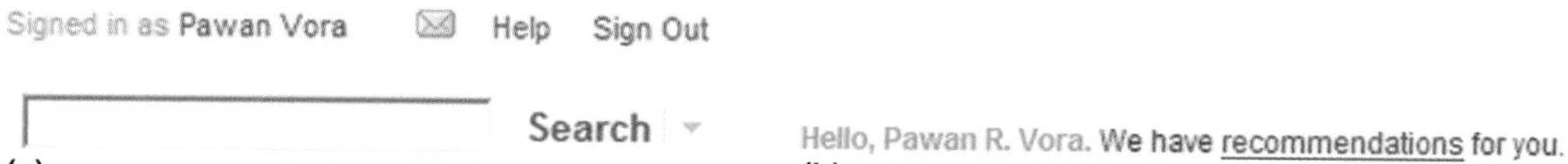

Signed in as **Pawan Vora** ✉ Help Sign Out

| Search ▾ | Hello, Pawan R. Vora. We have recommendations for you. |

(a) **(b)**

FIGURE 10.10 Greetings used by Flickr (a) and Amazon (b) are more appropriate for international audiences.

USE CULTURALLY RELEVANT METAPHORS

In North America, using a shopping cart is a valid metaphor for purchasing items because it easily translates to users' real-world experience. In Europe and Asia, however, a shopping cart icon could cause confusion because users are more familiar with shopping baskets than with carts. E-commerce sites should change labels and/or images when serving customers in those countries (Figure 10.9).

USE PLAIN LANGUAGE

Avoid confusing nonnative speakers by using plain language and refraining from slang and colloquialisms in text. In addition, be sensitive when using greetings such as "Welcome, <first name>" for applications that may be used by non-American users. North American culture is very informal compared to many other cultures, as evidenced by its low Power Distance Index in Hofstede's cultural dimensions (see *www.greet-hofstede.com/hofstede_united_states.shtml*). In Asia, such informality would be considered inappropriate, as people are usually addressed by their last name. Greetings used by Amazon or Flickr are more appropriate for web applications with international audiences (Figure 10.10).

In general, to make localization easier, avoid the following when developing web content (Hurst, 2007):

- Words with multiple meanings
- Abbreviations
- Mnemonics
- Acronyms
- Slang or jargon
- Gender notation
- Creation of new words
- Shortened plurals or word combinations
- Anything that portrays a way of life or culture specific to one country

Related design patterns

The patterns identified in Chapter 11—SEMANTIC MARKUP, UNOBTRUSIVE STYLE SHEETS, UNOBTRUSIVE JAVSCRIPT, and so forth—are also relevant for internationalization, as they help make web applications easy to localize.

DATE FORMAT

Problem

Using a date format common in one region can be confusing to users from other regions. For example, the date format used in the United States (mm/dd/yy or mm/dd/yyyy) would be confusing to European users because they are familiar with dd/mm/yy or dd/mm/yyyy formats and to Japanese users who use yy/mm/dd format.

Solution

Use the ISO 8601 recommended yyyy-mm-dd date format when showing dates, or use a format that eliminates confusion between the month and the year in a date (Figures 10.11 and 10.12).

Why

Although web applications designed to be used exclusively by a country or a region can depend on its native date formatting standard, users from other

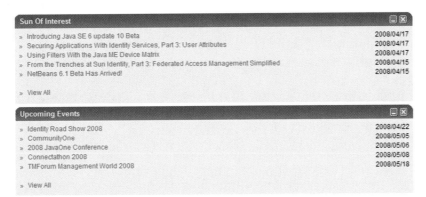

FIGURE 10.11 Sun uses the yyyy/mm/dd format for displaying dates (a slight variation from the ISO recommended yyyy-mm-dd format).

All Activity - Advanced View from Apr. 6, 2007 to Apr. 6, 2008			
Date	Type	To/From	Name/Email
Mar. 13, 2008	Bonus	From	PayPal
Oct. 4, 2007	Transfer	To	Bank Account

FIGURE 10.12 PayPal uses a date format of the abbreviated month, dd, yyyy to make the month and year obvious.

regions may find it confusing if it doesn't match their local conventions. For example, the date "02/04/03" may be interpreted as

- 2nd of April 2003 (Europe)
- 4th of February 2003 (United States)
- 3rd of April 2002 (Japan)

The international format defined by ISO (ISO 8601) addresses this problem by defining a numerical date system in the format yyyy-mm-dd. Showing dates in an ISO format or making the month and year obvious prevents confusion. In addition, this approach is computer friendly, as it makes chronologically sorting dates easier (see also *www.w3.org/International/questions/qa-date-format*).

However, the ISO date format is difficult to read, as it is quite different from most users' native date format. Therefore, when space and sorting are not issues, use a more readable format that spells out the month and makes the year obvious (e.g., February 4, 2003, or 4 February 2003).

How

Designers have two options to show dates:

1. Use a locale-neutral ISO 8601 recommended format. The ISO 8601 recommended format of yyyy-mm-dd is the solution most commonly adopted by web applications with a diverse user base, where:
   - yyyy is the year (all the digits, i.e., 2008).
   - mm is the month (01, January, to 12, December).
   - dd is the day (01 to 31).
   January 2, 2008 would then be shown as 2008-01-02.
2. Use a format that makes the month and year obvious. This approach uses a name for the month and four digits for the year. So the date can be written as January 2, 2008, or 2 January 2008. This approach is more natural to users, since it is easier to read. However, it occupies more space and, because it may affect sorting performance, is less computer friendly.

BE CAREFUL WHEN ABBREVIATING MONTHS

Abbreviating letters for months in dates (e.g., Jan. 2, 2008, or 2 Jan. 2008) may be problematic for users in some countries. For example, in French, the first three letters of June and July are the same—*juin* and *juillet*, respectively.

CONSIDER USERS' LOCALE PREFERENCES WHEN SHOWING DATES

For web applications, it's possible to capture users' locale preferences and display users' native date format using the Accept-Language HTTP header. However, this method of showing dates may be inappropriate if the content is not localized and therefore it is possible that the date format will not match

Edit the photo date

Date Taken   Date Posted

09/08/2006 | at 14:00:20

(a)

사진 날짜 편집

촬영 날짜   포스트 날짜

09/08/2006 | 시간 14:00:20

(b)

FIGURE 10.13 This pop-up calendar from Flickr, although it uses mm/dd/yyyy format (even for different languages), makes it easy to select a date from the calendar (a). The month in the pop-up calendar is localized to the selected language (b).

the language of the page. For example, if a page is presented in German, showing dates in the North American mm/dd/yyyy format may be confusing (even when users' locale preference is English), as users may be unclear if the page uses the mm/dd/yyyy format or dd/mm/yyyy format.

USE CALENDAR POP-UPS FOR DATE SELECTION

To minimize date input errors, consider using pop-up calendars. They help in several ways. First, they prevent data-entry errors caused by differing date formats (mm/dd/yy versus dd/mm/yy). Second, because users can see both the month and day, they can be sure that they have chosen the right date. When using pop-up calendars, show the calendar as soon as the date field has received focus to encourage users to pick a date from the calendar; however, do not prevent them from entering the date via the keyboard. In addition, when using a pop-up calendar, ensure that the month is clearly shown (Figure 10.13).

Related design patterns

Using a locale-neutral format requires more horizontal space than the U.S. format of mm/dd/yy or mm/dd/yyyy. Therefore, it's important that pages use an

EXTENSIBLE DESIGN to accommodate additional space requirements. In addition, consider using the GLOBAL GATEWAY pattern to capture users' country and language preferences.

TIME FORMAT

Problem

Like date formats, time formats vary from one region to another. Although each time format shows hours, minutes, and seconds, their presentation order and separators often vary in terms of a 12- or 24-hour format; the character used to separate hours, minutes, and seconds; leading zeros; the display of time zones; and the use of daylight savings times.

Solution

Whenever possible, show times in users' local time zones and use local conventions for showing time—that is, either the 12-hour AM/PM system or 24-hour system (Figure 10.14).

If time cannot be represented in users' native format, use ISO 8601 recommendations, which use the 24-hour system with either an **hhmmss** format or **hh:mm:ss** extended format, where:

- hh represents hours between 00 and 24.
- mm represents minutes between 00 and 59.
- ss represents seconds between 00 and 59 (or 60 in the exceptional case of an added leap second).

Why

Users are likely to be most familiar with the local convention for their time zone and may be uncertain about the time when presented with other conventions. In addition, when time is presented in a different country's time zone, users may not know how to convert it to their local time zone or may make errors when converting it.

How

Whenever possible, show time based on users' local time zones or stated preferences. In cases where the event or activity occurs in a different time zone,

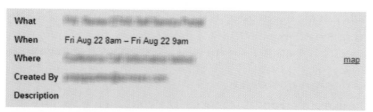

What	
When	Fri Aug 22 8am – Fri Aug 22 9am
Where	map
Created By	
Description	

FIGURE 10.14 Google Calendar localizes time to users' local time zone, even when the meeting is scheduled by someone in a different time zone.

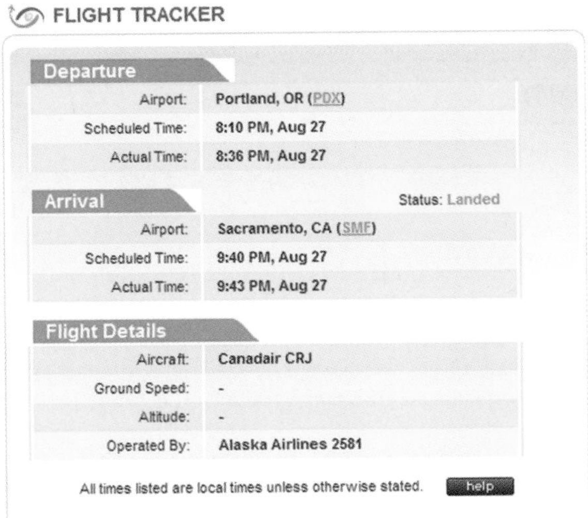

FIGURE 10.15 When showing flight status information, departure and arrival times should be shown using local departure and arrival times regardless of the time zone from which users are viewing the data (*www.flightview.com*).

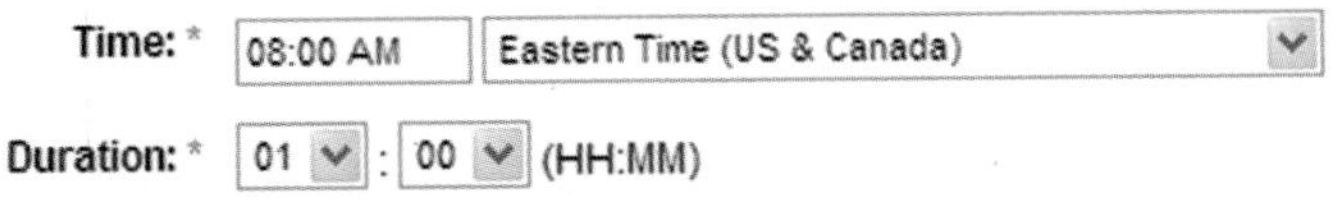

FIGURE 10.16 When creating a meeting or an event in ReadyTalk, users are asked to indicate both the time and time zone in which the meeting will occur.

show time using the event or activity's time zone as the point of reference. For example, when showing flight status, use local time zones from where the flight will depart and where the flight will arrive (Figure 10.15).

ALLOW USERS TO SPECIFY THEIR TIME ZONE PREFERENCE

When registering with an application or setting up a user profile, ask users for their preferred time zone (Figure 10.16).

For tasks such as scheduling meetings or setting up events, when showing local times, indicate the time zone and offset from GMT (Greenwich Mean Time) or UTC (Coordinated Universal Time or Universal Coordinated Time) (Figure 10.17). Because GMT and UTC are usually the same,[6] GMT is more commonly used because of users' familiarity with it.

Related design patterns

The localized DATE FORMAT pattern usually accompanies the TIME FORMAT pattern, because most applications that show time or require users to select

---

[6]GMT is based on the rotation of the Earth, whereas UTC is based on cesium-beam atomic clocks. The two times are usually the same, or no more than a second apart, as leap seconds are occasionally applied to UTC.

Name: [   ]
Enter your real name, so people you know can recognize you.

Username: [   ]   Your URL: http://twitter.com/**USERNAME**
No spaces, please.

Email: [   ]

Time Zone: [(GMT-08:00) Pacific Time (US & Canada)   ▾]

FIGURE 10.17 When editing account information, Twitter allows users to specify their time zone. Although it shows "GMT-08:00," it clarifies the time zone by indicating "Pacific Time" and the countries in which it is applicable, "(US and Canada)."

times usually show dates or require users to select dates. In addition, showing time zones and time zone offsets requires additional space, making use of the EXTENSIBLE DESIGN pattern as well.

NUMBER FORMAT

Problem

Conventions around the world for representing numbers vary in terms of group and decimal (i.e., fractional) separators, precision required, units of measure, and so forth.

Solution

Follow the conventions, formats, and regulations of the country from which users are accessing the application.

Why

There are no universally accepted conventions for representing numbers. They differ widely among countries. Since users cannot be expected to be familiar with conventions of other countries, the usable option is to present numbers in formats they are most accustomed to seeing.

How

When showing numbers, the whole (or integer) portion of a number is usually split into groups by a separator. The way the number groups are created and the separator is used varies around the world (Figure 10.18). In the United States, numbers are shown in groups of three, separated by commas (e.g., 1,000,000); in India, numbers are shown in one group of three and then in groups of two, separated by commas (e.g., 10,00,000); and in Japan, large numbers are created by grouping digits in 10000s separated by ideographic characters that represent powers of 10000 (e.g., 1億0000万0000).

United States	1,000,000,000	Groups of 3, separated by a comma (,)
Germany	1.000.000.000	Groups of 3, separated by a period (.)
Switzerland	1'000'000'000	Groups of 3, separated by an apostrophe (')
France	1 000 000 000	Groups of 3, separated by a space
India	1,00,00,00,000	First group of 3, then groups of 2, separated by a comma (,)
Japan	1億0000万0000	Groups of 4 separated by ideographic characters

FIGURE 10.18 Examples of grouping separators in different countries.

United States	1,123.45	Decimal separator is a period (.)
France	1 123,45	Decimal separator is a comma (,)
Switzerland (German)	1'123.45	Decimal separator is a period (.)
Switzerland (French)	1 123,45	Decimal separator is a comma (,)

FIGURE 10.19 Examples of decimal separators in different countries. Multilingual countries such as Switzerland use different decimal separators for different languages. A comma is used as the decimal separator, except when the amount is in Swiss Francs, in which case a period is used, and either an apostrophe or space is used for the thousands separator.

Like grouping separators, the separator between the whole and the fractional part of a number—known as a decimal point, decimal separator, and other terms—also varies from one country to another. It can be a decimal point (i.e., a period), comma, or another character (Figure 10.19).

USE UNITS OF MEASURE FAMILIAR TO USERS

Use units for weights and measurements to suit the target country's conventions as well. For example, using pounds, feet, and inches (English or British system) will not be effective in countries that use the Metric system, where the corresponding units of measure are kilograms, meters, and centimeters, respectively. Similarly, showing temperature in Fahrenheit will be confusing to users who are only familiar with the Centigrade system. Therefore, if an application is likely to be accessed by those familiar with different conventions, show units of measure and temperature in both Metric and English systems or allow users to switch from one measurement unit to another (Figure 10.20).

Because users may be unfamiliar with the terms "English" and "Metric" systems, when feasible, use explicit and familiar units of measurement such as °F and °C. Similarly, it is better to ask users to choose units of measurement, such as centimeters, meters, feet, yards, and so forth, instead of asking them to choose between English and Metric systems.

SHOW PHONE NUMBERS IN FAMILIAR FORMATS

Phone number formats also vary from one country to another in the total number of digits in the phone number and separators (Figure 10.21). Therefore, when possible, follow local conventions for showing phone numbers.

(a)

(b)

FIGURE 10.20 Weather information from *USA Today* (a) shows temperatures in both °F and °C. Weather.com (b) allows users to switch between "English" and "Metric" systems because it not only changes units of measure for temperature but also for wind, pressure, dew point, and visibility.

FIGURE 10.21
Local phone number formats.

Australia	61 (0403) 416 7216
New Zealand	64 021 525-582
United Kingdom	44 07700 954 321
United States	1 (954) 555-1234
France	33 06 87 71 23 45

An alternative is to use ITU-T E.123, which is the International Format that recommends the following (see also Figures 10.22 and 10.23):

§ 2.1: The international number should be printed below the national number, with corresponding digits lined up one under the other to facilitate understanding of the composition of the international number.

§ 2.5: If it is desirable to write only the international number, it should be written in the form: Telephone International + 22 607 123 4567.

Telephone	National	(607) 123 4567
	International	+ 22 607 123 4567

FIGURE 10.22 ITU-T E.123 recommendation for formatting national and international numbers.

FIGURE 10.23
Phone and fax numbers presented in this example are in an international format.

Location Information (Melbourne)

Park Hyatt Melbourne
1 Parliament Square off Parliament Place
Melbourne Victoria 3002
Australia

Tel: +61 3 9224 1234
Fax: +61 3 9224 1215

Related design patterns

Like other patterns, using localized NUMBER FORMAT requires additional space, and it's important that pages use an EXTENSIBLE DESIGN to accommodate additional space requirements. In addition, consider using GLOBAL GATEWAY to capture users' region and language preferences and present number formats accordingly.

CURRENCY AND CURRENCY FORMAT

Problem

Web applications (e.g., e-commerce applications) that show the value of products and services to users in regions around the world need to present prices in local currencies. However, not only are currencies different around the world, but their formatting in terms of the symbol and placement are different as well.

Solution

Show users currency in their native formats. In addition, where users may encounter prices in a currency other than in which they wish to transact, allow them to change it by specifying either country or desired currency (Figure 10.24).

(a)

(b)

(c)

FIGURE 10.24 Fontshop shows prices in U.S. dollars ($) (a), but allows users to select a different country from the country selection menu (b), which changes the currency, in this case, to Euros (€) (c).

United States $ 1,234.56
France   1 234,56 €
Brazil   R$ 1.234,56

FIGURE 10.25 The currency symbol and its placement differ among countries.

Why

Showing users price information in their local currencies and formats helps them because they know exactly how much they will pay for products (or services) and they do not have to rely on exchange calculators or other ways of converting prices to get correct amounts.

How

Web applications that support multiple currencies must take into consideration corresponding currency symbols, codes, and formats. This is because of the diversity in currencies and number formatting schemes used by different countries. For example, the currency symbol for the British pound (ISO code: GBP) is £ and for Japanese yen (ISO code: JPY) is ¥. In addition, the placement of the currency symbol varies from one country to another (Figure 10.25).

User interaction for changing currency is very similar to that of changing the language (see the LANGUAGE SELECTOR pattern later in this chapter). Depending on the number of currencies supported by an application, users may select the appropriate currency from either a dropdown list or a set of links (Figure 10.26).

When users change currencies to see prices in their local currency or a different currency, show the exchange rate along with the currency conversion (Figure 10.27).

To avoid potential confusion about the currency, show users the appropriate currency symbol (Figure 10.28), the ISO currency code, or both, as shown below. In addition, show the appropriate group and decimal separators based on users' locale preference

United States: $ 1,234,567.89 USD

Germany: € 1.234.567,89 EUR

France: € 1 234 567,89 EUR

MAKE THE CURRENCY SELECTION PERSISTENT

Do not require users to choose their desired currency every time they access the application and as they navigate the application pages. Make users' currency selection persist using cookies or as a preference tied to their login not only within the same session but also when they return to the application later.

Related design patterns

Prices are typically shown as numbers. Therefore, it is important that prices are not only shown in appropriate currencies and their formats but also follow

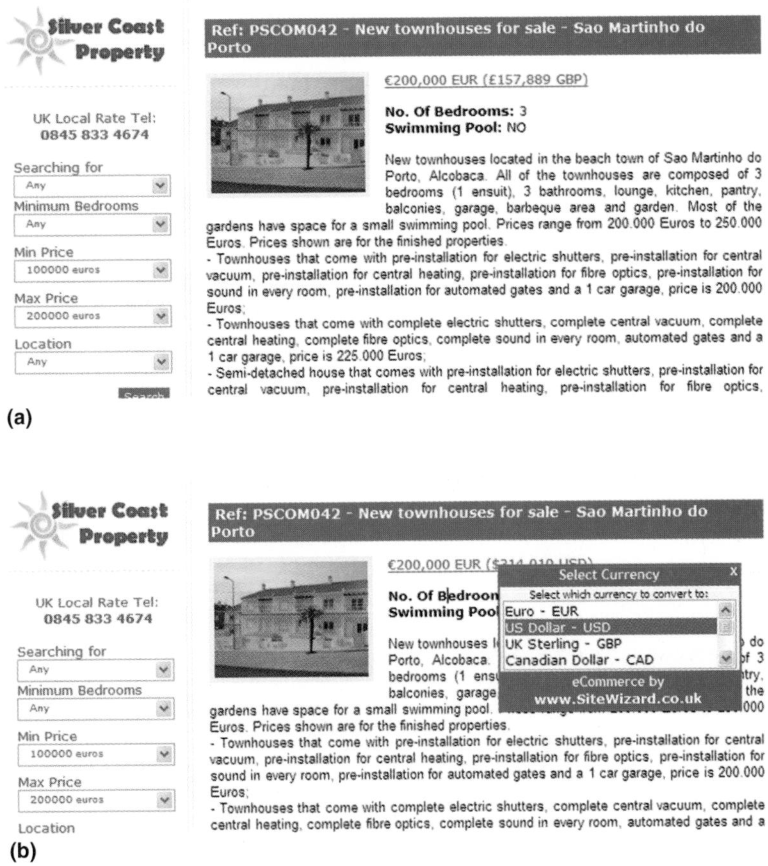

(a)

(b)

FIGURE 10.26 Silver Coast Property shows property prices in both Euros and GBP (Great Britain pounds) by default (a) and allows users to change the currency from GBP to U.S. dollars (USD), Canadian dollars (CAD), and others. Currency options are shown to users as a pop-up when users click the price link (b).

100,000.00 USD = **10,230,806.14 JPY**
United States Dollars   Japan Yen
1 USD = 102.308 JPY   1 JPY = 0.00977440 USD

FIGURE 10.27 Universal Currency Converter from XE.com shows users both the exchange rates for the source currency and the target currency, and vice versa.

local conventions for grouping and decimal separators (NUMBER FORMAT). In addition, to support different currency symbols and avoid using images for them, use the UTF-8 encoding. Showing the ISO code for the currency usually requires additional space, so it's important that pages use an EXTENSIBLE DESIGN.

Invoice Details

Specify the invoice details below. To increase the number of line items click the Add More Rows button. Tax can be optionally applied to each item by selecting the checkboxes in the Taxable column and specifying a Tax rate. Learn More

Currency:	Euros ▾ ?
Invoice Type:	-- Select Type -- ▾ ?
Email Subject: (optional)	
Note: (optional)	

Qty	Item ID	Description	Unit Price	Amount	Taxable
			€	€ 0.00	☐
			€	€ 0.00	☐
			€	€ 0.00	☐
			€	€ 0.00	☐
			€	€ 0.00	☐
			Subtotal: €	0.00	
			Shipping: € ▾	€ 0.00	☐
			Tax (%):	€ 0.00	
			Total: €	0.00	

FIGURE 10.28 When creating an invoice in PayPal, users are shown the appropriate currency symbol. Users may select a different currency, which updates the currency symbol accordingly.

GLOBAL GATEWAY

Problem

When localized applications are available, users need to be directed to the application designed for their region and language. This is particularly important for applications (e.g., e-commerce applications) where products and services offered by a company vary from one region to another. Even when localized applications are available using the appropriate country codes in their top-level domain (TLD) names[7] (e.g., *www.amazon.co.uk* for United Kingdom), users may not know the appropriate code or that a localized version exists and therefore they might go directly to the application's nonlocalized version.

Solution

To direct users to their localized version of the application, show them a global gateway page to allow them to choose their region (or country) and language (Figure 10.29). Once users have specified their preference, remember their selection so that they do not have to make the same choices again. However, do not lock users to their selection—allow them to change it (Yunkers, 2002).

---

[7]Many web applications use country-specific URLs by using the appropriate country code in their TLD name. Country codes for TLDs include .uk for United Kingdom, .jp for Japan, .fr for France, and so forth. See *www.iana.org/domains/root/db/* for a list of country code TLDs.

FIGURE 10.29 Coca-Cola takes users to a global gateway page and allows them to select the country of their choice. Additionally, the application remembers the selected option to avoid asking users to make the same selection again in the future.

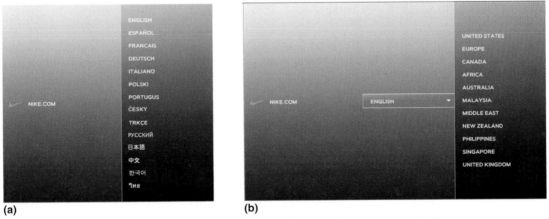

(a)   **(b)**

FIGURE 10.30 Nike asks users to select the language first (a), then the desired country (b).

Why

For many e-commerce applications, the products and services offered differ from one country to another. Allowing users to choose their country makes it easy for them to know exactly what they can purchase online and avoid the frustration of ordering items that may be unavailable in their country. Specifying the country also enables users to see localized prices, dates, currency, and so forth, further improving their experience interacting with the application.

How

Show users a list of available countries and/or languages, and allow them to indicate their choices and direct them to the localized version of the application for that region (Figure 10.30).

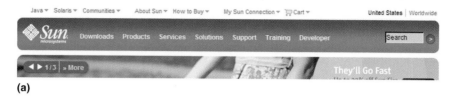

(a)

Some features, applications, and services are not available in all areas. See your carrier for details.

Some applications are not available in all areas. Application availability and pricing are subject to change.

(b)

FIGURE 10.31 (a) Sun places a "Worldwide" link in the top-right corner and, when clicked, shows users the "Global Gateway" page to allow users to select their country. (b) Apple places the "Apple.com Worldwide" dropdown list in the footer area and allows users to select a country directly.

ALLOW USERS TO CHANGE THEIR COUNTRY SELECTION ON EVERY PAGE

For many applications, especially e-commerce applications or applications that don't require users to login until they start transacting, users may access the application through pages other than the home page. To make it easy for them to switch to their country preference, allow them to select the country or access the global gateway page from every page within the application. The most common placements for the "Select Country" option are the top-right corner or the bottom in the footer region (Figure 10.31).

Related design patterns

Consider using the LANGUAGE SELECTOR pattern for users from multilingual countries who may want to change the application's language.

LANGUAGE SELECTOR

Problem

Users may prefer to view web application content in a language other than the one used by default. This is often the case when users are viewing a version of the application that is not localized or are directed to a localized web application in a foreign language because they are accessing it from a different country; this is because the web application uses the geolocation method to determine users' preferred language.

Solution

Show users the available language options, and allow them to change the language of the page content. To make it easy for users to determine if their preferred language is available, show language choices in their native script—that is,

FIGURE 10.32 Google India offers several language options to users and shows each language in its own script.

when viewing an application in Spanish, offer the language choice for English as "English," not "Inglés" (Figure 10.32).

Why

In countries such as Canada and India, where people with different language preferences and ethnicities may use the application, allowing users to switch to a different language is beneficial, since they may feel more comfortable viewing content in their native language. In addition, presenting language options in their own script makes it easy for users to understand available choices. This is similar to many interactive voice-response applications in the United States that, for the Spanish language option, prompt users in Spanish (e.g., *"para continuar en español, oprima el nueve"*) rather than English ("To continue in Spanish, press nine").

How

To make it easy for users to recognize languages, show users language choices in their own script and language rather than in the translated language. This makes it easier for users to navigate to their desired language if they made an incorrect choice for the language selection or if they are traveling and are presented with the localized version of the page and need to change the language (Figures 10.33 and 10.34).

DO NOT USE FLAGS TO REPRESENT LANGUAGES

Although Flags are acceptable for representing countries, there are several problems with their use when representing languages. Most important, flags represent countries and not languages. Some languages are spoken in many countries, and some countries speak many languages. For example, using the U.S. flag for English would be inappropriate because English is spoken in the United States, Canada, the United Kingdom, Australia, New Zealand, and several other

FIGURE 10.33
WordPress presents language options as if native speakers had written the menu option.

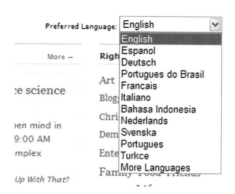

FIGURE 10.34 Blogger shows choices in their own script and language as well as the currently selected language.

countries. Using the Canadian flag would be an unambiguous selection, as many Canadians speak English and/or French. Similarly, using the Indian flag would not make it possible to determine users' preference for language because several languages are spoken in India, such as Bengali, Gujarati, Hindi, Kannada, Malayalam, Marathi, Oriya, Punjabi, Tamil, Telugu, and many others.

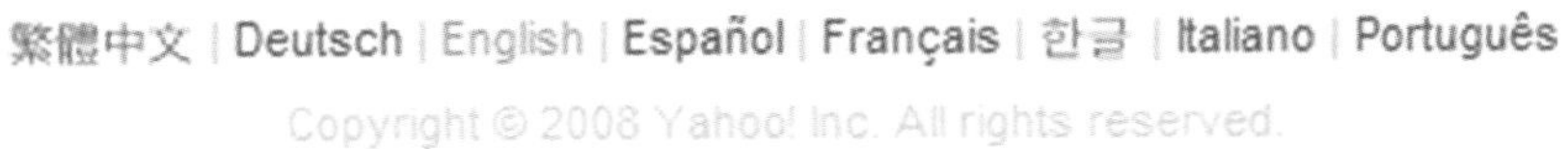

FIGURE 10.35 Language choices are offered as a set of links in the footer by Flickr.

FIGURE 10.36 When changing the language, Blogger keeps users on the same page in the newly selected language.

ALLOW USERS TO CHANGE THEIR INITIAL LANGUAGE SELECTION

Regardless of users' initial language selection, allow them to change it later. Users may want to change their language selection in case they are capable of comprehending multiple languages and prefer to view the page content in a different language. Language choice can be made using either a set of links or a dropdown menu depending on the available screen space (Figures 10.34 and Figure 10.35).

KEEP USERS ON THE SAME PAGE

Once a user changes the language, designers can either show users the page they are currently on in the selected language or take them to the "home" page of the application. Taking the user to the home page is appropriate for applications where a page may not be available in another language (e.g., Wikipedia) or if an application needs to serve the user using a different server and moving the session's data might be problematic. However, showing users the same page after selecting a different language is preferred, since users can easily switch the language on any page within the application and not have to worry about losing their place (Figure 10.36).

REMEMBER USERS' LANGUAGE CHOICE

Make users' language selection persist—that is, do not require them to make the choice again when they navigate to a different page within the application during the same visit or a return visit to the application in the future.

Related design patterns

Supporting multiple languages usually requires accommodating text expansion, making the best practices suggested in the EXTENSIBLE DESIGN pattern most important and relevant. In addition, language choices are often presented when users first visit an application and may be presented as part of the GLOBAL GATEWAY.

CHAPTER 11
Accessibility

INTRODUCTION

In the context of web applications, the term *accessibility* refers to designing web pages such that they are available to all users, including those with visual, physical, auditory, cognitive, or other disabilities.

When designing accessible web applications, it's important to follow the principle of PROGRESSIVE ENHANCEMENT—that is, design web pages in layers so that the basic content and interaction are available to all, and the more interactive (i.e., enhanced) options are available as capabilities of browsers and/or devices that can access the application increase. To allow for progressive enhancement, it's essential that application pages use SEMANTIC MARKUP, UNOBTRUSIVE STYLE SHEETS, and UNOBTRUSIVE JAVASCRIPT. Because user interaction with web applications is through forms, it's important they are designed to be accessible (ACCESSIBLE FORMS). In addition, other content presented on pages should be made accessible as well (ACCESSIBLE IMAGES, ACCESSIBLE TABLES, ACCESSIBLE NAVIGATION).

Although not a preferred option, there are situations where web applications cannot be made completely accessible in their current form and an alternative design may need to be built to ensure accessibility (ACCESSIBLE ALTERNATIVE). This is particularly the case with Rich Internet Applications (RIAs), which pose significant challenges to accessibility. To address this concern, the World Wide Web Consortium's Web Accessibility Initiative (W3C-WAI) has proposed a road map and working-draft versions for Accessible Rich Internet Applications (WAI-ARIA). While assistive technologies are catching up to W3C-WAI's recommendations, designers may want to start incorporating proposed markup in their designs.

Patterns in this chapter help in making web applications accessible and supporting the standards and regulations for web accessibility (see Standards and Regulations for Web Accessibility sidebar).

STANDARDS AND REGULATIONS FOR WEB ACCESSIBILITY

Several countries have adopted different laws and standards to ensure web accessibility. In the United States, the applicable standards and regulations include the Americans with Disabilities Act (ADA), Individuals with Disabilities Education Act (IDEA), and Section 508 of the Rehabilitation Act of 1973.

Perhaps the most important and comprehensive guidelines are the Web Accessibility Initiative's (WAI)[1] Web Content Accessibility Guidelines 1.0 (WCAG 1.0) and WCAG 2.0 in meeting the accessibility needs on the Web and complying with the regulations just noted. These guidelines detail how web developers can make their web sites and web applications usable for people with disabilities and are based on the following four principles:

1. *Perceivable.* Information and user interface components must be presentable to users in ways they can perceive.
2. *Operable.* User interface components and navigation must be operable.
3. *Understandable*. Information and the operation of a user interface must be understandable.
4. *Robust.* Content must be robust enough that it can be interpreted reliably by a wide variety of user agents, including assistive technologies.

For additional information on standards and regulations, see resources for Government Laws, Regulations, Policies, Standards, and Support at *www.uiaccess.com/access_links. html#government_laws_regs_policies.*

[1]The WAI is an organization within the W3C, the standards-making body for the World Wide Web. See *www.w3.org/WAI* for more information.

This chapter focuses on accessibility using core web technologies (i.e., HTML, CSS, and JavaScript) and does not address accessibility issues related to Flash and PDF. Readers interested in learning more about Flash and PDF accessibility should consider the following resources:

- Adobe Flash Accessibility Design Guidelines, *www.adobe.com/accessibility/ products/flash/best_practices.html*
- Adobe Acrobat Accessibility, *www.adobe.com/products/acrobat/solutionsacc.html*

NOTE

Because incorporating accessibility into web pages requires adapting HTML, CSS, and JavaScript, this chapter requires some familiarity with their basic concepts and syntax.

PROGRESSIVE ENHANCEMENT

Problem

Not knowing the browser and its version, platform, and assistive technology that users may utilize makes it difficult to predict how web applications will be used. As a result, exclusively relying on certain implementation approaches— even the recommended style sheets and JavaScript—may make a web application unusable or inaccessible to certain user populations.

Solution

Design web applications such that they support progressive enhancement. In other words, support users who have older browsers or assistive technologies to access the web application for content and functionality, while also offering users with newer browsers and more advanced technology to experience enhanced (i.e., more interactive) features in the web application (Champeon, 2003a, 2003b).

Why

Using progressive enhancement allows web applications the widest possible reach in terms of devices, browsers, and assistive technologies. In addition, by layering enhancements independent of each other, designers can avoid creating a separate accessible version (see the ACCESSIBLE ALTERNATIVE pattern later in this chapter), because regardless of the technology supported by the browser and/or assistive technology, users will be able to accomplish their tasks.

How

First and foremost, make web application content accessible by using web standards to mark up and structure page content and functionality without requiring client-side scripting technologies such as JavaScript (see the SEMANTIC MARKUP and ACCESSIBLE FORMS patterns later in this chapter).

Once content and functionality of a web application are made available to the widest possible audience, the next step is to improve its visual presentation using style sheets. However, make every effort to ensure that the incorporation of style sheets does not compromise its usability and accessibility for users whose browsers do not support them (see the UNOBTRUSIVE STYLE SHEETS pattern later in this chapter).

The final layer is to offer interactivity using client-side scripting approaches (e.g., JavaScript), which can make the application more responsive and efficient by supporting drag-and-drop, performing basic form validation without having to send data to the server, sorting table content, and so forth. Like style sheets, added interactivity should not affect users' ability to access web application content or functionality (see the UNOBTRUSIVE JAVASCRIPT pattern later in this chapter).

Finally, ensure that web applications using Ajax[2] work even when JavaScript is unavailable. This can be accomplished using the HIJAX approach as follows (Keith, 2007):

1. Begin by building a regular web application where users can request information from and send information to the server using links and forms. The server returns an updated version of the same page. Every time users click on a link or submit a form, the entire page is refreshed.

2. Use the Document Object Model (DOM) scripting approach (see UNOBTRUSIVE JAVASCRIPT pattern later in this chapter) to intercept (or "hijack," thus the term *HIJAX*) links and forms requesting information from and sending information to the server. Reroute these requests using Ajax such that the server sends back only the changed part of the page instead of returning the entire page.

Related design patterns

Incorporating PROGRESSIVE ENHANCEMENT requires web pages to be marked up using SEMANTIC MARKUP and then enhanced using UNOBTRUSIVE STYLE SHEETS and UNOBTRUSIVE JAVASCRIPT.

SEMANTIC MARKUP

Problem

It's difficult to ensure consistent presentation of web pages to all users without knowing the browser, platform, or assistive technology they use to access the web application. In addition, a page's information hierarchy established using images, style sheets, and layouts cannot be communicated visually because users' browsers and assistive devices may render visual information unusable.

Solution

Convey the document's meaning using structural markup such that it clearly conveys the relationship between page elements and maintains the reading order of the content irrespective of the browser's ability to use CSS and/or render images. In addition, delegate page presentation aspects to style sheets so that the page structure remains meaningful regardless of the browser type, platform, or assistive device.

This means that web designers must ensure that the order of page elements is communicated via headings and lists (i.e., <h1>, <h2>, <h3>, <h4>, <ul >, <ol>, and so forth), <table> tags are not used for page layout,, and page presentation aspects are absent from the markup. For example, additional space between

---

[2]*Ajax* stands for Asynchronous JavaScript and XML, and is a combination of technologies such as JavaScript, cascading style sheets (CSS), document object model, and XMLHttpRequest, which allow the creation of richer user experiences that are comparable to desktop applications (see Chapter 8 for additional details).

content paragraphs is not created using markup such as **<p> </p>**, and markup doesn't include **<ul>** or **<blockquote>** tags to achieve indentation.

Why

With semantic markup, users accessing a web application using screen readers or browsers with limited or no support for style sheets or scripting languages will be able to understand the content structure, the relationship among page elements, and the nature of content inside an element. This is extremely important for users with screen readers, which ignore style sheets and allow users to navigate using structural markup—for example, JAWS for Windows, a screen reader, allows users to navigate page headings using the "h" key. In absence of semantic markup, navigating among page elements and accessing appropriate sections within the page can become extremely difficult (Cannon, 2008).

Using semantic markup along with UNOBTRUSIVE CSS facilitates a clear separation of structure and presentation and affords the largest reach by supporting a variety of browsers and devices. In addition, separating page structure from its presentation simplifies the page design and makes it possible to easily adapt and optimize the presentation for different devices and technologies.

How

In markup, semantics is concerned with the meaning of an element and how that element describes the content it contains.
– Molly E. Holzschalg (2005)

At its most basic level, using semantic markup requires selecting and using HTML tags that match the desired structural intent of page elements and do not rely on their presentational effect as interpreted by browsers. For example, the **<blockquote>** tag is intended to quote text from an external source and not to indent text contained within the **<blockquote>** tags. Similarly, to emphasize text, the **<em>** tag should be used instead of **<i>**, and the **<strong>** tag should be used instead of **<b>**. Although **<b>** and **<i>** elements are not deprecated, even in recent versions of HTML or XHTML, the use of **<em>** and **<strong>** are more appropriate for adding emphasis to certain words or phrases. Screen readers can then use a different inflection when encountering them in text and convey the emphasis.

Similarly, headings, paragraphs, and lists within a page should be marked with available HTML markup tags such as **<h1>**, **<h2>**, **<p>**, **<ul>**, **<ol>**, and so forth, and not with tags such as **<div>** or **<span>**, which do not have any inherent meaning.

STRUCTURE DOCUMENTS USING HEADINGS AND LISTS

Organize web pages using heading-related tags such as **<h1>**, **<h2>**, **<h3>**, and so on. Heading tags establish page information structure and help users identify page hierarchy. Users interacting with the page using screen readers or other assistive technology can also use the page structure to navigate (see the ACCESSIBLE NAVIGATION pattern later in this chapter). They can jump from first-level headings (i.e., **<h1>**) to second-, third-, or lower-level headings (i.e., **<h2>**, **<h3>**, and so forth). They can also use assistive devices to "listen" to the page's outline in order to understand the page's structure (Cannon, 2008). For sighted users, using HTML-based headings helps determine the page's visual hierarchy because web browsers style headings in larger and bolder fonts than the rest of the text, even when style sheets are disabled.

Similarly, navigation menus, submenus, and lists within pages should be marked up using lists (**<ol>**, **<ul>**, **<dl>**, etc.). A general rule of thumb is to use ordered lists (**<ol>**) for lists that suggest some form of sequence or priority-based ordering, unordered lists (**<ul>**) for lists that have items without any suggested sequence or ordering, and definition lists (**<dl>**) when the items in the list consist of a term (marked up using **<dt>**) and its description (marked up using **<dd>**).

USE STYLE SHEETS FOR LAYOUT AND PRESENTATION

Use CSS to control the presentation and layout of a web page. Put all style declarations in a separate file to enable easy updates (see also the UNOBTRUSIVE STYLE SHEETS pattern next).

Do not embed style-related markup in a page using tags such as **<font>**, **<b>**, **<i>**, and so forth. In addition, do not use deprecated tags—that is, HTML tags that are no longer part of the HTML specification. *The Ultimate HTML Reference* (Lloyd, 2008) lists the following elements as deprecated: **<applet>**, **<base-font>**, **<center>**, **<dir>**, **<font>**, **<frame>**, **<frameset>**, **<iframe>**, **<isindex>**, **<menu>**, **<noframes>**, **<s>**, **<strike>**, **<u>**, and **<xmp>** (see also *www.w3.org/TR/REC-html40/index/elements.html for deprecated HTML 4.0 elements*).

DO NOT USE STYLE SHEETS TO SIMULATE STRUCTURAL MARKUP

Do not use CSS to give visual appearance of structural elements such as headings, paragraphs, and lists to **<span>** and **<div>** tags (Figure 11.1).

FIGURE 11.1 The page title in YouTube is marked up using the <div> element instead of the <h1>Rihanna – Disturbia</h1> or <h2>Rihanna – Disturbia</h2> element, making it difficult for screen reader users to navigate the page.

Screen readers and other assistive technologies rely on structural markup to communicate page structure to their users. Just because an item looks like a first-level heading, if it's not using <h1>, it will be presented as regular text to users of assistive technology. Therefore,

- Do this: <h1>Heading 1</h1>
- Not this: <div class="heading1">Heading 1</div>

Although both of these techniques use styles and achieve the same presentation results, the meaning of the first-level heading is lost without the <h1> tag.

Related design patterns

Once a page is marked up using structural tags, style sheets can be attached to make pages visually appealing. However, follow the UNOBTRUSIVE STYLE SHEETS pattern to ensure that the pages remain accessible.

UNOBTRUSIVE STYLE SHEETS

Problem

Pages using just structural markup do not look visually pleasing. Most designers rely on style sheets (e.g., CSS) to improve the appearance of pages by laying them out in multiple columns, using appropriate fonts and colors, and adding images. Although adding style sheets can significantly improve the appearance of pages, if used inappropriately, they could render the pages inaccessible to some users.

Solution

Add style sheets so that they can adapt to different usage and browser contexts—that is, CSS disabled, CSS unavailable, poor CSS support, user CSS, and so forth—so that they can satisfy the needs of the widest possible audience. In addition, develop style sheets so that users have the necessary flexibility to adjust the presentation to improve page readability.

Why

As discussed (see the PROGRESSIVE ENHANCEMENT pattern earlier in this chapter), style sheets are a way for authors to describe page presentation. However, the designer's preferred presentation may render a page inaccessible to people who have vision deficiencies if, for example, the page doesn't allow enlarging text size or changing colors. Allowing users to "layer" their own presentation over the one suggested by the designer/publisher not only makes the page more usable, but also improves its reach to text-only browsers, screen readers, screen magnifiers, Braille readers, and other assistive devices.

How

Following the principle of PROGRESSIVE ENHANCEMENT, structure the page first so that the page order makes sense (see the SEMANTIC MARKUP pattern

```
<link rel="stylesheet" href="name_of_cssfile.css" type="text/css" media="all" />

<style type="text/css">
            @import url(name_of_cssfile.css);
</style>
```

FIGURE 11.2 Two common approaches of referencing an external style sheet.

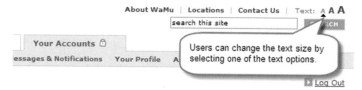

FIGURE 11.3 Washington Mutual allows users to change the text size by clicking on one of the text options in the top-right corner of the page.

earlier in this chapter). Then, add presentation-related markup using style sheets such that the addition of style sheets does not limit the page's accessibility.

KEEP PAGE MARKUP AND STYLE SHEETS SEPARATE

Keep all style sheet declarations in external CSS files rather than embedding them in individual pages or presenting them inline with markup elements. Style sheet files can then be referenced using either the **<link>** or **@import** tag (Figure 11.2).

By keeping all style declarations in a separate file, it's also easier to update one external file rather than go through every application page and make updates.

USE RELATIVE UNITS FOR FONT SIZES TO ALLOW USERS TO RESIZE TEXT

Using relative units, such as em, %, and keywords, allows users to enlarge or reduce text size as needed in web browsers such as Firefox, Safari, and Internet Explorer. Although px (pixels) is considered a relative unit, Internet Explorer (version 6 and older) doesn't allow text in the px-based layouts to be resized. Internet Explorer 7, however, allows user to zoom in and out of the page; this feature zooms in/out the entire page, not just the text.

It's possible that some users may not know how to resize text using browser controls. Therefore, consider providing users an explicit way to resize text (Figure 11.3).

ALLOW USER STYLE SHEETS TO OVERRIDE AUTHOR STYLE SHEETS

User style sheets are CSS files created by users and are used to override author style sheets to make pages easier to read. For example, a user might change the background color to black and the text color to yellow and set the font size larger to make the page easier to read. Most of the popular web browsers allow users to specify and use their own style sheet over the designer's/publisher's style sheet.

Browsers give preference to users' style sheets unless a style declaration is marked !important in the style sheets. Not being able to override the author styles can, in some instances, make pages unreadable for some users. Therefore, avoid using !important declaration in style sheets.

Related design patterns

Even when using CSS unobtrusively, it's important to use structural tags to mark up pages to ensure that pages are accessible without style sheets (SEMANTIC MARKUP). In addition, style sheets should be added only after the page structure has been created (PROGRESSIVE ENHANCEMENT).

UNOBTRUSIVE JAVASCRIPT

Problem

Using JavaScript on pages can offer users richer interactivity and make interaction more pleasant. However, not all web browsers support JavaScript, and users or system administrators may disable JavaScript because of their workplace security policy or personal preference. Therefore, web applications dependent on JavaScript may become inaccessible to at least some users.

Solution

Use JavaScript "unobtrusively"—that is, incorporate JavaScript within web pages in such a way that not having it available does not affect users' ability to use the web application.

Why

Using JavaScript unobtrusively and redundantly allows web applications to be functional without being dependent on it. When JavaScript is supported and enabled, the web application can offer enhanced interactivity.

How

Following the principle of PROGRESSIVE ENHANCEMENT, structure the page first (SEMANTIC MARKUP), add necessary presentation enhancements (UNOBTRUSIVE STYLE SHEETS), and then enhance browser interaction using JavaScript such that not having it available does not affect structural and presentation layers and the use of the web application.

KEEP PAGE MARKUP AND JAVASCRIPT SEPARATE

Keep all JavaScript for the web application in external JS files rather than in the page itself or embedded in the HTML markup, and reference them using the <script> tag as follows:

```
<script type="text/javascript" src="javascriptfile.js"></script>
```

```
<a href="javascript:doThis();">Link Anchor</a>
or
<input type="button" onclick="doThis();" value="Save Changes" />
```

FIGURE 11.4 "Obtrusive" ways of incorporating JavaScript—that is, calling JavaScript functions within the page markup.

```
var allLinks = document.getElementsByTagName("a");
for (var i=0; i<allLinks.length; i++) {
        allLinks[i].onclick = function() {
                ...
                return false;
        }
}
```

FIGURE 11.5 This code snippet accesses all links within the document (marked up using the **<a>** tag) and assigns the **onclick** behavior to it.

Keeping JavaScript files separate from page structure also makes it easy to change scripts without updating individual pages within the application.

USE THE DOM SCRIPTING APPROACH TO ATTACH FUNCTIONS TO PAGE EVENTS

Do not embed JavaScript functions within page markup. That is, do not call JavaScript functions that use the approaches shown in Figure 11.4.

Calling JavaScript functions from page markup may prevent pages from working correctly in browsers where JavaScript is unavailable or disabled. A better approach is to attach functions to events for different page elements using the DOM[3] Scripting approach (Keith, 2005). Use DOM methods such as **getElementById** and **getElementsByTagName** to find a specific element or a set of elements, respectively, and then assign behavior to specific events such as **click**, **mouse over**, and so forth (Figure 11.5).

DO NOT USE DROPDOWN LISTS TO INITIATE NAVIGATION OR FORM SUBMISSION

Do not use JavaScript to navigate to a different page or change effects on the web page when users change the option in a dropdown list. This is typically accomplished using the **onchange** event handler in JavaScript. Instead, allow users to select the menu item and then click an adjacent form button to go to the page corresponding to the item they have selected.

If a dropdown list is used to submit a form or to navigate to a different page, it will be extremely difficult, if not impossible, for keyboard users to select an appropriate option. For example, if a dropdown list is used to navigate to a different page as users select an item in the list, this would trigger the **onchange** event, and users would be immediately taken to the corresponding page.

---

[3]DOM, or Document Object Model, refers to a way of representing HTML and XML documents so that they can be manipulated using scripting technologies such as JavaScript. For more information, see *www.w3.org/TR/DOM-Level-3-Core/introduction.html*.

The only way for assistive technology users to select the last item in the dropdown list would be to repeatedly go back after selecting an option from the dropdown list, navigating to the page, and then select the next option in the list and so forth, until the last item is reached.

Related design patterns

Using JavaScript unobtrusively requires that pages be built using the principle of PROGRESSIVE ENHANCEMENT and that the "behavior" layer provided by JavaScript be completely separated from the structure and presentation layers (provided by SEMANTIC MARKUP and UNOBTRUSIVE STYLE SHEETS, respectively), such that its unavailability does not make the web application inaccessible.

ACCESSIBLE FORMS

Problem

Forms may become difficult to use if they are designed without regard to their use with keyboards and assistive technology such as screen readers or Braille readers.

Solution

Lay out form elements and incorporate appropriate accessibility tags in the markup to make forms accessible to assistive technology users. At a minimum, associate form elements with labels using <label> tags, group related form elements using <fieldset> tags, and set appropriate sequences for tabbing through form elements using tabindex attributes.

Why

Forms are the foundation of web applications. Making them accessible is essential to ensure the widest reach. Using <label> tags and grouping form elements using <fieldset> also adds meaning to elements and helps create a semantic structure in the markup (see the SEMANTIC MARKUP pattern earlier in this chapter). These techniques not only make forms accessible for users of assistive technology, but they also make them more usable and readable for users without disabilities.

How

First and foremost, follow the patterns in Chapter 2 to make forms usable and accessible. Ensure that forms are organized in a logical order and that it is easy for users to associate a form element with its label.

USE <LABEL> TAGS TO IDENTIFY CORRESPONDING FORM ELEMENTS

Use <label> tags to associate field labels to their corresponding form elements as follows:

```
<label for="firstName">First Name:</label>
<input type="text" id="firstName" name="firstName" />
```

FIGURE 11.6 In this form from Orbitz, users can click either on the highlighted areas or the radio controls instead of just clicking the radio button control to select an option.

In this example, the text field for first name has an id of "**firstName**" that is referenced in the **<label>** tag using the "**for**" attribute to associate the label **First Name** to the corresponding text field.

Not only does the **<label>** tag make it easy for screen readers to correctly associate labels to form control irrespective of where the form control is positioned, but it also helps sighted users when they interact with radio buttons and checkboxes. When used with radio buttons and checkboxes, the **<label>** tag allows users to click the label to select the corresponding radio button or checkbox. Thus, users have a larger clickable area and are not restricted to clicking the smaller radio button controls or checkboxes (Figure 11.6).

In addition, to ensure that screen readers present information to users in the correct order, place labels that relate to text fields or dropdown lists before the form element in the markup. This does not apply to radio buttons and checkboxes, where labels come after the corresponding controls.

GROUP FORM CONTROLS USING <FIELDSET> TAGS

Use the **<fieldset>** tag to group related form controls and use the **<legend>** tag to provide a heading to the grouped form controls (Figure 11.7). This helps screen readers identify and communicate groups to users. The tags **<fieldset>** and **<legend>** can also be styled using style sheets to make them visually appealing (Adams, 2008).

MAKE FORMS KEYBOARD ACCESSIBLE

Most browsers allow users to navigate among links, frames, and form elements on a page using the Tab key, which when pressed, moves the focus from one element to another in the order of their presence in the markup. In most cases, when the page is marked up correctly, the sequence in which users would move from one element to another would be correct. However, in cases, when the default tab sequence needs to be changed to provide a better form-filling experience, use the **tabindex** attribute for form elements (Figure 11.8; see also the KEYBOARD NAVIGATION pattern in Chapter 2).

Another way to make forms keyboard accessible and efficient to use is by using the **accesskey** attribute, which allows users keyboard access to frequently used

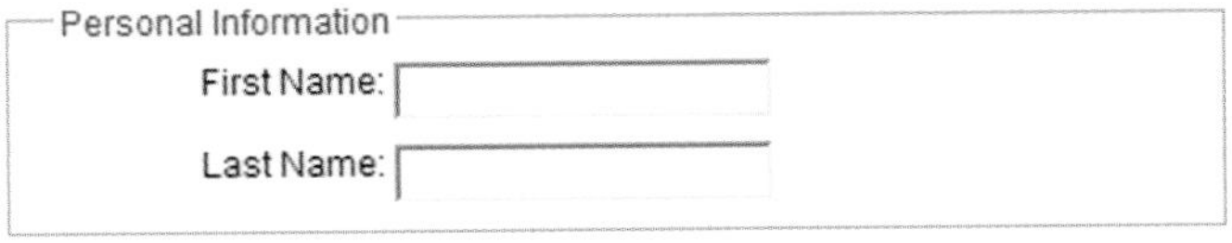

(a)

```
<fieldset>

        <legend>Personal Information</legend>

        <label for="firstName">First Name:</label>
        <input type="text" id="firstName" name="firstName" />

        <label for="lastName">Last Name:</label>
        <input type="text" id="lastName" name="lastName" />

</fieldset>
```

(b)

FIGURE 11.7 This form in (a) is created using the **<fieldset>** and **<legend>** tags shown in (b) along with a few style sheet rules (not shown).

```
<label for="firstName">First Name:</label>
<input type="text" id="firstName" name="firstName" tabindex="10" />

<label for="lastName">Last Name:</label>
<input type="text" id="lastName" name="lastName" tabindex="20" />
```

FIGURE 11.8 The **tabindex** attribute allows users to navigate form elements in a logical manner.

```
<label for="search" accesskey="S">Search:</label>

<input type="text" id="search" name="search" />
```

FIGURE 11.9 By adding the **accesskey** attribute of "**S**" to the **<label>** tag for the search box, we can allow users to focus on the search field by pressing the **Alt key** (or **Ctrl key** or another key combination) and the "**s**" key at the same time.

areas on a page or form (Figure 11.9). For example, the **accesskey** attribute can be used to navigate among primary navigation options in a web application and can also be used with a link to allow users to navigate to corresponding pages using the keyboard.

When the **accesskey** attribute is specified, users can press a combination of the "modifier" key(s) (e.g., Alt or Ctrl keys) in conjunction with the character specified in the **accesskey** attribute. See Figure 11.10 for a list of modifier key(s) on different browsers.

USE JAVASCRIPT UNOBTRUSIVELY WHEN USED FOR FORM VALIDATION

Many forms use client-side scripting technology, such as JavaScript, to manipulate forms or check for validity of users' data input. However, use of such scripting

Internet Explorer	ALT (PC), Ctrl (Mac)
Mozilla Firefox	ALT + SHIFT (configurable by typing about:config in the address field)
Opera	SHIFT + Esc
Konqueror (Linux)	Press CTRL and the accesskey in sequence

FIGURE 11.10 Modifier key(s) for different browsers when using the **accesskey** attribute.

technology may render forms inaccessible to users with assistive technology or those who have disabled JavaScript in their browsers. Therefore, perform the form validation on the web server regardless of whether it's done on users' browsers using JavaScript. This will ensure that forms remain accessible to all, including those using browsers that do not support JavaScript (see also the HIJAX approach discussed in the PROGRESSIVE ENHANCEMENT pattern earlier in this chapter).

Related design patterns

The patterns discussed in Chapter 2, such as LOGICAL GROUPING, REQUIRED FIELD INDICATORS, SMART DEFAULTS, FORGIVING FORMAT, KEYBOARD NAVIGATION, INPUT HINTS/PROMPTS, and ACTION BUTTONS, are all essential for designing usable and accessible forms.

ACCESSIBLE IMAGES
Problem

Images are not available to users with visual impairments.

Solution

Provide necessary text alternatives for images and minimize the use of superfluous graphics. There is a common misconception that to make a page accessible, all images must be removed. This is not true. Illustrations, graphics, and other images (including animated images) not only help improve comprehension for users without vision impairments but also help those with some forms of cognitive/learning disabilities (Brewer, 2005). By incorporating text alternatives for images, designers can possibly avoid building an alternative version of the web application.

Why

Making images accessible by providing a text alternative allows both screen reader users and those who have disabled images in their browsers to understand the purpose and function of the images. An added benefit is that it provides a meaning and description of images that can be read by search engines to improve searchability of pages. When used appropriately, images can make a page look visually pleasing and be incorporated in the page without impacting its accessibility.

How

Provide a text alternative for images describing the image's purpose. This is accomplished using the **alt** attribute for all image-related markup: **<img>** tags, **<area>** tags for hotspots on image maps, and **input** tags of **type="image"** (Figure 11.11).

```
<img src="btn_login.gif" alt="Log In" />
```
(a)

```
<map name="globalNav">
        <area coords="0,0,50,20" href="AboutUs.html" alt="About Us" />
        <area coords="51,0,100,20" href="CustomerSupport.html" alt="Customer Support" />
</map>
```
(b)

```
<input type="image" src="btn_login.gif" alt="Log In" />
```
(c)

FIGURE 11.11 Examples of **alt** text for images (a), image maps (b), and the input
(type = "image") tag (c).

USE AN EMPTY **ALT** ATTRIBUTE FOR DECORATIVE IMAGES

Decorative images refer to images that are used for presentation purposes
only—for example, spacer images, transparent images, or filler photographs.
Using the **alt** attribute to describe such images is not necessary because it
doesn't communicate any relevant information to users. Therefore, use an
empty **alt** attribute for images, such as **<img src="spacer.gif" alt="" />**.

When images are used only for decorative purposes, consider using them as background. Screen reader users will not see the image, and the need for an empty **alt**
text will not arise. This can be easily accomplished using CSS (Figure 11.12).

USE THE **LONGDESC** ATTRIBUTE FOR DETAILED IMAGE DESCRIPTIONS

Use the **alt** attribute for images when a short description for the image is sufficient. In cases where the image cannot be described succinctly, use the **longdesc**
attribute to reference and link to the page where the detailed image description
is provided (Figure 11.13).

Because the **longdesc** attribute is not supported by older assistive technologies,
often designers put a "d-link" (description link) next to the image that opens the
description file—the same file referenced in the **longdesc** attribute (Figure 11.14).

USE MEANINGFUL TEXT WHEN DESCRIBING IMAGES

When describing images using either the **alt** or **longdesc** attribute, indicate the
image's informational content and/or function as appropriate within its usage
context. For example, consider Figure 11.15. This example from WebAIM.org
illustrates a good approach in determining what would constitute a meaningful
text for the PDF icon image. Four potential values for the PDF icon's **alt** text are:

1. "Employment Application"
2. "PDF File"
3. "PDF icon"
4. "", because the image content is presented in context

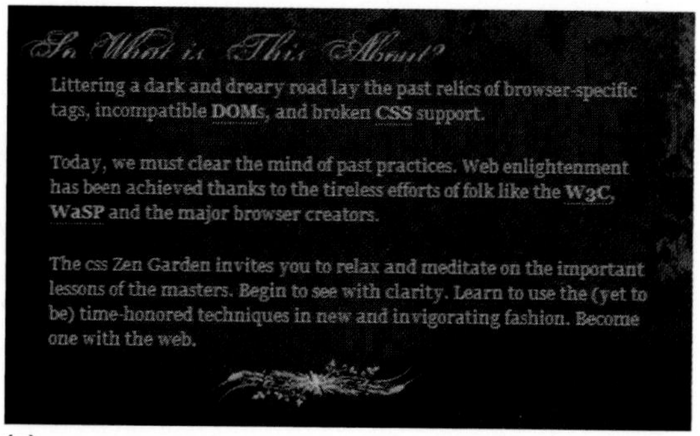

(a)

```
<div id="preamble">
          <h3><span>So What is This About?</span></h3>
          <p class="p1">.... </p>
</div>
```

(b)

```
#intro #preamble {
       background: transparent url(images/breakrule.gif) no-repeat center bottom;
       padding: 25px 0px 37px 0px;
       width: 464px; }
```

(c)

```
#intro #preamble h3 {
          background: transparent url(images/txt_sowhatisthisabout.gif) no-repeat left top;
          height: 25px;
          margin: 0px 0px -9px 27px; }
#intro #preamble h3 span {
          display: none; }
```

(d)

FIGURE 11.12 In this example from CSS Zen Garden, the designer has included a decorative image below the section in the background (a). This is evident in the HTML code for this section (b) and the corresponding style (c). The designer uses the breakrule.gif file as the background image and positions it at the bottom of the paragraph to use it as a separator between it and the next section. A similar approach is used for the section header, the text of which ("So What Is This About?") is enclosed within the `<h3><span>` tags (b), and its CSS shows the use of the image as background. The text is hidden from sighted users by setting its display to "none" but is still accessible to text reader users. Another option is to use a large negative text-indent value (e.g., –9999px). (Source: *www.csszengarden.com/?cssfile=/204/204.css&page=0.*)

The preceding are discussed in the online article, Appropriate Use of Alternative Text *(www.webaim.org/techniques/alttext/)*:

> Notice that the image is within the link. If it were not within the link, then the **alt** text might be different. In this case, because the image provides additional information about the function of the link, it's important that it

```
<img src="chart_sales.gif" alt="Sales from the year 2000 to 2003" longdesc="traffic_chart.html" />
```

FIGURE 11.13 When describing a chart, **alt** text ("**Sales from the year 2000 to 2003**") may not be sufficient to describe what the chart represents. To make it easier for users to understand the chart, summarize the content on a separate page (in this example, "**traffic_ chart.html**") and link it using the image's **longdesc** attribute.

```
<img src="chart_sales.gif" alt="Sales from the year 2000 to 2003" />
<a href="traffic_chart.html">D</a>
```

FIGURE 11.14 An example of a d-link that references the page and provides the detailed image description.

FIGURE 11.15 Using a link and an image together.

be within the link itself and is read with the link. This is vital because links are often accessed out of context from their surroundings.

Option A (**"Employment Application"**) is redundant with surrounding text so it is not the best choice. Option B is the best choice—it clearly provides the content that is being presented by the image—that the link is to a PDF file. The function (**"Download the Employment Application"**) is presented within the text of the link, so it does not need to be included within the **alt** attribute. Option C (**"PDF icon"**) describes the image itself, but is not most appropriate for this context. In another context, it may be important that the user know that this image is indeed an icon—in such a case, using the word **"icon"** in the **alt** text may be appropriate. Option 4 (null or empty **alt** text) would not provide the important information that the image presents.

NOTE

Another option is to use the PDF icon as a background image and position it using the style sheet and use the text PDF in the HTML markup as follows:

```
HTML:
<a href="/docs/employement_application.pdf" class="pdfdoc">
Download the Employment Application (PDF, 300KB)
</a>
CSS:
a.pdfdoc {
/* Assuming that the image is about 24px × 24px and 6px space to its
left is adequate */
background: transparent url(/images/icon_pdf.doc) no=repeat right;
padding-right: 30px;
}
```

AVOID USING TEXT IN GRAPHICS

Graphic formats (e.g., GIF, JPEG, and PNG) appear pixelated when zoomed in. When text is used in graphics, users who have magnified the screen to improve readability would end up reducing the page's readability (Figure 11.16). Readability is further compromised when text is overlaid on another image or a patterned background. Therefore, as much as possible, avoid using text in graphics; it also helps with internationalization (see the EXTENSIBLE DESIGN pattern in Chapter 10).

REGISTER NOW

FIGURE 11.16 Text used in graphics appears pixelated and thus is difficult to read when magnified.

Related design patterns

Using images should not compromise the SEMANTIC MARKUP. Therefore, use decorative images as background images using CSS so that they are not included in the page structure (see also the UNOBTRUSIVE STYLE SHEETS pattern earlier in this chapter).

ACCESSIBLE TABLES

Problem

Reading and understanding data presented in tables can be confusing to assistive technology users if they are unable to establish the relationship among the data elements. For example, if users are not able to associate data in table cells to corresponding headings, they may not know exactly what the data represent and how they relate to data in other cells.

Solution

Reserve the use of <table> tags for presenting tabular data and use style sheets for page layout (see the TABULAR LIST pattern in Chapter 7). Mark up tabular data such that table captions, column headings, and row headings are clearly identified. This helps screen readers understand and communicate the relationship between data presented in tables.

This is not to suggest that pages formatted using <table> tags are inaccessible. It is possible to build accessible pages using tables so that when content is "linearized"—that is, when all table-related tags are removed and content is presented in the order it appears in the markup—the resulting content order matches what users would expect and the page is accessible to assistive technology users. However, the same visual and structural result can be achieved

> **NOTE**
>
> With the new browsers supporting CSS tables using the display properties of **table**, **table-row**, and **table-cell**, soon there would be even fewer valid reasons to use HTML **<table>** tags for laying out pages (Andrew and Yank, 2008).

using style sheets, and there is no longer a valid reason for favoring **<table>** tags for layout (Andrew and Shafer, 2006). In addition, using tables for layout violates the SEMANTIC MARKUP pattern, which suggests that content be marked up using tags to match its structural intent and not to achieve a certain visual presentation.

Why

Associating data in tables to their column and row headings helps screen readers correctly communicate the relationship among data elements, and users establish appropriate context for their use.

How

Most important, clearly distinguish headings that indicate what the data represent from data cells (the actual values). This is achieved by marking up headings (both column and row headings) using **<th>** tags and data values using **<td>** tags.

USE THE **<CAPTION>** TAG AND **SUMMARY** ATTRIBUTE TO ESTABLISH CONTEXT

Use the **<caption>** tag to provide a short descriptive title indicating the table's purpose (Figure 11.17). The information within the **<caption>** tag is displayed to users and can be formatted using style sheets.

In addition, use the **summary** attribute to describe in detail what the table presents. Because information contained within the **summary** attribute is not displayed, its main purpose is to describe the data table's purpose and any relevant formatting information for assistive technology users (Figure 11.18).

IDENTIFY ROW AND COLUMN HEADERS OF DATA TABLES

Ensure that data values are correctly associated with their headings by using the **scope** attribute. Such a practice lets assistive technology users know if data are

```
<table>
        <caption>Sales Data for Past 3 years</caption>
        ... rest of the table markup
</table>
```

FIGURE 11.17 Use the <caption> tag to briefly describe the purpose of tabular data.

```
<table summary="Sales data for years 2005, 2006, and 2007 show an increasing trend, with
sales doubling from $1,200,000 in 2005 to $2,400,000 in 2007">
        <caption>Sales Data for Past 3 Years</caption>
        ... rest of the table markup
</table>
```

FIGURE 11.18 By using the **summary** attribute, users know what is relevant and important in the table and can help improve comprehension of the data presented in the table.

FIGURE 11.19
Knowing the scope of headings, users can clearly establish that sales in 2005 were $1,200,000.

```
<table>
<caption>Sales Data for Past 3 Years</caption>
<tr>
        <th></th>
        <th scope="col">2005</th>
        <th scope="col">2006</th>
        <th scope="col">2007</th>
</tr>

<tr>
        <th scope="row">Sales</th>
        <td>$ 1,200,000</td>
        <td>$ 1,500,000</td>
        <td>$ 2,400,000</td>
</tr>
</table>
```

tied to column headings (**<th scope="col">**), row headings (**<th scope="row"**), or both (Figure 11.19).

USE THE **HEADERS** ATTRIBUTE ON CELLS OF COMPLEX DATA TABLES

Use the **headers** attribute to specify the relationship among the headings for a given cell in more complex tables. This is accomplished by attaching an **id** attribute to any cell that you want to be a header cell and then adding the ids of those header cells to the **headers** attribute of the data cells (Figure 11.20).

Related design patterns

Data table presentation can be improved using style sheets so that the relationship between data values and headings are clear to those without vision impairments as well. (See Christie, 2008, for how CSS can be used to effectively present tabular data.) This is important for sighted users because attributes such as **summary**, **scope**, and **headers** are not displayed in web browsers. However, UNOBTRUSIVE STYLE SHEETS should be used to ensure that markup and presentation are layered independently as advocated in the PROGRESSIVE ENHANCEMENT pattern.

```
<table>
<caption>Travel Expense Report</caption>
<tr>
        <th><br /></th>
        <th id="meals">Meals</th>
        <th id="hotel">Hotel</th>
        <th id="transportation">Transportation</th>
</tr>
<tr>
        <td id="august-25" >25-Aug-03</td>
        <td headers="meals august-25">$ 37.74</td>
        <td headers="hotel august-25">$ 112.00</td>
        <td headers="transportation august-25">$ 45.00</td>
</tr>
<tr>
        <td id="august-26" >25-Aug-03</td>
        <td headers="meals august-26">$ 37.74</td>
        <td headers="hotel august-26">$ 112.00</td>
        <td headers="transportation august-26">$ 45.00</td>
</tr>
        <tr>
        <th id="total">Total:</th>
        <td headers="meals total">$ 196.27</td>
        <td headers="hotel total">$ 442.00</td>
        <td headers="transportation total">$ 162.00</td>
</tr>
</table>
```

FIGURE 11.20 In this example, the ids of the column headers are **meals**, **hotel**, and **transportation**, and the ids of the row headers are **august-25**, **august-26**, and **total**. Then the cell at row 2, column 3 would have **headers="hotel august-25"** or the other way around—that is, **headers="august-25 hotel"**—if that seems more appropriate.

ACCESSIBLE NAVIGATION

Problem

Most web pages are organized such that the main "content" area comes after persistent elements such as a logo, utility navigation, primary navigation, and secondary navigation. Although this practice is beneficial for users without vision impairments because they prefer a consistent location for navigation (see Chapter 5), it's disruptive for screen readers and keyboard users because they have to navigate through those links with every page load before they can reach the main content.

Solution

Allow users to access the page's main content without requiring them to go through persistent navigation and other elements located in the page's header area. In addition, structure the page so that users can easily navigate among the page's content areas.

Why

For users without vision impairments, it's easy to ignore persistent header and navigation sections of pages and focus on relevant content areas. Screen readers and keyboard users, however, are forced to access the page in a linear fashion, disrupting their experience. Built-in mechanisms to directly access a page's content via an explicit "skip navigation" link at the top of the page or through appropriate structural markup make interaction with web pages both efficient and pleasurable for assistive technology users.

How

Provide a link at the top of the page that allows users to skip over navigation links. The "skip navigation" or "skip to main content" link is just an HTML link created using the anchor **<a>** tag. If designers do not want to make the link visible, they may use CSS to hide it (Figure 11.21).

```
CSS:
a.skip-navigation {
        display: block;
        position: absolute;
        top: -9999px;
        left: -9999px;
}

HTML:
<a class="skip-navigation" href="#maincontent">Skip to main content </a>
… navigation and other persistent elements

<a name="maincontent" id="maincontent"></a>
<!-- Main Content Starts Here -->
```

FIGURE 11.21 Using this approach, the link is hidden for users without vision impairments but is read by the screen readers and is accessible to text browsers such as Lynx. As shown, the anchor for the "skip" link does not need to have any content.

NOTE

For sites with primary and secondary navigation, it's beneficial to provide separate skip navigation links: one for global (primary and utility) navigation and one for secondary navigation. The first "skip" link would then be "Skip Main Navigation" or "Skip Global Navigation" and the second "Skip Local Navigation," which then takes users to the page's main content.

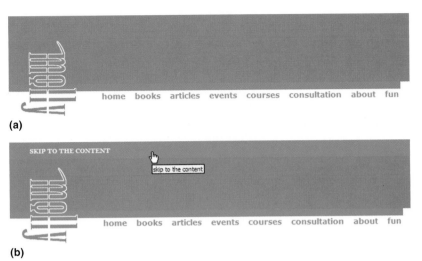

(a)

(b)

FIGURE 11.22 By default, Molly doesn't show users the "Skip to the Content" link (a). However, when users navigate to the link using the keyboard (or hover over it using a mouse), the link becomes visible (b).

Another common approach is to make the link visible when it receives focus (Figure 11.22). This makes the link available to those who are navigating the page using the keyboard.

USE HEADINGS IN THE MARKUP TO IDENTIFY PAGE STRUCTURE

Identify sections within the page using headings markup—that is, use `<h1>` through `<h6>`. This allows users with screen readers and browsers to navigate using a keyboard (e.g., JAWS for Windows users can use the "h" key to navigate the page content).

Related design patterns

It's also important that primary, secondary, and/or utility navigation features are marked up using appropriate SEMANTIC MARKUP. With the availability of working-draft versions of ARIA, consider marking up navigation elements using appropriate "role" attributes (see the Accessibility and Rich Internet Applications section later in this chapter).

ACCESSIBLE ALTERNATIVE

Problem

Sometimes it is not possible to make a web application accessible either because of the technology used (e.g. RIAs) or the way it is programmed.

Solution

Create an accessible alternative for the web application that offers the same content and functionality, and provide a link to the alternative application. This follows the recommendation by WCAG 1.0, which states:

> If, after best efforts, you cannot create an accessible page, provide a link to an alternative page that uses W3C technologies, is accessible, has equivalent information (or functionality), and is updated as often as the inaccessible (original) page.

And, from WCAG 2.0 (see Conformance Requirements at *www.w3.org/TR/2007/ WD-WCAG20-20070517/#conformance*):

> If the Web page does not meet all of the success criteria for a specified level, then a mechanism to obtain an alternate version that meets all of the success criteria can be derived from the nonconforming content or its URI [Universal Resource Identifier], and that mechanism meets all success criteria for the specified level of conformance.

Why

Ideally, web applications should be able to adapt to the needs and capabilities of browsers, assistive technologies, or users without maintaining separate versions. However, sometimes web applications use technology that offers important benefits justifying its use (e.g., better performance, richer interactivity, etc.) but are not well supported by assistive technologies.

RIAs are a good example. They offer important usability and performance benefits (e.g., Google Maps, Gmail). However, when used with assistive technology, mobile devices, or browsers that have JavaScript and CSS disabled, they break down. In addition, there may be legal requirements to use an exact copy of a document, making modifications to original documents impossible. In such instances, rather than excluding users, it's better to create an alternative version of the application with the same content and core functionality.

How

Once the alternative version is developed, two important WCAG 2.0 requirements are:

1. The accessible version provides the same content even with compromises in design and functionality.
2. At the beginning of the pages of the nonaccessible version, a link is provided to the alternative accessible version.

Approaches similar to those used for incorporating "skip navigation" link in the page markup can be used for providing the links to an alternative version of the application (see ACCESSIBLE NAVIGATION pattern earlier in this chapter).

Related design patterns

If Ajax or the use of JavaScript is making the application inaccessible, use approaches outlined in the UNOBTRUSIVE JAVASCRIPT and PROGRESSIVE ENHANCEMENT patterns to make the application as accessible as possible.

ACCESSIBILITY AND RICH INTERNET APPLICATIONS

Approaches used in developing RIAs (see Chapter 8) make extensive use of dynamic HTML and Ajax to offer a richer and more interactive experience. However, they pose significant accessibility challenges. For example, if page content changes without a page refresh, new content may not be available to people who rely on screen magnifiers or screen readers. RIAs also use complex interface controls such as sliders, progress bars, tabs, trees, and so forth, which are not natively supported in current versions of HTML/XHTML markup.

The W3C-WAI group has been working on addressing these challenges through their ARIA suite (WAI-ARIA; see *www.w3.org/WAI/intro/aria*). The purpose of WAI-ARIA is to offer a way to associate behavior and structure to interactive controls used on rich web pages with existing markup to make RIAs accessible to people with disabilities. It does so by incorporating *roles* and *states and properties* within existing markup.

Roles allow an RIA designer to provide proper type semantics on custom controls to make them accessible. For example, as indicated in the SEMANTIC MARKUP pattern, page navigation should be marked up using lists. However, if a page has several other types of lists, it's not easy for users to distinguish between navigation-based lists and other lists. ARIA specification provides help by using the notion of roles, which provide information about what the control is irrespective of the HTML markup that was used to create it. For example, an unordered list used for navigation can be marked up as:

```
<ul role="navigation">
    <li>Navigation Item 1</li>
...
</ul>
```

Roles are divided into *widget roles* and *structural roles*. Widget roles include widgets common in RIAs such as **progressbar, slider, combobox, tree, alert, dialog**, and others. Structural roles include roles such as **menubar, toolbar, breadcrumbs, search, liveregion** (in which content is changed without page refresh), **tab, navigation**, and so forth. Of particular importance for RIAs is the structural role of **liveregion**, which allows text in the live region to be spoken without giving it focus. Users can then be informed of any updates within the area tagged as **liveregion** without losing their place within the content.

While roles provide information about the type of control being used, the states and properties module of ARIA adds semantics about relationships and current states. For example, a slider control can have properties such as **value-now**, **valuemin**, and **valuemax**; a **liveregion** can have a state of "busy"; a **combobox** could have the property of **autocomplete**; a tree can have the state of "expanded" with a **treeitem** having an attribute of **level**; and so forth.

Currently assistive technologies such as Window Eyes 5.5+ , Jaws 7.0+ , and ZoomText have some support for WAI-ARIA–based markup with Firefox 2 or later; and Orca 2.20 supports WAI-ARIA with Firefox 3. Therefore, designers should start adding appropriate WAI-ARIA attributes in their markup to improve accessibility of RIAs. Because extra attributes will be ignored by browsers that do not support WAI-ARIA, there is minimal risk in their use. As support grows in browsers and assistive technologies, accessibility of RIAs continue to improve as well.

CHAPTER 12
Visual Design

INTRODUCTION

Although web applications are designed to facilitate task completion, visual design of them shouldn't be ignored. Not only does visual design play an important role in how usable an application is perceived (Kurosu and Kashimura, 1995; Tractinsky, 1997), but it also affects how credible it is considered by users (Fogg et al., 2002).

Among the first decisions that web application designers make is whether application content should adjust to the browser window width (LIQUID-WIDTH LAYOUT) or remain the same regardless of its width (FIXED-WIDTH LAYOUT). Although usability and accessibility generally favor liquid-width layouts, page aesthetics are often compromised with excessively large or small browser window widths. Using a PROGRESSIVE LAYOUT with defined minimum and maximum widths is a reasonable compromise because not only can it help maintain the aesthetic integrity but also better accommodate users who have either high- or low-resolution monitors.

The next important step is related to the placement and alignment of page elements to aid users by providing a clear visual page structure (GRID STRUCTURE, VISUAL HIERARCHY). Designers also may make certain page elements stand out (HIGHLIGHT) or use images that indicate important states and actions (ICONS) to further assist users in navigating pages and accessing features.

Visual design involves carefully balancing distinct components: layout, colors, graphics, fonts, contrast, and so on. Several books have been written on both the theory and practice of these components for web design (e.g., Baird, 2007; Lidwell et al., 2003; McIntire, 2008; Wroblewski, 2002). This chapter, however, emphasizes visual design patterns that are relevant for web application. Best practices for effectively incorporating other elements to create an effective design (e.g., colors, size and proportion, gestalt, typefaces), though not discussed, are important and must be considered for all designs.

LIQUID-WIDTH LAYOUT

Problem

Web page content (e.g., tabular data with many columns, image editors, portal applications with multicolumn layouts, etc.) requires considerable horizontal space. If presented using a preset width (FIXED-WIDTH LAYOUT), content would either appear too cramped to users with large monitors or require users with small monitors to scroll horizontally, which is typically not preferred (Nielsen, 2005).

Solution

Design web pages using a liquid-width layout such that as users widen or narrow the browser window, page content and data adjust to its width; this approach is also referred to as a *fluid* or *flexible* layout (Figure 12.1).

Why

It is very difficult to know or predict users' screen resolutions and browser window size preferences. Thus, designing for a specific width takes control away from users; instead of the design adapting to user preferences, users are forced to adjust to the design. Furthermore, with fixed-width layouts, much of the

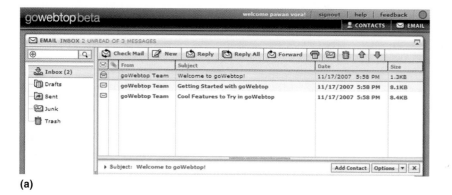

(a)

(b)

FIGURE 12.1 The gowebtop web mail application uses a liquid layout and adjusts its content to fit the browser's window size.

available screen space remains unused for users with high-resolution monitors. On the other hand, those using lower-resolution monitors may need to scroll pages horizontally to view the entire page.

Using a liquid-width design allows different page areas to adjust to browser window sizes and minimizes unnecessary horizontal scrolling. It also allows users to open sidebars for browser history and bookmarks without affecting their ability to view page content. In addition, users with vision deficiencies may prefer to use larger text sizes, which can be easily accommodated with liquid-width designs.

Although the study by Bernard and Larsen (2001) found no significant differences in user performance with liquid- or fixed-width layouts for reading and searching tasks, most users preferred a liquid layout. It could be argued that Bernard and Larsen's conclusion is dated because they used a monitor resolution of 1024 × 768, and almost 40 percent of users on the Web today use screen resolutions higher than 1024 × 768 and may have a different preference (see w3schools, *www.w3schools.com/browsers/browsers_display.asp*). However, using larger-resolution monitors does not necessarily imply that most users maximize their browser window to their maximum screen resolutions, and 60 percent of web users still use screen resolutions of 1024 × 768 or lower.

How

Designing a liquid-width or fluid-width layout requires page components—at least those occupying the main content area—to have a specific width relative to the browser's window width, which is usually accomplished by designing pages using percentage values. For example, overall content can be set to 100 percent, main content to 62 percent, and sidebar content to 38 percent (Clarke, 2007).

IT'S OKAY TO KEEP NAVIGATIONAL AREAS AS FIXED WIDTH

It's not necessary for all layout areas to expand proportionally for large windows. Page elements such as navigation, sidebars, and callouts, may be kept fixed to a certain width, while keeping areas occupied by main content flexible (Figure 12.2). This minimizes jumping and readjusting of page components when users resize their browser's window.

FIGURE 12.2 Gmail keeps left navigation fixed while expanding content areas.

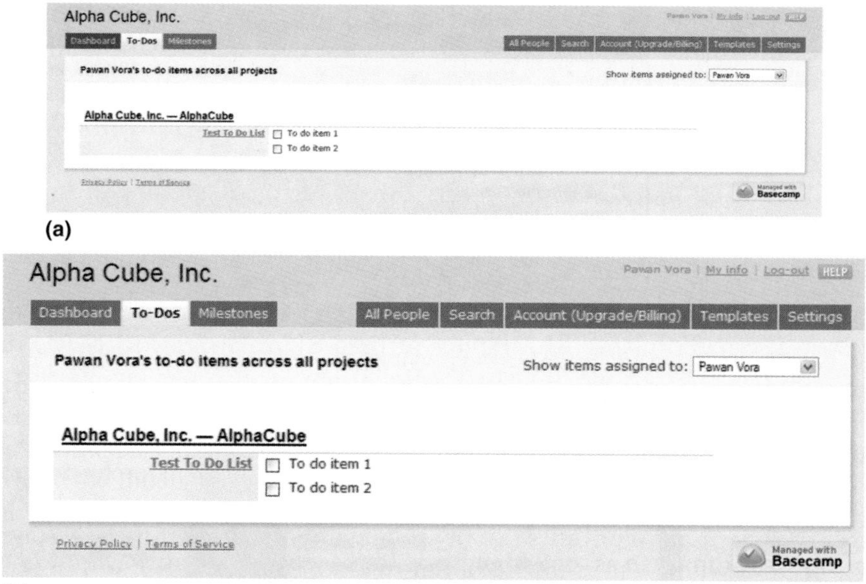

(a)

(b)

FIGURE 12.3 When users narrow (a) or expand (b) the browser window, Basecamp adjusts the background colors for body, header, and content areas as necessary. Utility navigation (in the header), the "powered by" logo (in the footer), and the "... assigned to" dropdown list maintain their right alignment with changing browser window widths.

ADJUST PAGE ELEMENTS TO BROWSER'S WINDOW SIZE

When using liquid-width layouts, page elements using background colors or images should fill up appropriately with expanding or narrowing browser window widths. The relative position of page elements—left- and right-aligned components such as headers, navigation bars, footers, and so on—should also maintain their alignment with varying window widths (Figure 12.3).

Related design patterns

As already mentioned, large screen resolutions are becoming common, and designers have started considering PROGRESSIVE LAYOUTS to ensure that pages' content readability does not suffer when users maximize browser window sizes.

FIXED-WIDTH LAYOUT

Problem

Liquid-width design can create excessive empty spaces between elements for pages with fewer elements. This not only makes pages appear sparse, disorganized, and disconnected but also less readable and visually unappealing.

Solution

Use a design that has a fixed width to ensure that page components remain together and appear coherent (Figure 12.4). *Fixed-width layout* means that the width of the page content is set to a certain pixel width irrespective of browser

FIGURE 12.4 Blinksale uses a fixed-width centered layout. The background is filled with the gradient if users are viewing the page in larger browser window sizes.

window size. Users cannot change the width by resizing the window or by changing the text size.

Why

For web applications that do not demand excessive horizontal space (i.e., mainly textual content and tables with just a few columns), a fixed-width layout is the most suitable, as information readability and scanability can be maintained even for large browser window sizes. In addition, with fixed-width layouts, designers have complete control over the placement of page elements, which allows them to ensure the layout appears almost identical in all major browsers.

How

Fixed-width layouts are typically designed by specifying the page width in pixels—an absolute unit of measure for text sizes. A downside of such an approach is that it doesn't scale well for users who have set text sizes larger or smaller than those specified by the designer. A common alternative is to use measurement units relative to the text size—that is, in em or ex. This layout is commonly referred to as an *elastic layout* because such a layout changes its size based on the text size users set. However, designs using elastic layouts are still unaffected by browser window widths and thus are fixed-width designs.

Optimal screen resolution for specifying the width of the layout is an important consideration when designing fixed-width layouts. Design for 800 × 600 resolutions to accommodate the largest number of users without introducing horizontal scrollbars. The width of the layout is then typically set to 750 to 770 pixels (with 30–50 pixels allocated for the browser chrome). In situations where the design is targeted for 1024 × 768 screen resolutions, the fixed-width container is set at 960 to 980 pixels. The goal, of course, is to prevent horizontal scrolling for the vast majority of the web application's users. Baekdal's (2006) research suggests that fixed-width designs for lower (i.e., 800 × 600) resolutions would support about 95 percent of users, whereas those designed for larger (i.e., 1024 × 768) resolutions would support only about 80 to 85 percent of users.

CENTER THE LAYOUT ON THE PAGE

Reduce the perception of empty space for users with larger screen resolutions by centering the layout so that the empty space is equally divided as the left and right margins. For example, viewing a design optimized for 800×600 resolutions (i.e., 770-pixel width) on a 1024×768 resolution screen would show an empty space of about 100 to 110 pixels on each side of the centered layout and 200 to 220 pixels worth of empty space on the right side for left-aligned layouts (Figure 12.5).

FILL THE PAGE BACKGROUND FOR LARGER BROWSER WINDOWS

Like centering the layout, filling the page background with an appropriate color, image, or texture makes empty space more acceptable and the page more visually appealing (Figure 12.6).

MAKE PAGES PRINTER-FRIENDLY

When web pages that are designed with fixed-width layouts are printed in a portrait or vertical (as opposed to landscape) orientation, information on the right usually gets clipped. This is because most printers cannot support more-than 600 pixels horizontally. If an application has pages likely to be printed by

FIGURE 12.5 Target centers the page so that there is an equal amount of white space on either side of the page.

FIGURE 12.6 Backpack (from 37signals) fills empty space with header and body background colors.

users, either offer users a "printer-friendly" link or create a separate style sheet for printing purposes such that printed pages show all relevant page content.

A separate style sheet for printing can be specified in one of the following ways:

1. Using an external cascading style sheet (CSS) file, which can work as a global style sheet and can be referenced by any page in the application:

```
<link href="print.css" rel="stylesheet" type="text/css"
media="print" />
```

2. Embedding CSS on pages that are most likely to be printed by users (e.g., an "Order Confirmation" page on e-commerce applications) as follows:

```
<style type="text/css" media="print">
… print specific selectors here…
</style>
```

The obvious downside is that the style sheet will need to be on every page likely to be printed.

Other approaches to specify style sheets for printing include the **@media** and **@import** rules. However, their support is inconsistent among browsers. For example, support for **@media** is buggy in IE 6.0 and IE 7.0 (see *www.reference. sitepoint.com/css/at-media*).

Related design patterns

Designers may want to consider a PROGRESSIVE LAYOUT, which offers a trade-off in that although it yields some design control to users by allowing the layout to adjust to the browser window width, it allows designers to put restrictions on minimum and maximum widths and still provide considerable control over the page's visual appearance.

PROGRESSIVE LAYOUT

Problem

Users with large screen resolutions (e.g., 1920×1200) may find pages using liquid layout difficult to read or scan with a maximized browser window. Users may not want to narrow the browser window size because they prefer larger widths for other applications, which may be available as tabs within the same browser window. On the other hand, users with smaller screen resolutions may find fixed-width designs difficult to use because they require them to scroll horizontally.

Solution

Use a progressive layout[1] with defined minimum and maximum widths to maintain page readability and aesthetic integrity. Pages designed using a progressive

---

[1]The definition of progressive layouts referred to in this chapter is different from that used by Adobe Flex developers. Their definition is to progressively display the application's content as it is initialized instead of waiting for the entire application to load (Szeto, 2004).

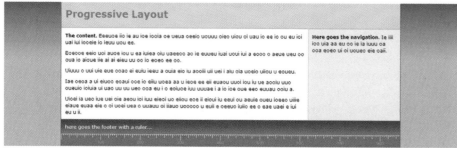

(a)   (b)

(c)

FIGURE 12.7 This example shows a progressive layout with a fixed width below 540 pixels of browser width (a), liquid between 540 and 1024 pixels of browser width (b), and fixed over 1024 pixels of browser width (c). The maximum width of this design is set at 850 pixels. (*Source*: Fulciniti, 2005.)

layout work as a liquid-width layout within a range of browser window widths. For browser window sizes below a certain minimum width and above a certain maximum width, the page behaves as a fixed-width layout (Figure 12.7).

Why

Progressive layout offers benefits of both liquid- and fixed-width layouts. It works as a liquid-width layout between a range of browser window widths and as a fixed-width layout above and below those widths. This helps satisfy the needs of users with either lower or higher screen resolutions. In addition, it allows designers reasonable control over a page's visual appearance.

How

Identify the minimum and the maximum design widths based on the target users' screen resolutions and design needs. Then design pages so that they remain at a fixed width below and above the minimum and the maximum browser window widths, respectively, and adjust to the browser window size between them.

Implementing such a design is possible by setting **min-width** and **max-width** style rules. However, because Internet Explorer versions 6 and 7 do not support **min-width** and **max-width** attributes, use of JavaScript is required to ensure that the design works correctly on all browsers (Fulciniti, 2005; Jesse, 2007a, 2007b).

Related design patterns

PROGRESSIVE LAYOUTS provide a graceful solution to counter arguments against designs using fixed- or liquid-width layouts. However, depending on the nature of the content presented by the application, either FIXED-WIDTH LAYOUT or LIQUID-WIDTH LAYOUT may be more appropriate and should be considered during design.

GRID STRUCTURE

Problem

Users need to clearly see and understand relationships between different page elements. Not using a systematic approach to lay out the page and its elements may lead to a cluttered design and make it appear unnecessarily complex.

Solution

Use a grid-based system for placing and aligning web page elements, giving web pages a visual structure and coherence and making it easy for users to understand the content's organization (Figure 12.8).

FIGURE 12.8 Using GRID STRUCTURE for positioning and aligning page components on this page is quite obvious. Not only does this make the page pleasing to the eye, but it also makes it easy to discern the visual hierarchy of page components (see the VISUAL HIERARCHY pattern next).

Why

A grid offers a consistent approach for designers to position and align various elements on a page and create appropriate visual hierarchies such that the resulting layouts are visually pleasing and easy to use. Laying out and aligning page elements using grids not only makes the pages appear simpler and visually pleasing, but the consistent placement of components within the grid makes the application easier to navigate as well.

How

When using a grid, pages are divided into rows and columns, and grid lines are used to position and align web page elements. The grid of rows and columns itself may be established using the rule of thirds or using columnar grids that create units in multiples of threes (Figure 12.9; Baird, 2007; Vinh and Boulton, 2007).

Once the grid is established, the next step is to position elements on the page that will be consistent throughout the application, such as logos, navigation (primary, secondary, and utility), headers, footers, and so forth. However, if content changes from one page to another, which may often be the case for web applications, it may be beneficial to position content within the grid first. The benefit of this "content-first" approach is that after placing the most important content on the page, it should become pretty clear whether navigation should be placed at the top or on the sides (left or right). For example, if content, such as reports or search results, demands horizontal space on pages, positioning navigation at the top may be the most appropriate.

Unlike printed pages, which have a fixed width and height, web pages provide limited control for vertical content, especially with a varying amount of

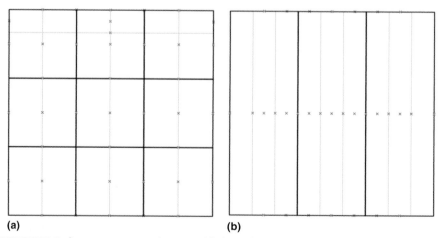

(a)   (b)

FIGURE 12.9 Among common columnar grids for web page layout are those based on the rule of thirds, which divides pages into rows and columns (a) or using only columnar grids in units of threes or fours (b).

page content occupying different amounts of vertical space. If the layout has to adapt to varying amounts of page content, maintain relative positions of elements within the page. A trivial example is the page footer, which could always appear after the page content no matter how much vertical space is needed by the page content.

CONSIDER USING THE GOLDEN RATIO

The *golden ratio*, also known as *divine proportion*, is the ratio between two segments such that the smaller (*bc*) segment is to the larger segment (*ab*) as the larger segment is to the sum of the two segments (*ac*), or $bc/ab = ab/bc = 0.618$ (Figure 12.10; Lidwell et al., 2003).

In general, layouts based on the golden ratio are considered to be aesthetically pleasing. Although the aesthetic superiority of designs based on golden ratios have limited evidence (Markowsky, 1992), most designers consider them superior and design their grid layouts accordingly. Although designs shouldn't be forced to fit the golden ratio, it should be considered whenever possible (Lidwell et al., 2003).

To use the golden ratio for a two-column, 770-pixel, fixed-width design—for example, multiply 770 pixels × 0.618. The result is approximately 475 pixels, which can be the main content column's width. The remaining width of 295 pixels (i.e., 770–495) can be used for the second column, which can be used for navigation or other secondary content (Baird, 2007; Clarke, 2007). The same approach also can be used for larger widths (Figure 12.11).

FIGURE 12.10 The golden ratio (bc/ab = ab/bc = 0.618).

FIGURE 12.11 This example from Apple shows a good application of the golden ratio. The total page content width is approximately 980 pixels. The content column "Select your Macbook Air" uses a width of 605 pixels (980 × 0.618), and the image column occupies the remaining width of 375 pixels.

ALIGN PAGE ELEMENTS ALONG GRID LINES

Align page elements along grid lines and with each other either vertically or horizontally. The objective is not only to create a minimal number of "invisible" grids on the page but also to do it in a way that reveals the structure of the page visually and makes it easy for users to understand and find different page elements. Creating effective alignment also helps lead a person through the design by associating related elements on the page (see the VISUAL HIERARCHY pattern that follows). Using alignment consistently on all pages within the web application improves the predictability of page elements within the design.

CREATE REUSABLE TEMPLATES

Once pages are laid out, they should be sliced into one or more page templates (depending on the number of page types) and used throughout the application. This ensures that designs work for the entire application and therefore prevents any guesswork on the developer's part as to how individual pages within the application should be designed.

Related design patterns

One of the important reasons for using the GRID STRUCTURE pattern is to ensure that the resulting design leads to a logical and predictable organization, improves comprehension, and makes it easy for users to find desired information (VISUAL HIERARCHY).

VISUAL HIERARCHY

Problem

Users need to make sense of information presented on web pages so that they can attend to the most important information first before moving to information of less importance.

Solution

Design pages such that the visual hierarchy is obvious to users. That is, use visual cues so as to clearly indicate grouping and the order of elements on a web page, and help guide users through the page so that they understand the page's purpose, comprehend its organization, and correctly assign importance to various page elements (Figure 12.12). As Lynch and Horton (1999) stated: "Graphic design is visual information management, using the tools of page layout, typography, and illustration to lead the reader's eye through the page."

Why

Establishing a visual hierarchy serves several important functions (Wroblewski, 2002):

- It creates a center of interest to attract users' attention.
- It creates a sense of order and balance.
- It establishes a pattern of movement to guide users through various page elements.

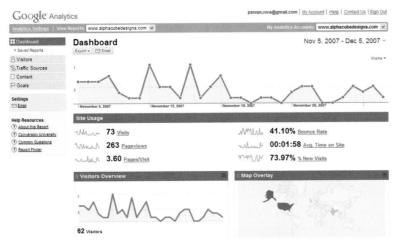

FIGURE 12.12 Google Analytics' "Dashboard" clearly identifies different groupings of page elements and leads users through it with an appropriate use of images, colors, and font sizes and their relative weights.

Creating an appropriate visual hierarchy, therefore, makes users more efficient and effective when interacting with web applications.

How

Because designers are attempting to correctly convey the importance of page elements through visual hierarchy, the obvious first step is to list page elements on a page in terms of their importance. The next step is to use one or more of the following visual components to order, position, and design those elements that reflect the desired visual hierarchy: contrast, chunking, images, alignment, white space, font sizes, shapes, colors, and others. For example, to elevate a page element to the top of the visual hierarchy—that is, provide the highest emphasis or importance to an element—it could be made larger, bolder, shown in a high-contrast color, separated from other elements using additional white space, wrapped into a bright-colored border, included with an image, and/or placed closer to the top left or top center of the page (Figure 12.13).

FIGURE 12.13 On Google's home page, the logo has the most prominence (at the top of the visual hierarchy) because it is larger, bolder, and more colorful; has a high contrast with the background; is surrounded by lots of white space; and is placed at the top center.

USE CONTRAST TO ESTABLISH VISUAL HIERARCHY

Contrast is a key design approach used to communicate visual hierarchy. It is created by visual difference between elements—the more two elements are different, the higher the contrast between them. In general, higher-contrasting elements grab users' attention first when compared with lower-contrasting elements. For example, black has the highest contrast with white and varying levels of contrast with different shades of gray. Value is not the only way two elements can contrast from each other. Contrast can also be created by using one or more of the following: size, texture, position, shape, color, and orientation (Figure 12.14).

By using a combination of these visual forms, an effective visual hierarchy can be designed, and desired elements can be emphasized to draw users' attention. Contrast can be applied to page elements at the text level as well. For example, headings and subheadings can be made to stand out from the rest of the text by using contrast forms such as size and color (Figure 12.15).

FIGURE 12.14
The primary forms of contrast. (*Source*: From Rutledge, 2007.)

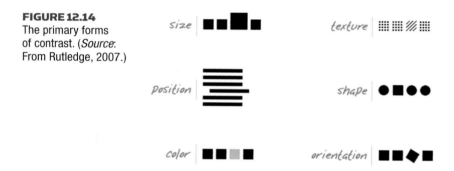

FIGURE 12.15 Blogger establishes a good visual hierarchy by using a large, colorful, high-contrasting logo; then moves users' attention to the center area with a prominent call to action, "Create Your Blog Now"; then to the images; and so forth.

It's important to remember that contrast does not just refer to background–foreground contrast but also about the contrast (i.e., differences) among page elements. If the background–foreground contrast is high, but the contrast among page elements is low, the web page will fail to establish a clear visual hierarchy. This can also make the page appear cluttered and disorganized to users because they will struggle to navigate through the page design to determine what to attend to first, second, and so forth.

GROUP RELATED INFORMATION VISUALLY

By grouping information visually and clearly indicating what the group represents, users can quickly decide whether to pay attention to it. When designed correctly, grouping makes pages appear simpler because it's easier for users to filter out (i.e., ignore) not-so-relevant information and focus on the areas of interest (Figure 12.16).

Visual hierarchy is important for both between groups and between elements within groups. Once users decide to focus on a logical group, they should be able to understand the importance of elements within the group. In Figure 12.16, Crazy Egg emphasizes different elements within the group to indicate their importance. For example, in the "Let's Get Started" section, "Create a Test" is higher in the visual hierarchy than the text "Setting up a test. . . ."

PLACE PERSISTENT ELEMENTS IN CONSISTENT LOCATIONS

Persistent elements on a page—that is, elements that appear on almost all pages within the application such as logos, navigation, headers, footers, and so

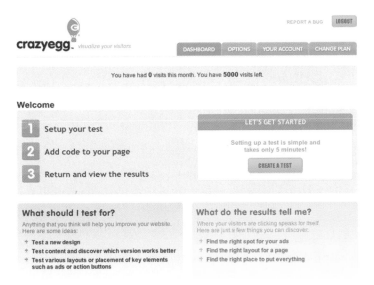

FIGURE 12.16 Crazy Egg groups different areas of the page using colors, font sizes, and white space to not only establish a good visual hierarchy but also to make the page appear simpler and visually pleasing.

FIGURE 12.17
Blinksale positions the header, primary navigation, utility navigation, page content, and related actions in consistent locations.

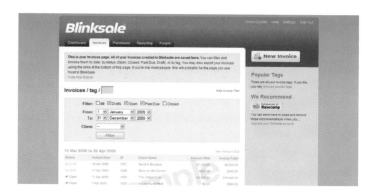

forth—should be placed in consistent locations. For each persistent element, establish its importance and position it accordingly. For example, navigation is important and should be appropriately emphasized and clearly delineated from other elements such as logos and headers (Figure 12.17).

Related design patterns

Aligning page elements is extremely important for establishing an appropriate VISUAL HIERARCHY and for guiding users through page elements. GRID STRUCTURE is typically used to ensure proper alignment of page elements and to facilitate content scanning. Knowing visual hierarchy of the page is also important for SEMANTIC MARKUP (see Chapter 11). The order of elements in the page markup should reflect the desired visual hierarchy so that when the page is rendered without style sheets and images, the visual hierarchy of page elements is still maintained.

HIGHLIGHT

Problem

Certain page elements need to stand out and grab users' attention, not only to establish their importance (VISUAL HIERARCHY) but also in response to users' actions (e.g., selecting an element) or to communicate to users a status change for page elements or individual data items.

Solution

Highlight selected or changed elements to direct users' attention to them (Figure 12.18). If necessary, indicate the "value" or the extent of the change.

Why

Highlighting is important to provide a visual feedback about selected elements as well as to direct users' attention to changes. It is also useful in the following ways (Mahemoff, 2006):

- Showing which particular element has focus.

FIGURE 12.18 Dell uses several highlighting approaches on this page: recommended options are highlighted with a green background, and changed and upgraded configuration items are highlighted in the "My Components" section with a yellow background.

- Showing which elements are selected.
- Indicating if an element is particularly important.
- Indicating an element is undergoing change.
- Prompting users to act on an element.

Highlighting is particularly important for pages communicating different states for a wide variety of elements, since it not only directs users' attention but also invites appropriate action.

How

There are several ways to highlight a page's elements to make them stand out: change the background color, change the text color, make the text bold or a larger size, change borders, use animation (see the patterns ANIMATIONS/TRANSITIONS and SPOTLIGHT/YELLOW-FADE in Chapter 8), dim some elements, or use icons. Ideally, use a combination of these styles (Figures 12.19 and 12.20).

HIGHLIGHT SELECTED ITEMS IN A LIST

Clearly indicate items with which users are working or will be taking action on by highlighting each selected item. Even when checkboxes are used for selection, highlighting is a better visual way of distinguishing selected items from unselected items (Figure 12.21).

USE TRANSIENT HIGHLIGHTING TO INFORM USERS OF PAGE CHANGES

Highlighting an item momentarily (typically by fading the highlight in and then fading it out) creates an animated effect and focuses users' attention on the changed area on the page (see the ANIMATIONS/TRANSITIONS and SPOTLIGHT/YELLOW-FADE patterns in Chapter 8).

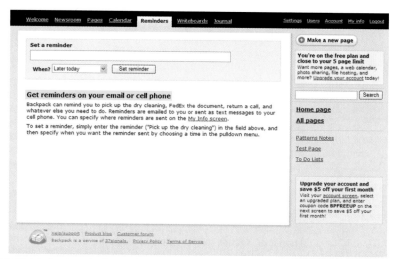

FIGURE 12.19 Backpack shows the current (i.e., selected) tab using a combination of background color, borders, font size, and font color. This page highlights the message "Get reminders on your email or cell phone" by changing its background color and making the font larger and bolder. Backpack also deemphasizes (i.e., "unhighlights") the utility navigation links in the footer by making them smaller and gray.

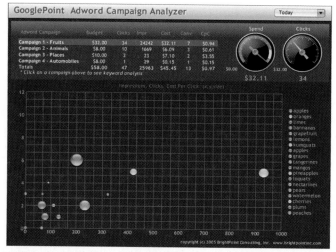

FIGURE 12.20 This demo dashboard from BrightPoint Consulting (*www.brightpointinc.com*) shows several different ways of highlighting page elements: the selected campaign is in a different background color, campaign totals are in yellow, and different bubble sizes highlight campaigns with higher ad spending.

USE A LIGHTBOX EFFECT TO HIGHLIGHT CHANGES THAT REQUIRE USER RESPONSE

In instances where a page element needs to be highlighted and users must interact with it before continuing (similar to a modal dialog box in desktop

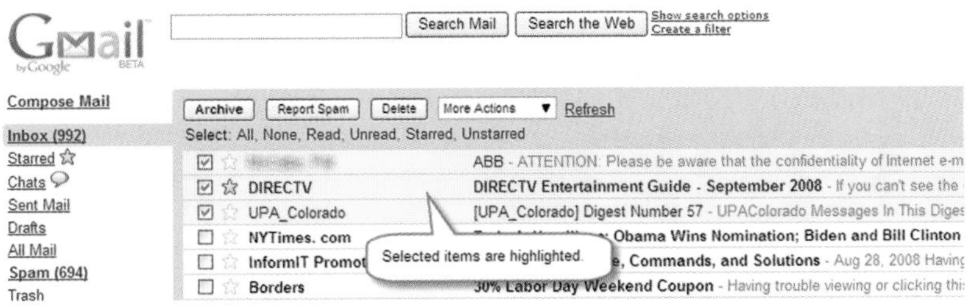

FIGURE 12.21 Gmail highlights selected items by changing their background color.

FIGURE 12.22 Picnik highlights the registration form by dimming the page's background, requiring users to either continue to create an account or to close the site by clicking on the close (×) icon.

applications), a useful way to get users' attention is to dim all elements on the page other than the highlighted element (Figure 12.22).

KEEP HIGHLIGHTING APPROACHES CONSISTENT

Keep highlighting approaches consistent throughout the application for similar interactions. Although the design may have different highlighting approaches for different contexts, such as selected items, messages (e.g., error, feedback, acknowledgment, and alert), selected navigation items, and so forth, they should remain consistent throughout the application. In Figure 12.21, Gmail uses a yellow background for selected emails, a blue background for the selected navigation item (in this case, "Inbox"), and a green icon for users who are currently online (in this case, Pawan Vora) for chatting.

Related design patterns

Animations and transitions are also useful ways to call users' attention to the changed elements (see the ANIMATIONS/TRANSITIONS and SPOTLIGHT/ YELLOW-FADE patterns in Chapter 8).

ICONS

Problem

Designers want to make different page objects and actions easily recognizable without requiring excessive space and, at the same time, want to make the interface visually pleasing and inviting to users.

FIGURE 12.23
Yahoo! mail uses icons for both objects (e.g., "Inbox," "Drafts," "Spam," etc.) and actions (e.g., "Delete," "Reply," "Forward," etc.).

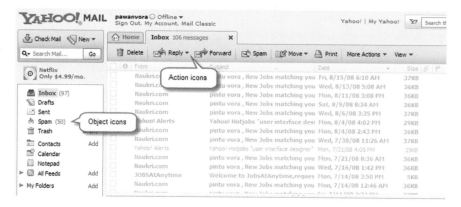

Solution

Use icons to represent commonly used objects and actions (Figure 12.23).

Why

Icons may be used in web applications for a variety of reasons:

- For many common objects and tasks, icons are more readily recognized and remembered.
- They take less space than corresponding textual links.
- Icons typically have more universal recognition than text; thus, when localizing a web application, icons, when appropriately used, have minimal layout impact. However, if icons are used with labels, label translation should account for text expansion when translating to other languages (see the EXTENSIBLE DESIGN pattern in Chapter 10).

How

Most important, use familiar icons (Nolan, 1989)—that is, use concrete (rather than abstract) icons and those that remind users of things already known. Use icons that clearly suggest the objects or actions they represent. Ideally, users should be able to recognize icons without any accompanying text labels.

SUPPLEMENT ICONS WITH LABELS

Undoubtedly, there will be objects and actions that are unfamiliar to users. Therefore, supplement icons with labels to make actions easier to identify. During users' initial interaction with an application, users are more likely to rely on labels, but as their use continues, their interaction will become more efficient as the icons become familiar.

When adding labels may take additional space, include tool tips for the icons. However, when dynamically changing the status of an icon, update the tool tip dynamically to indicate the changed state.

AVOID USING TEXT IN ICONS

Avoid using text as part of an icon's image, since it makes it more difficult to localize it (i.e., translate to other languages; see Chapter 10). Because of the smaller sizes of icons, text may also be difficult to read, and when used with a label, it may not be clear to users which label or text to consider for deciphering the icon's meaning. In addition, for users with vision deficiencies, the text may be difficult to read when zoomed in (see the ACCESSIBLE IMAGES pattern in Chapter 11).

USE MODIFIERS TO INDICATE OR CHANGE AN OBJECT'S STATUS

The same base icon can be used for multiple object states—for example, new email, read email, and responded-to email (Figure 12.24).

For monitoring applications, similar modifiers—referred to as "health badges"—are often used to indicate alarms or the status of objects. They are either placed side by side or to the bottom right or bottom left of the main icon (Figure 12.25). The modifier icon may be used over the main icon as long as the main icon is still recognizable and is not masked by the modifier icon (e.g., putting a "X" over an icon).

USE TOGGLE ICONS TO INDICATE ALTERNATE STATES

Toggle icons are used to indicate either the presence or absence of an attribute or to assign a state. For example, Figure 12.26 shows the star icon used as a toggle by Gmail to indicate the "starred" or "normal" states of an email. This is very similar to the "flagging" approach offered by desktop-based email systems

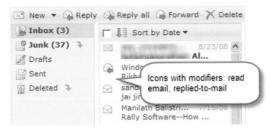

FIGURE 12.24 Hotmail uses the same base icon to show emails are new, read, and read and responded to.

FIGURE 12.25 In this example, modifier icons are placed next to the network icon to indicate the "health" of the network: (*left to right*) critical issues, major issues, minor issues, and normal status.

FIGURE 12.26 Gmail toggles the star icon to indicate a "starred" or "normal" state for an email.

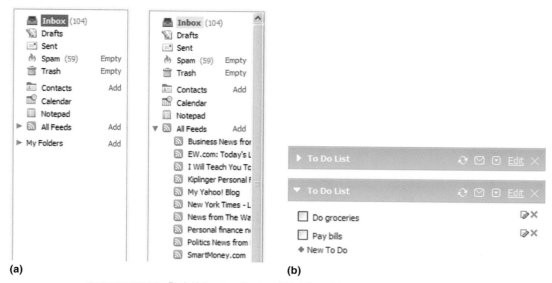

(a)   (b)

FIGURE 12.27 Both Yahoo! mail (a) and Netvibes (b) use arrow icons to expand or collapse sections.

FIGURE 12.28 Icons used by Mint use different shapes to make them clearly distinguishable from one another.

such as Outlook. Toggle icons are also used to indicate the disabled and enabled states of objects.

Some common uses of toggle icons are to show expanded and collapsed states in tree structures, for navigation, or for specific page elements (as in portlets) (Figure 12.27).

MAKE ICONS VISUALLY DISTINCT FROM ONE ANOTHER

It's important that icons are easily distinguishable from each other to help users find appropriate icons (thus, actions) quickly and minimize confusion. This is usually accomplished by making their shapes visually distinct from one another (Figure 12.28) and is particularly important when icons are used to suggest "status" information. For example, avoid using the same-shaped icons with different colors (e.g., red, yellow, and green) to indicate status. Instead, use different shapes in addition to colors such as, red octagon, yellow triangle, and green circle. Using multiple coding methods also helps users with color-vision deficiencies, as they can use the icon's shape to determine status.

USE THE SAME VISUAL STYLE FOR ICONS

Make sure that icons appear professionally designed and follow the same set of stylistic conventions—that is, the same base color set (matched to the site's brand) and the same visual styles and effects (Figure 12.29).

TIP
To test icons for their visual distinctness, fill nontransparent areas of icons with the same color and put them next to each other. The more distinguishable they are from one another by their shape, the better their discriminability.

(a) (b)

FIGURE 12.29 The icons used by Hulu (a) and Brightcove (b) use a consistent stylistic approach.

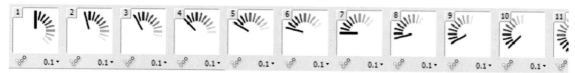

FIGURE 12.30 Animated icons are typically used to inform users that the application is processing information. This example shows 11 of the 24 frames used to create animated icon. (*Source*: www.ajaxload.info.)

USE ANIMATED ICONS ONLY WHEN ABSOLUTELY NECESSARY

Animation usually grabs users' attention and can be distracting. Therefore, use animated icons only when it's necessary to direct users' attention—for example, when users need to wait for the web application to finish processing (Figure 12.30).

Related design patterns

When used with health badges, icons are often used to highlight status change. Therefore, consider using other highlighting practices to ensure that users have noticed the change (HIGHLIGHT).

CHAPTER 13
Pattern Libraries

INTRODUCTION

As indicated in Chapter 1, design patterns have the potential to offer benefits such as proven design solutions and guidance for their use, improved design process, reusability and consistent interfaces, and so forth. To realize these benefits, however, it's important that design patterns be documented and made available in a format that promotes reuse. Several documented collections of patterns, commonly referred to as *pattern libraries*, currently exist. Some notable ones include Jenifer Tidwell's collection of interaction design patterns (Tidwell, 2006), Martijn van Welie's web site about design patterns (*www.welie.com*), Van Duyne et al.'s *Design of Sites* (2006), and Yahoo! Design Pattern Library (*developer.yahoo.com/ypatterns/*).

Despite the popularity of patterns and pattern libraries, currently there is no consensus on how patterns should be documented, maintained, and shared with others. Nor has there been any empirical research that evaluates the efficacy of existing pattern languages, libraries, and collections designed for user interfaces. Rather than analyze and discuss the pros and cons of different approaches (Dearden and Finlay, 2006; Dennis and Snow, 2006), this chapter presents a pattern library as a pattern and identifies its core elements, as well as offers best practices for its development.

PATTERN LIBRARY
Problem

In the absence of a formal process for reusing successful design solutions, the design process can be quite inefficient, because designers and developers spend time trying to solve user interface design problems for which successful design solutions have already been identified and implemented. This is often exacerbated when the rationale and context for previously used design solutions is not documented, making it difficult to justify their use.

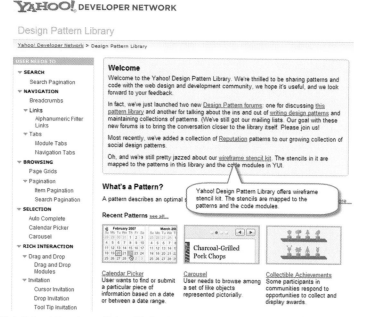

FIGURE 13.1 Yahoo! Developer Network's Design Pattern Library is available as an open-source pattern library. It offers interaction designers a stencil kit to facilitate development of wireframes and maps many patterns to code snippets in the YUI library to help with its use during development.

Solution

Develop a repository of design patterns (i.e., a pattern library), documenting the knowledge of design problems, solutions, rationale, and best practices for implementing the patterns (Figure 13.1). In addition, share the pattern library with other designers and developers, promote use and reuse of patterns by incorporating implementation code snippets (i.e., components), and encourage designer and developer participation.

Why

For large and/or distributed design teams within a corporation, it is common to find differing user interface designs and interaction approaches for the same design problem across different product lines; they often have different visual treatments as well. This results in inconsistent interfaces, which can lower usability of applications and weaken the corporate brand (Malone et al., 2005). By facilitating the reuse of design solutions, pattern libraries offer an effective way of documenting and sharing solutions for recurring design problems and help achieve desired consistency. Pattern libraries can also make the design process more efficient and increase the productivity of designers by reducing duplicate research and minimizing "reinventing the wheel" (Malone et al., 2005).

Although patterns are design solutions independent of specific implementation issues, design and development teams can further reduce the time spent on user interface development by building software components to support design patterns. After a design pattern is chosen, development teams can reuse and adapt software components and code snippets for implementing selected patterns (Sinnig et al., 2004). Reuse and efficiencies are also achieved since software components typically incorporate related design patterns. For example, a software component for the TABULAR LIST pattern can incorporate the SORTING and PAGINATION patterns and make it easy for developers to implement all three patterns in their designs.

Even when design teams are smaller and colocated, pattern libraries are beneficial because they provide a way to capture design best practices and promote reuse. Because of the limited design and usability resources available to smaller design teams, minimizing rework by reusing known successful design solutions are often of even greater importance than for larger design teams.

How

The first task when developing a pattern library is to determine how to document each pattern. As indicated in Chapter 1, pattern authors have used differing approaches (including this author) to document patterns, and a consensus on the most effective way of documenting patterns does not currently exist. However, they all contain the following core sections.

Pattern name. The name of the design solution to clearly communicate what the pattern stands for. An unambiguous (and preferably familiar) name is important to make it easy for designers to recognize, select, and remember patterns.

Problem. A brief description of the design problem and the trade-offs faced by the designers, if any.

Solution. A brief summary and an exemplar image that shows the successful design solution. The image may be a sketch or an actual screenshot; the latter is preferred because it shows the design solution in use and helps improve the strength of the pattern.

Reasons the design solution is effective (why). Some form of design rationale is essential to make the case for the pattern. This may be based on empirical research, user interface design principles (or heuristics), and/or user familiarity because of established conventions. This section may also include specific contexts in which the pattern is most appropriate.

Best practices for applying the design solution (how). In most instances, applying a design solution requires attending to additional considerations. For example, when using the DELAY/PROGRESS INDICATOR pattern (see Chapter 8), designers may need to know whether to show time elapsed or time remaining and in what contexts. Identifying best practices is essential to ensure the correct use of the selected pattern.

Related design patterns. Most patterns do not stand alone. They are related to other patterns either because their use requires incorporating other patterns or because they complete other patterns. For example, when creating a form, designers have to consider several patterns such as SHORT FORMS, ACTION BUTTONS, REQUIRED FIELD INDICATORS, ERROR MESSAGES,

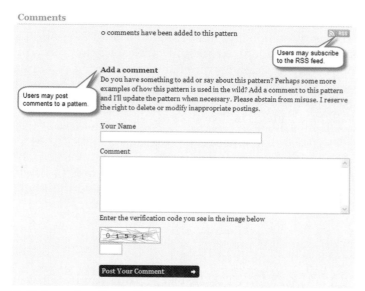

FIGURE 13.2 Welie.com's patterns allow users to post comments to discuss a pattern and to subscribe to the RSS feed if they want to stay informed of pattern changes.

and ACCESSIBLE FORMS, among others (see Chapter 2). Indicating such relations can help designers discover the relationships among patterns and ensure consistent and usable design. The related design patterns section sometimes reference similar patterns in other pattern collections as well.

There are other sections that may be beneficial, including:

Comments. To promote sharing and discussion among designers and developers, a pattern may include a discussion or comments section (Figure 13.2). This could help capture the "collective wisdom" of designers and can help improve patterns or at least document various scenarios in which a pattern was applied successfully or required changes. The comments section is common in publicly available libraries such as Welie.com, UC Berkeley Pattern Library, and Fluid Open Source Design Pattern Library.

Research evidence. To improve pattern validity and strength, it may help to include empirical or research evidence that demonstrates a pattern's benefits. Supporting research can be added in a section such as research evidence, usability results, or user feedback (Spool, 2006).

History or change log. Any changes made to patterns based on feedback from other designers and developers or from research evidence can be logged and shown in a history section (Figure 13.3).

For both smaller and larger design teams, developing pattern libraries may seem to be a monumental task.[1] Therefore, to get started with developing a pattern

---

[1]Interestingly, many of the popular pattern library repositories on the Web, such as Welie. com, ui-patterns.com, uipatternfactory.com, and designinginterfaces.com, are works of a single individual.

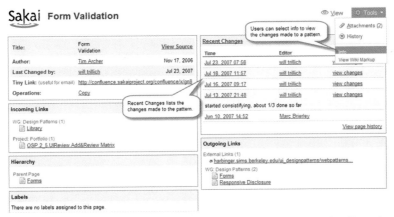

FIGURE 13.3 Sakai pattern library lists the changes made to a pattern in the "Recent Changes" section.

library, including only the core elements of a pattern may be sufficient; tapping from open-source pattern libraries is also a good way to seed pattern libraries. The benefits of pattern libraries are immediate in that with each pattern added to the library, the designs are available for reuse.

INCLUDE IMMEDIATELY (RE)USABLE DESIGN COMPONENTS

An important goal of a pattern library is to promote the reuse of design solutions. Pattern libraries should therefore consider offering artifacts that would make use of proposed solutions easier for both interaction designers and developers. For example, to facilitate reuse by interaction designers, pattern libraries can include sample site-maps, workflow diagrams, and wire-frames; these many be in the form of stencils or visual components (Figure 13.4).

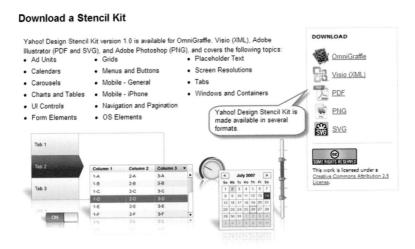

FIGURE 13.4 Yahoo!'s Design Pattern Library offers users a stencil kit in several formats (e.g., OmniGraffle, Microsoft Visio, PDF, etc.) to help in wire-frame design in designers' preferred tools.

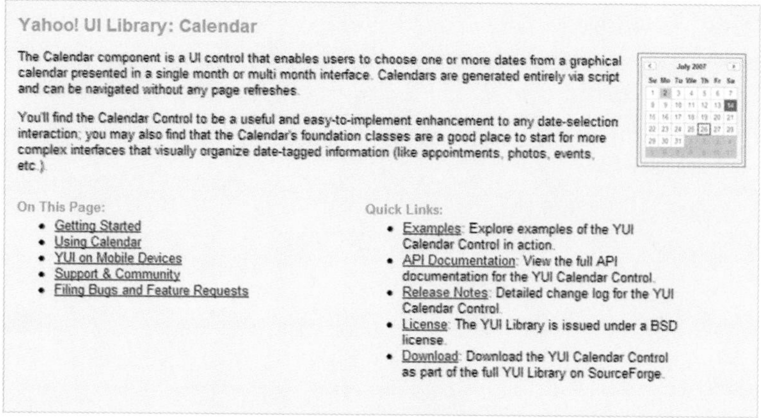

FIGURE 13.5 Yahoo! UI Library has several components to help implement their patterns. (They are not linked to the patterns, however.)

Similarly, to facilitate reuse by developers, include code snippets in HTML, CSS, JavaScript, PHP, ASP, JSP, and so on, as appropriate for a development team, to make it easy for them to copy and paste snippets in their code when building the application (Figure 13.5).

When offering software components for reuse, it's important to test them for necessary cross-browser compliance, performance, and interaction with other components before including them in the pattern library. It's also important to emphasize that components may not be completely pluggable solutions and may require some tweaking and updates. As development practices and technology change, review and retest components to ensure their continued usefulness.

INCLUDE MANY, MANY EXAMPLES

By definition, patterns prove their merit by their use (Winn and Calder, 2002). Without clear evidence of successful use, patterns may have limited "strength." Alexander's patterns (Alexander et al., 1977) and a few user-interface design pattern collections (Bochers, 2001; Graham, 2003) usually indicate the strength of a pattern using a star-rating system. Graham (2003, p. 52) states:

> Again, following Alexander, we have classified the patterns according to our degree of confidence in them. The pattern's "star rating," shown next to its name in orange, indicates this. Three stars means that we are totally convinced of the pattern's efficacy, having used it or seen it used successfully on many projects. Three stars may also mean, especially for abstract patterns, that there is a solid theoretical derivation or justification of the pattern in the literature and folklore of the subject. If there are no stars it means that we think this is a good idea but would like people to try and see. One and two stars are interpreted on the scale between these extremes in the evident manner.

Applying a star-rating system is difficult because it requires a judgment on the part of the pattern authors or the design team (one of the reasons for its absence in this book). In addition, applying a star-rating system in a corporate setting may be counterproductive, as it may appear to offer design teams leeway when they consider patterns with lower star ratings. Including several examples of usage of patterns is more effective because users can see instances of a pattern's use and determine its appropriateness for their design problem. Furthermore, patterns are often derived from actual use rather than theoretical constructs or principles, making it important to include a range of examples that show the use of patterns in a variety of applications (Figure 13.6).

In addition to actual screenshots that illustrate the pattern's use, consider showing users a list of applications where the pattern is used. This is particularly useful for corporate pattern libraries, where showing reference implementations of

FIGURE 13.6 UI Pattern Factory (*www.uipatternfactory.com*) shows a gallery of screenshots for each pattern. Users can also see additional screenshots on the accompanying public Flickr group.

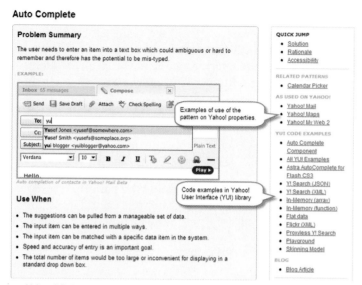

FIGURE 13.7 Yahoo! Pattern Library shows examples of the use of a pattern on Yahoo! properties (in the "As Used on Yahoo!" section) as well as code examples (in the "YUI Code Examples" section).

suggested patterns by even a few product lines within the corporation can both justify their use and allow designers and developers to explore different ways in which patterns are applied (Figure 13.7).

DEMONSTRATE RICHER INTERACTIONS

Many design patterns, especially for Rich Internet Applications (RIAs), are embodied in the user interaction. Such interactions can be made clearer if users can experience the interactivity suggested by the pattern. When such is the case, it's useful to allow users to experience the interactivity as an interactive proto-type, animation, or movie (Figure 13.8).

INCLUDE ACCESSIBILITY AND INTERNATIONALIZATION CONSIDERATIONS

If accessibility and internationalization-related design patterns are not sepa-rately documented, it's important to include relevant best practices with the patterns themselves; the necessary accessibility and internationalization hooks should be included in corresponding software components as well.

Although a few of the current pattern libraries include accessibility consider-ations (e.g., Yahoo! Pattern Library, UI Patterns, and Fluid Open Source Design Pattern Library; Figure 13.9), none currently include internationalization con-siderations. However, their inclusion is important for companies that plan to localize their applications (see Chapter 10 for details on internationalization considerations).

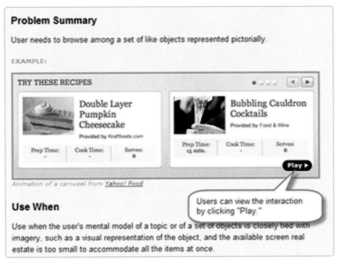

FIGURE 13.8 Yahoo! Pattern Library uses animation to illustrate relevant interactions.

Accessibility

Specific tips related to error messages from form validation:

- **Color perception**: Avoid using *only colour* to convey information. That is, use colour in addition to clearly labelled errors messages and success messages. (Red means "bad" but not everyone can distinguish red from green – so include the "bad" text as well.)
- **Navigation**: Consider moving focus to the area on the page where an error occurred or providing a quick way for users to jump down to the problem.
- **Workflow**: If multiple errors occurred, provide users with a summary or indication of the number of errors.

General techniques for form accessibility:

- **Labels**: Clearly label form elements. Use the <label> tag to explicitly associate form labels with their controls.
- **Sequence**: Ensure form fields are laid out in a logical order and can be easily controlled with the keyboard and other input devices. Use the "tabindex" attribute to provide convenient navigation when tabbing through form elements.
- **Sections**: Group related form elements together using the <fieldset> tag.

FIGURE 13.9 Fluid Open Source Design Pattern Library lists accessibility considerations for its patterns. This example shows the accessibility considerations for the LIST BUILDER pattern (see *www.uidesignpatterns.org/content/list-builder*).

CONSIDER INCLUDING ANTIPATTERNS

Antipatterns are inappropriate solutions that appear to be good solutions to a given problem; they are also referred to as *pitfalls* (Gamma et al., 1995). Although not mentioned by Christopher Alexander (Alexander et al., 1977), who proposed the notion of patterns, there may be some benefit to including antipatterns in the pattern library if the use of inappropriate design solutions seems to be a common practice.

A good example is the HOVER & COVER antipattern noted by Scott (2008), who described it as when the hover actually hides important contextual information around the object or gets in the way of other actions (Figure 13.10). Antipatterns observed by Scott also include MEANDERING WAY, TINY

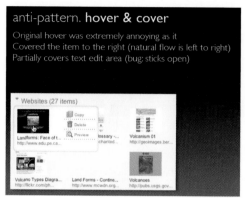

FIGURE 13.10 Description of HOVER & COVER anti-pattern. (*Source:* Scott, 2008.)

TARGETS, POGO STICK NAVIGATION, LINKITUS, ANIMATION GONE WILD, WINDOWS APLENTY, and MISSED MOMENTS, among others.

Because antipatterns are design practices that should be avoided, they should reference appropriate design patterns or suggest design practices to improve the design. An alternative to including antipatterns is to indicate the correct practice within the original pattern itself. For example, when describing a hover pattern, one of the best practices (or the "how") can indicate that when using the hover method, the contextual information or actions around the object should not be occluded (i.e., covered).

MAKE FINDING APPROPRIATE PATTERNS EASY

To encourage use, pattern libraries must make finding appropriate patterns easy. This can be accomplished by allowing users to browse patterns in multiple ways such as by user tasks, design requirements, application type, alphabetical list, and so forth (Figure 13.11).

When listing patterns, include a thumbnail of the pattern to make it easy to scan patterns and identify an appropriate match, as well as discover other relevant patterns (Figure 13.12).

Designers would also benefit if they were provided assistance in selecting appropriate patterns based on one or more design goals; this is especially helpful when choosing from a set of seemingly related patterns. As with the FILTERING pattern (see Chapter 6), users can adjust their design criteria to narrow or expand their pattern choices (Figure 13.13).

ENABLE AND ENCOURAGE PARTICIPATION

To encourage participation from other designers and developers, enable users rate patterns, post comments, and/or suggest ideas for new patterns (Figure 13.14).

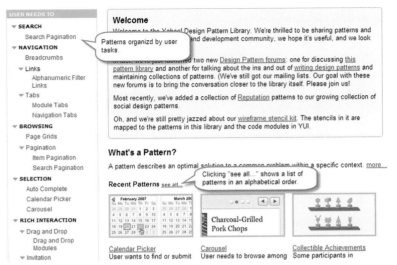

FIGURE 13.11 Yahoo! Design Pattern Library organizes patterns based on user tasks and alphabetically (when user clicks "see all..." next to "Recent Patterns").

FIGURE 13.12 User Interface Design Pattern Library, UI Patterns (*www.ui-patterns.com*), uses a thumbnail, pattern name, and brief description to make it easy for users to find the desired pattern.

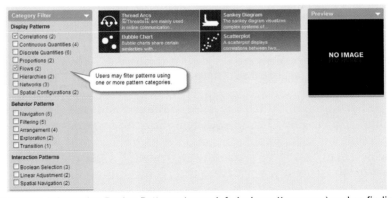

FIGURE 13.13 Information Design Patterns (*www.infodesignpatterns.com*) makes finding relevant patterns easy by allowing users to filter them using categories such as "Display Patterns," "Behavior Patterns," and "Interaction Patterns."

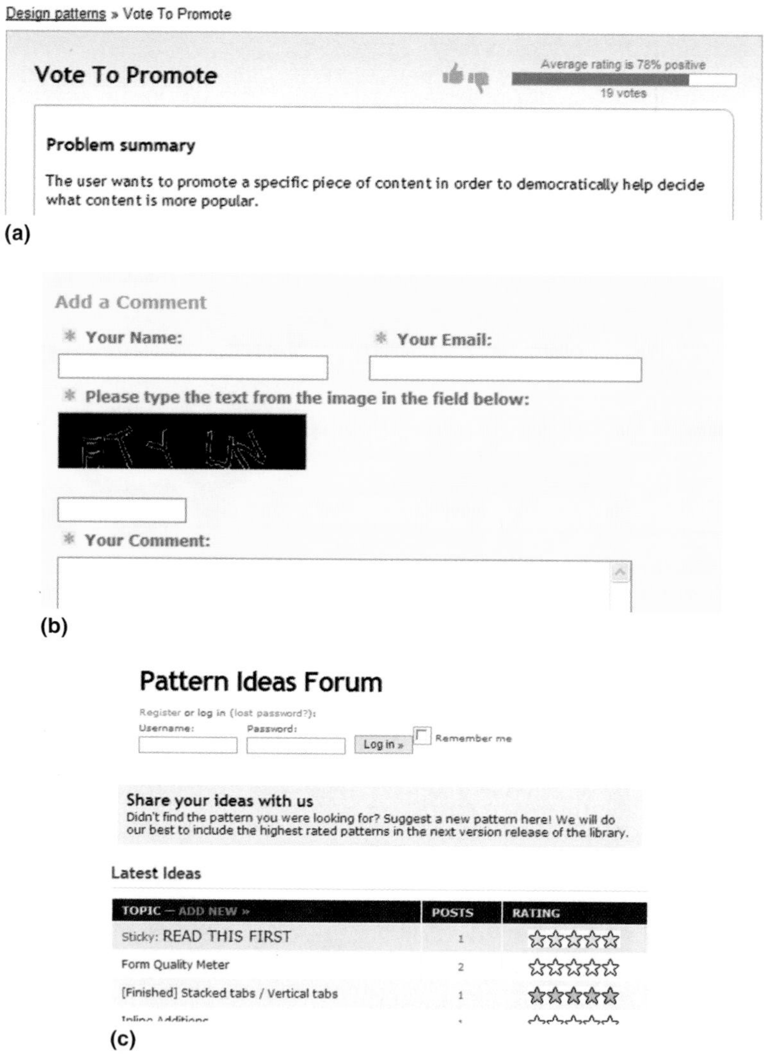

Design patterns » Vote To Promote

Vote To Promote

👍 👎   Average rating is 78% positive
19 votes

Problem summary

The user wants to promote a specific piece of content in order to democratically help decide what content is more popular.

(a)

Add a Comment

* **Your Name:**

* **Your Email:**

* **Please type the text from the image in the field below:**

* **Your Comment:**

(b)

Pattern Ideas Forum

Register or log in (lost password?):
Username: Password:

Log in »   ☐ Remember me

Share your ideas with us
Didn't find the pattern you were looking for? Suggest a new pattern here! We will do our best to include the highest rated patterns in the next version release of the library.

Latest Ideas

TOPIC — ADD NEW »	POSTS	RATING
Sticky: READ THIS FIRST	1	☆☆☆☆☆
Form Quality Meter	2	☆☆☆☆☆
[Finished] Stacked tabs / Vertical tabs	1	★★★★★
Inline Additions	.	~~~~~

(c)

FIGURE 13.14 Pattern libraries can encourage participation from other users in several ways: UI Patterns allows users to rate a pattern's usefulness by voting "thumbs-up" or "thumbs-down" (a); UC Berkeley Web Patterns allow users to post their comments and code (b); and UI Pattern Factory invites users to share their ideas and suggest patterns in a "Pattern Ideas Forum" (c).

Although not common, it helps to allow designers and developers to suggest and publish patterns in an open-source fashion. At a minimum, it should be made possible for them to submit examples and screenshots for existing patterns, which may be added as photo galleries. With each example, users may indicate how the pattern was used and their comments on the evidence of successful use or contexts in which its use was found to be inappropriate.

A good example is UI Pattern Factory. It allows users to contribute pattern examples using Flickr. Users can join the public Flickr group (*UIPatternFactory. com*), upload screenshots, tag them with the pattern name, and submit them

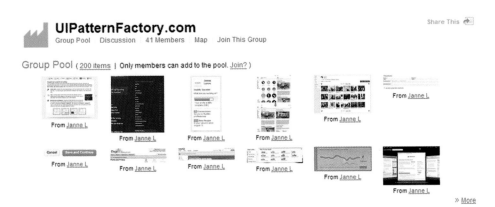

FIGURE 13.15 UIPatternFactory.com group on Flickr allows members to add their own screenshots to any of the existing patterns.

FIGURE 13.16 On Welie.com, users can subscribe to RSS feeds and stay informed of any changes.

to have them included with other examples for that pattern (Figure 13.15). In addition, participation from users should be acknowledged not only to recognize their contributions, but also to serve as an incentive for others to contribute.

To ensure that interested users can keep themselves informed of the changes, offer them the option to subscribe to RSS feeds (Figure 13.16).

ESTABLISH A PROCESS FOR MANAGING PATTERN LIBRARIES

Finally, and perhaps most important, pattern libraries should be managed just like any other software application. In particular, they should have a clear process around adding, updating, and archiving (or deprecating) patterns. It's also important to determine the process around the approval of patterns before publishing them. The process should indicate how patterns move from a draft or proposed stage to the approved stage, how participants provide feedback, how disagreements are resolved, how each proposal will be voted on, and so forth (Figure 13.17; see Crumlish, 2008; Malone et al., 2005). If software components are included in the pattern, it's important that the processes around code review and testing are included as well.

Pattern Library Workflow

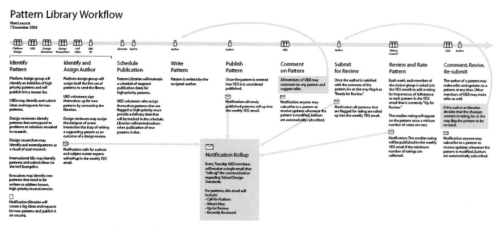

FIGURE 13.17 Pattern Library Workflow used by Yahoo! (*Source:* Malone et al., 2005.)

To ensure that the pattern library stays relevant and useful, it is important to monitor and refine or extend the patterns to ensure their continued efficacy and applicability. Some patterns may become obsolete because of improved design approaches. For example, the design pattern CAPTCHA (see Chapter 3), although appropriate now, may become obsolete as other technological approaches emerge to distinguish between humans and automated agents.

Alternatively, some patterns may not change in how they work but have to be updated because of improved implementations. For example, forms that were once laid out using tables may now be positioned using cascading style sheets (CSS). Any such changes made to the patterns must be marked as "updated" to inform designers and developers of the changes; the changes may be sent out via RSS feeds as well. To ensure that changes to patterns are not made in an arbitrary fashion, it's important to define and adopt some form of change control process.

CONSIDER USING A WIKI FOR DEVELOPING PATTERN LIBRARIES

A wiki should be considered for developing pattern libraries, since they make collaboration easier by allowing several people to add, change, and remove content (Figure 13.18). A wiki also maintains a history of changes and makes it possible to revert to a previous version, if necessary; such built-in version control makes a wiki useful for single-author pattern libraries as well. With features such as easy linking among web pages, a wiki also makes it easy to link related patterns. Finally, by supporting a discussion among its participants, a wiki makes participation easier.

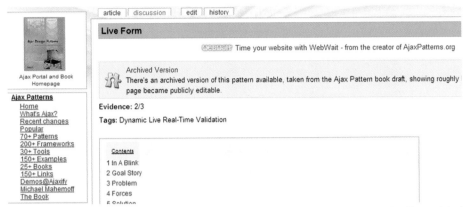

FIGURE 13.18 Michael Mahemoff maintains AjaxPatterns.org, a pattern library for Ajax-related patterns, as a wiki.

Related pattern libraries

Review the following user-interface design pattern libraries for inspiration:

- Fluid Open Source Design Pattern Library: *www.uidesignpatterns.org*.
- Jenifer Tidwell's collection of interaction design patterns: *www.designinginterfaces.com*.
- Martijn van Welie's web site about design patterns: *www.welie.com*.
- Sakai UI Design Patterns: *bugs.sakaiproject.org/confluence/display/DESPAT/Home*.
- UC Berkeley Pattern Library: *groups.ischool.berkeley.edu/ui_designpatterns/webpatterns2/webpatterns/home.php*.
- UI Pattern Factory: *www.uipatternfactory.com*.
- UI Patterns, User Interface Design Pattern Library: *www.ui-patterns.com*.
- Yahoo! Design Pattern Library: *developer.yahoo.com/ypatterns/*.

References

37signals. Getting Real: The Smarter, Faster, Easier Way to Build a Successful Web Application. Available from *gettingreal.37signals.com*, 2006.

Accessites.org. The Art of Accessibility. Available from *www.accessites.org*, 2008.

Adams, C. Fancy Form Design Using CSS. Available from *www.sitepoint.com/article/fancy-form-design-css*, 2008.

Adkisson, H. Identifying De-factor Standards for E-commerce Web Sites. M.S. Thesis, University of Washington, Seattle, 2002.

Aery, S. C. Breadcrumb Navigation Deployment in Retail Web Sites, Master's Paper for the M.S. in I.S. Degree. 2007. Available from *etd.ils.unc.edu/dspace/bitstream/1901/433/1/seanaery.pdf*.

AJAX and Accessibility. Available from *www.standards-schmandards.com/index.php?2005/03/01/16-ajax-and-accessibility*.

Alexander, C. *The Timeless Way of Building*. New York: Oxford University Press, 1979.

Alexander, C., S. Ishikawa, M. Silverstein, M. Jacobson, I. Fiksdahl-King, and S. Angel. *A Pattern Language*. New York: Oxford University Press, 1977.

Anand, S. S., and B. Mobasher (Eds.). Intelligent Techniques in Web Personalization. In *Lecture Notes in Artificial Intelligence*, Vol. 3169, pp. 1–37. Berlin: Springer-Verlag, 2005.

Andrew, R., and D. Shafer. *HTML Utopia: Designing Without Tables Using CSS*, 2nd Ed. Collingwood VIC, Australia: Sitepoint, 2006.

Andrew, R., and K. Yank. *Everything You Know About CSS Is Wrong*. Collingwood VIC, Australia: Sitepoint, 2008.

Apple Developer Connection. Internationalization Reference Library. Available from *developer.apple.com/referencelibrary/Internationalization/index.html*, 2008.

Apple OS X. Human Interface Design Guidelines. Available from *developer.apple.com/documentation/UserExperience/Conceptual/AppleHIGuidelines/OSXHIGuidelines.pdf*, 2007.

Aykin, N. (Ed.) *Usability and Internationalization of Information Technology*. Human Factors/Ergonomics Series. Marwah, NJ: Erlbaum, 2004.

Aykin, N. Designing Global Web Sites: Globalization and Localization Issues. A tutorial presented at the 6th Annual Human Factors and the Web Conference, Austin, TX, June 20–21, 2000.

Baekdal, T. Actual Browser Sizes. A Report. Available from *www.baekdal.com/ reports/Actual-Browser-Sizes/*, 2006.

Baird, J. *The Principles of Beautiful Web Design*. Collingwood VIC, Australia: SitePoint, 2007.

Ballard, B., and D. Malouf. Patterns Revisited. *Proceedings from Connecting 07*, San Francisco, October 19, 2007. Available from *www.slideshare.net/dmalouf/ patterns-revisited*.

Baxley, B. *Making the Web Work: Designing Effective Web Applications*. Berkeley, CA: New Riders, 2003.

Bernard, M. L. Developing Schemas for the Location of Common Web Objects, *Proceedings Human Factors and Ergonomics Society 45th Annual Meeting*, pp. 1161–1165, 2001.

Bernard, M., and C. Hamblin. Cascading versus Indexed Menu Design. *Usability News* 5(1). Available from *www.surl.org/usabilitynews/51/*, 2003.

Bernard, M., and L. Larsen. What Is the Best Layout for Multiple-Column Web Pages? *Usability News* 3(2). Available from *www.surl.org/usabilitynews/32/ layout.asp*, 2001.

Bernard, M., R. Baker, and M. Fernandez. Paging vs. Scrolling: Looking for the Best Way to Present Search Results. *Usability News* 4(1). Available from *surl.org/usabilitynews/41/paging.asp*, 2002.

Blake, R. Topix.net Forums on Fire: The Ni-chan Paradox. Available from *blog.topix.com/archives/000106.html*, March 31, 2006.

Bluestein, J., I. Ahmed, and K. Instone. An Evaluation of Look-Ahead Breadcrumbs for the WWW, *Proceedings HT '05*, Salzburg, Austria, September 6–9, 2005

Borchers, J. *A Pattern Approach to Interaction Design*. New York: John Wiley & Sons, 2001.

Boulton, M. Five Simple Steps to Designing Grid Systems. Available from *markboulton.co.uk/articles/detail/why_use_a_grid/*, 2006a.

Boulton, M. Why Use a Grid? Available from *markboulton.co.uk/articles/detail/ why_use_a_grid/*, 2006b.

Brath, R., and M. Peters. Dashboard Design: Why Design Is Important. DM Direct. Available from *www.dmreview.com/dmdirect/20041015/1011285-1.html*, 2004.

Brewer, J. (Ed.). How People with Disabilities Use the Web. Working-Group Internal Draft. Accessed May 5, 2005. Available from *www.sitepoint.com/ article/fancy-form-design-css*.

Calbucci, M. A 10% Improvement on Conversion with One Change. Available from *marcelo.sampa.com/marcelo-calbucci/brave-tech-world/A-10-improvement-on-conversion-w.htm*, July 15, 2008.

Cannon, A. Importance of HTML Headings for Accessibility. YouTube. Available from *www.youtube.com/watch?v=AmUPhEVWu_E*, 2008.

Card, S. K., J. D. Mackinlay, and B. Shneiderman (Eds). *Readings in Information Visualization: Using Vision to Think*. San Francisco: Morgan Kaufmann, 1999.

Cederholm, D. *Bulletproof Web Design: Improving Flexibility and Protecting against Worst-Case Scenarios with XHTML and CSS*, 2nd Edition. Berkeley, CA: New Riders, 2007.

Champeon, S. Progressive Enhancement: Pacing the Way for Future Web Design. Available from *www.hesketh.com/publications/progressive_enhancement_paving_way_for_future.html*, 2003a.

Champeon, S. Progressive Enhancement and the Future of Web Design. Available from *www.hesketh.com/publications/progressive_enhancement_and_the_future_of_web_design.html*, 2003b.

Chen, E. Design Patterns: A Bridge Between Usability and Design (Panel), *Usability Professionals' Association Conference*, Scottsdale, AZ, 2003.

Chi, E. H. Scent of the Web. In *Human Factors and Web Development*, J. Ratner (Ed.), pp. 265–285. Mahwah, NJ: Erlbaum, 2003.

Chi, E. H., P. Pirolli, and J. Pitkow. The Scent of a Site: A System for Analyzing and Predicting Information Scent, Usage, and Usability of a Web Site, *Proceedings Human Factors in Computing Systems, CHI '00*, Hague, The Netherlands, pp. 400–407, 2000.

Childers, T. L., and M. J. Houston. "Conditions for a Picture-Superiority Effect on Consumer Memory." *The Journal of Consumer Research* 11(2):643–654, 1984.

Christie, R. Top 10 CSS Table Designs. Available from *www.smashingmagazine.com/2008/08/13/top-10-css-table-designs/*, 2008.

Clarke, A. *Transcending CSS: The Fine Art of Web Design*. Berkeley, CA: New Riders, 2007.

Colter, A., K. Summers, and C. Smith. Exploring User Mental Models of Breadcrumbs in Web Navigation. Available from *www.angelacolter.com/site/breadcrumbs/index.html*, 2002.

Crumlish, C. *The Power of Many: How the Living Web Is Transforming Politics, Business, and Everyday Life*. New York: John Wiley & Sons, 2004.

Crumlish, C. Designing with Patterns in the Real World. Lessons from Yahoo! and Comcast. *Proceedings from IA Summit*, Miami, April 14, 2008.

Dearden, A., and J. Finlay. Pattern Languages in HCI: A Critical Review. *Human–Computer Interaction* 21(1):49–102, 2006.

del Galdo, E. M., and J. J. Nilesen. *International User Interfaces*. New York: John Wiley and Sons, 1996.

Denning, P. J., and P. Yaholkovsky. Getting to "We." Solidarity, Not Software, Generates Collaboration. *Communications of the ACM* 51(4):19–24, 2008.

Dennis, T., and K. Snow. Comparative Analysis of Web Design Patterns and Pattern Collections. Center for Document Engineering, Technical Report (CDE2006-TR04), p. 16, University of California, Berkeley, April 30, 2006.

Denton, W. How to Make a Faceted Classification and Put It on the Web. Available from *www.miskatonic.org/library/facet-web-howto.html*, 2003.

Dixon, H. E-Mail Marketing—CAN-SPAM Act—What Does the Law Require? Available from *www.privacyspot.com/?q=node/view/465*, 2004.

Dryer, D. C. Wizards, Guides, and Beyond: Rational and Empirical Methods for Selecting Optimal Intelligent User Interface Agents, *Proceedings Intelligent User Interfaces (IUI) 9*, pp. 265–268, Orlando, 1997.

Edelman Trust Barometer. The Ninth Global Opinion Leaders Study. Available from *www.edelman.com/trust/2008/TrustBarometer08_FINAL.pdf*, 2008.

Enders, L. (2008). Zebra Striping: More Data for the Case. Available from *www.alistapart.com/articles/zebrastripingmoredataforthecase*, September 9, 2008.

Erickson, T. Lingua Francas for Design: Sacred Places and Pattern Languages. Available from *www.visi.com/~snowfall/LinguaFranca_DIS2000.html*, 2000.

Faraday, P., and A. Sutcliffe. Designing effective multimedia presentations. *Proceedings of ACM CHI '97*:272–279, 1997.

Few, S. *Information Dashboard Design: The Effective Visual Communication of Data*. Sebastopol, CA: O'Reilly, 2006.

Fincher, S. Perspectives on HCI Patterns: Concepts and Tools (introducing PLML). *Interfaces*, 56:26–28. Also available from *www.bcs-hci.org.uk/interfaces.html*, 2003.

Fleming, J. *Web Navigation: Designing the User Experience*. Sebastopol, CA: O'Reilly, 1998.

Flickr Design Patterns Group. Available from *www.flickr.com/groups/designpatterns/*, 2008.

Fluid Open Source Design Pattern Library. Available from *www.uidesignpatterns.org*, 2008.

Fogg, B. J., T. Kameda, J. Boyd, J. Marshall, R. Sethi, M. Sockol, and T. Trow-bridge. Stanford–Makovsky Web Credibility Study 2002: Investigating What Makes Web Sites Credible Today. Research Report, Stanford Persuasive Technology Lab and Makovsky and Company, Stanford University. Available from *www.webcredibility.org*, 2002.

Fulciniti, A. Progressive Layout. Available from *webdesign.html.it/articoli/ leggi/545/progressive-layout/1/*, accessed May 18, 2005.

Galitz, W. O. *The Essential Guide to User Interface Design*, 2nd Ed. New York: John Wiley & Sons, 2002.

Gamma, E., R. Helm, R. Johnson, and J. Vlissides. *Design Patterns: Elements of Reusable Object-Oriented Software*. Reading, MA: Addison-Wesley, 1995.

Garrett, J. J. AJAX: A New Approach to Web Applications. Available from *www. adaptivepath.com/publications/essays/archives/000385.php*, 2005.

Gauri, D. K., A. Bhatnagar, and R. Rao. Role of Word of Mouth in Online Store Loyalty. *Communications of the ACM* 51(3):89–91, 2008.

Gladwell, M. *The Tipping Point: How Little Things Can Make a Big Difference*. Boston: Little, Brown and Company, 2000.

Glass, B. Designing Your Reputation System (in 10 Easy Steps), IA Summit, Miami. Available from *www.slideshare.net/soldierant/ designing-your-reputation-system*, 2008.

Goldberg, D., D. Nichols, B. M. Oki, and D. Terry. Using Collaborative Filtering to Weave an Information Tapestry. *Communications of the ACM* 35(12): 61–70, 1992.

Golder, S. A., and B. A. Huberman. Usage Patterns of Collaborative Tagging Systems. *Journal of Information Science* 32(2):198–208, 2006.

Graham, I. *A Pattern Language for Web Usability*. Boston: Addison-Wesley Professional, 2003.

Griffiths, R., and L. Pemberton. Don't Write Guidelines, Write Patterns! Available from *www.it.bton.ac.uk/staff/lp22/guidelinesdraft.html*, 2001.

Halvey, M., and M. T. Keane. An Assessment of Tag Presentation Techniques, *Proceedings WWW '07* poster paper, Banff, Alberta, May 8–12, 2007.

Hearst, M. A. User Interfaces and Visualization. In *Modern Information Retrieval* edited by R. Baeza-Yates and B. Ribeiro-Neto, pp. 257–323. New York: Addison-Wesley Longman, 1999.

Hearst, M. A. Design Recommendations for Hierarchical Faceted Search Interfaces, ACM SIGIR Workshop on Faceted Search, Seattle, August 6–11, 2006.

Henry, S. L. *Just Ask: Integrating Accessibility Throughout Design.* Available from *www.Lulu.com*, 2007.

Hoekman, R. Jr. *Designing the Moment: Web Interface Design Concepts in Action.* Berkeley, CA: New Riders, 2008.

Holzschag, M. E. Integrated Web Design: The Meaning of Semantics. Available from *www.peachpit.com/articles/article.aspx?p=369225*, 2005.

Hornbæk, K., B. B. Bederson, and C. Plaisant. Navigation Patterns and Usability of Zoomable User Interfaces with and without an Overview. *ACM Transactions on Computer–Human Interaction* 9(4):362–389, 2002.

Horton, S. *Access by Design. A Guide to Universal Usability for Web Designers.* Berkeley, CA: New Riders, 2006.

Hull, S. S. Influence of Training and Exposure on the Usage of Breadcrumb Navigation. *Usability News* 6(1), 2004. Available from *www.surl.org/usabilitynews/61/breadcrumb.asp*.

Hurst, S. How to Internationalize Your Website. White Paper, SDL. Available from *www.sdl.com/en/globalization-knowledge-centre/whitepapers/default.asp*, 2007.

Instone, K. Location, Path and Attribute Breadcrumbs, Poster presentation at ASIST 3rd Annual IA Summit, Baltimore, March 16–17, 2002. Available from *www.instone.org/files/KEI-Breadcrumbs-IAS.pdf*.

International, Dr. *Developing International Software*, 2nd ed. Redmond, WA: Microsoft Press, 2003.

Internationalization (I18n) Activity: Getting Started. Available from *www.w3.org/International/getting-started/*, 2007.

Ishida, R. Ishida ≫ blog. Available from *www.rishida.net/blog/*, 2008.

ISO 8601. Data Elements and Interchange Formats—Information interchange—Representation of Dates and Times. Available from *www.iso.org/iso/iso_catalogue/catalogue_tc/catalogue_detail.htm?csnumber=26780*, 2000.

ITU-T E.123. Notation for National and International Telephone Numbers, E-mail Addresses and Web Addresses. Series E: Overall Network Operation, Telephone Service, Service Operation and Human Factors. Telecommunication Standardization Sector of ITU. Available from *www.itu.int/rec/T-REC-E.123/en*, 2001.

Jesper, R.-J. Usability of Pagination Links. Available from *www.justaddwater.dk/2008/01/03/usability-of-pagination-links/*, 2008.

Jesse, D. *CSS-Layouts—Praxislösungen mit YAML* (in German). Galileo Press, 2007a.

Jesse, D. Bulletproof and Flexible Layouts Made Simple. Available from *www.yaml.de/en/home.html*, 2007b.

Kalbach, J., and T. Bosenick. T. Web Page Layout: A Comparison between Left- and Right-Justified Site Navigation Menus. *Journal of Digital Information* 4(1). Available from *journals.tdl.org/jodi/article/view/jodi-111/93*, 2003.

Kalbach, J. *Designing Web Navigation*. Sebastopol, CA: O'Reilly, 2007.

Katz, M. A., and M. D. Byrne. Effects of Scent and Breadth on Use of Site-Specific Search on e-commerce Web Sites. *ACM Transactions on Computer–Human Interaction* 10(3):198–220, 2003.

Kaushik, A. Five Rules for High-Impact Web Analytics Dashboards. Available from *www.kaushik.net/avinash/2007/03/five-rules-for-high-impact-web-analytics-dashboards.html*, 2007.

Keith, J. *DOM Scripting: Web Design with JavaScript and the Document Object Model*. New York: Friends of ED, 2005.

Keith, J. *Bulletproof Ajax*. Berkeley, CA: New Riders, 2007.

Kliehm, M. Accessible Web 2.0 Applications with WAI-ARIA. Accessed April 09, 2007. Available from *www.alistapart.com/articles/waiaria*.

Koch, N., and G. Rossi. Patterns for Adaptive Web Applications, *Proceedings 7th EuroPlop*, 2002.

Koerner, B. I. (2003). What Does a "Thumbs Up" Mean in Iraq? Available from *slate.msn.com/id/2080812/*, March 28, 2003.

Krug, S. *Don't Make Me Think!: A Common Sense Approach to Web Usability*, 2nd Ed. Berkeley, CA: New Riders, 2006.

Kurosu, M., and K. Kashimura. Apparent Usability vs. Inherent Usability: Experimental Analysis on the Determinants of the Apparent Usability. *Conference Companion on Human Factors in Computing Systems*, pp. 292–293, Denver, May 7–11, 1995.

Laasko, S. User Interface Design Patterns. Available from *www.cs.helsinki.fi/u/salaakso/patterns/index.html*, 2003.

Leacock, M., E. Malone, and C. Wheeler. Implementing a Pattern Library in the Real World: A Yahoo! Case Study. Available from *www.leacock.com/patterns/leacock_malone_wheeler.pdf*, 2005.

Lida, B., and B. Chaparro, B. Breadcrumb Navigation: Further Investigation of Usage. *Usability News* 5(2), 2003. Available from *www.uie.com/brainsparks/2005/09/26/value-of-breadcrumbs/*.

Lidwell, W., K. Holden, and J. Butler. *Universal Principles of Design*. Gloucester, MA: Rockport Publishers, 2003.

Linderman, M. Web Interface Design Tip: The Yellow Fade Technique. Available from *www.37signals.com/svn/archives/000558.php*, 2004.

Linderman, M., and J. Fried. *Defensive Design for the Web*. Berkeley, CA: New Riders, 2004.

Lloyd, I. *The Ultimate HTML Reference*. Collingwood VIC, Australia: Sitepoint, 2008.

Lynch, J. P., and S. Horton. *Web Style Guide: Basic Design Principles for Creating Web Sites*. New Haven: Yale University Press, 1999.

Mackay, W. E. Triggers and Barriers to Customizing Software, *CHI '91 Proceedings*, pp. 153–160, 1991.

Mahemoff, M. J., and L. J. Johnston. Pattern Languages for Usability: An Investigation of Alternative Approaches. In J. Tanaka (Ed.), *Proceedings Asia-Pacific Conference on Human Computer Interaction* (APCHI), pp. 25–31, Los Alamitos, CA: IEEE Computer Society. Available from *www.mahemoff.com/paper/candidate/*.

Mahemoff, M. *Ajax Design Patterns*. Sebastapol, CA: O'Reilly, 2006.

Malone, E., M. Leacock, and C. Wheeler. Implementing a Pattern Library in the Real World: A Yahoo! Case Study. Boxes and Arrows. Available from *www.boxesandarrows.com/view/implementing_a_pattern_library_in_the_real_world_a_yahoo_case_study*, accessed April 29, 2005.

Markowsky, G. Misconceptions about the Golden Ratio. *The College Mathematics Journal* 23(1):2–19, 1992.

Marlow, C., M. Naaman, b. boyd, and M. Davis. Position Paper, Tagging, Taxonomy, Flickr, Article, ToRead. Available from *www.semanticmetadata.net/hosted/taggingws-www2006-files/29.pdf*, 2006.

Mayhew, J. D. *Principles and Guidelines in Software User Interface Design*. Englewood Cliffs, NJ: Prentice-Hall, 1992.

McIntire, P. *Visual Design for the Modern Web*. Berkeley, CA: New Riders, 2008.

Microsoft Development Network (MSDN) Go Global Developer Center. Available from *msdn.microsoft.com/en-us/goglobal/default.aspx*, 2008.

Morville, P., and L. Rosenfeld. *Information Architecture for the World Wide Web*, Third Edition. Berkeley, CA: O'Reilly, 2006.

Mulpuru, S. *Which Personalization Tools Work for eCommerce—And Why*. Cambridge: Forrester Research, Inc, December 27, 2007.

Nielsen, J. Search and You *May* Find. Available from *www.useit.com/alertbox/9707b.html*, July 15, 1997.

Nielsen, J. Reset and Cancel Buttons, Alertbox. Retrieved April 16, 2000, from *www.useit.com/alertbox/20000416.html*.

Nielsen, J. Search: Visible and Simple. Available from *www.useit.com/ alertbox/20010513.html*, May 13, 2001.

Nielsen, J. Scrolling and Scrollbars. Alertbox. Available from *www.useit.com/ alertbox/20050711.html*, accessed July 11, 2005.

Nielsen, J. Breadcrumb Navigation Increasingly Useful. Available from *www .useit.com/alertbox/breadcrumbs.html*, April 10, 2007.

Nielsen, J., and R. Molich. Heuristic Evaluation of User Interfaces, *Proceedings of the CHI '90 Conference*, pp. 249–256, Seattle, April 1–5, 1990.

Nolan, P. R. Designing Screen Icons: Ranking and Matching Studies. *Proceedings of the Human Factors Society 33rd Annual Meeting*, pp. 380–384, 1989.

Paivio, A., T. B. Rogers, and P. C. Smythe. Why Are Pictures Easier to Recall Than Words? *Psychonomic Science* 11(4):137–138, 1968.

Pemberton, L. The Promise of Pattern Languages for Interaction Design, Human Factors Symposium, Loughborough, UK Available from *www .it.bton.ac.uk/staff/lp22/HF2000.html*, 2000.

Penzo, M. Label Placement in Forms, UX Matters. Available from *www .uxmatters.com/MT/archives/000107.php*, 2006.

Peterson, H., and D. Dugas. The relative importance of contrast and motion in visual perception. *Human Factors* 14:207–216, 1972.

Pirolli, P., and S. Card. Information Foraging. *Psychological Review* 106(4): 643–675, 1999.

Porter, J. *Designing for the Social Web*. Berkeley, CA: New Riders, 2008.

Raskin, J. Intuitive Equals Familiar. *Communications of the ACM* 37(9):17, 2004.

Raskin, A. Never Use a Warning When You Mean Undo. Available from *www .alistapart.com/articles/neveruseawarning*, July 13, 2007.

Resnick, P., R. Zeckhauser, J. Swanson, and K. Lockwood. The Value of Reputation on eBay: A Controlled Experiment. *Experimental Economics* 9(2):79–101, 2006.

Rivadeneira, A. W., D. M. Gruen, M. J. Muller, and D. R. Millen. Getting Our Head in the Clouds: Toward Evaluation Studies of Tag Clouds, *Proceedings of CHI '07*, San Jose, CA, April 28–May 3, 2007.

Rossi, G., D. Schwabe, and R. M. Guimarães. Designing Personalized Web Applications, *Proceedings WWW10*, pp. 275–284, Hong Kong, May 1–5, 2001.

Rutledge, A. Contrast and Meaning. A List Apart. Available from *www.alistapart. com/articles/contrastandmeaning*, 2007.

Sakai UI Design Patterns. Available from *bugs.sakaiproject.org/confluence/display/ DESPAT/Home*.

Schafer, J. B., J. Konstan, and J. Riedl. Recommender Systems in E-commerce, *Proceedings E-Commerce '99*, pp. 158–166, Denver, 1999.

Schwartz, B. *The Paradox of Choice: Why More Is Less.* New York: HarperCollins, 2004.

Scott, B. Looks Good, Works Well. Posts with Label: Antipatterns. Available from *www.looksgoodworkswell.blogspot.com/search/label/antipatterns*, 2006.

Scott, B. When Designers Get Too Clever. eBig 2008. Available from *www. looksgoodworkswell.blogspot.com/2008/02/ebig-talk-slides-available.html*, 2008.

Shaikh, A. D., and K. Lenz. Where's the Search? Reexamining User Expectations of Web Objects. *Usability News* 8(1). Available from *www.surl.org/ usabilitynews/81/webobjects.asp.*, 2006.

Singh, S. Social Networks and Group Formation: Theoretical Concepts to Leverage. Available from *www.boxesandarrows.com/view/social-networks*, 2007.

Sinnig, D., H. Javahery, J. Strika, P. Forbrig, and A. Seffah. Patterns and Components for Enhancing Reusability and Systematic UI Development. *Proceedings of BIR*, Rostock, 2005.

Smarr, J., M. Canter, R. Scoble, and M. Arrington. A Bill of Rights for Users of the Social Web. Available from *www.opensocialweb.org*, 2007.

Smith, G. *Tagging: People-Powered Metadata for the Social Web.* Berkeley, CA: New Riders, 2007.

Smith-Ferrier, G. *.NET Internationalization: The Developer's Guide to Building Global Windows and Web Applications.* Boston: Addison-Wesley Professional, 2006.

Spool, J. Design Patterns: An Evolutionary Step to Managing Complex Sites. Available from *www.uie.com/articles/design_patterns/*, 2003.

Spool, J. Value of Breadcrumbs. User Interface Engineering (UIE) Brainsparks. Available from *www.uie.com/brainsparks/2005/09/26/value-of-breadcrumbs/*, 2005.

Spool, J. The Elements of a Design Pattern. Available from *www.uie.com/articles/ elements_of_a_design_pattern/*, 2006.

Spool, J. Producing Great Search Results: Harder Than It Looks, Part 1. Available from *www.uie.com/articles/search_results/*, 2008a.

Spool, J. Producing Great Search Results: Harder Than It Looks, Part 2. Available from *www.uie.com/articles/search_results_part2/*, 2008b.

Szeto, J. Building Flex Applications with Progressive Layout. Available from *www.adobe.com/devnet/flex/articles/prog_layout.html*, accessed October 20, 2004.

Teng, H. Location Breadcrumbs for Navigation: An Exploratory Study. Master's thesis, Dalhousie University, Faculty of Computer Science, Halifax, Nova Scotia, 2003.

Thatcher, J., P. Bohman, M. Burks, S. L. Henry, B. Regan, S. Swierenga, M. D. Urban, and C. D. Waddell. *Constructing Accessible Web Sites.* Birmingham, U.K.: Glasshaus, 2002.

Thatcher, J., M. R. Burks, C. Heilman, S. L. Henry, A. Kirkpatrick, P. H. Lauke, B. Lawson, B. Regan, R. Rutter, M.Urban, and C. D.Waddell. *Web Accessibility: Web Standards and Regulatory Compliance.* New York: Friends of ED, 2006.

Tidwell, J. *Designing Interfaces.* Cambridge, MA: O'Reilly, 2006. Also available at *www.designinginterfaces.com.*

Tractinsky, N. Aesthetics and Apparent Usability: Empirically Assessing Cultural and Methodological Issues. *CHI '97 Conference Proceedings*, pp. 115–122, Atlanta, March 22–27, 1997.

Turnbull, G. *Your Life in Web Apps. Short Cuts*, p. 24. Boston: O'Reilly, 2006.

UC Berkeley Pattern Library. Available from *groups.ischool.berkeley.edu/ui_ designpatterns/webpatterns2/webpatterns/home.php*, 2008.

UI Patterns. Available from *www.ui-patterns.com*, 2008.

Vander Wal, T. Folksonomy. Available from *www.vanderwal.net/folksonomy.html,* accessed February 2, 2007.

van Duyne, D. K., J. Landay, and J. I. Hong. *The Design of Sites: Patterns, Principles, and Processes for Crafting a Customer-Centered Web Experience.* Boston: Addison-Wesley, 2002.

van Duyne, D. K., J. Landay, and J. I. Hong. *The Design of Sites: Patterns for Creating Winning Web Sites*, 2nd Edition. Boston: Addison-Wesley Professional, 2006.

van Welie, M. *Design Patterns.* Available from *www.welie.com.*

Venners, B. Patterns and Practice: A Conversation with Erich Gamma. Part IV. Artima Developer. Best Practices in Enterprise Software Development. Available from *www.artima.com/lejava/articles/patterns_practice.html*, 2005.

Vinh, K., and Boulton, M. Grids Are Good. Available from *www.lifeclever.com/ khoi-vinh-mark-boulton-grids-are-good/*, accessed November 1, 2007.

von Ahn, L., M. Blum, and J. Langford. Telling Humans and Computers Apart Automatically. *Communications of the ACM* 47(3):57–60, 2004.

Vote to Promote Pattern. Yahoo! Developer Network. Design Pattern Library. Available from *developer.yahoo.com/ypatterns/pattern.php?pattern= votetopromote*, 2008.

W3C Internationalization (i18n) Activity. Available from *www.w3.org/ International/*, 2008.

W3C. Web Accessibility Initiative. Available from *www.w3.org/WAI/*.

Web Accessibility in Mind (WebAIM). Available from *www.Webaim.org/articles/*.

Wellhausen, T. User Interface Design for Searching. A Pattern Language. Available from *www.tim-wellhausen.de*, 2006.

Wickham, D. P., D. L. Mayhew, T. Stoll, K. J. Tolley III, and S. Rouiller. *Designing Effective Wizards: A Multidisciplinary Approach.* Upper Saddle River, NJ: Prentice Hall, 2002.

Windows Vista User Experience Guidelines. Available from *download.microsoft. com/download/e/1/9/e191fd8c-bce8-4dba-a9d5-2d4e3f3ec1d3/ux%20guide.pdf*, 2007.

Winn, T., and P. Calder. A Pattern Language for Pattern Language Structure. *Proceedings of the Conference on Pattern Languages of Programs,* Vol. 13, pp. 45–58, Melbourne, Australia, 2002.

Wroblewski, L. *Site-Seeing: A Visual Approach to Web Usability.* New York: Hungry Minds, 2002.

Wroblewski, L. *Web Form Design: Filling in the Blanks.* Brooklyn: Rosenfeld Media, 2008.

Wroblewski, L., and Etre Ltd. Primary and Secondary Actions in Web Forms. Available from *www.lukew.com/resources/articles/PSactions.asp*, 2007.

Yahoo! Design Pattern Library. Available from *www.developer.yahoo.com/ ypatterns/*, 2008.

Yunkers, J. *Beyond Borders: Web Globalization Strategies.* Berkeley, CA: New Riders, 2002.

Index